THE LONG ROAD TO CHANGE

THE LONG ROAD TO CHANGE
AMERICA'S REVOLUTION, 1750–1820

Eric Nellis

UNIVERSITY OF TORONTO PRESS

Library and Archives Canada Cataloguing in Publication

Nellis, Eric Guest, 1938–
The long road to change : America's revolution 1750–1820 / Eric Nellis.

Includes bibliographical references and index.
ISBN 978-1-55111-110-0

1. United States—History—Revolution, 1775–1783. 2. United States—History—1783–1815.
3. United States—Politics and government—To 1775. 4. United States—Politics and government—1775–1783. 5. United States—Politics and government—1789–1815. I. Title.

E210.N45 2007   973.3   C2007-900281-1

We welcome comments and suggestions regarding any aspect of our publications—please feel free to contact us at news@utphighereducation.com or visit our Internet site at www.utppublishing.com.

North America
5201 Dufferin Street
North York, Ontario, Canada, M3H 5T8

2250 Military Road
Tonawanda, New York, USA, 14150

ORDERS PHONE: 1-800-565-9523
ORDERS FAX: 1-800-221-9985
ORDERS E-MAIL: utpbooks@utpress.utoronto.ca

UK, Ireland, and continental Europe
NBN International
Estover Road, Plymouth, PL6 7PY, UK
ORDERS PHONE: 44 (0) 1752 202301
ORDERS FAX: 44 (0) 1752 202333
ORDERS E-MAIL: enquiries@nbninternational.com

The University of Toronto Press acknowledges the financial support for its publishing activities of the Government of Canada through the Canada Book Fund.

To the memory of my parents.

CONTENTS

LIST OF MAPS AND TABLES

ACKNOWLEDGEMENTS

This book is the result of a long engagement with early American history, and the academic literature that has enriched it. My interest in colonial and revolutionary America was sparked by David Flaherty and Ian Steele at the University of Western Ontario and sustained by Alan Tully at the University of British Columbia and the University of Texas. I am grateful for their guidance. For a survey text, the greatest thanks must go to the historians who have probed the complex issues raised by the subject. I owe much to the generations of scholars of monographs, essays, biographies, and surveys who have stimulated me. This book is a reflection of that scholarship, and the names of those mostly American scholars who have influenced the tone of this volume will be prominent in the bibliography. I have benefited from the inevitable contributions of a great many students, and I thank them for their questions, challenges, and insights over the years. I thank the archivists and librarians who have assisted and guided me in my various research projects, and the colleagues who in recent years have provided discussion, support, and friendship. In particular, I thank James Hull, Maury Williams, Duane Thomson, Sahadeo Basdeo, Bob Fuhr, Katie Bindon, John Lent, and Sylvie Zebroff. Richard Johnson and the members of the Northwest Early American Workshop in Seattle offered sound advice and encouragement when I presented the proposal for this book. Karen Taylor not only reviewed the manuscript for style but provided valuable editorial advice. My wife Vicky McAulay not only worked with the manuscript but her enthusiastic support made the project a happy one.

INTRODUCTION

In the seventeenth century, the word "revolution" in the English language came to describe the removal of an established government, usually by the governed themselves, followed by the replacement of that government by a new one or a new form or system of government. The word had found its way into common usage by the eighteenth century. As a major event in modern history, the American Revolution fits the definition. The term "event," however, is perhaps a bit misleading, and the Revolution is more profitably seen as a series of *events* that merged over several decades into the United States of America. When it began, the colonists were identifiably British, or British American, but within a few decades became simply American, in a way that identified a nationality. The initial opposition to Parliament's authority in the 1760s had a limited objective, to seek a moderation of new imperial policies; but it adapted over time to changing circumstances and opportunities. The Declaration of Independence was not the American Revolution, nor was the War for Independence, nor the ratification of the Constitution, nor Jefferson's election in 1800; but these were points along a line defined by factors as varied as persistent British policies and actions, colonial reactions and assertions of older rights, and finally the search for a republican framework for the independent states. The process was a lengthy and complex affair, fluid, creative, and adaptive.

Since independence, the Revolution has been credited, largely by implication (and largely by Americans), as a model for the rise of democracy in the Western world and as the wellspring of a host of natural, human, and civil rights. However, as historian Jack Greene notes, the Revolution's "half life" as a model for other peoples was very short and never wholly successful. The succession of Latin American independence movements, wars, and constitutional imitations that began in the immediate wake of the American Revolution could not replicate the basic formula of the American Revolution even if the ideals of early nineteenth-century Latin American revolutionaries San Martin, Bernardo O'Higgins, or Simon Bolivar rang with the rhetoric of 1776 or 1787. In the first half of the twentieth century, the distinguished colonial historian Charles McLean Andrews argued that modern democracy would have come to Americans regardless of whether they had stayed in the British Empire or not. It came to Britain, after all, albeit in a slow and piecemeal way, but it was a British version of democracy, shaped by British historical experience and not by any model drawn from the American Revolution. By any definition, Canada, Australia, and New Zealand, for example, the so-called "white dominions" of the later British Empire, are as democratic as the United States. They became democratic without the republican ideals of

1787 and without the need for the violent overthrow of the Empire. Democratic institutions and values evolved in various ways in various places at different times, and
while the United States ascribes its democratic character to a set of revolutionary ideas
and institutions, those ideas and institutions have not been readily transferable to
other societies.

Most European forms of representative or parliamentary democracy, as constitutional monarchies or republics, were arrived at without any significant borrowing
from America. Closer to home, it is worth noting that modern Canada emerged from
the Revolution as a next door neighbor predicated on *not* being like the United States,
by avoiding the republican model. The historian David Brion Davis is right when he
says that Thomas Paine's claim for America as "the cause of all mankind" was never a
reality, and then points to the fact that the United States spent much of the latter half
of the twentieth century *suppressing* revolutions all over the world. While America has
been a magnet for masses of migrants over the last three centuries, drawn to its opportunities and openness, and has exported many of its cultural and economic values, its
political system has been a difficult one to replicate because it came out of a rare set of
conditions.

British North American society in the 1760s and 1770s had no parallel in the
Western world, and the creation of the United States of America must first be seen as a
particular rather than a general example of revolution. Indeed, the vaunted "colonists"
who rose up against British rule might be better understood as "colonizers" who had
claimed eastern North America for the Empire and who had colonized native and
African peoples along the way. When they later resisted official British intrusions into
their established political identities, they did so not to change the world but to preserve
the one they had made for themselves. Our understanding of the Revolution begins
there, with those colonizers and the particular circumstances of the communities,
institutions, and values they had developed by the middle of the eighteenth century. As
all revolutions are unique to their time and place, the American Revolution was
uniquely a product of the people who made it. It is also unique by the very fact of its
success. No other major modern anti-colonial or ideological revolution or national
liberation movement can make that claim. The anti- and post-colonial revolutions in
the twentieth century have been either thwarted or limited in their outcomes. While
the rhetoric of the American revolutionary experience is often invoked elsewhere, it is
usually the more radical model of the French Revolution or more commonly the
Marxist imperative that informs "from the bottom up" revolutions. As models, however, there is irony in the short-term failure of the French Revolution itself and the
haphazard trail of misery and authoritarianism that has followed in the name of Marx.
The message to be drawn from any history of planned political revolutions is that so
few succeed or survive as intended.

The American Revolution was not an uprising of economically oppressed peoples.
It began as a conflict over legal rights, became a struggle of competing political authorities, and ended with a redefinition of the constitutional status of British subjects in

North America. As the German-born philosopher-historian Hannah Arendt notes in her 1963 treatise *On Revolution*, "The superior wisdom of the American founders in theory and practice is conspicuous and impressive enough, and yet has never carried with it sufficient persuasiveness and plausibility to prevail in the tradition of revolution. It is as though the American Revolution was achieved in a kind of ivory tower into which the fearful spectacle of human misery, the haunting voices of abject poverty, never penetrated." What she means is that the causes of the American Revolution lacked some of the human characteristics of the French or Russian Revolutions, or the Mexican or Chinese Revolutions for that matter. Her "tradition of revolution" suggests the attempt to exterminate "human misery" and "abject poverty." This was absent in the American Revolution when we allow that the revolutionaries did not consider natives or African slaves as part of their mandate. Nevertheless, she appears to approve of the American Revolution because in the end it satisfied the people who saw it through. Robert Palmer, one of the outstanding students of the subject, in his magisterial 1959-1964 study, *The Age of Democratic Revolution: A Political History of Europe and America, 1760-1800*, claims that the Revolution was in fact a reference point for modern politics because it demonstrated the potential for large scale and decisive change towards participatory and inclusive political systems.

A familiar, even shop-worn, question arises from any comparative approach: "How revolutionary was the American Revolution?" What was the nature of the social, economic, cultural, and political *changes* for peoples who were satisfied with their identities before the Revolution? What brought those peoples together in the first place? The South Carolina slaveholder, the backcountry settler, the Boston merchant, and the Pennsylvania Quaker were not drawn together as a cultural, social, neighborly collective to throw off the British. No, they were drawn together by shared concerns about their respective political status, institutions and rights, and their economic futures because of external imperial pressures. The Revolution was inspired by concerns over political status and resulted in political innovation. Its cultural and social causes and consequences are more difficult to determine. The political outcomes of the Revolution and the war that accompanied it can be traced in a fairly straightforward way. But how much social change took place?

The academic literature is rich, controversial, and voluminous, and adds complications, contradictions, and ongoing revisions to interpretations of the Revolution. As methodologies and perspectives of historical enquiry have changed so has the meaning of the Revolution. When Arendt and Palmer were pondering its global place, natives, African Americans, and women were generally left out of their studies. Since at least the 1960s, American historians have retained Palmer's political framework, which he saw as grafting a set of modern, mostly European ideas onto colonial institutions to create the seedbed for modern democratic society. Historians must now allow that the American Revolution involved minorities and dissent, progress and reaction, inclusion and exclusion, and a range of issues that do not fit the older version of a Revolution by and for, and to the memory of white, protestant males. Still, the search for a single or dominant explanation for the causes and major consequences of the Revolution goes on, and the sheer abundance of studies suggests that the project will continue. For example, there has been a recent revival of economic determinism. Historians have recently noted that late eighteenth century America was increasingly a consumer society and British policies interfered with rising material expectations. Thus the boycotts, embargoes, and non-importation movements in the 1760s and later were part of lively consumer behavior that continued well after independence, fusing, as it went, with political demands. That version of economic explanation should be judged in the light of older frameworks such as Charles Beard's "progressive" thesis of a century ago that saw the revolutionary mandate and the Constitution in particular as being guided by a self-interested economic elite that sought a national economy as its objective. The other side of that historiographical coin, largely a product of the 1960s but still active, sees a growing class problem in late colonial America. Landless men, insecure urban artisans, and growing numbers of poor created an unstable social environment that fed the revolutionary impetus and then challenged the middle-class politics of the era. A recent reinterpretation of the Revolution by historian Gary Nash, *The Unknown American Revolution* (2005), is a superbly researched and argued synthesis of the class, gender, and race variables of recent scholarship on the Revolution. In an oblique way, it tends to qualify Arendt's judgment by discussing poverty and exclusion as vital parts of the engine of revolutionary change. It is a valuable reminder that the revolutionary generations were not an undifferentiated mass of patriotic ideologues, headed toward an historical inevitability.

Any approach to understanding the American Revolution must acknowledge its timing. The long era that embraced the various stages of the Revolution included the Enlightenment in its various forms, religious upheaval and debate, the market and industrial transformations in all Western cultures and the rhetoric of rights and egalitarianism. The American Revolution coincides with vast changes in the politics, economics, and sociology of the European and Atlantic worlds. The revolt arose in a set of pre-industrial societies hemmed in by the Appalachian Mountains. Three generations later, settlement had crossed the Mississippi River, and the territorial claims of the United States of America reached all the way to the Pacific Ocean, and, while it was still largely agrarian, the new nation had embraced modern industrial innovation, modern banking systems, consumerism, and a market economy. The slave-based economies of tobacco, rice, and other agricultural commodities in the colonial south had given way to the mass production of cotton. Cultivated and harvested by new managerial techniques and a more disciplined forced labor regime, it fed a new textile industry, the foundation of the modern industrial economy, in dozens of locations in the northern states. While Benjamin Franklin's storied experiments with electricity survive as an example of American enterprise, it was profit-oriented mechanical tinkering and steam that gave the Republic a technological and industrial kick-start.

The present survey acknowledges the enormous volume of research and stimulating recent literature on the subject and places both in a political narrative following

Hannah Arendt's comment on the largely political ends of the Revolution and what was arguably the first *new* nation of the modern era. Its legacy has given Americans a unique historical perspective. Consider the titles given to college survey texts on American history such as *The Enduring Vision; The American Promise; Liberty, Equality, Power; The Great Republic; The American Pageant; Give Me Liberty; Created Equal; Out of Many,* and so on. Those emotive phrases are not at all considered extravagant by Americans in the twenty-first century. The language was used as readily in the 1770s as today and Americans assume "liberty," "promise," "vision," and "equality" as defining distinctively American values. In most respects, American political values are derived from Americans' understanding of the Revolution, and from how they wish to project that understanding to the world.

The political crisis that led to independence was brought on initially by British policy and not by Americans clamoring for change. Indeed, it stands in contrast to the other great revolution of the era, the French. The French revolutionaries honestly set out to start the world anew, to redefine human relations, politics, and social and cultural norms. If it was ultimately a more disordered and brutal affair than the American Revolution, it was also more idealistic about the possibility of pure and universal egalitarian reform and the end of class divisions, but it ended as a failed attempt at social engineering. The American revolutionaries, by contrast, initially set out to preserve or continue the world they had, in fact, to make it more secure. Over time, however, the Revolution came to be seen as a "radical" break with the past, and an ideological and a potential political beacon for future generations of Americans and the world. If it has not served as a revolutionary template, the United States has nevertheless profoundly affected world affairs, from its modest beginnings in the late eighteenth century to the present. The Revolution was a creative, exciting, and at times a fearful experience lasting over several decades. It was as exclusionary as it was egalitarian and as radical in its political outcome as it was conservative in many of its origins, objectives, and ideals. Its social impact was moderate and even conservative at first, even if it loosened the relationships between all classes of white males. Politically, it bound together a set of formerly provincial, colonial societies, but it left unfinished problems of regional and local conflict. It formalized sectional and constitutional problems that were still not resolved a half century after the Declaration of Independence, and left a racial divide, the residue of which remains. When the American Revolution began, Quebec, Nova Scotia and Newfoundland, parts of the Caribbean, along with the thirteen contiguous mainland colonies comprised the British Empire in America. Only half the colonies left the Empire, a fact that suggests the unique historical and geographical character of the thirteen departees. The "birth of the Republic" was shaped by the common spatial and political baggage of its participants. To do justice to the Revolution requires a long view of its origins and immediate consequences. We simply cannot begin when the British began to reform their American colonies in 1763 and end with the first United States Congress in 1789. The dissenters and protesters who resisted imperial change in the 1760s were British, their successors, three generations later, were Americans.

Suggested Reading

After four decades, Hannah Arendt, *On Revolution* (1963; New York: Viking, 1965) stands up as a thoughtful and articulate contemplation on the nature of modern revolutions and makes incisive comparisons, in particular between the French and American revolutions. R.R. Palmer, *The Age of Democratic Revolution: A Political History of Europe and America, 1760-1800*, 2 vols. (Princeton, NJ: Princeton University Press, 1959-1964) demonstrates Palmer's scholarship and places the American Revolution in the mainstream of modern world history. Charles M. Andrews, *The Colonial Background of the American Revolution*, rev. ed. (New Haven: Yale University Press, 1931) and Charles Beard, *An Economic Interpretation of the United States Constitution* (1913; New York: Free Press, 1965) can still be read with profit, not simply as historiographical artifacts but as guides to understanding the context of the American Revolution. For an example of the way historians experiment with new approaches to the Revolution, see T.H. Breen, *The Marketplace of Revolution: How Consumer Politics Shaped American Independence* (New York, Oxford, 2004).

David Brion Davis, *Revolutions: Reflections on American Equality and Foreign Liberations* (Cambridge, MA: Harvard University Press, 1990) and Jack P. Greene, *The American Revolution: Its Character and Limits* (New York: New York University Press, 1987) focus on the limitations of the American Revolution as a model for others. Gordon S. Wood, *The Radicalism of the American Revolution* (New York: Knopf, 1992) is important for its suggestion that colonial America was a deferential civilization that was transformed by the Revolution into a modern, radical polity and culture. It should be read along with Gary B. Nash, *The Unknown Revolution: The Unruly Birth of Democracy and the Struggle to Create America* (London: Viking Press, 2005) and Alfred F. Young, *The Shoemaker and the Tea Party: Memory and the American Revolution* (Boston: Beacon Press, 1999), both of which study the Revolution from the perspective of the rising power of the lower classes in America. Young, in particular, is eager to show that the working-class role in independence was co-opted by the middle and upper classes in the wake of the Revolution.

CHAPTER ONE

THE COLONIAL BACKGROUND TO THE AMERICAN REVOLUTION

Rule, Britannia, rule the waves;

Britons never shall be slaves.

— James Thomson and David Mallett, *Alfred: A Masque* (1740)

Time Line

Pre-Columbian native population of the Americas: ca. 50 million; of North America north of Mexico: ca. 2-4 million; of the area from the Atlantic to the Mississippi and from the Great Lakes to the Gulf Mexico: ca. 500,000-1 million; in the area of the original thirteen colonies: ca. 200,000. These are recent and tentative estimates, subject to revision.

1492	Columbus reaches the Caribbean (West Indies).
1521 35	Start of the Spanish conquests in Central and South America.
1603	The union of the crowns of Scotland and England.
1607	First permanent English settlement in America at Jamestown, Virginia.
1607 1763	The English create or acquire over 20 colonies on the North American mainland, in the western Atlantic, and in the Caribbean.
1608	First French permanent settlement in America at Quebec.
1619	Slaves arrived in Virginia. The first representative assembly in the Americas, the House of Burgesses, met at Jamestown.
1642-49	English Civil War.
1651	The first of many Navigation Acts to control trade between the British colonies and Britain.
1660	The Restoration of the Stuart monarchy in Britain.
1688-89	The Glorious Revolution in Britain.
1689-97	King William's War (in America) or the War of the League of Augsburg.
1702-13	Queen Anne's War (in America) or the War of the Spanish Succession.
1707	The union of the Scottish and English parliaments.
1730s-50s	The Great Awakening in America.
1733-35	The Zenger trial in New York.
1740-48	King George's War (in America) or the War of the Austrian Succession.
1750	The white population of the 13 mainland colonies approaches 1 million.
1756-63	The French and Indian War (in America) or the Seven Years' War.
1763	The Treaty of Paris and the British acquisition of Canada.

The Mature British Empire in North America

In 1775, the first British Empire had reached its apogee. In the western Atlantic alone, there were 26 colonial jurisdictions stretching from Newfoundland and Nova Scotia in the north to the Lesser Antilles in the Caribbean and from the Atlantic Ocean to the Mississippi River, including the new province of Quebec, and northwest to Hudson Bay. The thirteen colonies that left the Empire were similar to each other in important ways and differed from all the other North Atlantic and West Indian parts of the Empire. The former had well-established permanent populations who had governed themselves routinely through local representative institutions for several generations. This was in contrast to Newfoundland, for example, which was home to only about 10,000 people in a few scattered permanent settlements while serving a transient white population of unknown size in the offshore fishing economy. Elsewhere, the settlements in the Caribbean, that is the British West Indies, ranged in size and importance from the small and prosperous St. Kitts to the small and obscure Anguilla. The large island of Jamaica and the densely populated Barbados were wealthy and very important to the British economy but were managed by resident governors and controlled to some degree by absentee owners pulling strings in Parliament. Their small resident white populations of planters, overseers, and government officials were shrinking minorities in the 1770s in increasingly slave-dominated populations. Only Jamaica and Barbados had total populations comparable in size to some of those on the mainland, but, in 1775, only 18,000 whites resided among 193,000 black slaves in Jamaica. That 90-plus per cent black majority applied in general to the British Caribbean. While several of the southern mainland colonies also had large slave populations, even South Carolina, with a near 60 per cent black majority, the closest mainland colony to the Caribbean's demographics, contained a white population of nearly 50,000 who were permanent land holding residents. Nova Scotia and the vast, newly acquired Province of Quebec had neither the density of population of the thirteen older mainland colonies, nor their customary representational politics. The 80,000 or so French speaking *habitants* were concentrated in a long, narrow strip along the shores of the St. Lawrence River. Nova Scotia's population was approximately 26,000 in 1770, including former New Englanders who had experience with representative government, but when the Revolution came the people showed little enthusiasm for it.

The Navigation Acts of the middle to late seventeenth century had established a controlled economic system, a "mercantilist" design in which the metropolis (England) drew raw materials from its Atlantic colonies, provided them with finished goods, and determined the shipping rules for the imperial network. The purpose of mercantilism here was to limit the contacts between the colonies and other trading nations such as France and Holland. Before that time, the mainland settlements had operated as mostly private religious or commercial enterprises, and, even after the onset of trade regulations, they retained much of their self-determination. The newer colonies, created between the Restoration of the Stuarts in 1660 and the early eighteenth century, were each granted charters that allowed distinctive social and political character-istics to develop. From the start, the New England settlements of Plymouth (1620) and Massachusetts Bay (1630) and those in the Chesapeake in Virginia (1607) and Maryland (1634) were settled by people who came to stay. Even Virginia, a transient economic venture to some, was intended to attract permanent white settlers. It became the most populous British American jurisdiction in the revolutionary era because the survivors of the first generation of instability and strife went on to form permanent, localized, and self-consciously "Virginian" communities by 1700. The early English investments in the Caribbean, or Newfoundland or Bermuda, by contrast, were not primarily set on "planting" permanent communities, and what first separates the mainland colonies from all the others was the commitment of the white settlers in the former to maintain permanent communities, along with institutions of representa-tional government.

The British Caribbean in the Eighteenth Century

The Caribbean is a series of archipelagos, a large maritime region of islands of various sizes and topographies. Before the English integrated their Atlantic economy in the late seventeenth century and invested in the Caribbean, the islands had been havens for pirates, deported political dissenters, fugitive criminals, outlawed religious radicals, exiled protestant Frenchmen, and a mélange of proletarian refugees and opportunists. Even after the establishment of thriving sugar colonies, there was not much residential permanence. Where the pre-1660s communities of the mainland did encounter some parts of the Caribbean's floating human detritus, the established societies of New England or the Chesapeake either rejected or assimilated them. The Caribbean began not as a melting pot of religious and ethnic groups but as a stew of the outcast, the out-lawed, the marginalized and restless. Even New Providence in the Bahamas, which was to be a Puritan religious community, became a haven for pirates. Historian Richard Dunn catches the contemporary impression of Barbados when he cites Henry Whistler's apt description of the island in 1655 as "a dunghill whereon England doth cast forth its rubbish. Rogues and whores and such like people are those which are gen-erally brought here" (spelling modernized). Another characteristic of the West Indies was that it was in a constant military and economic flux as the major European powers wrestled for control of the most strategic or economically promising islands. In the end, the "dunghill" of Barbados became one of the most prosperous British colonies of the eighteenth century, but it was a slave society and its raison d'être was the pursuit of wealth and not the transplantation of English society. In 1673, the Barbadian popula-tion comprised 21,000 whites and 33,000 blacks, virtually all of whom were slaves, and, by the time the British abolished slavery in 1834, those figures were 12,700 and 80,800 respectively. Not only had the percentage of whites dropped from about 40 per cent of the whole to about 14 per cent but also, in real numbers, whites did not replace themselves in Barbados.

In the century after the Restoration, the white populations of the cash crop mainland colonies, in particular Virginia, grew at healthy and steady rates even as the proportion and numbers of slaves rose. South Carolina owed much of its early growth to the migration of white slaveholding West Indians, and the white populations of the Carolinas grew steadily throughout the eighteenth century even as their economies became slave dependent. In broad terms, the ratio of whites to blacks in the New England colonies in 1775 was 35 to 1; in the middle Atlantic colonies of the mainland, about 14 to 1; in the Chesapeake colonies of Virginia and Maryland, about 1.7 to 1; and, in the lower south, about 1.3 to 1, with a small black majority in South Carolina. In the British West Indies, the ratio was 1 to 9, a black majority of nearly 90 per cent. These numbers become even more compelling when the residential habits of the white population are considered. Not all slaveholding planters in the Caribbean and the Atlantic island of Bermuda were absentee owners, but enough were to create, at best, an irregular pattern of social and political commitment. White merchants, artisans, slave drivers and overseers, and Royal government officials rotated through the island societies and back to Britain. Even the slave population, while growing, also required steady replacement because of high mortality rates.

Table 1.1: Racial Composition of the British Caribbean Population, 1660-1760 (percentages in brackets)

These figures are aggregate figures. The ratio of whites to blacks was roughly similar in each colony but there was some variation from island to island.

	White		Black		Total
1660	33,139	(50.3)	32,732	(49.7)	65,871
1710	27,461	(17)	133,800	(83)	161,261
1760	42,686	(12)	313,177	(88)	355,863

Adapted from Jack P. Greene, *Pursuits of Happiness: The Social Development of Early Modern British Colonies and the Formation of American Culture* (Chapel Hill: University of North Carolina Press, 1988), 178-79.

By the beginning of the eighteenth century, there were hardly enough natives left in the Caribbean to count, and the large Arawak and Carib populations, numbering in the hundreds of thousands when Columbus arrived, had been exterminated.

The Thirteen Mainland Colonies
Before the Revolution, there were three models for creating colonies in mainland British North America. All involved the issuing of a charter by the Crown, not unlike

those of the East India Company (1600), the Hudson's Bay Company (1670), or the Royal African Company (1672), which established trade and administrative monopolies. Charters were also issued to joint stock companies such as the London Company of 1606 (later the Virginia and Plymouth colonies of 1607 and 1620 respectively) or to a religious corporation of covenanting congregations, such as the Massachusetts Bay Company of 1629, or to existing settlements, such as Connecticut and Rhode Island in the 1660s. These English settlements were organized by company-appointed governors and officials. In the course of accommodating immigrants, granting land, and laying out towns, these companies designed their own representative assemblies. Twelve years after the initial settlement of Virginia, the House of Burgesses was created, making it the first representative political chamber established by Europeans in the Americas. Its representational system was based on the needs and participation of the landed minority, which would come to control Virginia's politics in the seventeenth century. The Massachusetts Puritans set up a governing General Court upon their arrival in America in 1630. Regardless of what they were called, or their precise mandates or operations, similar institutions were firmly in place in all the colonies by the early eighteenth century as the engines of local authority. By then, they were increasingly referred to as the "General Assembly" or simply the "Assembly." A second charter model was the "proprietary" grant, such as the 1634 charter given to the second Lord Baltimore (Cecilius Calvert) for Maryland, or to William Penn in 1681 for Pennsylvania. In these cases, the proprietor appointed the governor and made allowance for a law making body. Exceptions to the individual proprietary grants occurred in the Carolinas in the 1660s, when a group of proprietors was named in the original charter, and in Georgia in 1732, when a philanthropic Board of Trustees was given a charter to settle the defined area with the poor and destitute of London. The third model was the Royal charter, a monopoly granted by the Crown, in effect, to itself. Here the Crown appointed the governor but again required an elected legislative body, which was normally drawn from resident landholders.

Decades of probing in the western and northern Atlantic had preceded the issuing of the first charters. In the earliest phase of colonization, there was no consistent policy or strategy for empire, and the medley of settlements and charters attest to that. At the very level of policy, or the lack of it, really, British America's origins are significantly different from those of the colonies established by other major imperial powers of the age. The arbitrary grants to groups, companies, or individuals made scant reference to the natives who were assumed, in most cases, to be absorbed under the new colonial authorities. One has to strain through the dense pages of the Massachusetts Bay Charter of 1629, for example, to find very brief references to natives such as encouraging the Company to "incite the Natives...to the Knowledg and Obedience of the only true God and sauior of Mankinde, and the Christian Fayth." From north to south, the mainland colonies were established as follows:

New England

Massachusetts was settled in 1630 under the Massachusetts Bay Charter of 1629. It absorbed Plymouth Colony in 1691, which had been settled in 1620 by Church of England separatists, the "Pilgrims," from a part of the London Company grant. The Massachusetts Bay Company sought to create a Christian commonwealth to "purify" the Church of England in America. The Maine area was attached in 1677. The original company charter was withdrawn in 1684, and Massachusetts was part of the Dominion of New England until 1689. A royal charter was issued in 1691. Most of New England was settled by congregations on small family farms in organized towns.

Connecticut was settled in the mid-1630s by Puritans from Massachusetts, who established settlements, including New Haven, which were combined as Connecticut under a private charter in 1662. That charter survived the War for Independence.

Rhode Island was originally settled by dissidents led by Roger Williams from Massachusetts in the 1630s. Anne Hutchinson, another dissident, was expelled from Massachusetts for challenging Puritan orthodoxy and made her way into the colony. A thriving Puritan settlement at Providence was chartered in 1662, and that private charter survived to the Revolution.

New Hampshire's first permanent white settlers arrived as a group in 1623, and the settlement was governed without a charter until 1679 when it was made a crown colony. There had been small and isolated settlements all along the New England coast from the first decade of the seventeenth century. These disappeared or were absorbed into the four eighteenth-century provinces.

Middle Colonies

New York: The Dutch were the first Europeans to settle there and, after 1613, developed a thriving economy based on the interior fur trade. The English wrested the colony from the Dutch in the 1660s, and a formal charter was granted to the Duke of York in 1664. There was a brief resumption of Dutch control in 1673-74, and the colony was administered as part of the Dominion of New England from 1686 to 1689. It became a royal province in 1691.

New Jersey was settled permanently by the English from New York in the 1660s. Proprietors then gained charters for East and West Jersey, and the two were combined as a royal colony, as New Jersey, in 1702.

Pennsylvania was carved out of the remaining large tract of land open to white settlement on the mainland between New York and Virginia with a charter given to the proprietor, the Quaker William Penn in 1681. It remained in his heirs' hands until the Revolution. It did, however, change the terms of the proprietary authority in 1701 to allow more open settlement. Thereafter, as Pennsylvania became known as the "best poor man's country," it attracted the most diverse ethnic and religious population in the British Empire. The Pennsylvania grant indicated the scale of the

Map 1.1 Colonial North America in 1750

colonial American land mass. Penn was granted title to land that was larger than England in area.

Delaware was originally settled by the Swedish in 1638. The territory was then made part of the Pennsylvania grant and became a separate proprietary colony in 1703.

South

Virginia began with the establishment of Jamestown in 1607 and was the first permanent English settlement in America. The successor to the London Company of 1606, the Virginia Company, a joint stock enterprise, ultimately failed in 1624 after revisions to the original charter, and was replaced with a crown charter.

Maryland shared the Chesapeake with Virginia. It was created in 1632 with a proprietary charter and settled initially in 1634 by English Catholic refugees. It developed in much the same way as Virginia, but on a smaller scale.

North Carolina was settled by Virginians in the 1650s. It was then chartered to eight nobles in 1663 as part of the larger Carolina grant and gradually drew away from the southern portion. Between 1691 and 1712, the two colonies went their separate ways, and each was made a royal colony in 1729.

South Carolina became wealthier than North Carolina within a few decades as cash crops and a huge slave population made it the most slave dependent economy in the south by the late eighteenth century.

Georgia was the last of the thirteen colonies to be created. The 1732 charter combined proprietary and royal grant authority. It was founded by the philanthropist James Oglethorpe and a board of trustees as a refuge for English paupers and funded by Parliament as a buffer between British America and Spanish America. Slavery was banned, initially, but the prohibition was violated. When Parliament ended the experiment in 1752, Georgia became a royal colony, and open settlement and huge slave importations followed.

Population Growth in Mainland British North America

The white settlement of mainland North America has been described by at least one historian as "swarming." By the middle of the eighteenth century, war, disease, territorial expropriation, and assimilation had scattered and in some places eliminated native populations. In most of Spanish or French North America, white settlement remained sparse, and miscegenation was tolerated and even encouraged. Although diseases ravaged native populations everywhere and war was a factor in all European and native contacts (especially in the Spanish sixteenth-century invasions of Central and South America), there was nothing in New France or Spanish North America to compare with the displacement of indigenous peoples in the settled areas of British America. After a century of settlement, a Caucasian population, accompanied by an African minority, had transformed the human landscape. On the other hand, white populations remained thin until well after American independence on the edges of the North American Empire — in Newfoundland, Nova Scotia, and

Rupert's Land (the area around Hudson Bay, north and west of New France).

The causes of the Revolution are sometimes read back from 1776 to see the colonies preparing themselves for independence. Political institutions, such as representative assemblies, cultivated ideas of political rights, and a maturing of social settings and growing white populations ended up with what historian Jack Greene described as a metaphorical "parent-child" relationship, with the Empire as parent or guardian. That view takes a shift in British imperial policy in the middle of the eighteenth century as a trigger to a nascent colonial separatism. We might assume, however, that mainland North America's evolution into a white dominant settler community was a self-conscious extension of Britain rather than a proto-form independence movement and that the permanent and increasingly "British" communities of mainland North America were close and affectionate extensions of the mother country. Still, the thirteen colonies did revolt, and, if they were not heading that way all along, they were developing cultural and political qualities that made them mature enough to resist British attempts to change the imperial relationship.

In 1750, there were an estimated 1,170,760 people living in the thirteen colonies (or provinces as they were increasingly and formally identified) of mainland North America. The number of black people in that population was 236,420, or about 20 per cent of the whole, with a considerable concentration south of Pennsylvania. All but about 5 per cent of blacks were in bondage, and, in fact, there were more slaves in Virginia (nearly 100,000) than there were whites in each but four of the other colonies. There are no reliable estimates of the ratio of African-born to African Americans in the black population, and the number of natives in that total population is unknown. Slaves were counted as slaves without much concern for nativity, and local tax and poll lists and various other censuses ignored natives in their counts or factored them into the gross numbers without identifying them.

Tragically, as the native population was being systematically reduced, it was also invisible to the extent that the first official census of the United States in 1790 did not appear to include natives in the totals. Some anthropological and ethnographic estimates put the number of natives in 1750 in the settled areas of the thirteen colonies at about 20,000, a paltry number and only 10 per cent of what it had probably been when the first whites arrived. The white population passed 1,000,000 in the early to mid-1750s and would double in the next 25 years in a continuing high rate of natural increase and steady immigration. We can be sure that, despite colonial anti-miscegenation laws and practices, there was some racial mixing in the population, but anyone of mixed racial parentage would normally be assigned the status of native or black. Between 1750 and 1770, the population had nearly doubled, to an estimated 2,121,326, including 457,097 blacks. By 1780, during the War for Independence, the estimated population, including Vermont, Kentucky, and Tennessee, was 2,780,369 including 575,420 blacks. Even as that war dragged on, immigrants arrived in large numbers, along with a steady stream of slaves. The sources for the following figures take no notice of natives in the counts.

Table 1.2: Selected Population Figures for the Mainland North American Colonies W. = White. B. = Black.

New England

		New Hampshire	Massachusetts	Rhode Island	Connecticut
1720	W.	9,205	88,858	11,137	57,737
	B.	170	2,150	543	1,093
1750	W.	26,955	183,925	29,897	108,270
	B.	550	3,035	3,347	3,010
1770	W.	61,742	*261,336	54,435	178,183
	B.	654	*5,229	3,761	5,698
1780	W.	87,261	*317,760	**50,275	200,816
	B.	541	*5,280	**2,671	5,885

* Includes the Maine counties of Massachusetts, which were listed separately after 1750. The Massachusetts figures for 1770 included 30,783 whites and 475 blacks in the Maine counties; for 1780, the figures were 48,675 and 458 respectively.

** Rhode Island's population declined as the British wartime occupation of Newport drove many inhabitants into neighboring provinces.

Total New England population in 1780:
White: 656,112
Black: 14,377 (a drop of 975 persons from the 1770 figures).

Middle Colonies

		New York	New Jersey	Pennsylvania	Delaware
1720	W.	31,179	27,433	28,962	4,685
	B.	5,740	2,385	2,000	700
1750	W.	65,682	66,039	116,794	27,208
	B.	11,014	5,354	2,872	1,496
1770	W.	143,808	109,211	234,296	33,660
	B.	19,112	8,220	5,761	1,836
1780	W.	189,487	128,987	319,450	42,389
	B.	21,054	10,460	7,855	2,996

Total Middle Colonies population in 1780:
White: 680,313
Black: 42,365

Southern Colonies

		Maryland	Virginia	North Carolina	South Carolina	Georgia
1720	W.	53,634	61,158	18,270	5,048	—
	B.	12,499	26,599	3,000	12,000	—
1750	W.	97,623	129,581	53,184	25,000	4,200
	B.	43,450	101,452	19,800	39,000	1,000
1770	W.	138,781	259,411	127,600	49,066	12,750
	B.	63,818	187,605	69,600	75,178	10,625
1780	W.	164,595	317,422	179,133	83,000	35,240
	B.	80,515	220,582	91,000	97,000	20,831

Total Southern Colonies Population in 1770:
White: 779,390
Black: 509,528

All Colonies

	*** Totals for 1770	*** Totals for 1780
White	1,688,254	2,204,949
Black	459,822	575,420
Total	2,148,076	2,780,369

*** The aggregate totals include some 14,000 whites and 2,700 blacks in Kentucky and Tennessee and 10,000 whites and 25 blacks in Vermont in 1770 as well as about 46,000 whites and about 9,000 blacks in Kentucky and Tennessee and 47,750 whites and about 50 blacks in Vermont in 1780. The figures for those territories and settlements are not listed among the state populations in the foregoing charts.

Source: Data from U.S. Bureau of the Census, *Historical Statistics of the United States, Colonial Times to 1970* (Washington: Bureau of the Census, 1975), Part 2, Section 7, pp 1168ff.

Those figures, while estimates, are reliable enough to make several observations. After the first generation of English settlement in mainland North America, the total population of non-natives was about 50,000, including 1,600 blacks in 1650. The doubling every generation thereafter of the white population and the sensational growth of the black slave population in the south after 1700, while the native population was almost disappearing, must rank as one of the great demographic transformations to occur anywhere in the modern Western world. In the period between 1700 and the outbreak of the War for Independence, an estimated 350,000 whites and 200,000 slaves came to the mainland colonies of British America. There was never an even distribution of white or black arrivals. Nor was there an even growth of the native-born white population. New England, for example, contained a much higher proportion of American-born adults than would be the case in North Carolina or Pennsylvania. Not only would some colonies have higher ratios of Caucasian immigrants, but there was also an obvious skewing of the slave population. For every African slave brought into Massachusetts in the middle of the eighteenth century several hundred were delivered to Charleston, South Carolina. On the eve of the Revolution, Virginia's slave population contained higher ratios of English-speaking slaves than did South Carolina and Georgia, simply because Virginia's and Maryland's communities of slaves had been producing offspring since before the turn of the eighteenth century. The demand for slaves in the far south after about 1750 seemed insatiable as the Carolina and Georgia economies boomed.

The slave who arrived in the lower south in the eighteenth century was a tragic immigrant indeed. The trade itself was a lethal mechanism that began in some of the interior regions of Africa with prisoners of war or with straightforward kidnapping of peoples, followed by the brutal transit of shackled slaves to the coast and onto packed ships to be deposited, terrorized, and socially alienated, in most cases, on the shores of the Americas. The records indicate that nearly 100,000 slaves were landed at Charleston between 1700 and 1775, most of these after 1740. For every 100 slaves who reached Charleston, as many as 25 died en route from disease, depression and suicide, and the rigors of corporal punishment. Slavery was a linked series of crimes, and the slave merchants, traders, and carriers were the first criminals in the chain.

The Social Geography of the Colonies

The American mainland population was spread over territory that ran in a north-south line from the tenuous northern reaches of New England, on the border of New France, to the boundary between southern Georgia and Spanish Florida. The distance between the French to the north and the Spanish to the south was about 1,200 miles as the crow flies. Each of the thirteen colonies began at the Atlantic Ocean to the east, and most tapered out toward the Appalachians. The latter includes a number of smaller cordilleras and other landforms and is best thought of as a raised braided belt running in a southwestern to northeastern line from the Gulf of Mexico plain to the Gaspe Peninsula in eastern Quebec. The Blue Ridge Mountains, Great Valley, Cumberland Plateau, Great Smoky Mountains, and Catskill, Green, and White Mountains of New England are all part of the Appalachians, one of the great geographical features of North America. To the east of the Appalachians and including the Piedmont (foothills), the range of soil types and vegetation was extensive, and climate differences were significant not only in a north to south graduation but from the seaboard to the western limits of settlement. In northern New England, there were only about 150 frost-free days annually compared to as many as 350 days in coastal South Carolina and Georgia. Boston's mean annual temperature of about 50 degrees Fahrenheit compares to 45 in western Massachusetts. Charleston's 66 degrees drops to 60 in the western uplands of the Carolinas. At its widest, the distance from the Atlantic to the spine of the Appalachians is about 300 miles. Thus, the British settlements in North America were confined to a long and narrow band on the Atlantic, in striking contrast to the range of French and Spanish probing and contact in North America. British settlement was concerned with filling in a well-defined area with farms and plantations, towns, and parishes, in communities of resident permanent populations. The relatively small Spanish settlements of the area north of Mexico were strung out from Florida to the Pacific, and the French, apart from concentrations of populations in Acadia and New France, were sparsely distributed in a web of trade and exploration that extended westward beyond the Mississippi and into the higher latitudes of eastern North America. There was no such horizon or vision or activity in the settlement patterns of pre-revolutionary British colonists, but the ill-defined borderlands between the British, French, and Spanish territorial claims were increasingly tested by confrontational land seeking British colonists. By the 1740s, farmers and fur traders began to seep west through the mountain passes into the Ohio Valley, into territory that was still heavily populated by native peoples and claimed by the French.

In some respects, the British colonies on the Atlantic seaboard functioned like separate countries, with well-defined social, economic, and political cultures and clear territorial boundaries. They were linked by language, citizenship, and imperial attachment, but, in many ways, existed in parochial separation from each other. The hundreds of thousands of farmers, planters, merchants, lawyers, artisans, and slaves ranging over a thousand miles of coastline were Virginians or New Yorkers or New Englanders, and they represented a medley of European origins, mostly English but also Dutch, German, Scotch-Irish (or Ulster), Scots, Irish, and others. What these colonial Americans had in common, however, were political, legal, and literary values, and, even as they matured as New Englanders or Marylanders, they retained much that was British, and they retained it collectively.

Cultures

Historian David Hackett Fischer describes colonial American regions as modified transplantations of the donor cultures of the British Isles. Thus, the Puritans who founded New England fused their English origins to both their mission and their need to adjust to the climate, space, and opportunities. Similarly, the frontier societies established by migrant Scots, Scotch-Irish, and others reflected their Celtic backgrounds and sometimes intense religious habits. Those basic premises applied to the Virginia planters and the slaveholding grandees of South Carolina, many of whom had descended from servants but all of whom imitated parts of what they perceived to be British gentry behavior. By meshing original purpose and subsequent development into what he called "seeds," Fischer then studied the product of those seeds — *four* distinct cultural regions — as the main characteristics of American society from the colonial period to beyond the Revolution.

What Fischer calls "greater" New England extended to northern New York and Long Island. The population was characterized by high levels of literacy, town government,

19

nuclear families, a strong emphasis on basic education, and the availability of higher education at domestic institutions such as Harvard (1636) and Yale (1701). There was a very low incidence of violence and crime in general. New Englanders enjoyed a rough equality of economic status, and land holdings were small by other American standards. Towns helped bind the nuclear families into communal networks. The Congregational church model was still dominant into the middle of the eighteenth century and probably enhanced local, neighborly, and family coherence. Residential persistence was high, with more than 75 per cent of adults remaining in the same place for more than ten years. The original Calvinist orthodoxy in Massachusetts had been modified by the middle of the eighteenth century, but the Calvinists' civil structure, the town, remained a significant social and political legacy. The basic social feature was order, but of a kind that Fischer pronounced "ordered liberty." Massachusetts can be seen as both dominant and culturally representative of the region.

A second regional distinction can be seen in the so-called "middle colonies" or "mid-Atlantic" region that included New Jersey, Pennsylvania, Delaware, and the northern counties of Maryland, but not New York. The ethnic and religious mix of the populations in this region resulted in some political, cultural, and economic pluralism. According to Fischer, these societies maintained high levels of basic education but showed no penchant for higher education. Farm communities and farm clusters and mostly nuclear families dominated the social landscape. While there was still a strong Quaker influence in religious matters in Pennsylvania and neighboring areas, there was a substantial Presbyterian presence and sufficient varieties of other Protestant churches to offset the possibility of a fixed ecclesiastical dominance, especially after 1750. The area was marked by a strong political and economic egalitarianism and close-knit community relations. The area was the most ethnically mixed one in America. Land grants were about double the size of those in New England and about 35 per cent of the Tidewater acreages. The Delaware Valley was culturally and economically representative of the region as a whole, and personal liberties were reciprocated by a balance of interests and economic variation.

A third region, the Tidewater south, was distinct from the so-called "back country" of the south, and even from the Piedmont (the various sets of foothills in each colony). The Tidewater was, and remains in name, a band of coastal territory running south from the Chesapeake to the Georgia coast. It was home to the colonial period's greatest concentration of slavery and wealth. The outstanding features of this society were lower levels of general literacy; the importance of parishes, courts, and plantations in local government; and the prevalence of extended families and the absence of anything resembling an urban culture. Neither Virginia nor Maryland had a port with international connections, and the tobacco trade was conducted on wharves that dotted the banks of the area's navigable rivers. Education standards were weak at the basic level and strong at the higher levels, where the wealthier planters hired tutors and sent their sons to Britain for learning. It was a more violent society than New England's. There was more pronounced class deference than in New England, and land grants were on average nearly six times larger, which favored a moneyed minority. The dominant religion was Anglican (Church of England), and churches were located in parishes that in many cases were little more than a scattering of rural hamlets. Virginia dominated the Tidewater region and, even with the rising power of the colonies farther south, remained the key political force in the region. The Virginia Tidewater slave society spread into the rolling terrain of the Piedmont by the middle of the eighteenth century to extend the plantation system as far inland as the soils and climate would allow. Power in the Tidewater was based on something Fischer called "hegemonic liberty," which is taken to mean that freedom for the individual was guaranteed by, and mostly for, elites. Four of the first five presidents of the United States were Virginians.

Historians other than Fischer have long identified the southern highlands as a fourth colonial region. The backcountry culture on the frontier or fringes of eighteenth- and early nineteenth-century America was the destination of the largest numbers of white immigrants and inter-colonial migration. Inland North Carolina had the highest rate of population growth of any part of colonial America by the middle of the eighteenth century. Participation in formal education was low, as was literacy, and the family unit was more likely characterized by an extended clan relationship than by either the strict nuclear or extended family relations evident in other regions. The geographical mobility of frontier peoples resulted in only 25 per cent to 40 per cent of adults retaining the same domicile after ten years, compared to the more than 75 per cent rate in New England. The culture was marked by more pronounced male dominance than was found in any of the other settings. Pre-nuptial pregnancy rates were high compared to New England and the middle colonies, and higher even than in the Tidewater south. No towns of any consequence existed in the area, there were few concentrations of farms, and the "folk" habits of the population were clearly influenced by North British and Celtic traditions. Presbyterianism was the dominant but far from the exclusive religious affiliation. The courts exercised political authority. There was a high incidence of conflict with natives whose territorial claims were being challenged by force and threat and treaty. The "natural" or highly personalized liberty of the population indicates a very subjective set of interpersonal relations and limited formal politics. In most of the southern backcountry, there were communities whose residents seemed exotic, remote, and even wild to the Tidewater or British visitor.

In the late 1760s, the Anglican Church missionary Charles Woodmason ventured into the backcountry of South Carolina and reported scenes and conditions that caught some of the region's social atmosphere. His journals and other writings, edited by Richard J. Hooker and published in *The Carolina Backcountry on the Eve of Revolution*, provide an impassioned critique of backcountry religion and of the elite response to it. Woodmason criticized the ruling classes of South Carolina, "so rich, so luxurious, so Polite a People," for ignoring the religious needs (their Anglican Church responsibilities) and economic condition of the frontier settlements. Those leaders, he noted, "look upon the poor White People in a Meaner Light than their Black Slaves, and care less for them." What annoyed Woodmason more, it seems, was the

"Republican Spirit" of the Carolina grandees and the fact that they "seem not at all disposed to promote the Interest of the Church of England [Anglican Church]." Indeed, they had spent a fortune to attract "over 5 or 6000 Ignorant, mean, worthless, beggardly Irish Presbyterians, the Scum of the Earth, and Refuse of Mankind…solely to ballance the Emigrations of People from Virginia who are all of the Established [Anglican] Church." The "wild Peoples" Woodmason observed dressed and behaved in a way that left him aghast, and resulted in the following colorful impression:

> The men with only a thin Shirt and a pair of Breeches or Trousers on — barelegged and barefooted — The Women bare-headed, barelegged and barefoot with only a thin Shift and under Petticoat… The Young Women have a most uncommon Practice, which I cannot break them off. They draw their Shift as tight as possible to the Body, and pin it close to shew the roundness of their Breasts, and slender Waists (for they are generally finely shaped) and draw their Petticoat close to their Hips to shew the fineness of their Limbs — so that they might as well be in Puri Naturalibus — Indeed Nakedness is not censurable or indecent here, and they expose themselves often quite Naked, without Ceremony — Rubbing themselves and their Hair with Bears Oil and tying it up behind in a Bunch like the Indians — being hardly one degree removed from them — In few Years, I hope to bring about a Reformation, as I already have done in several Parts of the Country.

One might be forgiven for doubting Woodmason's prospects.

There were, of course, smaller cultural or ethnic enclaves and subdivisions such as the Dutch in New York and New Jersey, Caribbean planters in the Carolinas, and a northern frontier abutting New France, so Fischer's models must be tempered. But he is right to suggest that the transfer of English and other British and European traditions to America and their persistence in modified form had contributed to regional variation. Thus, America's foundations were formed not simply from the effects of climate, terrain, economic ambition, or religious utopianism, but also from large-scale migratory and cultural patterns. Colonial Americans, according to Fischer, were modified Britons in segmented regional societies. To put that another way, revolutionary activists in New England were products of the imprint left by the social habits, familial organization, and cultural norms of the first generation and their localized English origins, modified by time and space.

Social and Economic Environments
Social historians continue to probe into the relationships between social settings, economic and occupational status, and culture. For example, eighteenth-century frontier society was characterized by a higher ratio of single males to females than was normal in other colonial settings and by generally lower standards of living. While land seemed abundant, it was not easily farmed, and any marketable surpluses were difficult to distribute. The frontier included the far northern and western parts of New York, western Pennsylvania and Virginia, and much of the southern highlands noted

above. On the other hand, the small family farm and its economy comprised the setting for the majority of white Americans in the middle and northern colonies, on the frontier, and in parts of the Tidewater south. These small holdings were run by the combined labor and skill of family units. Subsistence agriculture was the lot of the great majority of New Englanders and of those white landholders in the south who did not farm cash crops or own slaves. Males in these settings were usually multitalented and could turn to shoemaking, weaving, and even blacksmithing and carpentry to augment farm production and to complete the local rural community's other material needs. It was rare to find full-time craftsmen or artisans in most subsistence farm communities. The highly personalized economic relationships in those communities led to societies that encouraged a blend of collective interdependence and responsible individualism. In the Chesapeake and Tidewater Carolinas, the proportion of white planters with slaves was about 25 per cent, which meant that much of the local white population was engaged in subsistence or marginal farming. All of that led to greater disparities in income and social status in the southern white population than in the white population of the middle colonies and New England.

A different kind of agrarian economy was found on the larger grain and livestock farms of the middle colonies and in the tobacco, rice, and indigo plantations of the Chesapeake and south. This profit-based commercial agriculture produced surpluses for the imperial economy. Not only did the tobacco of Maryland and Virginia and elsewhere and the rice of lowland South Carolina produce wealth and status but so did the manors of New York and the successful livestock and grain farms of Pennsylvania, whose surpluses often went to the West Indies to feed slaves. Commercial farm labor was provided by slaves in the south and, in the north, by family units supplemented by white servants, and sometimes slaves. There were higher proportions of commercial farm units in Pennsylvania, for example, than in Massachusetts or the North Carolina backcountry. The economics of the middle colonies also made more use of full-time tradesmen, rural retailers, and landless white laborers. The smallest demographic environment in the eighteenth century, the urban port, was as vital to the colonial economy as any other. By the 1770s Boston, New York, and Philadelphia led the way as America's major entrepôts, but seaports such as Newport, Rhode Island, Salem, Massachusetts, and Charleston, South Carolina were also, by contemporary standards and definition, "urban." Only 5 per cent or so of the colonial population lived in towns of more than 2,500 people. Boston, including the several towns immediately adjacent to it, was home to less than 10 per cent of the Massachusetts population. Even Philadelphia, the largest city in the late eighteenth century with 40,000 people, represented a small numerical minority of the regional population. What primarily separates the urban setting from all others was the occupational range. Merchants, tradesmen, sailors, government officials, and skilled workers associated with printing, manufacturing, and specialized crafts economies thrived in these urban environments. The ports were the information and trade doorways to the Atlantic and simultaneously to the colonies' respective rural societies.

Colonial Classes and Social Mobility

Over forty years ago, historian Jackson Turner Main used the image of a social and economic ramp to describe revolutionary America, but his occupational and social taxonomy came with very real economic and class distinctions. At the lower end, he lumped together landless males, servants, mariners, some subsistence or marginal farmers, and unskilled laborers, husbandmen, and some tradesmen such as tailors and shoemakers. This group accounted for about 20 per cent of the entire population. While it was fairly evenly distributed, there were fewer "lower sorts" in some settings and more in others, such as the backcountry, the crowded towns of eastern New England, and the port cities. The "middling sorts" constituted the largest general group, according to Main, and most social historians agree that a competent middle class existed in colonial British America. In the rural areas in all colonies, the more successful full-time small farmers and most small-scale commercial farmers constituted a great middling stratum of Americans. In the larger towns and seaports, most of the successful craftsmen, professionals such as practicing physicians and lawyers, some retailers, and small-scale merchants made up a substantial middle class society. Perhaps as much as 50 per cent of the population fit the various social and economic criteria that Main and others have used to describe a middle stratum. An upper middle class of perhaps 20 per cent of the whole consisted of the more successful of the agricultural "middling sorts," including rural mill owners, an array of urban merchants, shipbuilders, distillers, printers, and craftsmen. Among the latter, one can place Benjamin Franklin (1706-90), a printer and entrepreneur, and Paul Revere (1735-1818), the Boston silversmith, whose artistic virtuosity enhanced his occupational status. There was an upper class of the "better sorts" whose roles in the various colonies inevitably involved political influence. Thomas Jefferson (1743-1826), a Virginia planter-slaveholder, and John Hancock (1737-93), a prominent, successful Boston merchant, lived in quite different social and cultural worlds, but shared an upper class status in their respective communities that translated into political authority.

An interesting wealth comparison can be seen in the following averages per free white male in the 1770-75 period:

Table 1.3: Net Wealth per Free White Person in British America and Total Wealth by Region, c. 1775

Net wealth is determined as the combination of assets.

Per free white person

Continental colonies, aggregate	74 pounds sterling, per capita.
Chesapeake and the South	132 pounds sterling, per capita.
Middle Colonies	51 pounds sterling, per capita.
New England	33 pounds sterling, per capita.

West Indies
Jamaica   1,200 pounds sterling, per capita.

Total wealth by region
New England   19,000,000 (aggregate wealth)
Middle Colonies   30,000,000 (aggregate wealth)
Upper and Lower South   86,000,000 (aggregate wealth)
Jamaica   18,000,000 (aggregate wealth)

Source: Adapted from John J. McCusker and Russell R. Menard, *The Economy of British America, 1607-1789* (Chapel Hill: University of North Carolina Press, 1985), 61.

These are averages and measure real and personal worth, but they are less than satisfactory in gauging well-being. For example, the Jamaica figure is what the planter class realized in assets and profits. Earlier in the eighteenth century, the worth of the wealthiest planters was in the 3,000 pounds sterling range, but the median income was under 400 pounds sterling. The white non-planter class in the West Indies was negligible. On the southern mainland, a core of wealthy planters probably did reach the 1,000 pounds sterling range, but, when the paltry incomes of small holders and landless white males are taken into account, the averages are meaningless. In the middle colonies and New England, the averages, however, were probably closer to the median worth of the population. Certainly that would be the case in large areas of rural Pennsylvania and southern New England. What the figures do show is the relative wealth of each region. In aggregate terms, Virginia was a richer colony than Massachusetts, but the latter's assets were more equally distributed than were Virginia's, and the local social and political status of a New Englander with an income of 500 pounds sterling per annum would be as great as any Virginian grandee who might need two or three times that much for similar status.

Women, the White Poor, and Slaves
Data on eighteenth-century white males have little to say about women, slaves, or poor, destitute, and marginalized peoples. To be sure, Fischer's cultural sociology brings women directly into his sketches, but what needs to be stressed is the way women helped define colonial life with their productive labor and their childbearing and nurturing. The social harmony that existed in agricultural communities can be inferred in many ways from the statistical and literary record, but it began in the emotional and intimate internal workings of the farm family. The planter's wife in the Chesapeake was involved in the business of the plantation, and widows in the south often retained central roles in the fortunes of the miniature communities of parish and plantation. However, in the increasingly hierarchical societies of the south, planters' wives were subordinate to males in the structured pecking order. The roles of poorer women in the south and of most small-farm women in the north can best be seen in the image of women pulling rough plows and raising vegetables as they helped the thousands of

small household economies survive. The central importance of domestic service to the cohesion of small communities, where young women moved from their own homes to the households of neighbors, is one of the truly significant influences on the shaping of American rural values. Yet, as central as women were to shaping the rhythms of everyday life, they were formally excluded from political roles. In legal terms, women's civil rights in most colonial American societies were conditional, truncated, or denied. Still, the strict gender separation of domestic and economic roles that would appear gradually in later decades had not yet developed in America's pre-industrial farm environment. Some older gender roles were specific, and farmwomen served as midwives, pharmacists, and medical consultants. However, by the late eighteenth and early nineteenth centuries, male professional physicians began to replace women as the communal health overseers. The New England "goodwife" survived as a transplant from England and adapted to American conditions as an agent of social integration, but, in the end, even America's more fluid environment did not encourage any tendency toward acknowledging formal equality for women.

The history of the African in all of British America was a process of steady degradation and legal exclusion. From a slow start in the middle of the seventeenth century, race-based slavery expanded until it defined the economies, the cultures, and the politics of the Chesapeake and then the lower south. The numbers alone are astonishing, but the historical significance of the system was its deeply etched legal and institutional severity. As physically and emotionally difficult as was the slave's immediate condition, the system created a more depressing legacy for African slaves and their progeny by condemning them to two centuries of institutionalized moral and social oppression. The sociologist Orlando Patterson once described slavery as "social death," but historians in recent years have shown that, over time, slaves created distinct and vibrant societies and cultures within the institution. But it was an *institution*.

The Chesapeake colonies in the 1660s had drawn a sharp legal and moral dividing line between the African servant and the Christian white population. A major Maryland slave code of 1664 announced that "all Negroes...already within the Province And All Negroes...to bee imported...shall serve *Durante Vita* [for life] And all Children born of any Negro...shall be Slaves as their ffathers were for the terme of their lives." The statute goes on to assign the same fate to the children of white women and "Negro" men. The "single drop" policy was born. Thereafter, anyone with any African "blood" was identified as black. Eventually, what resulted was a crude equation: black = slave = black. By 1705, Virginia had written a code that said "Slaves are the Negroes, and their Posterity, following the Condition of the Mother, according to the Maxim, *partus sequitur ventrem*. They are call'd Slaves, in respect of the time of their Servitude, because it is for Life."

These codes are extremely important in American history. The actual stripping away of slaves' moral identity when supplemented with law created a racially determined caste in America, one that was subjected to the tightest regulations and control in the Western Hemisphere. Moreover, the use of color as a marker became a commonplace, and the terms "negro" and "black" were used as adjectives and nouns. As the "single drop" principle took hold in the eighteenth century, the term "mulatto" appeared in the records to define a person of mixed African and Caucasian and even native parentage. In advertisements for runaway slaves or for slaves for sale, persons would be described as "light skinned" or "brown" and even "yellow" to indicate the presence of African lineage. By the nineteenth century, the term "colored" began to be used with some frequency to catch all the permutations that miscegenation produced.

The image of a social and economic ramp, rather than a ladder, should not blind us to the existence of poverty among the white population of late colonial America. Poor people existed at the edges of all communities, and in the midst of some. There were poor landless laborers, tramps, beggars, and idlers in most areas, and persistent numbers of working poor in the seaports. Imperial wars boosted coastal economies. But when those economic spurts collapsed in the wake of the treaties that ended the wars, economic insecurity returned. As land became scarce in eastern New England, the volume of rural transience rose. Still, it is not clear that there were higher percentages of poor people in the population overall or merely larger numbers of poor as the population rose everywhere and not only in New England. Rural communities had always treated needy families with charity, and chronic poverty was rare, but permanent almshouses and workhouses could be found in the seaports of Boston, New York, Philadelphia, and Charleston. In Boston, for example, in the second half of the eighteenth century, at least 5 per cent of the population was receiving relief at a given time. The same individuals did not always receive relief, and the total numbers of people who received charity or formal relief, even temporarily, in any given year in any of colonial America's ports constituted a proportion of the population much higher than 5 per cent. Widows and orphans were especially vulnerable, given that male mortality rates, while lower than those in Europe, were still high enough to create needy survivors.

There was not, however, a permanent or large population of dependent poor in colonial America. The people of British North America were healthier than those in the British Isles, and far healthier than those in the British West Indies. In fact, slaves, as more valued economic investments, would become healthier in British mainland America than their counterparts in Brazil and the Spanish and French Caribbean. Their diets and material conditions, but not their status, improved into the nineteenth century. The ramp was there for the majority of whites and for whites only, and the cliché that, in America, land was plentiful but people scarce held true throughout the colonial period. At one end of the ramp were clusters of economic, intellectual, and political elites who provided local and provincial leadership. At the other end were the masses of farmers, moving along the grade to competence and security and the means to transmit improved standards to their children.

The children of colonial America were miniature reflections of their parents' class and environment. Farm boys were in the fields as young as eight and nine years old, grooming themselves for an agricultural future and learning some useful skills, such as weaving or carpentry along the way. Farm girls were often sent to work as domestic help for neighbors. They were groomed for an agricultural future based on their upbringing and prospects for marriage to a suitable young farm adult with some acreage. For the economically better off children, say for instance the Boston merchant class or the plantation elites, the future might be in law or trade. Pre-adolescent boys studied accounting and classics, translated Latin or practiced bookkeeping and became the Adamses and Dickinsons, the Jeffersons and Madisons of revolutionary leadership. The daughters of the well-to-do were coached in manners and domestic protocol and, like the daughters of the middling and lower sorts, prepared for suitable marriage.

Politics in Eighteenth-Century British North America

The charter system and the establishment of representative assemblies resulted in roughly similar political structures in all thirteen mainland colonies. The colonies adopted and then adapted what was considered a transatlantic mirror of the "mixed" English system. The governor served as chief executive, responsible for appointments and administration, and a council served as a combination advisory body and upper chamber of legislation. The assembly discussed, made and forwarded laws, and represented the will and instructions of the electorate. To the colonial mind, these arrangements appeared to be local versions of the Crown, Lords, and Commons in the British system. From the earliest points of settlement, and according to the various charter instructions, colonists in North America had adapted English (or more appropriately in the eighteenth century, British) customs, laws, processes, and institutions to their local needs. Not only was the framework of government itself seen to be British, but residence rights, poor laws, marriage and inheritance laws, and a host of legal, social, and political habits were transplanted to America. These were intended to create customary forms of order and justice but were modified for use in America. America was not Britain. There was far more economic mobility in the colonies than in the old country, and property ownership in the colonies reached levels that were impossible in Britain. The colonial assemblies could not be versions of Parliament's House of Commons because of the way electoral participation in Britain was slight and almost static, with a minuscule number of eligible members for the Commons, even fewer hereditary Lords, and a very small electorate. The British electoral and legislative practices were the most open of European systems, but they were tightly controlled and manipulated by tradition, and by Parliament itself.

As Bernard Bailyn notes in his brief and trenchant *The Origins of American Politics* (1968), the importance of the colonial assemblies in the eighteenth century was the way they reflected local political values and expectations while referring to their inherent British constitutionality. Bailyn's conclusion is that, as colonial societies grew and matured, they developed assumptions of local prerogative. The private colonies of the early seventeenth century had formed local political systems out of necessity, but, after the Restoration of the Stuarts in 1660 and certainly by the Glorious Revolution of 1688-89, something like a formal and administered Empire had been matched in America by a more refined, focused, and innovative set of colonial governments. Eligibility, in say the Massachusetts General Court or the Maryland General Assembly, for example, expanded a bit during the seventeenth century, but as the original charter-holding groups disappeared, the process of inclusion and of competitive elections changed more rapidly after the start of the eighteenth century.

One way to understand the dynamics of assembly politics is to observe the role of the governor in the often charged atmosphere of legislative behavior. Governors, whose appointments were made by the Crown, were often backed by British patrons, and their written instructions stipulated unrealistic levels of personal influence and authority. The right to veto legislation and access to local patronage in appointing judges, tax assessors, customs agents, and others, including administrative assistants and deputies, appeared to give governors leverage in local politics. But all along, and especially after the early eighteenth century, those privileges were usually retarded or negated, as the assemblies assumed more responsibilities and self-assurance and as they reduced the independence of governors with tax legislation and procedures for appointments. Moreover, as Bailyn has emphasized, assemblies were continuous and longer lasting than governorships. Not only did most appointed governors see their appointments as short-term opportunities, but often their sponsors in Britain, who had wangled their appointments, fell from grace or favor and could not support their colonial clients. Proprietary and royal governors, with some notable exceptions, lasted on average about three years while assemblies tended to be continuous, repeatedly electing experienced and long-serving local members. By and large, the governor's role, while ostensibly central to colonial administration, was shaped more by local conditions than by formal definition, and, as time went on, governors began to depend on the cooperation of assemblies and thus were drawn into the dynamics of local politics.

A remarkable feature of colonial history is that every colony evolved into something quite different from, and even at odds with, the original intentions of the settlement mandate and the original settlers' hopes and intentions. It was not a static world and neither were the colonies' political or constitutional identities fixed or unchanging. By the 1760s, eight of the thirteen mainland colonies were royal colonies, with charters that were ostensibly owned by the Crown and administered by governors appointed by the Crown. As noted, two colonies, Rhode Island and Connecticut, retained their private charters, and three were still under proprietary control: Maryland, Pennsylvania, and Delaware. But if the Crown had nominal administrative control of eight of the colonies, the Crown had not, in fact, ever settled and directly operated any colony. This alone sets the mainland societies apart from the other European ventures in the New World. The royal charters either had replaced earlier private charters or had been granted after informal or migratory settlement had taken root. For the most part, they either were grafted on to existing political cultures or were obliged to accommodate developing ones.

From the cliques and elites in the southern colonies to the heated partisan politics in Pennsylvania to the lively town-based representations in New England, political culture in the colonies was dynamic. There were coups and attempted coups as these societies grew and matured. One such domestic revolt failed: Bacon's Rebellion in Virginia in 1676 attempted unsuccessfully to break down the power of the planter elite. At the imperial level, the ousting in 1689 by New Englanders of Governor Andros of the short-lived Dominion of New England was a major demonstration of the vitality of colonial self-determination. Those are among the more conspicuous political tremors that ran through mainland British America. A common political theme during the period was the often contentious and always lively relationship between the various colonial assemblies and their respective governors. The most dramatic example of those energies was the John Peter Zenger libel action in New York in 1733-35.

The Zenger Affair

Along with its neighbors in the mid-Atlantic region, New York had a more varied ethnic and religious composition than New England or the south. New York had a large Dutch minority and the largest black population in numbers and percentage (nearly 15 per cent of the whole) of any colony north of the Chesapeake. The large manors that dotted the Hudson River Valley had no parallel in the north in wealth, size, or in the status of their white tenant populations. New York had a firm resource and agricultural economy, and New York City had become a shipping and commercial hub for the region between Boston and Philadelphia. For all its social and cultural distinctiveness, its political structure was not unlike other royal and proprietary colonies: a governor, a council, and an elected assembly. Its political history was similar to that of other colonies, which, at one time or another, had gone through rancorous governor versus assembly confrontations and power struggles. The Zenger affair is important not only for the precedents it set but also for what it revealed of colonial political values in the 1730s. It is a vivid example of the clash between governor and assembly, of the rising importance of factions, and of the principle of opposition in local politics. It reflects too on the way local colonial political factions referred to English political theory in their debates and, in particular, on how English Whig political theory informed the practical politics of the American assemblies.

William Cosby, wryly identified by the *Dictionary of American Biography* as "the *unenlightened* royal governor of New York and New Jersey, 1731-1735/6" (emphasis added), began to exercise what he saw as his gubernatorial privileges soon after taking office by making a series of patronage appointments and sinecures. He was supported by a faction in the assembly led by James Delancey. In 1733, Cosby suspended the Chief Justice of New York, Lewis Morris, and appointed Delancey to the position. Morris, who was New York-born, saw the issue as a usurpation of the "time-honored traditions" of English constitutional practices. He protested the patronage as a blatant corruption of assembly rights that violated parliamentary protocol and theory. He and others started *The New York Weekly Journal*, printed by the German-born John Peter Zenger. They began a steady and vituperative attack on Governor Cosby, the members of the council in his favor, and the assembly faction that had supported his actions and that now was in the Delancey camp. Soon enough, the issue polarized the political community. In a steady editorial assault on Cosby, Delancey and the so-called "Court" party, the provincial American Morris used the tracts of the English radical pamphleteers John Trenchard and Thomas Gordon, tracts referred to as "Cato's Letters" and originally published in London in 1720-23. This association of the Cosby-Delancey axis with the "Court" politics of royal favoritism and parliamentary patronage in the English politics of the age rested on the principle of legitimate opposition, the right of the political "outs" to seek redress of the wrongs committed by the political "ins."

Morris and Zenger, however, crossed the line into what was considered libel. The law held that the printer of any material for public use was in fact the de facto publisher and so responsible for the content. In early 1734, Zenger was charged with seditious libel for denouncing a high-ranking royal official, William Cosby, and was held incommunicado for about ten months by an angry administration before being tried by jury in 1735. The prosecution refused to receive testimonials on the accuracy of the attacks on Cosby, but a superb defense by Zenger's lawyer, the Philadelphian Andrew Hamilton, led to an acquittal. The jury was convinced that Zenger had not published seditious libels but rather that Cosby had been too zealous in stifling dissent and too biased in his patronage appointments. The outcome showed that, in New York, and by implication elsewhere in the colonies, the freedom to criticize was assured in law, and the Morris-Zenger attacks had been legitimized as opposition tools in an open political system. In denouncing a royally appointed governor's behavior as "corrupt" and getting away with it, a more assertive body politic had revealed itself. The case confirmed the openness of assembly practices and served as a brake on governors and their cronies.

What Morris had demonstrated was an American dependence on English constitutional principles and the assumption that American governments were miniature versions of the real Parliament. Those enthusiastic if superficial parallels were understatements by 1735 because American assemblies were representing a larger percentage of a more diverse white population than Parliament ever did. The councils in the colonies were made up of successful and respected citizens, but ordinary citizens for all that, while, in Britain, the House of Lords was exactly that, a bastion of privilege defined by heredity and permanence. Otherwise, Morris's and others' assumptions about the assemblies' authority would not stand up to Parliament's claim to full and ultimate constitutional supremacy, an issue to be raised on a later day, during the 1760s. In 1735, the rights of the colonial assembly had been vindicated in the Zenger trial. In New York, Morris and his supporters in the assembly and elsewhere, the "Morrisites," formed a "popular" party and launched further attacks on the Cosby administration and the Delancey faction. The Morrisites demanded some remarkable reforms, such as fixed annual or triennial elections, courts established by acts of the assembly, and, in direct response to Cosby's dismissal of Morris and appointment of Delancey, judges appointed on "good behavior" rather than "at pleasure." The party also demanded annual elections of mayors, sheriffs, and other public officers in all chartered towns and a system of regional representation based on population. Cosby was gone by 1736, and Morris's party controlled the lower house by 1737.

The Great Awakening

The Great Awakening was the greatest single popular movement in pre-revolutionary America, an explosion of religious passion that reverberated through all the colonies in the 1730s and 1740s. Its residual effects trailed into the revolutionary era. In some ways, this ecclesiastical, sociological, and emotional event was also political. On the surface, it was a surge of faith-based revivalism, spurred by a small army of itinerant and unorthodox preachers and proselytizers who unleashed popular alternatives to the conventional clerical establishment in every colony. They succeeded in creating a tempest of debate and resistance to existing local religious and political structures and the conversion of masses of colonists to intellectually simpler and politically freer expressions of Christian devotion. Briefly stated, the Awakeners sought to revive religious commitment in America by attacking the complacency and orthodoxies of the conventional religious institutions and clergy. It was not a controlled movement in the usual sense, but it was sustained by aggressive proponents, and its broad, universal message seemed to touch on local conditions everywhere. In some areas, such as Connecticut, it inspired a New Light-Old Light controversy that was deeply political. In fact, James Davenport, a spectacularly passionate and emotional Awakener, was charged with inciting riot and then used by Old Light conservatives as a caricature of the dangers of "enthusiasm" and itinerancy. He was parodied further by being charged and then cleared of being *non compos mentis*. But if the erratic Davenport could be used by the conservative church, he was also the quintessential disturber. The Connecticut congregational establishment would never again be free of the temptations of revivalism. So it was throughout the colonies.

The indefatigable English zealot George Whitefield was the greatest of the Awakeners, and was also perhaps the most persuasive public orator of his age. He made seven strenuous tours of the colonies. He gave some 18,000 sermons all over the English-speaking world in his long career, perhaps addressing more people than any individual before him in the history of Christian preaching. He started an orphanage in Georgia but was equally at home sermonizing to thousands in a field in Pennsylvania. He was by turns a social reformer and a political conservative. While he denounced slavery at times, he later owned some slaves. He was equally at home with sophisticated, literate audiences and with illiterate frontier settlers. He fired the Awakening with his riveting, theatrical performances, and his reputation added a popular cachet to the revivals. This mobile dynamo was the heart and soul of the revival's transcolonial reach, but some conventional religious figures were also caught up in the exuberance. The Awakeners inspired the traditional clergy to react, and some, such as Jonathan Edwards, the greatest mind of that New England generation, clearly recognized the potent appeal of the Awakeners' message of faith over reason. Edwards spent the last active years of his life attempting to restore a more disciplined theology to New England. On the other hand, Theodorus Frelinghuysen, a Dutch immigrant, saw the need for an educated *itinerant* ministry, and the log cabin college he helped establish in New Jersey became Princeton College. William Tennent, an Irish Presbyterian immigrant, and his son, the American-born Gilbert, came close to instilling a kind of religious democracy in their wake, and their denunciation of the conventions of organized churches bordered on ecclesiastical anarchy.

The Awakening paralleled some serious social change in the colonies. By mid-century the Church establishments were weak, where they existed at all. Even in places like New England and Virginia, where the Congregationalist and Anglican churches respectively were established, alternative churches had already weakened their political power. Christianity remained the guide to spiritual and moral identity and behavior, but much of the population had become apathetic and lazy. In 1750, there were about 1,300 churches (chapels, meeting houses, and parish buildings) in the colonies, or about one church per 800 of population, and even if attendance was strong, the tactics and ultimate appeal of the Awakeners show that audiences were ready for a revisionist approach to worship and faith. As important as the Awakening was in upsetting the assumptions of the older churches, it was not the reason for the absence of a state religion in America after the Revolution. There was no likelihood of that. But by driving a wedge between the public and the authority of the organized churches, the Awakening confirmed and advanced the principle of institutional separation. The Awakening gave a distinctly American face to Christian practices by showing how belief could be reinforced even as conservative established church organizations were being splintered. And, while religion would still be used to advance political agendas, no large-scale church organization could hope to influence politics in the revolutionary or early national periods because no inter-colonial church establishments existed on any effective level. Finally, the Awakening indicated the potential for popular protest and collectivism even as it preached individual responsibility in faith. There was also a class-related tone to the Awakening. One of the first things the established churches recognized was the popular appeal of the revival. Did the Awakening indicate a "democratic" or egalitarian upheaval, or did it simply vent reactions to gradual social change through reformed and popular Christian expressions? For all the flux that the Awakening revealed, there was no revolt or even serious challenge to the normal organs of authority. By the eve of the Revolution, political leaders in each of the colonies persisted in their roles. The revolt against British policy in the 1760s and 1770s was led by a traditional political and social leadership that quietly survived the Awakening's loosening of local authority. More than anything, the Awakening revealed a population that was capable of acting in its own interest.

The British Empire and the Atlantic Economy in the Eighteenth Century
In 1707, the Scottish and English parliaments were refashioned into the joint Parliament of the United Kingdom, and, for the Scots, the Treaty of Union created a legacy of debate on its value that survives to this day. The Scots acquired 45 seats in the Commons and 16 in the Lords, a ratio of about one to ten in terms of Scottish to English representation when the population ratios were closer to one to six. What impelled the Scottish proponents of the union was the hope that, by surrendering

some constitutional sovereignty, Scotland would benefit economically from being part of an increasingly powerful state enterprise.

The treaty gave birth to the United Kingdom of Great Britain, and what had been "the empire" was now the more impressive "British Empire." Englishmen, Scots, and colonial Americans now belonged to "Great Britain" and became "Britons" with the potent cultural image of "Britannia." The Act of Union coincided with the rising influence in world affairs of British arms, economics, and diplomacy that, even after the loss of the American colonies, would result a century later in the most expansive imperial system in history. The burgeoning British Empire of the eighteenth century concluded a phase of international expansion that had been inspired by Elizabeth in the sixteenth century and constructed by the Stuarts in the seventeenth. The Empire that had stuttered into existence at the Restoration in 1660 was, by the middle of the eighteenth century, a globally integrated economic system that benefited from the political stability that developed in England after the tempestuous events of the Civil War of the 1640s and the Glorious Revolution of 1688-89. The relationship between the Monarchy and Parliament was harmonized with the rise of coherent majority parties in Parliament. The Succession Act of 1701 ended a long struggle between aggressive royal prerogatives and the growing power of Parliament. The Monarch had, in effect, given way to Parliament's superior role in general government while retaining a key role in administrative matters such as official appointments to government and judicial offices. As head of state, the Monarch continued to influence foreign policy. As for the British economy, it was marked by increased administrative competence and a rising military presence in America, the wider Atlantic world, Africa, and beyond into the Indian Ocean and the Indian subcontinent.

Trade figures reveal the growth of the imperial economy. The Atlantic was the crucible of the new world economy, and, as Europe, America, and Africa were joined in a series of triangular trade relations, the British economy thrived and added India's tea and spices to the mix. The Atlantic economy grew steadily through the eighteenth century as the staples flowing from the French, Spanish, Dutch, and British trading systems fuelled economic development in Europe and, by extension, Asia and Africa. But these competing systems were driven by seventeenth-century theories of mercantilism and understood in part in zero-sum principles. That notion held that the world's economy was a fixed pie-like whole from which nations took larger or smaller slices depending on their rivals' abilities, territorial assets, and trade and political alliances. Sugar, tobacco, rice, and indigo created a set of slave societies that ran south from the Chesapeake to southern Brazil. North of the Chesapeake, the timber, furs, fish, and agricultural staples added value to the Atlantic economy with little or no slave labor. The Americas consumed a great variety of European finished and refined commodities, and depended on the more advanced kinds of manufactured items for common or luxury use. Still, the most significant imports into all the Americas in the eighteenth century were slaves. Of the estimated 11 to 12 million slaves taken to the Americas in the three and half centuries of the slave trade, about 7 million were transported between 1700 and 1800. Tragically, as a measure of economic development, the slave, a "labor producing commodity," is the greatest indicator of the scale of the eighteenth century Atlantic economy. The majority of slaves were transported on British ships.

The Empire and Colonial Economic Development

Economic historians of colonial America continue to look at new models and old data to test the state of the mainland economies in the eighteenth century. They ask the same questions that were asked by British and colonial merchants and politicians in the eighteenth century: where exactly did the colonies fit in the economy of the Empire, and what were the benefits of the imperial economy to the colonies and the mother country respectively? As for the colonies themselves, were their separate economies growing in tandem with each other, and were they sharing in the Empire's aggregate wealth? While the Revolution's origins cannot simply be reduced to economic determinism, neither can economic factors be ignored in the run-up to the colonies' defiance of Britain after 1763. Despite colonial murmurings about restrictive trade practices and British problems with colonial violations of the Navigation Acts, there was no tendency on either end to interrupt the relationship at least until 1750. At that time, Lord Halifax as head of the Board of Trade did recognize the growing importance of America to the Empire's wealth and began to tighten up the political and administrative involvement of the Crown in colonial affairs. Whatever reforms his policies might have achieved were shelved by the Seven Years' War, and what did follow resulted in fundamental changes. Today's economic historians agree with eighteenth century economic theorists, politicians, and merchants that the Empire was growing wealthier in mid-century. The place of export staples in that growth was indisputable, but the consumption habits of the mainland colonial population created a demand for British commodities that was unmatched by any other European imperial jurisdiction.

By 1750, the population of England was 6.2 million. There were nearly 1.2 million subjects, including slaves, in the American mainland colonies, about the same as the population of Scotland. What those figures do not show is that the colonial population had grown by 400 per cent, while the population of England and Scotland had grown by less than 10 per cent. Ireland, which was governed by the British as a colonial extension, was an exception. Its population was very fast growing and rose from about 2.5 million to about 3.5 million in 1750. It was not, however, a fully functioning cog in the imperial network, and its largely Catholic peasant population served mostly to accommodate a transplanted English gentry. Ulster, in the north of Ireland, was home to a rising population of Protestant Scotch-Irish descended from the Scottish migrations of the seventeenth century. Otherwise, as Britain grew, it grew most prodigiously in the American colonies. Thus, as Britain's economy grew, the colonists were contributing substantially to the Empire's investment capital pool, as consumers and producers. Britain's trade shifted its emphasis away from a broad international strategy to an increasing dependency on its American, West Indian, and African sources and markets. The following figures indicate those trends:

Table 1.4: Selected Average Annual Values of British Imports and Exports
Note: Figures are in 1000s of Pounds Sterling.

Imported from America (including the West Indies) and Africa
1699-1701	1,107	(19 per cent of all British imports)
1752-54	2,684	(33 per cent of all British imports)
1772-74	4,769	(37 per cent of all British imports)

Exported to America (including the West Indies) and Africa
1699-1701	539	(12 per cent of all British exports)
1752-54	1,707	(33 per cent of all British exports)
1772-74	4,176	(42 per cent of all British exports)

Source: Adapted from John J. McCusker and Russell R. Menard, *The Economy of British America, 1607-1789* (Chapel Hill: University of North Carolina Press, 1985), 41.

Table 1.5: Selected Average Annual Values of English Imports and Exports to and from the Mainland North American Colonies
Note: Figures for Scotland were kept separate to the end of the Revolution. The figures are in 1000s of Pounds Sterling.

Imported by England and Scotland from the mainland colonies of British America
1700	395	no figures for Scotland
1750	814	127 by Scotland
1770	1,015	224 by Scotland
1774	1,373	253 by Scotland (136 of it from Virginia)

Note: The figure for England reached 1,920 in 1775 and fell to 103 in 1776. With the start of the revolutionary war, imports dropped immediately. In 1777, they amounted to a paltry value recorded as 12 thousand Pounds Sterling.

Imported by the thirteen mainland colonies from England
1700	344	no figures for Scotland
1750	1,313	160 from Scotland
1770	1,925	482 from Scotland
1774	2,590	473 from Scotland

Source: Data from U.S. Bureau of the Census, *Historical Statistics of the United States, Colonial Times to 1970* (Washington: Bureau of the Census, 1975), Part 2, Section Z, pp. 1176-77.

By the 1760s, the mainland colonies' proportion of the triangular trade was beginning to favor the mother country. North Americans were consuming more than they were exporting, and the value of imports was running at twice what they were exporting to Britain. Even with the non-importation movements in the 1760s and into the 1770s, colonists were buying more than they were selling. Rising material expectations had created a steadily expanding consumer culture in colonial America, but, after 1750, the trade imbalance began to register some alarm in the colonies. The problem of trade deficits for North Americans continued into the revolutionary period, but British merchants and Parliament had stumbled upon economic policies that made the American colonies economically valuable. The Navigation Acts dictated trade relations in America for Americans, but the British *home* economy managed to intrude into other markets such as Spain and Portugal, whose goods were excluded from direct import into Britain's colonial markets. In other words, colonial producers, consumers, and merchants were locked into a closed British system while producers, consumers, and merchants in Britain were not. The mercantilist nature of the Navigation Acts was ironically bolstered by an open system of consumption as British America's population and affluence rose steadily. The demand for slaves and for manufactured and refined products grew. France was another story. Not only had the French developed a tight mercantilist system, but they competed directly with the British in India and Africa and were the only Europeans capable of limiting Britain's influence in the global economy and in European international relations. The eventual measure of British and French differences was not simply British economic genius, but Britain's growing military establishment. By the middle of the eighteenth century, the combination of economic growth, military power, and naval reach put Britain ahead of its rivals in those areas of state activity. Britain "ruled the waves," and the performances of the mainland and West Indian economies were central to her successes.

The Wars of Empire, 1689-1748

Most of the modern nation states of Europe were forged in war. A striking example of this was the final stage of the Reconquista, the military recovery of Spain from centuries of Moorish domination and the union of Castile and Aragon in the 1470s. Spain became a major European and world force in the space of a few decades at the beginning of the sixteenth century. The smaller Portugal had won its independence in the twelfth century and, by the 1440s, had edged its way tentatively into the Atlantic and down the coast of West Africa. The consolidation of France's various regions and authorities into Europe's largest nation was made possible by militarism. Very quickly, the Dutch Netherlands emerged as a formidable small power in the early seventeenth century after its wars of independence against Spain. Prussia, the "army masquerading as a state," forged a political identity through warfare in the eighteenth and early nineteenth centuries. As European dynasties became nation states and empires, the need for military policy became fixed. Indeed, the Europeanization of the Americas was achieved in large part by war. Indigenous peoples were always subject to military pressure, but so too were the Europeans themselves, who from the beginning of colonization had fought each other. In North America, France and Britain were the major belligerents in the struggle for domination. Although faulty administration, weak political institutions, and economic shortcomings were factors in the ending of the French empire in North America in the 1760s, it was war with Britain that killed the great French experiment.

War, in fact, had been crucial in the consolidation of the modern British state. The Norman Conquest in the eleventh century had begun a process of military expansion in the British Isles. The absorption of Wales, wars with Scotland, and periodic regional, baronial, and dynastic conflict marked England's domestic history into the late Middle Ages. The civil "Wars of the Roses" in the late fifteenth century moved national unity closer. The Tudor-Stuart dynasties and the conquest of Ireland continued the process of territorial amalgamation and the creation of constitutional monarchy and a national secular authority in Parliament by the seventeenth century. The union of the Scottish and English crowns in 1603 and the settlement of Ireland as a colony of the English and Scots coincided with the beginning of British colonization of the western hemisphere. The Civil War of the 1640s and the Glorious Revolution of 1688-89, by definition a civil war, capped a long history of internal military conflict in the British Isles. The suppression of the two Stuart uprisings in Scotland in 1715 and 1745 and the brutal military reprisals that followed the latter confirmed the permanence and power of the state and were the last full-fledged wars to occur on British soil. Britain was not only a unified state by the eighteenth century but also a fully militarized one.

England had also warred with its European rivals in intermittent fashion. The "Hundred Years' War" with France was important in defining late medieval international relations, but the growth of a militaristic foreign policy matured in the Elizabethan era. The defeat of the Spanish Armada in 1588 was the threshold of an aggressive English nationalism, and the English waged an informal war against the Spanish seaborne empire through the latter part of the sixteenth century and into the seventeenth century. A generation of romantic military adventurers boosted English pride in warfare. Sir Francis Drake, Sir George Grenville, and Sir Walter Raleigh were patriots, warriors, and national celebrities. As Drake's 1586 sack of Cartagena and other ports shows, privateers routinely attacked Spanish interests on the high seas and even more boldly in the Caribbean. The seventeenth century revealed a more formal face to English activities in the western Atlantic, and the English cleared the Dutch out of mainland North America and wrested Jamaica from the Spanish. In the English mainland colonies themselves, major white-native encounters — such as the Powhatan War of 1622 in Virginia, New England's Pequod war of 1637, and King Philip's war, an especially vicious affair in 1675-76 — highlighted what was constant warfare against native resistance. Wars against natives persisted beyond the early period. The Yamassee Wars in Carolina in the early eighteenth century and the native involvement in every imperial war of the eighteenth century kept America in a state of near constant organized warfare. At various times, militia or government forces were used to settle domestic issues, such as the imposition of martial law in Virginia in 1609, and in celebrated cases, such as Bacon's Rebellion in 1676 in Virginia and Leisler's Rebellion in New York in 1689. As North America grew in importance, the struggles between France and Britain intensified. Four major wars were fought between Britain and France and their allies between 1689 and 1763. Each war raised the stakes of the previous one, as each seemed to demand another. These were essentially European wars with formal North American focus.

The War of the League of Augsburg of 1689-97 was known in America as King William's War. It began when the League of Augsburg was formed to resist Louis XIV's ambitions in the Rhineland Palatinate. The Glorious Revolution in Britain and the ousting of the Catholic James II had brought William of Orange to the British throne as William III. The Anglo-Dutch alliance that followed was a Protestant-based attempt to curb France's continental ambitions. The conflict spread to Africa, India, the West Indies, and North America, where it sputtered into the far north and west. Even Hudson Bay was disputed. The French populations in the St. Lawrence and Acadia were small, but French advantages lay in military competence and a unified command structure. Decades of trade and diplomacy had led to effective alliances with natives from Maine to the western Great Lakes. They had built well-located forts, but, because of the large New England population, major campaigns by the French into British North America were usually out of the question, and they and their native allies were reduced to making small frequent raids along the frontier, with occasional forays deeper into British territory. In 1690, a New England militia army captured Port Royal on the Bay of Fundy on the western shore of what is now Nova Scotia only to lose it a year later. It was the most significant and yet the most symbolically desultory military campaign of the American phase of the war. In 1697, the Treaty of Ryswick affirmed the *status quo ante* in America. The French responded to it by expanding into the Mississippi Valley, establishing a Louisiana settlement and building forts along their trade routes. With Christian diplomacy, they set up fresh missions among the natives of the interior. The terms of the Treaty of Ryswick were too feeble to keep the peace in either Europe or America, and, in 1702, war was resumed.

The War of the Spanish Succession of 1702-13 broke out shortly before the death of King William in 1703 and was known in America as Queen Anne's War, for William's daughter and successor. It began in a familiar way, as a dynastic conflict. Britain's allies included the Dutch and notably the Holy Roman Emperor. Their objective was to prevent France, in alliance with Bavaria, from settling the Spanish crown on a French favorite and tipping the balance of power in Europe toward France. Spain's spiraling decline had created the potential for global problems. When Charles II died in 1700, the power of the Spanish Habsburgs collapsed, and the succession was ripe for French intervention. The long European phase of the war was fought at great cost by professional armies and had serious economic consequences for Louis XIV. The previous war had depleted French financial resources, but French military efforts in Europe were sustained by its huge manpower pool and strong military traditions. Still, the war confirmed rising British political and economic power, and the European campaigns revealed the military flair of John Churchill, the Duke of Marlborough, who was the first in a string of new British military heroes to match the Elizabethan icons. As British national pride soared in the eighteenth century, Marlborough was followed by other military celebrities such as James Wolfe and Robert Clive in the Seven Years' War and later, after an absence of star performers in the War for Independence, by the Duke of Wellington and Lord Nelson in the Napoleonic Wars.

In America, French manpower was limited, and native alliances and an effective administration once again saved most of France's assets, but not before the New England militias and British naval superiority had scored decisive victories. Acadia (parts of present day New Brunswick and Nova Scotia) was occupied, and Port Royal once again fell to colonial militias. In the south, British colonists with their own native allies attacked St. Augustine and then destroyed over a dozen French missions in the Carolina-Louisiana borderlands before being stopped. French success in Newfoundland meant nothing in the long term because of their inability to hold the island permanently. New England's francophobia was deepened with the Deerfield, Massachusetts raid of 1704 by native allies of the French. The incident demonstrated the ability of northern warriors to penetrate into southern New England settlements but also became a byword in Massachusetts for native savagery and French immorality. It mattered not that the British use of native allies invoked similar responses from French traders and missionaries. What mattered was that cultural bias in New England would always distinguish the purer ethics of Protestant colonists from French deceit.

The war in Europe exhausted the combatants, but the Peace of Utrecht in 1713 resulted in some British rewards. Newfoundland, Acadia, and claims to Hudson Bay were relinquished by France, and the British occupied Spanish Gibraltar and Minorca in the Mediterranean and were granted the *asiento*, a lucrative license to carry African slaves into the Spanish American plantations. Again, however, the end of the war pointed to another one in the future, and the balance of power in Europe remained in flux not only in the short term but through several more wars all the way to the defeat of Napoleon a century later. When Louis XIV died in 1715, he had secured for France a pre-eminent position among Europe's contentious kingdoms, duchies, and nation states, and, while he is popularly remembered for his alleged claim that "*l'État c'est moi*" ("I am the state"), the greatest legacy of his absolutist reign was the emergence of France as a European powerhouse. France was not only the most populated nation in Europe ("twenty million Frenchmen" as the symbolic phrase goes) but also the richest. It had all the apparent means and the ambition to be an international superpower. Louis had provoked Britain in ways that brought the latter directly into European affairs and encouraged an accelerated British imperial strategy. Louis's successors embarked on a program of trade and exploratory expansion into the North American interior. The French planned a cordon of forts at strategic trading sites, developed permanent transportation routes, and, in 1720, built the great citadel at Louisbourg at the tip of Cape Breton Island to guard the entrance to the St. Lawrence. British colonial authorities also prepared for further conflict in America. The founding of Georgia in 1732 was established as much for defense as to provide a sanctuary for poor Englishmen. The Yamassee Wars of 1715-28 on the Carolina frontier with French-supported Spanish Florida to the south encouraged a British strategy of containment south and west of South Carolina.

The War of the Austrian Succession (King George's War) of 1740-48 resulted from strains in the Habsburg Empire, and another set of alliances emerged to complicate shifting dynastic ambitions. While Prussia opposed Austria over the Polish borderlands in Silesia, the rivalry was also inspired by the highly personalized politics of autocratic rulers such as Frederick II of Prussia and Maria Theresa, who was also opposed in her pursuits by Louis XV of France and Spain's Philip V. The latter contested Austria's attempts to control as much of Italy as possible. These various continental convolutions drew in Britain as a broker for any power that would oppose France. Britain's energies could constrain the French in the Atlantic and Mediterranean, and on land in America and India. In America, the war was a familiar mixture of small engagements and a major effort by the French to recover Port Royal (now renamed Annapolis Royal by the British). A hugely successful campaign in 1745 by a combined New England militia force and the Royal Navy captured Louisbourg in a triumph of tactical bravado. To the consternation of New Englanders, while the victory was being celebrated for its symbolic and strategic value, the fortress was returned to the French at the war's end in 1748. The British negotiators were damned for their action, but, in fairness to them, there was exhaustion all around, and the Treaty of Aix-la-Chapelle was shaped as much by military fatigue as by diplomacy. The war's major effect in Europe was the emergence of Prussia as an influence in continental affairs. In America, not much had been decided by the war. The door was left open for another showdown between France and Great Britain.

The Great Imperial War in America

The Seven Years' War of 1756-63 began as the French and Indian War in 1754, and it settled the struggle for hegemony in North America. The high stakes in the war became obvious as it spread from skirmishes in the forests of the Ohio Valley to Europe, the Indian Ocean, the Caribbean, and Africa. The objectives of both France and Britain shifted from merely negotiating the inevitable treaty from a position of strength, to waging a decisive war for permanent superiority. The Seven Years' War resulted in crushing French losses in America and India and immediately changed the course of modern history.

After the Treaty of Aix-la-Chapelle of 1748, the French strengthened their alliances with the natives in the Ohio Valley. Although Pennsylvanians and Virginians had been moving into the Ohio Valley throughout the 1740s, in 1747, the newly formed Ohio Company encouraged larger numbers of eager settlers into French-claimed territory. The French resisted and attacked a British trading post at Pickawillany in 1752 and began building forts in the area. British authorities had meanwhile urged the northern colonies to make treaties with the Iroquois, whose commitment to the British cause in America seemed to be weakening. At the Albany Congress in 1754, delegates from New England, New York, Pennsylvania, and Maryland supported Benjamin Franklin's call for a union of all the colonies under a single executive authority. The plan excluded Nova Scotia and Georgia. As the British appealed to the Iroquois, war preparation was well underway, and the need for collective colonial action was implicit in the Albany proposal. It was rejected by the colonial assemblies because it seemed to limit their flexibility and by the Crown because it seemed too cumbersome. With the threat of a major war with France in the offing in 1754, there was marked indifference to trans-provincial cooperation. A little over ten years later at the Stamp Act Congress, in a collaboration to renounce an act of Parliament, the colonies acted with amazing collective urgency. The significance of the events of that ten-year period changed colonial perceptions of what the Empire was all about.

Meanwhile, in 1754, the Scots-born Lieutenant-Governor of Virginia, Robert Dinwiddie, wanted to build a fort at what is now Pittsburgh, at the strategic junction of the Ohio, Monongahela, and Allegheny Rivers. But the French beat him to it and built Fort Duquesne on the site. In a portentous decision, Dinwiddie sent the twenty-two year old militia colonel George Washington (1732-99) and 150 militiamen into the area to remove the French. Despite a spirited performance, Washington and his troops had to withdraw, with two important consequences: the event propelled a more serious confrontation between the British military authorities and the French, and George Washington was exposed to military opportunity. The future commander of the Continental Army in the War for Independence, the first President of the United States, and the most enduring symbol of American patriotism got his start fighting France for Britannia. Washington was a Virginian, and proud of it, but he was proud too of his British identity. This duality would be tested later, but, in the decades of the 1750s and 1760s, most colonial Americans shared that palpable loyalty to the Empire while bound to their local communities. Defending the one was in effect defending the other. So it was that, when the British commander of His Majesty's forces in America, General Edward Braddock, took 1,400 regular British troops into the upper Ohio in 1755, he was accompanied by 450 enthusiastic colonial militiamen commanded by Washington. Disaster befell them at the Battle of the Wilderness when a force of about 1,000 French and natives scattered the British and killed Braddock. The French and Indian War had begun in earnest.

Braddock was replaced by the hero of Louisbourg, William Shirley, who failed to complete a campaign against Fort Niagara and was subsequently relieved as Governor of Massachusetts. Before he left for a new post in the West Indies, however, Shirley, who understood imperial-colonial relations very well, identified a problem that would plague the British effort in the war, the failure of the various colonial militias to commit to the general campaigns and their propensity to defend only their local interests while refusing longer service beyond their localities. Also in 1755, Sir William Johnson (1715-74), who had kept the Six Nations from allying with the French during King

George's War, continued his remarkable career as a solid link between the Empire and the native peoples of the northern frontier. With a force of 3,500 militia and 400 natives, he defeated a smaller French force at Lake George, New York, and, although he failed to take Crown Point on Lake Champlain, the gateway to New France, he secured the northern border for the British. Farther east, the British Army destroyed many Acadian settlements in the Bay of Fundy by the end of 1755 and eventually expelled approximately 6,000 French-speaking settlers to other colonies to the south. The British policy was based in part on the suspicion that the Acadians might serve as a fifth column, leaving Halifax vulnerable to French seizure, but the geographic logic for the war in America had been revealed, Britain would concentrate its efforts in the north, inside or at the edge of French territory.

In 1756, the war moved to Europe. France seized the Mediterranean island of Minorca from the British, and a full-fledged European war, and by extension a world war, was underway. A British-Prussian-Hanoverian coalition was faced with a French consortium that included Austria, Russia, Sweden, and Saxony. These familiar players, always shifting and re-forming in European affairs, were overshadowed by an expanded confrontation between France and Britain for dominance outside Europe. The war led to the return of William Pitt (the "Elder" and later Earl of Chatham) after the failure of the first Newcastle government. The experienced Pitt had earlier been excluded from government but now returned as Secretary of State for War. He began his tenure by reorganizing British resources and strategies to deal with the war's growing intensity and scale. For Pitt, this would not be a repeat of the earlier imperial wars with France. As the war went on, he stretched the resources of Britain by putting greater than ever pressure on French finances and logistical abilities. Robert Clive and the East India Company secured Bengal for the British with a complete victory over French-supported Indian forces at the battle of Plassey in 1757, an event that ranks with the later fall of Quebec as a turning point in the global war. Yet, for most of 1756–58, the war went badly for the British in America and to some degree in Europe.

The French appointed the Marquis de Montcalm as commander of French forces in America, and he arrived in Quebec with several thousand regular troops. He quickly outclassed his opponent, the Earl of Loudoun, and destroyed Fort George, Oswego, and Fort William Henry. Pitt ordered Loudoun to attack Louisbourg, but his fleet was delayed and damaged by a storm at Halifax, and the French navy took the time to reinforce the great sentinel. Loudoun now complained bitterly of the failure of colonial assemblies to wholeheartedly support the war effort. This criticism was not new, of course, but coupled with the failures of 1757, it began to resonate at Whitehall, and the newly formed Pitt-Newcastle ministry began to look seriously at new strategies. First, Pitt, now in a position of real authority, designed a policy of unlimited war against the French in America, the Caribbean, and Europe. He reinforced the army in America, expanded the Royal Navy, and extended material and financial subsidies to his European allies. This grand plan required a great deal of money. The British had sent 25,000 regular troops to America by 1760, with as many as 15,000 in the colonies at peak times, and Pitt persuaded Parliament to raise taxes and seek war loans, much of the latter coming from members of Parliament. This plan also put money and supplies into the colonies for militia recruitment and outfitting. In addition to the local militias, some 5 per cent of the British Army in America consisted of colonial-born enlistees, and another 5 per cent were "foreigners." The bulk of the army, the "American Army" as it was called, was, by 1757, a veteran force of older longer serving regulars. During 1758, the war began to turn in Britain's favor.

The Fall of Quebec and the Treaty of Paris

Loudoun was replaced by the equally flawed James Abercromby who with an army of 12,000 was soundly beaten by Montcalm's much smaller force near Ticonderoga. Just as it appeared that incompetence would continue to dog the British effort, Generals Jeffrey Amherst and James Wolfe took a fleet of 40 ships, 9,000 regular troops, and 500 colonial militiamen and captured Louisbourg, thus securing the mouth of the St. Lawrence. At the eastern end of Lake Ontario, the British captured Fort Frontenac (present day Kingston, Ontario). At the same time, the war was taken to the Ohio Valley, the French were forced to abandon Fort Duquesne, and the tide began to favor the British. Abercromby was replaced by Amherst, and Pitt devised the grand strategic assault on the heart of French America, a three pronged attack aimed at Niagara, the Lake Champlain corridor, and Quebec itself. By July, Amherst had taken Crown Point on Lake Champlain, and another force that included William Johnson and 100 or so Iroquois had taken Fort Niagara. But the *pièce de résistance* was the attack on Quebec. General Wolfe with 9,000 troops and a fleet of warships laid siege to Quebec in the summer of 1759 and, in September, surprised Montcalm above the town. The battle that ensued not only vindicated Pitt's policies but also guaranteed a huge diplomatic and territorial breakthrough for the British Empire. Montreal fell in 1760, and the French formally surrendered Canada. The Battle of Quebec (or The Plains of Abraham) ended in the dramatic and symbolic deaths on the field of battle of the two heroic adversaries, Montcalm and Wolfe. Generations of British and Canadian schoolchildren grew up with the images of brave men struggling for mastery and dying nobly to shape history, but the real hero of the Seven Years' War was surely Pitt.

Meanwhile, a popular American hero emerged in the person of Major Robert Rogers whose rangers had performed splendidly during the war. He enhanced his reputation for courage and innovation by receiving the surrender of the French forts around Detroit and in the west. Yet he would later waver between the patriot and the British cause in the War for Independence, and ended his days in England. In 1760, he was committed, like most Americans, to the Empire. Later, many Americans would follow Rogers's example when the choice between rebellion and "loyalty" was offered. It is worth noting that General Wolfe regarded the American rangers as being poor soldiers, a British attitude that would persist into the future. By the time Detroit fell, the British victory began to take on greater meaning. In a rash move in 1761, Spain indicated its support for the French and Austrian cause. Britain declared war on Spain and campaigned against the French and the Spanish jointly in the Caribbean and the Far East. Martinique, St. Lucia, and Spanish Havana fell to the British navy, and, in Asia, another British fleet took Manila. This was a staggering coda to the war, and the French eagerly sought peace, but, before sitting down with the British, they ceded New Orleans and their claims to territory *west* of the Mississippi to the Spanish as compensation for Spain's efforts and in an effort to hasten peace talks.

When the Treaty of Paris was signed, it revealed on paper the full import of Britain's victories. France surrendered its continental American claims, including all of Acadia, Cape Breton, and Canada to Britain. Canada turned out to be the French ace in the hole. They had taken British territory in the West Indies and demanded either Canada or the lost French West Indian islands, Martinique, Guadalupe, and St. Lucia in exchange. The pre-war status of separate claims in India was recognized, confirming British control of fertile and strategic Bengal. Minorca was returned to the British, and France agreed to end its occupation of parts of Hanover. A separate peace concluded the German phase of the war. The British returned Cuba to Spain in exchange for East and West Florida, and removed forts they had built in coastal Honduras. A new world in North America was created, and a century and a half of French and British colonial history was ended. The British Empire was ascendant, and its navy did in fact "rule the waves." But there was a cost. In America, there was a clear need for a re-evaluation of colonial policy now that France was gone. A substantial French population needed to be accommodated by the British, and a huge new expanse of territory needed to be administered. The British treasury was broke. The national debt had doubled between 1753 and 1763 to about 70 million pounds sterling as the costs of the war reached 24 million pounds sterling a year. War loans had to be repaid, and the costs of administering the new Empire seemed prohibitive. The Peace of Paris of 1763 required extensive reforms to the British Empire in America, and, when those reforms began in 1763, colonists reacted with opposition. The era of the American Revolution was underway.

Conclusion

At the end of the Seven Years' War, there appeared to be permanence in the British American Empire. We need to ask, therefore, what, if any, late colonial characteristics could later inspire a pan-colonial movement to question the colonies' place in the Empire. By the Seven Years' War, the colonies had grown in size, complexity, wealth, and competence. The lower houses of assembly had emerged as efficient and aggressively responsible institutions. The Great Awakening had served to loosen the formal controls of local religious authority and revealed an energetic and volatile general population. At the same time, there were local political and economic leaderships in every colony committed to their local communities. Was the rise of urban poverty or the restlessness of an increasingly land hungry population a signal that a revolt against Britain was in the works? No. These expanding, competent, and permanent American colonial societies did not decide individually or collectively to leave the Empire. When the British, of necessity, had to redefine the Empire, the colonial world was first shaken and then, on the basis of the way it had matured, responded. By the second half of the eighteenth century, the colonies had reached a stage of growth that would cause them to react to the changing Empire. That reaction, rather than a conscious trend to confrontation, is the key to the troubles that followed the end of the French regime in America. In 1763, American history was still British history. On another level, while France had lost America, it would continue to influence its history. Into the nineteenth century, the British, British American colonists, and then independent Americans and the French would interact in a variety of ways as the consequences of the Seven Years' War unfolded.

Suggested Reading

An extensive bibliography is included here because of the long time frame of this chapter and the broad range of topics and themes contained in the chapter.

Two excellent introductions to colonial American history are Alan Taylor, *American Colonies: The Settling of North America* (New York: Penguin, 2001) and R.C. Simmons, *The American Colonies, from Settlement to Independence* (London: Longman, 1976). Simmons's book is a dense, encyclopedic study. Taylor's book is an ambitious comparative survey of all the European and indigenous cultures of North America that reflects a generation of scholarship on social history, historical geography, ethnography, and environmental studies.

Beginning in the early 1960s, historians of early America began to look in earnest at the social structures of the colonies. The case studies and syntheses that resulted produced an imaginative and imposing body of social, legal, and political studies. The New England town, the Virginia parish, the South Carolina plantation have since been subjected to microscopic examination, and the family, women, African-Americans, and the poor of colonial America, who had been largely left out of the literature, are now seen as agents in the shaping of British American society. Ethnographic studies have brought the native presence more clearly into historians' versions of the American past.

Some ambitious syntheses resulted from the "new (now old) social history." Jackson Turner Main's *The Social Structure of Revolutionary America* (Princeton, NJ: Princeton University Press, 1965) still stands as a useful overview of how Americans arranged themselves as clusters of economic and social classes that often transcended regional or colonial boundaries. David Hackett Fischer's *Albion's Seed: Four British Folkways in America* (New York: Oxford University Press, 1989) sees American society in the revolutionary era as a set of regionally defined adaptive British traditions. Richard Hofstadter in his unfinished *America at 1750: A Social Portrait* (New York: Knopf, 1971) spoke of a "middle class world." Jack P. Greene, *Pursuits of Happiness: The Social Development of Early Modern British Colonies and the Formation of American Culture* (Chapel Hill: The University of North Carolina Press, 1988) sees the colonial experience as resulting in a set of discrete communities seeking a common end in America, an optimum condition of "happiness."

Colonial historiography has moved into increasingly diverse themes and subjects, but the models created by Fischer, Greene, and Main offer ways of seeing the regional, class, and cultural contours of British North America. See also Bernard Bailyn, *The Peopling of British North America* (New York: Alfred A. Knopf, 1986). Daniel Vickers, ed., *A Companion to Colonial America* (Malden, MA: Blackwell, 2003) is a comprehensive set of essays on the major topics and recent literature on the period. The resistance to the Empire in the 1760s and 1770s was formulated in the politics of the colonial period and in the long development of political systems and ideas. See Bernard Bailyn, *The Origins of American Politics* (New York: Knopf, 1968) for a forceful introduction to the principles and institutions of colonial American politics. See also Alan Tully, "Colonial Politics," in *A Companion to Colonial America*, ed. Daniel Vickers, cited above. Andrews, *The Colonial Background*, cited in this book's introduction, remains as clear and persuasive as ever. Jack P. Greene, *Peripheries and Center: Constitutional Development in the Extended Polities of the British Empire and the United States, 1607-1788* (Athens, GA: University of Georgia Press, 1986) is an invaluable study of colonial and imperial political relations. Contrast the older George Louis Beer, *British Colonial Policy, 1754-1765* (New York: The Macmillan Company, 1907) with Linda Colley, *Britons: Forging the Nation, 1707-1837* (New Haven: Yale University Press, 1992) and Anthony McFarlane, *The British in the Americas, 1480-1815* (New York: Longmans, 1994). See also the theories and themes offered in Anthony Pagden, *Lords of All the World: Ideologies of Empire in Spain, Britain and France c.1500-c.1800* (New Haven: Yale University Press, 1995).

The growing attraction of "Atlantic history" is dealt with in McFarlane, *The British in the Americas*, Vickers, *A Companion to Colonial America*, and Eliga H. Gould and Peter S. Onuf, eds., *Empire and Nation: The American Revolution in the Atlantic World* (Baltimore: Johns Hopkins University Press, 2005). Ian Steele, *The English Atlantic: An Exploration in Communication and Community, 1675-1740* (New York: Oxford University Press, 1986) and D.W. Meinig, *The Shaping of America*, vol. 1, *Atlantic America, 1492-1800* (New Haven: Yale University Press, 1986) have influenced a generation of scholars and help balance the fascinating revisionist survey by Peter Linebaugh and Marcus Rediker, *The Many Headed Hydra: Sailors, Slaves, Commoners and the Hidden History of the Revolutionary Atlantic* (Boston: Beacon Press, 2000). On the Caribbean colonies, see McFarlane, *The British in the Americas*; Vickers, *A Companion to Colonial America*; and Richard S. Dunn, *Planters and Slaves: The Rise of a Planter Class in the English West Indies, 1624-1713* (Chapel Hill: University of North Carolina Press, 1972). On French and Spanish America, see Taylor, *American Colonies*, and Vickers, *A Companion to Colonial America*. After twenty years John McCusker and Russell Menard, *The Economy of British America, 1607-1789* (Chapel Hill, NC: The University of North Carolina Press, 1985) retains its value as a study of the colonial economy, and its bibliography runs to 80 pages of pre-1983 scholarship.

Natives are prominent in much of the social, military, and demographic literature on colonial America, and are central to any understanding of the period's history. The best introduction to native-European contacts and relations in the colonial period is Colin Calloway, *New Worlds for All: Indians, Europeans and the Remaking of Early America* (Baltimore: John Hopkins, 1997) or Ian Steele, *Warpaths: Invasions of North America* (New York: Oxford University Press, 1994). See also the imaginative William Cronon, *Changes in the Land: Indians, Colonists, and the Ecology of New England* (New York: Hill and Wang, 1983).

War was central to British colonial policy and to colonial settlement. John Brewer, *The Sinews of Power: War, Money and the English State, 1688-1783* (London: Knopf, 1989) is a good overview. On the Seven Years' War, see Fred Anderson, *The Crucible of War: The Seven Years' War and the Fate of Empire in British North America* (New York: Knopf, 2000) and Stephen Brumwell, *Redcoats: The British Soldier and War in the Americas, 1755-1763* (Cambridge: Cambridge University Press, 2002). See also Taylor, *American Colonies*, and Colley, *Britons*. Colley is useful for British domestic politics; for the early eighteenth century shift in British domestic political function, see J.H. Plumb, *The Growth of Political Stability, 1675-1725* (London: Macmillan, 1967).

Race-based slavery became entrenched in eighteenth-century America. Chapters 1 and 2 in Peter Kolchin, *American Slavery, 1619-1877* (New York: Hill and Wang, 1993) are commendably brief and comprehensive. The vast literature on the subject is well represented in Ira Berlin, *Many Thousands Gone: The First Two Centuries of Slavery in North America* (Cambridge, MA: Harvard University Press, 1998) and Philip D. Morgan, *Slave Counterpoint: Black Culture in the Eighteenth Century Chesapeake and Lowcountry* (Chapel Hill: The University of North Carolina Press, 1998). See also two outstanding older studies: Edmund S. Morgan, *Slavery and Freedom: The Ordeal of Colonial Virginia* (New York: Vintage Books, 1975) and Winthrop D. Jordan, *White Over Black: American Attitudes Towards the Negro, 1550-1812* (Chapel Hill: The University of North Carolina Press, 1968). Gary B. Nash, *Red, White and Black: The Peoples of Early North America*, 5th ed. (Englewood Cliffs, NJ: Prentice Hall, 2006) and Russell Menard, *Migrants, Servants, and Slaves: Unfree Labor in Colonial British America* (Burlington, VT: Ashgate, 2001) help put slavery in a class context.

The best general history of women in the colonial period is Carol Berkin, *First Generations: Women in Colonial America* (New York: Hill and Wang, 1996). See also Carolyn Merchant, *Ecological Revolutions: Nature, Gender, and Science in New England* (Chapel Hill, NC: University of North Carolina Press, 1989), which has a useful section on New England. Laurel Thatcher Ulrich, *Good Wives: Image and Reality in the Lives of Women in Northern New England, 1650-1750* (New York: Vintage, 1991) and Kathleen Brown, *Good Wives, Nasty Wenches, and Anxious Patriarchs: Gender, Race, and Power in Colonial Virginia* (Chapel Hill: University of North Carolina Press, 1996) are excellent regional studies of the roles and experiences of colonial women.

CHAPTER TWO

THE NEW BRITISH EMPIRE
REFORM AND PROTEST, 1763-1774

You are happy in the cession of Canada: we, perhaps, ought to think ourselves happy that you have acquired it. Delivered from a neighbor whom they have always feared, your other colonies will soon discover that they stand no longer in need of your protection. You will call on them toward supporting the burthen which they have helped bring on you, they will answer you by shaking off all dependence.

— Comte de Vergennes, French diplomat, c. 1763, in a letter to a British friend

Time Line

1760	The Accession of George III.
1763	The Treaty of Paris.
	Pontiac's Rebellion.
1764	The American Revenue Act (The Sugar Act).
	The Currency Act.
1765	The Quartering Act (the first of several).
	The Stamp Act.
	The Stamp Act Congress.
1766	Repeal of the Stamp Act.
	The Declaratory Act.
1767	The Townshend Duties.
1768	The non-importation movement.
1770	The Boston Massacre.
1772	The *Gaspee* Incident.
1773	The Boston Tea Party.
1774	The Coercive Acts.
	The Quebec Act.

The New Empire of 1763

Despite Vergennes' prophetic musings, the Empire seemed very secure in 1763. One of the immediate causes of the French and Indian War had been the movement of land-hungry British colonists across the Appalachian Mountains. The pressure on land continued during the war, as colonial population increased by about one third or by some 350,000 people. The thirteen mainland colonies were filling up. Militias and regular army units had moved through the colonies to the northern and western frontiers to engage the French but, for the most part, had not interrupted life in the sprawling agri-cultural landscape. Atlantic ports had hummed with the movement of troops, naval preparations, and fleet assemblies; and merchants and farmers alike had benefited from Pitt's commitment to support large numbers of regular British Army soldiers in America. From the production of naval supplies to food and accommodations, the war in America had created local profits, according to the observations of British officials. The war had also demanded a greater participation from the colonial assemblies, in money and men, than had been forthcoming. Complaints from royal governors and their agents and from the British military command generally fell on deaf colonial ears. The end of the war in 1763 also ended the wartime economy, just as had hap-pened after King George's War in 1748, and although merchants feared another reces-sion in the short term, the decisive nature of the war promised a buoyant future of territorial expansion and economic development.

The absence of adequate interior transportation routes had not dulled the lure of the upper Ohio Valley, Kentucky, and the western slopes of the southern Appalachians. Settlements had been established in the west. New Englanders, for example, could not continue to subdivide their small holdings for their progeny, and, while there was land in the river valleys of New Hampshire and Maine, the northern forests were not as receptive to agriculture as was the Ohio Valley. A similar overflow of population was developing in the middle colonies as the stock of open fertile land dwindled. What was true for the compact town economies and the small farms of Massachusetts was also true for the planter class in the Chesapeake and the lower south. Usable land was not infinite, and, in the south, poor agricultural practices and soil exhaustion caused by the rigors of tobacco cultivation, for example, demanded a constant breaking of new ground. The south's expansion in this period can be judged by the rise in the slave population. Between 1756 and 1760, more slaves were brought into Charleston, South Carolina than in the previous ten years. The bulge in population on the southern white frontier was equally impressive and was accompanied by a relentless demand for arable and pasture land. North Carolina's population grew by about 75 per cent during the war, much of it from white movement into the backcountry, while slave growth fueled the coastal plantation economy. Growth occurred everywhere, and in urban Boston, Philadelphia, and New York, the merchants, artisans, and laboring classes all shared an optimistic view of prosperous futures. The expulsion of the French sug-gested a brilliant new era for the Empire, the instrument designed for the improve-ment and nurturing of the colonies: a protective partner. The results of the war seemed to confirm that view.

In politics, the rise of the lower houses of the colonial assemblies and the restless, questioning Protestant upheavals of the Great Awakening were pre-war portents of what was becoming, even in the early 1750s, an "uneasy connection," as the historian Jack Greene put it, between colonists and Parliament. In their various ways, the colonies had matured into self-conscious communities. The dual attachment to the virtues of locality and the umbrella of Empire meant that colonists could now rejoice in the "Blessings of being Britons," as James Horrocks stated in a 1763 sermon in Virginia. Britons, he claimed, had "set the World a fair Example that the highest Ambition of Princes shou'd be to govern a free People." The war, in this version, had been waged to protect and advance British "liberty," which, according to Horrocks, was the source of "all Blessings." The equation seemed obvious: Britannia and liberty were synonymous. Horrocks had been in America for only two years, but he caught the general mood of the imperial mentality. To Parliament and the King, however, the blessings of liberty needed to be adjusted to the exigencies of economics, the administration of vast new territories, frontier tensions with natives, and future international relations. What was seen in much of colonial America as a windfall in territorial acquisition was seen in London as the beginning of a new Empire, with new rules.

The Proclamation of 1763 and Pontiac's Rebellion

Just as the new Empire was being defined in 1760, King George II died. The House of Hanover had been made the successor to Anne after 1713, and one of the things the second George is noted for was the fact that he was the last British monarch to see military combat, bravely, it seems, in the War of the Austrian Succession. He was also an enthusiastic patron of music and a strong supporter of Handel, even if he did not care for other artistic forms such as "boetry" and "bainting," as he pronounced them in his German accent. He was prone to long absences in Hanover, and, while his father George I ("German George") learned only a bit of English in his lifetime, George II made a greater effort to assimilate but remained more Hanoverian than British, according to his detractors. Yet, the otherwise ordinary George II contributed to the harmonizing of Parliament's rights with royal administrative prerogatives and to a stable constitutional monarchy to which he generally deferred. He had for over a decade refrained from an active role in national or international politics. The accession of his grandson George III, however, brought to the throne an activist King, a wilful politician who was something of a revisionist. George III was 22 years old in 1760 and had been tutored by the Earl of Bute who became his great friend and advisor. Bute had instilled in George an assumption of royal prerogative in government policy making and had encouraged him to push the constitutional role of the Monarch to its limit. George understood Parliament's power and would not go so far as to imitate the disgraced seventeenth century Stuarts, but he relished his role as chief executive and took a direct hand in the administration of the nation's business. As much as any individual, George III provoked colonial opposition to British policy, and his fierce determination encouraged a growing and very dangerous disaffection among colonists. He seemed to relish the changed times and the way the war had sped up the bureaucratization of the state and enhanced executive and ministerial imperatives. His choice of ministers made him a central figure in the imperial crisis of the 1760s and 1770s. The colonial joy of early 1763 soon gave way to befuddlement and concern due in part to his inflexibility on imperial matters.

Lord Shelburne of the Board of Trade had devised a plan for the territory west of

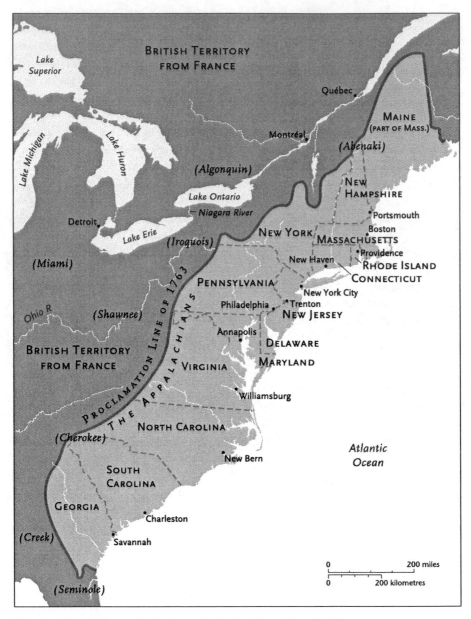

Map 2.1 The Thirteen Colonies and the Proclamation of 1763

the Appalachians that prohibited settlement beyond the mountains and used the divide as a boundary between the large native populations to the west and the colonies to the east. A small area in the upper Ohio was set aside for settlers who had already crossed the divide but that allowance was rescinded before the year was out. While the design of the new provinces (Quebec and East and West Florida) was being refined, the native tribes in the lower Great Lakes grew impatient with British trade controls and, inspired by the "Delaware Prophet" began demanding lower prices on trade goods and better supplies of firearms ammunition. The Prophet's disciple Pontiac, an Ottawa chief, began destroying British forts in the autumn of 1763. The widespread violence of the uprising provoked first a concentrated suppression of the rebellion and then a tightening of the Appalachian boundary. The revised plan, the "Royal Proclamation" hit colonial America like a bombshell. The Crown, a term that implies both the royal administration and the Monarch in combination with Parliament's constitutional authority, had moved to a strategy of excluding all colonists from the west. The Proclamation of 1763 promised to protect the natives of the west by barring everyone else, including those in the newly established provinces of Quebec and the Floridas. Unfortunately, its language was especially hostile to the older colonies. It attacked colonists as troublemakers and forbade any land deals with natives, not only in the former French territories but in the older colonial settlement areas too. It announced, antagonistically, that "We do…strictly enjoin…all Persons whatever who have either wilfully or inadvertently seated themselves upon any Lands…still reserved to the… Indians…forthwith to remove themselves." It is not clear how many colonists were settled in the "Indian Lands" of the Ohio or the southwest, but they were being told to leave. Open westward movement, previously limited by French power, was now being prevented by British law. Any expectation that the Proclamation would attract New Englanders to move north into the newly acquired Canadian territories was not realized. In early 1763, William Pitt was being celebrated in the colonies as America's liberator, and streets and towns were being named in his honor. By the end of 1763, he was being burned in effigy. The first small wedge had been entered between the colonists' local interests and their pride of membership in the Empire.

Taxation and Troops: The Shape of Imperial Reform

The Proclamation hinted at a betrayal of colonial expectations, but, to most, it appeared at first glance to be merely a short-term security measure. Pontiac's Rebellion did suggest the perils of freewheeling settlement in the west, and royal governors and councils were quick to support the Empire's right to its own security and its authority to plan and design future settlement patterns. However, in practice, the Proclamation appeared to be unenforceable. Imperial resources were not adequate to regulate white settlement, and the boundary was soon moved farther west. In 1763, a group of settlers from Paxton, Pennsylvania (the "Paxton Boys") killed some twenty peaceful Conestoga natives near Lancaster as reprisal against earlier native attacks on white settlements in the area. The Conestoga massacre was part of an older pattern of frontier confrontation that was now complicated by the departure of the French, but it was also a harbinger of a more deadly frontier.

Within months of the Proclamation, a second bombshell hit the colonists. In April 1764, Parliament passed the American Revenue Act (or Sugar Act) to raise money in the colonies for Parliament. There appeared to be no precedent for this. The act was intended to defray some costs of the late war and to help pay for the administration of trade regulations. It amended and extended the old Molasses Act of 1733, and while it reduced the duty on foreign molasses by half, it maintained the duty on raw sugar and increased the duties on foreign refined sugar. It introduced new or higher duties on non-British goods such as Spanish and Portuguese wines, textiles, and coffee that were imported directly into the colonies. It doubled the duties on any foreign product shipped from Britain to the colonies and expanded the number of colonial goods that could be carried only in British ships and only to British ports. Finally, the act banned foreign rum and all French wines from the colonies. Lord Grenville, the Chancellor of the Exchequer, announced that about 45,000 pounds sterling a year could be returned to the Treasury from these new regulations. To have any hope of success, the act needed teeth and Grenville, noting that the customs service in America returned only a quarter of what it cost to run it, tightened collections services and, most important, established a vice admiralty court in Halifax to circumvent the presumed leniency of local colonial courts.

On the heels of the Sugar Act, the Currency Act of 1764 arrived to further perplex and annoy colonists. It forbade the issuance of paper money by colonial assemblies and hit Virginia especially hard because it had issued large sums during the war and the notes were still in circulation. The Currency Act was deflationary and arbitrary and spelled out a new era in imperial relations and an end to what Edmund Burke referred to in 1775 as the decades of "salutary neglect" of the Navigation Acts and Board of Trade regulations. The trend was now away from lax administration and the rubber stamping of colonial legislation. While the Currency Act had aroused the Virginians, the most outspoken opposition to it came from Massachusetts, which had been subject to similar currency controls since 1751. A depressed economy and thwarted hopes of expansion coupled with the Sugar and Currency Acts aroused the Boston Town Meeting to issue a formal denunciation of Parliament's tax policies telling the Crown, "You will remember that this Province has been at very great Expence in carrying on the late War, and that it still ly under a very grievous burden of debt." This, of course, was the very reverse of Parliament's claim that it needed revenues to retire the debt it had incurred in defending Massachusetts and the rest of the American provinces. The Bostonians also hit on a condition that predated the war, the balance of trade deficit that by 1760 was running at a near two to one advantage to the British economy: "We are in short … yielding large supplys to the Revenues of the Mother Country while we are labouring for a very moderate Subsistence for ourselves." Then the Town Meeting declared its pride in the Empire by asserting "The unshaken Loyalty of this Province and this Town — its unrivalled Exertions in supporting His Majestys Government …

its acknowledged Dependence upon and Subordination to Great Britain." These sentiments would come to be part of American political discourse for another decade. That is to say, the colonists were loyal and devoted subjects and respected the supremacy of the British constitution and the Empire but had exhausted their resources in the war and should not be taxed further to support the tightening of imperial administration. In addition to the sarcastic claim that its people could not afford to buy British goods, the Boston Town Meeting introduced a striking rationale for a boycott by merging financial plight with political principle: "It strikes at our British Privileges which as we have never forfeited them we hold in common with our Fellow Subjects who are Natives of Britain: If Taxes are laid upon us in any shape without ever having a Legal Representation where they are laid, are we not reduced from the Character of Free Subjects to the miserable state of tributary Slaves."

The Massachusetts Assembly created a Committee of Correspondence to contract the other provinces to boycott or restrict certain imported luxuries. James Otis (1725-1783), one of Boston's provincial representatives, repeated the gist of the town's sentiments in a long pamphlet that included the curt comment that "no parts of His Majesty's dominions can be taxed without their consent," a phrase that found its way into the idiom as "no taxation without representation." The Sugar and the Currency Acts had now given already troubled colonists a slogan that would become a philosophical position and ultimately an ideological mantra. By the end of 1764, the movement had spread, and the New York Assembly claimed it had a right to be exempted from taxes imposed by Parliament and that the canceling of its own paper currency was arbitrary and punitive. More important was New York's argument that it had paid its way in the war according to its means, a statement that ran contrary to what Parliament had insinuated.

Meanwhile, the extended presence of large numbers of British regular troops raised questions about the Empire's motives. The war had brought America's varied, self-assured and mobile population into frequent contact with the rank and file of the British Army and with its officers, the latter usually well-bred men with aristocratic affectations. The result was the creation of a set of scornful prejudices that, from the British perspective, painted the colonial militias as sloppy, irreverent, and tentative soldiers and their communities as unformed backwaters. Some colonists stereotyped British soldiers as disciplined pawns and their officers as coddled, arrogant, condescending, and ultimately incompetent poseurs. None of these caricatures would have mattered had the British Army gone home after the war. It did not. The Quartering Act of 1765, the first of several, was intended to garrison British troops in the colonies at colonial expense. The act was expanded the following year to include inns and various unoccupied private and public buildings as suitable places for billeting troops. This brought the British Army directly and apparently permanently into Boston, New York, and other centers in an ominous and puzzling way. Why did the Crown have a full-time military contingent settled among the population? The French and Spanish surely posed no threat, and the native populations to the west were out of the reach of most of the colonial population. The individual pamphleteers and the various assembly notices couched their language in appeals rather than demands and simply asked Parliament to respect the special status of the provincial populations and their representative institutions. Each appeal reasserted the colonists' devotion to the Empire by stressing that they were Britons, regardless of what side of the Atlantic they were on. But that very claim and the colonists' growing insistence on their exclusive taxing prerogatives revealed a paradox. The colonists were subject to Parliament's constitutional supremacy, and the colonies themselves were "creatures" of the Crown's making, founded initially by the Crown's authority. But then, the colonial logic insisted that their equal status when matched to their special circumstances, three thousand miles from Whitehall, gave them certain powers that countered Parliament's supremacy. In other words, if Parliament could not tax the colonists without their consent because there were no colonial representatives sitting in Parliament, could Parliament expect to pass any specific laws for the colonies without the consent of the colonists? In 1764 and 1765, that issue was beginning to reshape relations between Britain and its American subjects, and the passing of the Stamp Act in March 1765 gathered together the colonists' scattered appeals and forged them into a collective protest with historic consequences.

The Stamp Act

The Stamp Act was a mechanism for raising money directly from the colonies for the Crown's use. The preamble announced "An act for granting and applying certain stamp duties, and other duties, in the British colonies and plantations in America, towards further defraying the expences of defending, protecting, and securing the same." With dense detail, it enumerated every imaginable legal transaction and applied a surcharge to each by way of an attached compulsory stamp to be purchased from a crown agent. The costs ran from a few pence for a posted notice of goods for sale to a few shillings for a newspaper to 10 pounds sterling for formal appointments to official offices such as Justice of the Peace. It applied to packs of cards and sets of dice. It listed dozens of categories and scores of particular documents and introduced each category, repetitively, with the words "For every skin or piece of vellum or parchment, or sheet or piece of paper, on which shall be ingrossed, written or printed [the following particulars]." It was a monument to bureaucratic minutiae, and the reference for the clerks who would collect the tax. It hit lawyers, merchants, local politicians, and newspaper publishers directly. It was seen right away as an affront to colonial rights, and the technical delay in its introduction to the first of November meant that some activist groups were allowed time to organize, calling themselves "Sons of Liberty." Isaac Barré (1726-1802), an MP, had used the phrase in the House of Commons in a speech opposing the act. In America, the Sons of Liberty were organized groups of artisans, retailers, laborers, and seamen in New York and Boston, led by some of the leading merchants and civic officials in those cities extending a long tradition of urban protest in colonial America. The working classes of the seaports routinely gathered to protest prices or to celebrate holidays, such as the famous "Popes Day" parades in Boston. Those parades were New England versions of the British "Guy Fawkes" day, a holiday that celebrated the aborted Catholic plot to blow up the English Parliament on November 5, 1605. The purposes of those earlier popular gatherings changed in 1765 with anti-imperial protests, and, by summer, the Sons of Liberty had forced the removal of practically all the appointed Stamp Act agents in the colonies. In Boston, crowds burned the records of the local vice-admiralty court, ransacked the home of the currency comptroller, and, in the most publicized and far reaching demonstration of anger, looted the home of Chief Justice Thomas Hutchinson (1711-1780), the native born intellectual, historian, and member of Boston's civic elite, who was already disliked by James Otis and other activists. The demonstrators' aims foreshadowed future political motivations; Hutchinson was singled out for abuse because he publicly defended the legality of the Stamp Act.

The Stamp Act Congress and Resolutions

By the time the wave of protest and violence had passed — it receded with the resignation of the stamp tax collectors — the issue had brought together nine of the thirteen colonial authorities to the Stamp Act Congress in New York in October 1765. The imperial world was redefined by that meeting and by the violence that had preceded it. Yet the colonists continued to affirm their loyalty, struck a conciliatory pose, and appealed as Britons for a repeal of the Stamp Act and a consideration of their "special circumstances." Only nine of the thirteen provinces sent delegates, three of which were unofficial. Virginia, North Carolina, Georgia, and New Hampshire did not attend, but the meeting was a momentous act of political collectivism by the provinces. There was no precedent for it. In the resolutions released by the Congress ("The Declaration of the Stamp Act Congress"), the term "His majesty's liege subjects" was a signal that, so far, the colonists were in and for the Empire. James Otis's position on Empire as a single commonwealth was accepted as a given, but the Congress thought his idea of colonial representation in Parliament logistically impossible and politically impractical, and the idea was rejected. The resolutions had a clean and direct message for the Crown, one that introduced Britain to a new colonial solidarity.

> [No] taxes should be imposed upon them [the colonists], but with their own consent, given personally, or by their representatives.... That the people of these colonies are not, and from their local circumstances cannot be, represented in the House of Commons in Great Britain.... That the only representatives of the people of these colonies are persons chosen therein, by themselves; and that no taxes ever have been or can be constitutionally imposed on them but by their respective legislatures ... [and it is] inconsistent with the principles and spirit of the British constitution, for the people of Great Britain to grant to His Majesty the property of the colonists.

James Otis had helped set up the Stamp Act Congress and was the most influential advocate of an integrated Empire with equal *actual* representation. This clashed with

Parliament's assumption that every member of Parliament represented every person in the Empire *virtually* (indirectly). Even though Otis's idea of a physical (actual) colonial representation in the Commons was not feasible, his general theory was sound. His position was that there could be no degrees of citizenship among Britons and that Parliament had implied an inferior constitutional status for colonists. He was important in the seeding of ideas that would challenge British assumptions concerning colonial status, but he took no part in the Revolution's more active phase. After his starring role in the Stamp Act crisis, he became moderate in his politics even as his pamphlets continued to fuel the debate. After 1771, it is reported that he became mentally ill and was looked after by his brother. He then receded from the main political stage and died from a lightning strike in 1783. Otis was one of the originals in the redefinition of colonial status, and his influence was wide and long lasting. Another potent voice of dissent was Maryland's Daniel Dulaney (1722-1797) whose 1765 essay "Considerations on the Propriety of Imposing Taxes in the British Colonies" had anticipated the language and thesis of the Stamp Act resolutions. But Dulaney represented a paradox. He may have questioned the right of Parliament to raise internal taxes in America but was not prepared to separate from Britain because of it. Eventually, he opposed independence and became one of America's most famous loyalists.

Perhaps the most memorable figure to emerge from the Stamp Act Congress was John Dickinson (1732-1808) of the Pennsylvania delegation. Dickinson was a paragon of political moderation who was involved in all the major political issues after 1764. He belonged to that fascinating revolutionary species, a conservative who changed with the tide and ended up as a delegate from Delaware to the Constitutional Convention of 1787. He was a superb pamphleteer, eloquent and reasonable, and attempted at every turn to reconcile the colonies with the Empire. He had shrewdly argued that the Stamp Act could only harm the British economy, and his *Letters From A Farmer in Pennsylvania*, written after the crisis, were hopeful appeals to Britain to communicate a respect for colonial concerns. However, he did insist on the colonial right to resort to force if absolutely necessary. He supported non-importation while he sought reconciliation, in part, by writing a *Petition to the King* in 1774. As a delegate to both the first and second Continental Congress in 1774 and 1775, he angered the militant New England delegates by urging moderation. He voted against the Declaration of Independence but then volunteered for service in the War for Independence. He opposed separation, but, when it occurred, he embraced it and came to embody the principle that no people can be governed without their consent. From the time before the Stamp Act crisis to the first United States Congress in 1789, Dickinson traveled the rocky road from colonist to republican citizen.

Parliament repealed the Stamp Act in 1766. In truth, it had no choice really, given the impossibility of collecting the tax without military force. Also, the uproar in America had led to an interesting opposition to the tax in the House of Commons. While George Grenville had sought a mandate to use military force, William Pitt argued for repeal by using the colonists' principle of actual representation or, in short, consent. Much of the movement to repeal had come from British merchants who feared a decline in trade. From the American perspective, the various colonial agents, representatives of the colonies in England, gave accounts of the hardships caused by the reforms. Most telling was Benjamin Franklin's testimony that Pennsylvania had spent 500,000 pounds sterling on the war but had received only 60,000 pounds sterling from the Crown in compensation. Parliament's position was that the Treasury had gone into debt to defend the colonies and to secure the Empire for the sake of all Britons. Colonists rejoiced when the Stamp Act was repealed. They then ignored the Declaratory Act, which followed in 1766. That act granted that the Stamp Act was ill conceived but declared that its repeal did not affect Parliament's sovereignty and that Parliament "had, hath and of right ought to have, full power and authority to make laws and statutes of sufficient force and validity to bind the colonies and peoples of America, subjects of the Crown of Great Britain, in all cases whatsoever." The colonists believed that the repeal of the Stamp Act had conceded their position. Parliament did not agree, and its unequivocal and forceful summary in the Declaratory Act was a forecast of an even deeper imperial crisis. It was business as usual at Whitehall, and the new Empire would proceed according to Parliament's dictates.

The Townshend Duties

Within a year of the Declaratory Act, Parliament revived its colonial revenue program, and the Townshend Duties, as they are known, were passed as the American Import Duties Act of 1767. This act was sensitive to the colonists' objections to internal taxes, but still imposed onerous surcharges on a range of imported consumer goods. Charles Townshend was a powerful figure in Parliament and had been appointed Chancellor of the Exchequer in 1766. According to his logic, if colonists had made the distinction between unacceptable "internal" taxes and acceptable "external" duties, then surely they should have no complaints about duties. His blandishments missed the point. Merchants, who controlled the assemblies in some of the northern colonies, were in no mood to pay more for imported luxuries and immediately campaigned for another non-importation movement. At the same time, the New York Assembly was suspended because it had balked at paying for quartering British troops at the request of General Gage, the Seven Years' War veteran who was now commander of the British Army in America. In his "Letters," John Dickinson described the Townshend Duties and the suspension of the New York Assembly as unconstitutional, and the moment of comfort after the repeal of the Stamp Act had passed. Just as the first bitter wave of opposition to the duties reached Britain, the fifty-two year old Townshend died of a "neglected fever," and his ultimate successor, Lord North, was left to deal with the fallout from the program. Lord North held the Treasury post for a remarkable 15 years. He was prime minister during 12 of those years.

A rhythm now appeared in imperial relations. If Parliament made a law for the administration of any aspect of colonial trade or government, the colonies reacted, increasingly in concert. In the case of the Townshend Duties, the obvious reaction was non-importation, and the merchants of Boston, Newport, New York, and Philadelphia (and subsequently in all the ports of entry) began a steady and coordinated boycotting of all luxury items. By the end of 1768, the ban was extended to include any of the items identified in the Townshend Duties. A year later, only New Hampshire continued importations of interdicted goods. The Massachusetts Circular Letter of February 1768 that had requested collective action was condemned by Massachusetts Governor Francis Bernard (1712-1779) as sedition. Secretary of State Lord Hillsborough ordered Bernard to dissolve the General Court, but the House of Representatives (the Massachusetts lower house) defied him. Bernard was gone by the end of 1769 by which time other colonies had issued their own circular letters. A Royal Navy warship then appeared in Boston harbor to protect royal customs agents who were being denied duties and threatened by locals. The warship was snubbed, and crowds in Boston harassed and assaulted customs officials and sent them running to the safety of Castle William in the harbor. A few months later, two regiments of British regulars landed in Boston to be billeted. Meanwhile, the Boston Town Meeting, with amusing tongue in cheek, had urged inhabitants to arm themselves on the pretence of a fresh outbreak of war with France. This public taunting was more than frustrated mischief. Ninety-six towns sent delegates to an informal political convention in Boston. It broke up before the troops landed. The protests of 1768 were more direct and confrontational than those of 1763 and 1764. Constitutional theorizing was still in the air, but it was mixed now with tests of Parliament's patience and, more important, the difficulties of British colonial representatives to operate safely in the colonies.

British Political Concerns

Between 1721 and 1756, there had been only four prime ministers in Britain, all of them Whigs. As the list below shows, the rate of turnover sped up during and after the Seven Years' War, and, while the Whigs maintained control of Parliament for most of the period of the American Revolution, nine of the first ten prime ministers after the loss of America were Tories. The term "*Prime Minister*" was not constitutionally recognized until the early twentieth century, but it had applied in practice to every majority party leader after Walpole. In a generalized sense, Whig and Tory followed from the seventeenth-century terms "Country" and "Court" respectively, which sometimes referred to affiliations with either the Commons (Whig) or the Monarchy (Tory). These terms were also used to identify what we would consider, respectively, liberal or conservative political affinities and social values. Each term was used originally as an insult. The word "Tory" derived from a term for Irish bandits and "Whig" from the definition of a Scottish Presbyterian rebel. As parliamentary factions evolved in the eighteenth century from highly personalized associations to more rigorous party organizations, the terms became more formal. American colonists were familiar with the terms, and, during the Revolution, "Tory" came to be used as a specific reference for loyalists, while British officials and loyalists tended to see the American "rebels" as "Whigs." The terms continued to define parties into the nineteenth century in Britain and Canada but gradually petered out. The word "Whig" is seldom used today in political discourse, but "Tory" retains its power as a synonym for the Conservative Party in Britain and also for its namesake in Canada. In the 1830s in the United States, a coalition of smaller political organizations opposed to Andrew Jackson referred to themselves as "Whig" and applied the term in a way that echoed its original usage, with Jackson's Democratic Party administration ironically representing the "Court."

Table 2.1: British Prime Ministers, 1721-1801

Sir Robert Walpole	1721-42
Spencer Compton, Earl of Wilmington	1742-43
Henry Pelham	1743-54
Thomas Pelham-Holles, Duke of Newcastle	1754-56
William Cavendish, Duke of Devonshire	1756-57
Thomas Pelham-Holles, Duke of Newcastle	1757-62
John Stuart, Earl of Bute	1762-63
George Grenville	1763-65
Charles Watson-Wentworth, Marquess of Rockingham	1765-66
William Pitt the Elder, Earl of Chatham	1766-68
Augustus Fitzroy, Duke of Grafton	1768-70
Frederick North, Lord North	1770-82
Charles Watson-Wentworth, Marquess of Rockingham	1782
William Petty, Earl of Shelburne	1782-83
William Cavendish Bentinck, Duke of Portland	1783
William Pitt the Younger	1783-1801

All but Bute and Pitt the Younger can be identified as "Whigs." There is a touch of irony in the fact that American rebels (patriots) were also referred to as Whigs while at war with a British Prime Minister, Lord North, who was a Whig. The terms need to be used carefully. Note that Pitt the Elder was a Whig, but his son identified himself as a Tory. Lord North had some Tory connections and leanings but is rightly seen as a Whig in the contemporary political culture.

The turnover in parliamentary leaders in Britain belies what was otherwise a stable period in domestic politics, even though Britain was at war almost continuously from the end of Walpole's tenure to the 1780s. Only Walpole, Pelham, Newcastle (second term), and North managed to last for more than two years. Walpole's 21-year run and Pitt the Younger's 18-year leadership after 1783 bracket the list. Between those two ministries, the turnover is brisk, and the average length of service was about a year and a half between 1762 and 1770. Lord North's 12-year leadership corresponds to the war years, but, in 1782-3, five prime ministers appeared in the turmoil of the war's aftermath. The influence of George III on this period of political musical chairs cannot be underestimated. He exploited the American "crisis" with zest. Bute, who had groomed the King-to-be and who was briefly the royal favorite in the early 1760s, fell out of favor after 1763. George's skilful patronage, single-mindedness, and awareness of the partisan issues of the day worked well. This can be attributed to his yielding to party politics when necessary, recognizing the limits of monarchical power, and advancing his personal objectives when he could. To the colonists, George was the real power in Britain. It was he who allowed Parliament to subvert the constitution by signing their acts into law, and it was he who authorized the use of force. It was at his "Majesty's pleasure" that lackeys were appointed to administrative and judicial positions. George III, in many ways, was an aberration to the extent that he managed policy during the decades of the American crisis. Opponents of his American policies were aware that "the influence of the crown has increased, was increasing, and ought to be diminished" as a belated parliamentary proposal put it in 1780. That proposal was the result of clashing interests in a war-weary Parliament, but, in the 1760s and 1770s, the King's approach prevailed, driven by colonial actions that tested British authority in America. In that sense, the King was often reacting to American behavior. Was the colonial tail wagging the royal dog? Perhaps, but for the most part, until 1776, the Crown directed the action and ignored or overruled colonial opposition.

By 1769, the non-importation movement was reaching into the British economy while doing no good for the colonial economy. In May, the Virginia Resolves were announced as a result of George Washington's initiatives and the work of George Mason (1725-1792), a fifth generation Virginian. These were yet another blast against Parliament's denunciation of the circular letters and its threats to remove American troublemakers to Britain for trial. Again, the issue of taxation rights was raised. The resolves led Patrick Henry (1736-1799) and Richard Henry Lee (1732-1794) — both of whom were lawyers, native Virginians, and future revolutionaries — to petition the King to relent, but to no avail. The Virginia Assembly was dissolved by the royal governor, so its members simply met informally and drew up and adopted the Virginia Association, yet another non-importation agreement that spread to Maryland and the Carolinas.

Imports into the colonies as a whole fell by as much as 80 per cent during 1768-1769. In New York, the decline was even greater. While British trade in Europe and Asia was stable or growing, the loss of substantial parts of the colonial American market, especially when accompanied by colonial political alienation, raised talk by the Board of Trade about modifying the Townshend Duties. At the start of 1770, Lord North began his long tenure as chancellor of the exchequer and de facto prime minister. He saw the folly of continuing the Townshend Duties but knew that a complete repeal would be seen as appeasement. His calculations were correct in the short term. Parliament passed a bill that effectively gutted the duties, leaving only the tea tax in effect and so causing the quick collapse of the various non-importation movements. The Boston Town Meeting resisted at first but gave in to the tide of official and public acceptance of North's initiative. As merchants resumed trading, and assemblies resumed the business of local government, the Quartering Act expired and the agitation that had marked colonial life for several years began to abate. But the fundamental issue of sovereignty had not been dealt with. Merchant interests in the non-importation movements had been drawn into the political sphere, and activists such as James Otis, John Dickinson, George Mason, and others had fused the question of economic sovereignty with political sovereignty. The ending of the Townshend Duties led to a brief lull in the sovereignty debate, but could not hope to resolve it.

Parliament's claim of "virtually" representing the colonies in the way that British MPs represented a largely unfranchised British population had been summarily dismissed by the Stamp Act Congress. The concept of consent had bubbled up during the Stamp Act debate and continued to simmer, and the "no taxation without representation" thesis became axiomatic in the petitions, appeals, and pamphlets directed at Parliament. These verbal exchanges gave way to an unexpected resumption of violence at the end of 1769. Scuffles in New York City in a dispute over appropriations for the Quartering Act brought out the Sons of Liberty. A riot resulted in a rash of injuries, many of them inflicted by British bayonets. In an imprudent official decision, Alexander McDougall (1732-1786), a Sons of Liberty leader, was imprisoned for criticizing the Crown-influenced New York Assembly. Like so many others in this period, his experience was an apprenticeship of sorts, and he ended up in the thick of the Revolution as an important Continental Army officer during the War for Independence. British actions were contributing directly to a growing urban resistance and politicizing it along the way.

The Boston Massacre
As the New York courts dealt with McDougall's alleged sedition, a more persistent series of petty clashes between civilians and soldiers climaxed in Boston in March 1770 in what was immediately labeled "the Boston Massacre." The deaths of five Bostonians in a confrontation with British soldiers became an instant sensation. The quartering of troops in Boston in 1768 had hatched frequent clashes between soldiers and townspeople. Much of the time, tensions were released verbally, but tavern and street brawls did occur, and soldiers had on one occasion dispersed an angry crowd by firing their muskets into the air. The prelude to the incident occurred in a working class environment. British soldiers often sought employment on the city's waterfront, on wharves, and in rope-works, a sector of the shipbuilding industry, and, on March 5, 1770, a fist fight between a worker and an off duty soldier led to a small street protest. Troops were called out to restrain a belligerent gathering near the Province House (the seat of government in Massachusetts). As the crowd pressed forward, an unidentified voice called out for the troops to open fire. They did, directly into the crowd, killing five people, three instantly and two from their wounds. Lieutenant Governor Hutchinson sensibly had the garrison leave town, and, in a remarkable turn of events, the officer in charge, Captain Preston, and six soldiers were tried in civil court and defended by two important locals, John Adams (1735-1826) and Josiah Quincy (1744-1775). All but two of the accused were acquitted; the others were convicted of manslaughter, and each was branded on the hand.

The authority of the Massachusetts court likely quieted the population, but, as people's anger subsided, Samuel Adams (1722-1803), the busy and belligerent street politician and second cousin of the sober-minded and judicious John Adams, was happy to fan the embers of unrest. He contributed to a dramatic publication, *A Short Narrative of the Horrid Massacre in Boston*, put together by a group whose later careers meshed with the patriot cause in the Revolution. Among the group was James Bowdoin (1726-1790), a Boston merchant and erstwhile moderate, who was not only active later in the Revolution but also helped draft the first Massachusetts Constitution and served as governor. Paul Revere (1735-1818), another major revolutionary figure, emerged from the "Massacre" with a patriotic reputation. His stylized engraving was and remains one of the most potent images of the event and shows a line of British troops firing point blank into an unarmed group of well-dressed Bostonians. The Boston-born Revere is one of the Revolution's most celebrated and legendary figures because of his 1775 "ride," but his engraving of the Boston Massacre might be just as decisive a contribution to the Revolution. Despite the hubbub over the affair, tensions eased in New England as the repeal of the majority of the 1767 duties encouraged an easing of non-importation. But the "Massacre" had made an impression on Massachusetts, and it would not take much to revive the antagonisms between the province's executive and an increasingly volatile population.

Activists and Reactionaries

A long simmering internal problem in the backcountry of North Carolina heated up in the years after 1768. In contrast to the political collaborations of working and merchant classes and of urban and rural interests in Massachusetts, the people in the western regions of North Carolina had for a long time opposed the province's political and economic leadership. This kind of geographical and social division affected all the southern colonies from the Chesapeake to Georgia. Economic and political power was skewed in the south, and class factionalism colored the politics of the region. Bacon's Rebellion in 1676 had confirmed the power of the coastal planters. Their status had been maintained since then as they distributed land to their offspring and friends and quite routinely controlled the franchise. These long-standing divisions lasted well into the nineteenth century. The backcountry societies, especially in the Carolinas, were poorer, looser, and more radical in their religious behavior and more egalitarian and informal in their politics than the Tidewater communities. There was a much-diminished level of slaveholding and a high incidence of "natural" justice in the foothills and highlands.

Over several decades, the growing populations in the backcountry became increasingly vociferous in their complaints against planter-controlled assemblies. There, protest against local elected authority, *not* against the British, was a complicating trend in the colonial-imperial debate. In North Carolina, a group of flamboyant militants calling themselves "Regulators" raised the flag of rebellion and took the law into their own hands near Hillsboro. Their declared nullification of North Carolina's elected authority aroused a predictable reaction. Governor William Tryon led 1,200 militiamen into the backcountry and quashed the incipient rebellion at Alamance Creek. One of the leaders of the Regulators was summarily executed, and six others were hanged later as traitors. Over 6,000 backcountry settlers were forced to swear allegiance to the government. Their actions had been deemed treason. Eventually, courts were set up in the backcountry of North Carolina as they had been in South Carolina, where the Regulator movement was earlier appeased by this gesture. A local conflict had been revealed that had nothing directly to do with the larger imperial issue but rather would coincide with it as the internal antagonisms added complexity to the revolutionary movement.

While the Regulators were troubling North Carolina, the peaceful interlude in New England after the "Massacre" ended with a spectacular display of anti-imperialism. On June 9, 1772, the *Gaspee*, a customs schooner used to track smugglers, went aground near Providence, Rhode Island while in pursuit of another vessel. In an act of symbolic vandalism, eight boatloads of men left Providence and attacked the stranded ship. They set the crew ashore before burning the vessel to the waterline, a vivid example of the "propaganda of the deed." A royal announcement naively offered a 500 pounds sterling reward to anyone who could identify the culprits. When no one came forward, it was assumed that the entire Rhode Island community was conspiring against the Crown. A Commission of Enquiry was set up and met for several months, hoping to identify the perpetrators and put them on trial in England. The Commission included the chief justices of Massachusetts, New York, and New Jersey; the vice-admiralty judge of Boston; and the Governor of Rhode Island, but the hearings were handicapped, predictably, by an uncooperative public. The Commission was a predictable failure, but its intention to take Rhode Islanders to Britain for trial alarmed even moderates in the New England population. While the *Gaspee* Commission was being adjourned, an executive governmental decision in Massachusetts exacerbated the deteriorating relations between New England and the Crown. Governor Hutchinson declared that henceforth he and the judges of Massachusetts would receive their salaries from the Crown instead of from the Massachusetts Assembly. The elected representatives would thus lose an important financial check on royal government, and Hutchinson, who had lost public trust in 1765, was seen as the chief agent of a growing assault on traditional rights. In his defense, Hutchinson saw only the criminality of New Englanders' political behavior. His loyalty to the Empire seemed to radicals to supersede his communal attachment to Massachusetts, his home. But Hutchinson's Massachusetts lineage was as long as any, including those of Samuel Adams, Otis and Hancock, and other Boston durables who were now becoming solidly opposed to the way the Empire was operating in the colonies. Here lay the revolutionary paradox: the local, mature native-born American who could be equally devoted to the Empire and to the local community. In Hutchinson's case, however, and for the tens of thousands like him who became loyalists, the fear was that a breakdown of the Empire would leave an ungovernable mess in the colonies. Everything Hutchinson saw frightened him, from the Stamp Act riots to the non-importation movements to the *Gaspee*

incident. His readings of the opposition pamphlets confirmed that they were dangerous assaults on Massachusetts's rightful place in the Empire.

When the news of Hutchinson's announcement reached the patriot circle in
Boston, Samuel Adams called for the towns of the province to form associations to
respond. Some patriots in Boston, including John Hancock, questioned the militant
approach, but it was gaining favor with the public and helped bring a new Committee
of Correspondence into existence. Boston created its own standing committee of 21
members who were commissioned to spread the town's views to the rest of the
province and beyond. James Otis was made chairman and the Town Meeting approved
the usual litany of complaints about British violations of colonists' rights. As it was, the
Hutchinson loyalists were also present in the Boston Town Meeting, and the fiery rhetoric of Otis and Samuel Adams was relayed to the loyalist administration. When one
considers that in the early 1770s the radical anti-British element in New England politics was a minority of the population, the British reaction to the committees of correspondence was plausible; they saw the same old malcontents leading a vociferous and
simple-minded rabble. It would be some time before the British in America understood that in Samuel Adams's noisy behavior was a rather obvious truth: the reformed
Empire had been alienating significant sections of the colonial population. Indeed,
by the start of 1773, committees of correspondence were circulating anti-imperial
propaganda everywhere, and, by early 1774, only Pennsylvania and North Carolina
were outside this loop. In Virginia, the Committee included future luminaries Thomas
Jefferson, Richard Henry Lee, and Patrick Henry. The opposition that had ebbed
and flowed since 1763 was gelling. Not since the Stamp Act Congress had there been
a comparable display of opposition. The committees were remarkably well organized
and acted as information conduits to link the assemblies. As the British forced the
issue over the next two years, the precedent of the Stamp Act Congress and an articulate and ideologically coherent system of communications served to encourage a more
radicalized resistance.

Tea

Over the winter of 1772 and 1773, the East India Company amassed an inventory of
nearly 8,000 tons of surplus, marketable tea in England. The Company managed much
of India for the Empire and for its shareholders, much as the Hudson's Bay Company
did in the far reaches of British North America. Along with tobacco, sugar, and spices,
tea had become a major commodity in the consumer culture of Britain and the
colonies. It had become a staple of colonial beverage consumption along with milk,
ciders, beer, wine, and rum. The colonies produced all of their beverage needs except
for wine and tea. Wine remained a drink for the "better sorts," but tea, on the other
hand, was more widely popular and accessible. Colonial merchants and retailers
bought consignments of tea from middlemen, and prices in the colonies reflected the
costs of the British export duty (tea went from India to Britain and then by re-export
to European and American markets) and the costs of the middlemen, the import duty

in America, and, finally, the merchants' mark up. The duties on tea were the last of the 1767 Townshend Duties still in effect. While there was lingering disapproval of them, there was no great clamor for the repeal of either the British export charge or the import duty. However, in a completely unexpected move, Parliament passed a bill in April 1773 ending the export tax on tea and allowing the East India Company to sell directly to its own selected agents and retailers in the colonies, thus bypassing the colonial wholesalers who normally bought at auction in Britain. This was a shocking reversal of fair trade practices; it lowered the price of tea to a point where even smuggled tea from Holland and elsewhere could not compete, but it also undermined the colonial merchants who had honestly taken part in the tea market. While the change seemed to offer a boon to consumers, it was translated immediately by merchants into another political crisis.

With its mandate in hand, the East India Company authorized the shipment of roughly 250 tons (500,000 pounds) of tea to its own selected merchants in Boston, New York, Philadelphia, and Charleston. Within weeks, colonial merchants condemned the unseemly monopoly and managed to get all of the Company's consignees to resign, except for those in Boston. In New York, the Sons of Liberty charged the consignees with violating local ethics. Boycotts were threatened, and harbor pilots were warned by an angry broadside not to guide the tea fleet to New York wharves. In Charleston, the only shipload of tea that arrived could not be unloaded after the Company's agents on shore were persuaded to resign. Import regulations stated that unclaimed cargoes had a 20-day grace period before being apprehended for duties, so the tea was landed by customs agents and stored. It sat unclaimed until July 1776 when the rebel government of South Carolina auctioned it to raise money. In Boston, meanwhile, embattled Governor Thomas Hutchinson was drawn vicariously into the matter. His two sons and a nephew were among the Company's agents in Boston, and, once again, Hutchinson found himself in an untenable position. If he acceded to the demands of the population, he would be endorsing illegality. His value system and conscience led him to support the Company's position because it had been authorized by an act of Parliament. For Hutchinson, the act was ill advised. He clearly saw the problems with it, as he had with the Stamp Act, but he insisted on Parliament's right to pass and enforce its laws, even those of questionable logic. When three tea-laden ships appeared in Boston Harbor, Bostonians in large meetings twice called for the cargoes to be sent back to England. Hutchinson refused to issue an order. The scene was set for what we now know as the "Boston Tea Party."

The leading merchants of Boston joined with the town's working and crafts classes in organizing a physical response to Hutchinson's stubbornness. While Hutchinson realized that there was a problem in getting the tea unloaded, he insisted on the letter of the law that said that the ships could not leave port until the import duty, which remained at 3d a pound, was paid. The 20-day regulation was applied, as in Charleston. What followed, the "destruction of the tea," was not spontaneous, but a calculated act of property damage for political ends. On the eve of the twentieth day, a reported 8,000 people assembled near Boston's South Church and listened while Samuel Adams was informed by the ship's owners that the governor still refused to let the ships leave port while duties remained unpaid. Immediately, some thirty men dressed as Mohawk Indians rushed to Griffin's Wharf. They were joined by as many as a hundred more and, in a prearranged action, boarded the three ships and dumped 342 chests of tea into Boston Harbor. The spectacle was watched from the wharf by an estimated 2,000 people, the largest of the many protests that had taken place anywhere in the colonies during the imperial imbroglio. The merchants of Boston had an obvious financial stake in the tea issue, but 8,000 people, perhaps a majority of Boston's inhabitants, had earlier lent their support to the demonstration. The economic and ideological interests of John Hancock meshed with the civic egalitarianism of the silversmith, the shoemaker, the sailor, the carpenter and the wharfinger. The Boston "mob" that gathered on December 16, 1773 was as varied as any cross section anywhere among free white males in urban America. Crowds of that size and complexion were available in America's other major port cities. New York and Philadelphia each had large floating dockside and seafaring populations eager to protest against privilege or unemployment or the price of bread. Substantial numbers of literate, politically engaged urban artisans, small retailers, and local officials resided in all the seaboard towns, but it was Boston that produced the most theatrical and decisive resistance to the Tea Act.

Boston Politics

Colonial Boston was a tightly coordinated municipality with a long-standing corporate mentality. Civic government was intrusive; it drew the entire population into a network of institutions through the Town Meeting and the open and popular election of town selectmen (councillors). The Town Meeting elected or appointed the myriad of civic officials needed to run the town's affairs and was open to all taxpayers. It supervised public works, regulated poor relief and residence requirements, but remained subject to the superior taxation, judicial, and legislative authority of the province of Massachusetts. Like all towns in the province, Boston had been created by the colonial government in the first place. A defined civic leadership was drawn annually from a mid-eighteenth century pool of about 200 merchants, lawyers, and other professionals. The class structure of Boston, from the church and merchant hierarchy down to the destitute and dependent, shared an intimate urban environment; the dense, compact town of about 16,000 in 1770 contained 12 neighborhood wards and several miles of busy waterfront. There was deference, to be sure, but there was a respect for citizenship, too, so that John Hancock and the instigators of the assault on the tea fleet could enlist small retailers, tradesmen, mariners and laborers to the cause. There was also a political hierarchy in New York and in Philadelphia, the "private" city that governed itself differently from Boston. Many of Philadelphia's civic operations were run by non-governmental agencies. Port cities had a lot in common with each other, and though New York or Philadelphia merchants supported non-importation movements and published broadsides protesting British actions — and crowds of artisans, dock-workers, and sailors in those two cities mustered to confront British officials and troops — Boston's more integrated citizenry offered the best coordinated defiance of British authority.

Boston produced activists such as Samuel Adams and James Otis on the one hand and John Hancock and John Adams on the other. The former were seen by the British as rabble-rousers, capable of inciting mob action. Samuel Adams was a brewer, a pamphleteer, and a tavern brawler rolled into one. John Adams and Hancock were sterling members of Boston's upper class. Yet all of them could persuade ordinary people to see the Empire's motives as detrimental to Boston's corporate ethos, so that Hancock's economic interest in defying the East India Company was taken up as a political issue by Boston's working class population. This collectivism did not end class distinctions, nor did it ease the poverty that was growing in the port cities, but it allowed for concerted action. Political dissent penetrated all levels of society, and the string of British actions over the previous decade, from the Proclamation to the Tea Act, gave tangible evidence to phrases like "corruption" and "tyranny." Was there more at stake for the merchants of Boston than for the working classes? Was the shoemaker who helped dump the tea coerced? Did John Hancock seduce the deferential shoemaker from a position of authority? The complex problem of trying to make the inarticulate speak through their actions cannot be solved easily. What we do know is that the Boston community, acting across class lines, destroyed the tea in December 1773. It was not a "party," and it would not be referred to as a "party" until decades later. What it represents is an act of communal rebellion. It was bloodless and even polite, and no other ships' properties were harmed, but it included, at one level or another, almost the entire Boston population directly or in sympathy. What differentiated Hancock, for example, from Thomas Hutchinson or the Oliver family, were temperament, ideology, and perhaps common sense.

In Thomas Hutchinson, the community saw a fellow citizen who ran against the will of the majority of his own class and of the broader community. He had been attacked for it in 1765, and, by the time of the "Tea Party," the conservative Hutchinson had become a pariah. He stuck to the letter of the law even when he saw ill considered British action and, by 1773, had become notorious for defending the British position in America. He had been dubbed a "courtier" by John Adams a few years earlier and would be driven to England in opprobrium by a hostile citizenry with epithets such as "tool of tyrants" and "damn'd arch traitor" and "Machiavellian" schemer. He attracted the shared scorn and distrust of much of Boston's political *cognoscenti*. To his opponents, Hutchinson's personality, political career, and ambitions blinded him to New England's legitimate concerns over changing imperial policies. He was the obvious choice to succeed Governor Barnard, first as acting governor in 1769 and then fully in 1771. His association with Barnard revealed his desire to rise in the imperial world, but his unwavering support for Parliament's authority in the colonies was genuine. By 1773, Hutchinson's reputation was so demeaned that he was likely beyond saving, but even he could not have predicted the dramatic event that brought his world crashing down. While he was alienating Massachusetts with his position on the East India Company's privileges, it was revealed that he and Lieutenant Governor Andrew Oliver (1706-1774), his friend and relative through marriage, had been corresponding secretly with a member of the Grenville and North ministries between 1767 and 1769. During the struggles over the Townshend Duties, he had recommended tougher measures against colonial dissenters. Benjamin Franklin made the letters public and was chastened for his breech of ethics. Samuel Adams had the letters printed so that, even before the tea arrived in Boston, Hutchinson's fate was sealed. To Bostonians, the letters were evidence of a conspiracy, and an apparent attack on the liberties of Massachusetts, in a pact between a native-born agent of the Crown, Hutchinson, and the Crown itself.

The Coercive Acts

At the beginning of 1774, Benjamin Franklin appeared before the Privy Council in London on behalf of the Massachusetts House of Representatives to complain about the Crown's paying the salaries of Hutchinson and Chief Justice Peter Oliver. The latter was the brother of Andrew Oliver and was seen by the Boston radicals as a Hutchinson toady just as Andrew had been. When news of the "Tea Party" reached London, Franklin was attacked as a deceiver and dismissed as Deputy Postmaster for America. At the same time, the Massachusetts House impeached Peter Oliver for accepting a salary from the Crown in contravention of the House's custom and prerogative. Hutchinson used his authority to dismiss the elected assembly. Boston bubbled with expectation. The intentions of the Crown's best known agent in New England, Thomas Hutchinson, were now out in the open. He was suspected of dismantling the legislature in order to prevent it from putting Peter Oliver on trial, and the first high-ranking royal loyalists were exposed. The tea troubles had by this time moved down the coast from Boston. This indicated to the British an incipient breakdown of civil order on a scale greater than the Stamp Act disturbances and non-importation. A new shipment of tea was dumped by the Sons of Liberty into New York Harbor. Another ship and its load were burned at Annapolis, Maryland, and a warehouse of tea was destroyed in New Jersey. If Americans, and especially Bostonians, were angry with the Crown, the feelings were mutual, and, in the spring of 1774, the Crown reciprocated by introducing the aptly named Coercive Acts, a set of hardnosed reprisals against Massachusetts. Tea had been destroyed in New York, New Jersey, and Maryland as well as in Boston, but the Crown decided that Massachusetts was the cockpit of American dissent.

Parliament made the decision in anger. The destruction of the tea and the general riotous mood in Boston outraged Britain's merchant and political classes. Moderates such as William Pitt and the redoubtable Edmund Burke tried to temper Parliament's punitive mood but were brushed aside in the rush to make an example of Massachusetts. The majority in Parliament had long sought to apply severe strictures on New

England. The organized destruction of the tea had been completed with a remarkable degree of order and even decorum, but Parliament could see only an unruly snub of its authority. The insistence on preserving that authority was to be expected, but the full-scale application of arbitrary rule, for that is what the Coercive Acts amounted to, appeared to Bostonians to be a case of persecution for persecution's sake. The term "coercive" speaks to Parliament's frustration, and to its belief that sanctions backed by military force would restore imperial order in Boston.

The four separate Coercive Acts were passed in sequence from the end of March to the beginning of June 1774. The first was the Boston Port Bill of March 25, signed into law by the King (given "Royal assent") on March 31 to be effective on June 1. It shut down the port of Boston except for cargoes of military supplies, food, and fuels. Even those goods had to be cleared by customs agents who were now located at Salem. The port of Boston was to remain closed until the East India Company and His Majesty's Customs were compensated for the dumping of the tea in December 1773. How this money was to be found or raised was not stipulated, but, if Parliament expected the merchants of Boston or the Town Meeting or the Massachusetts House of Representatives to come forward with apologies and compensation, they were disappointed. In any case, Parliament hit Massachusetts even harder two months later with the Administration of Justice Act, one of the key features of which was the provision that any royal official charged with a serious offence in provincial court could have the trial removed to England for the official's personal safety.

The third of the Coercive Acts was the most devastating. The Massachusetts Government Act, effective August 1, voided the Massachusetts charter and shut down the provincial government. It denied the House its prerogative in selecting members to the upper chamber, the Council, and gave the King the authority to appoint council members at pleasure. The Governor could now remove lower court justices, sheriffs, the Attorney General, and justices of the peace, and replace them at will. Even the Chief Justice of the Massachusetts Court, the highest civil judicial office in the province, was subject to the Governor's direct control. The Governor could nominate candidates directly to the King for his approval. Local authority was ended because, according to the Crown, the towns had been seedbeds for public riot. The towns of Massachusetts and all of New England were vital mechanisms in political representation and governance. To end the local prerogative in local affairs, at least to the point where only the Governor could authorize meetings and elections, was in effect to declare all civil government in Massachusetts null and void. The fourth of the acts was yet another Quartering Act, more severe than any of its predecessors. It applied to all the colonies and allowed the British Army to claim any unused buildings for billeting troops. Massachusetts was placed under modified military rule with the appointment of General Thomas Gage as military-civil executive. He succeeded the disgraced and exiled Thomas Hutchinson, whose safety was in jeopardy up to the time he left Boston that spring.

The Quebec Act

While the shocking news of the Coercive Acts or "intolerable" acts, as the colonists' epithet had it, was being digested, Parliament passed the Quebec Act in May of 1774. This was the final or delayed application of a government plan for the trans-Appalachian west. It took the terms of the Proclamation of 1763, which had banned colonial penetration into most of the former French territories, and created a civil government for Quebec in territory that stretched from the St. Lawrence Valley to the Ohio River. The territory south of the Ohio to the boundary with Spanish territory was to be reserved for natives. No charter was issued for any part of the territory, and its council and administrators were to be chosen by the Crown. No jury trials were allowed for any civil case, a feature of French colonial administration but alien to the traditions of British America. There was immediate outrage, especially in Virginia, Pennsylvania, and Massachusetts, all of which had claims to the territory. Just as vexing was the granting of French language privileges in law and the confirmation of the Catholic faith as a legal and protected institution. The tone of the Quebec Act was an affront to colonial sensibilities:

> Article V ... And, for the more perfect security and ease of the minds of the inhabitants of the said province [Quebec], it is hereby declared, That his Majesty's subjects, professing the religion of the church of Rome of and in the said province of Quebec, may have, hold and enjoy, the free exercise of the religion of the church of Rome....

> Article VIII ... And be it further enacted ...That his Majesty's Canadian Subjects, within the province of Quebec [except the churches] ... may also hold and enjoy their property and possessions, together with all customs and usages thereto, and all other their civil rights, in as large, ample, and beneficial manner....

Colonial leaders, who were historically anti-Catholic, noticed that Catholics in Great Britain did not have the legal rights suggested by the Quebec Act. In a sweeping set of laws, applied in what seemed like a flash of time, colonial British America was being redesigned and the colonies' futures reformulated. Martial law in Massachusetts, troops being quartered in all provinces, the renewed and dreaded specter of a "standing army," and the elevation of French language and religion to legality all seemed like a complete corruption of British justice. Colonial territory had been expropriated, it seemed, for the sanctuary of an enemy of two hundred years. How long would it be before the 80,000 French Catholics in the St. Lawrence Valley began to make their way into the Ohio country? How long would it be before the suspension of representative government west of the Appalachians would be applied to the thirteen colonies? And if Britain could extinguish civil and representative government in Massachusetts and replace it with military rule, what would prevent it from doing the same in any other American jurisdiction if there was dissent?

Reaction to the Coercive Acts was swift. At the local and popular level, sermons and public gatherings attacked the acts. Ebeneezer Baldwin, a Congregational Church pastor in Danbury, Connecticut, denounced the acts as part of a larger scheme to end chartered governments in the British colonies. As he put it,

> If we view the whole of the conduct of the ministry and parliament, I do not see how any one can now doubt but there is a settled fix'd plan for *inslaving* the colonies, or bringing them under arbitrary government.... Now notwithstanding the excellency of the British constitution, if the ministry can secure a majority in parliament... they may rule as absolutely as they do in *France* or *Spain*, yea as in *Turkey* or *India*.

Baldwin's long essay hit the nail on the head. He saw the unwritten British constitution being violated. The ancient constitution itself had been an excellent protector of free and open civil rights, but wilful men were now abusing it. Baldwin's attack and others in a similar vein suggested that the King's ministers had arranged a majority in Parliament to extinguish the rights of "freeborn Englishmen" or "Britons" in British North America for nefarious ends.

Questioning the Legitimacy of Parliament

By August of 1774, reactions to the Coercive Acts in the mainland colonies were marked by dismay and foreboding. Parliament had fallen into the hands of wicked men. In Pennsylvania, James Wilson (1742-1798) posed the question directly by asking rhetorically how colonists could possibly have abdicated their citizenship rights by leaving Britain and settling in America. Wilson, a practicing lawyer, was himself an immigrant of Scotch-Irish descent who had come to the colonies in 1765 in the midst of the Stamp Act crisis. He studied law with John Dickinson, whose theory of representation he had imbibed. Wilson's logic was sound. If Parliament could make separate and arbitrary laws for the colonies, it could redefine citizenship by fiat. Wilson's treatise *Considerations on the Authority of Parliament* is a stylish, rational, and persuasive essay on the assumed roles of King and Parliament as separate parts of the administration of law. Wilson referred to historical precedent and the legal constitutional theories of Sir Edward Coke, the great English jurist who had questioned royal prerogative in the early seventeenth century, noting that the role of the monarch was as guarantor of rights rather than lawmaker. He also cited the eighteenth-century jurist Sir William Blackstone's theory of dependence based on the rights of conquest, a condition that did not apply to the original settlers and their dependents who were British to begin with. What Wilson did not acknowledge was Blackstone's assertion that "[Parliament] has sovereign and uncontrollable authority [in all civil and ecclesiastical matters, and] can, in short, do anything that is not naturally impossible." But, in 1774, Americans were on their way to disproving Blackstone's thesis. Colonial allegiance and "obedience" to the King required a reciprocal protection of the subjects' rights to representation. Wilson was in fact back at the Stamp Act resolutions. His essay took a familiar tack with its complex mix of history and theory, and, while he claimed that a common definition of citizenship applied to colonists and residents of the British Isles, he insisted that special circumstances pertained to America because of the impossibility of actual representation in Parliament. Wilson insisted that colonial America was both equal and different at the same time, and Parliament's hardliners saw impertinent colonists demanding to have their cake and eat it too.

In August 1774, Thomas Jefferson entered the debate with a rousing address to the King in which he attacked Parliament's aims in America and accused the King of collusion. Jefferson addressed the deeper meaning of the Coercive Acts in a pamphlet sent to Virginia's delegates to the Continental Congress in September. *A Summary View of the Rights of British-America* is remarkable for its presaging the language and themes of the Declaration of Independence, written two years later. Jefferson came to the defense of Boston's merchants and citizens and revealed the far-ranging common ground of colonial leaders in their increasing dismissal of Parliament's presumptive authority. As had Wilson in his essay, Jefferson retailed a long set of historical precedents and current events and fused them to a theory of consensual politics; no government could simply assume sovereignty unless it maintained the consent of the governed. Here he argued the same case that Wilson had, charging the King with responsibility for curbing Parliament's aggressive victimization of the colonies. It could hardly have escaped Wilson's or Jefferson's notice that the King was locked solidly into Parliament and had fudged his constitutional separation from the legislative powers of Parliament. Jefferson noted

> That we ... consider the conduct of his majesty, as holding the executive powers of the laws of these states [a significant use of the term], and mark out his deviations from the line of duty: By the constitution of Great Britain, as well as of the several American states, his majesty possesses the power of refusing to pass into a law any [parliamentary] bill. [Here Jefferson claims that George III and his predecessors had simply respected the prerogative of the House of Lords and the House of Commons in matters pertaining to the British Isles.] ... But by change of circumstances ... the addition of new states to the British empire has produced an addition of new, and sometimes opposite interests. It is now, therefore, the great office of his majesty, to resume the exercise of his negative power [veto], and to prevent the passage of laws by one legislature of the empire [Parliament], which might bear injuriously on the rights and interests of another [the colonial assemblies].

The earlier tone of appeal had become defiance. Wilson and Jefferson in so many ways were simply embellishing the principles of the Stamp Act resolutions, but in other ways were less conciliatory and rather more audacious in demanding that the King do his duty. Jefferson raised issues that had not so far been discussed, including a rather ridiculous charge that British law and Parliament's connivance had led to the introduction and growth of slavery in the colonies and that the Crown could have and should have forbidden those laws, mostly by refusing to allow duties. Another example of Jefferson's tendency to exaggerate was his inflation of the size of the American population in order to make a point, as in the rhetorical "Can any one reason be assigned why 160,000 electors in the island of Great Britain should give law to four million in the states of America, every individual of whom is equal to every individual of them ... ?" Jefferson's claimed population of America was double what it actually was, but it made more effective his claim that it was governed by a British electorate of "160,000 tyrants." At the end of *A Summary View,* Jefferson claimed that the status quo could not stand, that trade restrictions were unconstitutional and a violation of ordinary good sense, and that "our properties within our own territories [cannot] be taxed or regulated by any power on earth but our own." This essay warrants further attention. In it, Jefferson anticipated the culmination of a decade or more of grievances, and the design of *A Summary View* is in the form of a warning to the King to limit Parliament to British or imperial affairs and to safeguard traditional colonial prerogatives. Indeed, the last few lines of the essay would reappear in slightly different form when Jefferson began the Declaration of Independence with his lament of a broken relationship. In the 1774 disquisition, the eloquent Jefferson left his protest with these words:

> The God who gave us life gave us liberty at the same time; the hand of force may destroy, but cannot disjoin them. This, sire, is our last, our determined resolution; ... that you will ... interpose ... to procure redress of ... our grievances, to quiet the minds of your subjects in British America, against any apprehension of future encroachment, to establish fraternal love and harmony through the whole empire ... to the latest ages of time, is the fervent prayer of all British America!

Thomas Jefferson was not only one of the greatest minds of the age but also a political touchstone from the 1770s to his death in 1826. He could be warm and generous, aloof and quiet, prolific in writing and often orally shy in direct encounters. There were ambiguities in his character and inconsistencies in his behavior. He has been praised for his intellect and literary skills and criticized for his personal and ethical evasions, especially in the case of Sally Hemmings, his slave with whom he is alleged to have fathered children in what some historians have claimed was hypocrisy and deceit. But in certain important ways, Jefferson embodies the great spirit of the Revolution. He was not alone in seeing the ideological and institutional opportunities offered by the situation, but the reputation he achieved in the brief period from 1774 to 1776 stayed with him as he moved from protester to constitutionalist and idealist, and from president to sage and elder statesman. With Washington, John Adams, James Madison, Franklin, and Alexander Hamilton, he sits atop the pantheon of America's revolutionary idols. *A Summary View* and the Declaration of Independence vaulted Jefferson into a leadership role in the independence movement. There were many others, of course, from Tom Paine to Richard Henry Lee, who pushed the issue, but it is Jefferson's articulations that are most commonly remembered. His 1774 argument shows that the patient appeals to the King now would be couched in threatening language. Yes, Jefferson closed with yet another plea for conciliation, but only after he had warned the King to stop and reverse Parliament's oppressive reforms. George III would not, of course, not because he chose not to rebuff Parliament, but because he too was bent on redefining the Empire in America.

The language of protest, resistance, and political theory, as compelling as it was, could not have influenced the course of events without a corresponding level of physical display. As the Stamp Act protests and the Boston Massacre had shown, and the *Gaspee* incident and the Tea Party had confirmed, violence and crowds were as politically effective as any treatise. The visual propaganda of cartoon caricature and serious pictorial journalism such as Revere's Boston Massacre etching had also raised a conscious defiance in the colonies. And just as Jefferson's structured and cogent language made its way to the various colonial activists, another phase of physical opposition began and grew rapidly, everywhere in America, even before the Coercive Acts went into effect. As General Gage arrived in Boston in May 1774 to oversee matters, the soon-to-be banned Town Meeting called for economic sanctions against British interests and repeal of the Coercive Acts. Elsewhere, there were calls from several colonial bodies, from places such as Philadelphia and Providence, Rhode Island, for an intercolonial conference to attempt to bind the colonies in a movement to discuss, identify, and coordinate a complete program of non-importation and non-compliance. In June, the Massachusetts House of Representatives declared its support for an intercolonial congress. It was under threat of dismissal after August when the Massachusetts Government Act would go into effect. The Boston Committee of Correspondence went ahead with a "Solemn League and Covenant" to bind the committee members to end all business dealings with Britain and suspend consumption of all British goods. Even in advance of the Continental Congress in Philadelphia, the Bostonians had thrown down a gauntlet that was clear in its intention: an end to business dealings with Britain was but a first step in severing all relations. Meanwhile, every province except Georgia held conventions to select delegates to the Philadelphia congress. Jefferson's *A Summary View* was in the hands of the Virginia delegation, and the Massachusetts delegation churned with anger at the specifics of the Coercive Acts. This proposed congress would soon reveal in the clearest way that the Coercive Acts were everyone's business and that the threat to civil liberties in Massachusetts was a threat to those liberties everywhere.

Conclusion
The end of the Seven Years' War meant that British colonial administration in America would require a major shift in the Empire's institutional and policy makeup. Not only was a territorial adjustment needed but the French capitulation and the terms of the 1763 Treaty of Paris left Britain with a huge and potentially hostile native population to deal with. There was also a substantial French and Catholic population to the north in Quebec that would require considerable attention. The British Treasury had doubled the national debt during the war and needed to recover what it could. All these circumstances led to the banning of colonial settlement in the newly acquired territory

west of the Appalachians and tighter regulations of trade and politics in the existing thirteen mainland colonies. The Stamp Act raised the issue of actual versus virtual representation. The trade wars that resulted from British taxing legislation created a growing resistance to British authority in the colonies. After the Boston Tea Party, Parliament cracked down with the Coercive Acts, in effect declaring martial law in Massachusetts. The Quebec Act of 1774 appeared to close the west to conventional colonial growth and expansion; at least it ended the colonies' claims to the territories. The mild and conciliatory language of 1763 had, by 1774, given way to angry confrontational language. The colonial assemblies then agreed to meet in congress to present a formal demand for the end of the Coercive Acts.

Suggested Reading

One of the seminal studies of the Revolution is Bernard Bailyn, *The Ideological Origins of the American Revolution* (Cambridge, MA: The Belknap Press of Harvard University Press, 1967). This celebrated thesis argues that the Revolution was driven by ideas and ideologies. It should be seen alongside more prosaic theories such as Pauline Maier, *From Resistance to Revolution: Colonial Radicals and the Development of American Opposition to Britain, 1765-1776* (New York: Knopf, 1972) and Edmund S. Morgan and Helen M. Morgan *The Stamp Act Crisis: Prologue to Revolution* (Chapel Hill: University of North Carolina, 1953). T.H. Breen, *The Marketplace of Revolution: How Consumer Politics Shaped American Independence* (New York, Oxford, 2004) suggests an economic undercurrent to American concerns. The central role of the American seaports' working populations in the coming of the Revolution is convincingly recounted in Gary B. Nash, *The Urban Crucible: Social Change, Political Consciousness, and the Origins of the American Revolution* (Cambridge, MA: Harvard University Press, 1979). For an equally influential view of the popular involvement in the prelude to rebellion, see Alfred F. Young, *The Shoemaker and the Tea Party: Memory and the American Revolution* (Boston: Beacon Press, 1999).

Two older but useful summaries of the Revolution's early political problems are Ian R. Christie, *Crisis of Empire: Great Britain and the American Colonies* (New York: W.W. Norton, 1966) and Lawrence Gipson, *The Coming of the Revolution, 1763-1775* (New York: Harper and Row, 1954). John Shy, "The Spectrum of Imperial Possibilities: Henry Ellis and Thomas Pownall, 1763-1775" in *A People Numerous and Armed: Reflections on the Military Struggle for American Independence*, rev. ed. (Ann Arbor: University of Michigan Press, 1990) is a sharply observed commentary on the convolutions of Britain's American policy. See also John Shy, *Before Lexington: The Role of the British Army in the Coming of the American Revolution* (Princeton: Princeton University Press, 1965). The Revolution's limited impact on the rest of Britain's Atlantic empire is clearly revealed in Andrew Jackson O'Shaughnessy, *An Empire Divided: The American Revolution and the British Caribbean* (Philadelphia: University of Pennsylvania Press, 2000) and in George A. Rawlyk, *Revolution Rejected, 1775-1776* (Scarborough, ON: Prentice-Hall, 1968). A solid and durable commentary is J.B.

Brebner, *The Neutral Yankees of Nova Scotia: A Marginal Colony during the Revolutionary Years* (1937; New York: Russell and Russell, 1970). For natives, see the early chapters in Douglas R. Hurt, *The Indian Frontier, 1763-1846* (Albuquerque: University of New Mexico, 2002).

CHAPTER THREE

THE CONTINENTAL CONGRESS, WAR, *COMMON SENSE*, AND THE DECLARATION OF INDEPENDENCE, 1774-1776

Pickering's observations, and Mr. Adams' in addition, "that it [the Declaration of Independence] contained no new ideas, that it is a commonplace compilation, its sentiments hacknied in Congress for two years before" ... may all be true.... Richard Henry Lee charged it as copied from Locke's treatise on Government.... *I know only that I turned to neither book nor pamphlet* [John Locke's book or James Otis's pamphlet] *while writing it. I did not consider it as any part of my charge to invent new ideas altogether and to offer no sentiment which had ever been expressed before.*

> — Thomas Jefferson, Letter to James Madison, August 30, 1823
> (emphasis added)

Time Line

1774   The First Continental Congress.
1775   The Battle of Lexington-Concord.
         The Second Continental Congress.
         Creation of the Continental Army.
         The Battle of Bunker (Breed's) Hill.
         The Olive Branch Petition.
1776   Thomas Paine's *Common Sense*.
         The Declaration of Independence.

Beyond Boston: Rural Massachusetts and the Coercive Acts

Colonial political institutions, merchant networks, legal establishments, the printing presses for newspapers and pamphlets were located chiefly in America's seaports. Large crowds and major demonstrations were possible only in port cities, such as Boston. Yet 90 per cent of the population of Massachusetts was rural, as was roughly 90 per cent of the entire colonial population. From the Tidewater plantations and Virginia estates to the farms of Pennsylvania, the manors of New York, and the new settlements in the backcountry, American communities were small, agrarian, and sometimes isolated. Communication was sufficiently refined so that events in New

York City or Boston or Charleston were known to the mass of the rural population within hours or days. In rural New England and in Massachusetts particularly, reaction to the Coercive Acts was immediate. There was a stunning suddenness to the imposition of martial law, and, in eastern Massachusetts, the impact was felt as soon as the British Army took up residence in Boston. Because representation in the Massachusetts legislature was town based, the suspension of local civil authority added political insecurity to the economic anxieties of the 1770s. About half the population of Massachusetts lived within a fifty-mile radius of Boston and had already felt the effects of the imperial crisis.

Crowding threatened a lower standard of living for the landless young males who remained in southern New England. In 1775, there were 212 towns in Massachusetts, and the population had doubled in the previous 25 years. The land base for new farms had all but disappeared in the older settled areas. Out migration to western and northern New England eased some of the crowding, and the spread of the New England community to the west, a trend that would last a hundred years, was underway. But, in the shorter term, the towns within the Boston hub were ripe for involvement in the incendiary atmosphere of 1774 because of a shared political history. There was transgenerational continuity in the towns throughout the various New England colonies that identified a distinct New England society. The integrated network of social habits and religion had been modified by the Awakening, but the church remained a focal point of community values and organization. Even in the western and northern extensions of the region, familiar composite towns dotted the landscape. The integrated labor of men, women, children, relatives, and neighbors sustained the economic rhythms of town life. Adult men served the town and the province with taxes and political participation. While participation in local militias was often an easygoing get-together for town males, it added to the communal bond and was in fact a long-standing tradition on both sides of the Atlantic. In America, militiamen had fought against natives and against the French and their native allies throughout the seventeenth and eighteenth centuries. Carolina militias had fought in the Yamassee Wars of the 1720s, and Virginia militiamen had accompanied Washington into Ohio in the 1750s. New England militiamen had captured the mighty French fortress at Louisbourg in 1745.

Massachusetts officials claimed that three-fifths of provincial revenues had gone to supporting the militia during the Seven Years' War. Whatever the accuracy of that estimate, it was generally believed in Massachusetts that the province had more than paid its way for the good of the Empire. To an already land-starved and economically depressed people, Parliament's policy of bleeding the province financially and sending in troops to suppress legitimate opposition added insult to a long train of injuries. With the Coercive Acts and Gage's arrival in Boston, the rural Massachusetts militia stirred. It was about to play a vital part in the shaping of the Revolution, and, ultimately — for all the urban articulation of principle, street protest, and political organization, — the rural Americans would fight the War for Independence. The intolerable acts spurred a martial response in rural Massachusetts even as the province's delegates were leaving to attend the Continental Congress in Philadelphia. When that congress urged the people of Massachusetts to arm, it was addressing a rural population that was already doing so.

The First Continental Congress

Benjamin Franklin had earlier called for an interprovincial meeting to discuss common concerns but had been ignored. The events of 1774 changed all that. At the eager request of several legislatures, the Continental Congress met at Philadelphia on September 5, 1774 and lasted seven weeks. The delegates were unanimous in their desire to resolve the crises in Massachusetts. Serious efforts to find a compromise had been made weeks earlier by conservatives, and Joseph Galloway (1731-1803) of Pennsylvania was chief among delegates who opposed the hard line of Jefferson and others. As it turned out, the Virginia delegation itself had found Jefferson's comments extreme and had tempered them. Galloway began with a dire warning that the radical delegates' confrontational approach might overwhelm any hope for an amicable resolution. He was correct. On September 17, the radicals succeeded in having the Congress adopt a set of resolutions that effectively called on Massachusetts to commit itself to rebellion. The Suffolk Resolves, the work of a local convention in Suffolk County (Boston), Massachusetts, were delivered to the Congress in great haste by Paul Revere and received Congress's approval. The Congress took a major step towards formal nullification of Parliament's authority when it declared the Coercive Acts unconstitutional and therefore void. That was only the start. The Suffolk manifesto pressed the people of Massachusetts to form an alternative government that would collect the taxes for normal operations and refuse to submit them to the military government unless the Coercive Acts were repealed. A third resolve recommended the usual economic sanctions against Britain. The most dangerous of the suggestions from Suffolk was the recommendation that the people defy the military authority and arm the local militias.

Galloway, meanwhile, appealed to the conservatives in the 56-delegate-strong Congress to counter the Suffolk Resolves with an alternative plan. He proposed a "Grand Council" made up of representatives from all the colonies under the administration of a royally appointed president-general. This "Plan of Union" was bold in its way because it proposed a federated union of the colonies that would combine the interests of each in a single agency. But while it insisted on the retention of each colony's internal "constitution," it did place too much power in its council. It also made the president-general and the grand council "an inferior and distinct branch of the British [Parliament]." The Plan was defeated by a vote of six to five, but, as close as it was, the delegates nevertheless chose to remove the proposal from the record. The Continental Congress was breaking new ground. The insurrectionary tone of the Suffolk Resolves was in contrast to the imaginative, cautious, but unworkable Galloway plan. The Crown was in no mood to entertain any modification of its sovereign power in America, even Galloway's idea. The ten resolutions issued by the

Continental Congress in October 1774 summarized the history of grievances and claims of the previous dozen years and were offered to the King and Parliament as legitimate claims to equality. The declaration demanded redress for the offences that had been committed against colonists since the Seven Years' War. It was patently clear that the Coercive Acts had put the Parliament and the now harmonized colonies on a collision path. The united will of the Congress can be seen in the preamble of the resolutions: "That the inhabitants of the English Colonies in North America, by the immutable laws of nature, the principles of the English constitution, and the several charters or compacts, have the following Rights." The resolutions went on to make the following claims:

1. The colonists' right to "life, liberty & property" could not be "ceded to any sovereign power whatever...without their consent."
2. The colonists' "ancestors" were "free and natural-born subjects" of Britain.
3. Because the original emigrants had not surrendered their rights, those rights were passed on to "their descendents," including the present generation of colonists.
4. The various colonies had the right to a "free and exclusive power of legislation ...in all cases of taxation and internal polity."
5. Any colonist could appeal to common law and had the right to trial by jury and in local courts. This was clearly an attack on several attempts by the Crown to try colonists in some cases in Nova Scotia or Britain.
6. English statutes in force at the time of colonization that had been satisfactory to colonists should be retained. This was a direct claim, again, for the constitutional legitimacy of local prerogative.
7. Local laws passed under the terms of the original (mostly royal) charters were valid. This claim repeated much of the preceding appeal.
8. The Congress had a right to exist as a congress. This resolution was particularly presumptuous and anticipated charges of the Congress's illegality. Colonists had a right, it said, "to assemble, consider of their grievances, and petition the King" and any denial of that by the King would be "illegal."
9. "[T]he keeping of a Standing army in these colonies, in times of peace, without the consent of the legislature of that colony, in which the army is kept is against the law": A brilliant, pithy précis of decades of tracts on the issue of standing armies.
10. "[T]he exercise of legislative power in several colonies, by a council appointed, during pleasure [arbitrarily], by the crown, is unconstitutional, dangerous, and destructive to the freedom of American legislatures."

The resolutions then called for revocation of a host of post-1763 laws, now demanding rather than merely requesting that the Crown recognize their authority in local matters. This was heady stuff, and the ripples were soon felt in Britain. The Continental

Congress had now identified the problem as a clash between political authorities — colonial and imperial — of which the former had equal status on most issues and exclusive jurisdiction and sovereignty on others. The Congress was unilaterally redefining the Empire. One can understand Galloway's concerns. He and other conservatives may have disliked the trend in the Crown's policies and actions, but, like Hutchinson and others before them, they could not yet question the Crown's superior and ultimate authority, as the Declaratory Act of 1766 had claimed, "in all cases whatsoever." On the other hand, radicals had never accepted the Declaratory Act, and by 1774 had renounced it. The Congress backed up its tough talk by agreeing to meet on May 10, 1775 if its demands were not met.

Divisions: Loyalists and Separatists

The Continental Congress had certainly marched the colonists closer to a collective, full-blown rejection of Parliament's authority. The Continental Association for example, borrowed heavily from the Virginia Association, which in August 1774 had instituted yet another trade embargo and had set a list of non-importation and non-consumption actions that denied almost all trade with Britain. Among the more notable items on the list was a proposed ban on the importation of slaves after December 1, 1774. The Continental Association went further than any of the earlier trade organizations in that each colony pledged to boycott any non-complying colony. Georgia, which had not attended the Congress, nevertheless signed on and agreed with the Continental Association's enforcement mechanism. Each American community — town, parish, county — was to elect a committee to regulate the boycott, and this extralegal agency was sanctioned to punish violators.

An innovative idea had emerged from the Congress in the form of the "dominion" theory of government, where the colonies would conduct their own internal business unhindered by Parliament while the Monarch served as an administrative authority. A similar plan underwrote the British North America Act of 1867 that created the Dominion of Canada, and Jefferson and Wilson had implied such a model in their 1774 pamphlets. Parliament had no authority in the colonies, according to this theory, but colonists, as Britons ("free born Englishmen") would swear allegiance to the King. Allegiance perhaps, but on a closer look, these proposals did not suggest unalloyed obedience. Over the winter of 1774-75, John Adams published a series of "letters" under the pseudonym of "Novanglus," and there the Latinized "New Englander" advanced the case against Parliament's claims for jurisdiction in America. The phrase "Massachusetts is a Realm" was used with the qualifier that, although the King was sovereign in that realm, Parliament was not. Adams was responding to Galloway and others such as Samuel Seabury and Daniel Leonard in New England and Jonathan Boucher in the Chesapeake, all of whom simply stood the radicals' thesis on its head by charging their proposals as unconstitutional.

The term "loyalist" is appropriate here, but is used with caution. One could safely claim that Adams, Jefferson, and others were "loyalists" at this point. They may have expressed stern opposition to Parliament but were essentially "loyal" in wishing to remain in the British Empire. They would abandon that view soon enough, and "loyalists" would come to identify those who chose to support not only the King and the Empire but also the sovereignty of Parliament. The potent line "better to be ruled by a tyrant 3,000 miles away than by a thousand tyrants at home" illustrates the mentality of a substantial minority of Americans. The sentiment was not as reactionary as it sounded. Most of Galloway's ideas did call for readjustment, and, when his "Plan of Union" was published, it appeared to be a reasonable way around the imperial impasse. The radical confrontationists at that point were treating the "no taxation without representation" issue as being too soft. Unless the King responded favorably and directly to the pleas of Jefferson and others and to the resolutions of the Congress, the radicals would not be in a position to maneuver. The King, in effect, had been given an ultimatum. Galloway was right to see the larger danger. Was there a possibility of separation, and, if so, would anarchy follow? What kind of a "realm" was Massachusetts? The broad movement that had begun as a protest against new imperial policies had not articulated anything clearer than the Galloway plan. In calling for the union of the colonies, he had offered a distinct alternative to the status quo. He was in some way ahead of the Continental Congress in that, while its resolutions expressed a collective position, they left legislative authority in the hands of separate and autonomous units, the individual colonial societies that Jefferson had already called "states." As it was, neither the radicals nor the moderates could have known what the spring of 1775 would bring, but the Congress's resolutions were painting Americans into a very dangerous corner.

Armed Insurrection

Even before the Continental Congress convened, General Gage had begun to fortify the narrow land link to the Boston peninsula. Several thousand militiamen had assembled in Cambridge, across the Charles River from Boston, to protest the British Army's seizure of some provincially owned artillery pieces. The atmosphere was tense with rumor as British troops moved steadily through the area. The Massachusetts Lower House met in Salem and appointed John Hancock to head a Committee of Safety, which was authorized to call up militia units, if needed. These so-called "minutemen" were vital to Congress's resolve because they were prepared to act, figuratively, at a minute's notice. While the Massachusetts militia's rebuff of the British troops at Lexington and Concord in April 1775 was apparently extemporaneous, there had been some preparations. Paul Revere once again showed his talent for delivering vital messages. As he had done with the Suffolk Resolves at Philadelphia, he delivered a timely alert to the Portsmouth, New Hampshire militia of a plan by the British to reinforce their garrison there. The result was that the local militia managed to seize some arms from the small British unit on site. Events were now moving faster than Parliament's ability to know of them. Gage could respond to what he encountered in New England, but Parliament's larger strategic picture was influenced by the slowness in communicating North American news to London. By the time the full import of the Congress's resolutions and the Continental Association's mandate had reached Parliament, New Englanders were ready for armed conflict.

The moderates in Parliament now feared that American affairs were headed for disaster. Lord Chatham (William Pitt) carried a message from the Lords requesting the removal of British troops from Boston. It was turned down. He went further and asked Parliament to recognize the Continental Congress and to replace arbitrary taxing by a system of revenue requests. All the colonists would have to do would be to recognize the King's "supreme legislative authority and superintending power." The suggestions were rejected, and, within a few days, Massachusetts was considered to be in a state of "rebellion." The only compromise that emerged during the debates was a grudging agreement to review and revise the imperial taxing authority and to allow colonists more say in the definition of regulatory and defense taxes. Further restraints were then placed on the New England colonies' ability to trade with jurisdictions other than British, effectively stifling the New Englanders' own boycott by edict and by force if necessary. Then, when Parliament learned of the several colonies' ratification of the Continental Association agreement, it laid restraining orders against them. Once again, Boston's troubles became the concerns of the rest, hurried along by Parliament's actions. While Parliament was discussing the issues, the Massachusetts Assembly met again, illegally. John Hancock and Joseph Warren (who would be killed at the Battle of Bunker Hill) drew up military plans that inspired Patrick Henry's bellicose comments at the Virginia Convention in March 1775.

> If we wish to be free — if we mean to preserve inviolate these inestimable privileges for which we have been so long contending... we must fight! I repeat it, sir, we must fight! An appeal to arms and the God of hosts is all that is left us.... It is vain, sir, to extenuate the matter, Gentlemen [at the Virginia Convention] may cry Peace, peace! — but there is no peace. The war is actually begun.... I know not what course others may take; but as for me, *give me liberty or give me death.* (Emphasis added.)

Henry could read the signs as well as anyone, and, as if to confirm his melodramatic flourish, a letter from Secretary of State for the Colonies Lord Dartmouth reached General Gage on April 14, 1775. It was sent at the end of January 1775 and ordered the army to crack down on any sign of military preparation and to step up enforcement of the Coercive Acts. A confrontation between militia and the British Army at Salem at the end of February had ended without violence. However, the next confrontation would be lethal, and while Patrick Henry had been adding one of the most vivid phrases to the revolutionary lexicon, in Britain, Edmund Burke was warning Parliament that military action was the worst possible response to the situation. In his famous long speech, *On Conciliation With The Colonies*, Burke attempted to persuade Parliament to consider the colonies as assets to be treated more fairly. As he said, those "who wield the thunder of the state may have more confidence in the efficacy of arms. But I confess...my opinion is much more in favour of prudent management than of force, considering force not as an odious, but a feeble instrument for preserving a people so numerous, so active, so growing, so spirited." Burke had hit on a central problem for any military policy. Even if the colonists were subdued in the short term, they would not be controlled in the long term.

Lexington and Concord

The orders to General Gage to crack down on the gathering Massachusetts minutemen led to the opening salvoes of the American War for Independence. What followed on April 18-19, 1775 immediately opened a catalogue of great American historical events. Paul Revere's patriotic ride to warn the residents of Concord, 21 miles from Boston, and the plucky resistance by militia irregulars against a disciplined British Army unit of 700 regulars have stitched the Battle of Lexington-Concord into the fabric of American legend. "The shots heard around the world" were initially heard only locally, but that brief military encounter would, in fact, have global consequences. General Gage's decision to act on Lord Dartmouth's orders produced first a military blunder and then a disaster. Dartmouth's letter to Gage is a study in military arrogance. To suppress the illegal activities in Massachusetts, "the first essential step to be taken...would be to arrest and imprison the principal Actors and Abettors in the [extralegal] Provincial Congress." Gage knew better, that the leadership of the resistance could not be arrested, but the rest of Dartmouth's letter was even more careless. He told Gage that, because "any efforts of the people, unprepared to encounter with a regular Force, cannot be very formidable...it will surely be better that the Conflict should be brought on, upon such ground, than in a riper state of Rebellion." In other words, rebel control of Massachusetts could be nipped in the bud by seizing people like Joseph Warren, Samuel Adams, and John Hancock and scattering the projected small group of "people" by military intimidation. The trouble was that the bud had in fact blossomed by the time the order was received. Still, Gage willingly complied because it suited his own autocratic assessments. He assembled a force to go to Concord where the illegal Massachusetts government had begun to cache arms. He did this in Boston in full view of the Committee of Safety. The Committee sent Paul Revere and William Dawes to raise the alarm. Revere was captured by a British patrol just past Lexington and never did reach Concord, although one of his companions did. In any case, at Lexington, Revere had already aroused Samuel Adams and John Hancock.

The fight at Lexington was brief and embarrassing for the few minutemen present. But hundreds, and then thousands, of militia were headed into the area, and, by the time the advance British force reached Concord, it was in trouble. As his forward platoon was attacked and bloodied, the British commander Lieutenant Colonel Smith withdrew and headed back down the road to Lexington, thence to Boston. He was reinforced at Lexington, to his temporary relief, but the throngs of militia who gravitated to the area eventually numbered between 3,500 and 4,000. Their constant small attacks panicked the regulars who hastened to Charlestown and the security of the garrison across the river at Boston and the warships in the harbor. While fewer than 100 militiamen were reported dead, wounded, or missing, there were nearly 300 British casualties and missing, including 73 dead. In the course of the war that followed, those numbers would be repeated hundreds of times, but on April 20, 1775, in the aftermath of the battle, the images from Lexington-Concord loomed large in the minds of the officers at British headquarters in Boston and among the citizenry in the towns and farms of New England. A "police action" had become an armed insurrection.

The Second Continental Congress and an American Army

Within days of the fight at Lexington and Concord, the Massachusetts Provincial Congress issued a call for over 13,000 men to serve in the conflict. The levy was ambitious and mostly successful as the other New England colonies committed nearly 10,000 militiamen to the cause. There were fewer than 9,000 British troops in the colonies and only about 5,000 in eastern Massachusetts. The New England countryside was in a state of great agitation, and the formal appointment of Artemus Ward (1727-1800) as commander of the combined New England force signaled the commitment to organized armed rebellion. Despite realistic fears of strenuous British reaction, the Congress acted with great decisiveness. At the end of April, Ethan Allen (1738-89) and Benedict Arnold (1741-1801) with a very small force captured Fort Ticonderoga and Crown Point on Lake Champlain and finally Fort St. John's (St. Jean) on the Quebec side, although the latter was abandoned as untenable. The Americans suffered no casualties and secured some valuable military supplies to the chagrin of the British regulars, one of whom recorded his embarrassment for being overrun by a "Sett of ragamuffins." This was heady stuff, colonial "ragamuffins" defeating the King's Army. The success at Ticonderoga was all the more impressive considering it was about 250 miles from the center of action at Boston. The farmers and artisans of New England were rising in large numbers, even as sober logic suggested that it would not be long before the Crown reacted with energy. The British had been caught by surprise, but sensible rebels knew that there would be a reckoning.

The Continental Congress met as planned, in Philadelphia on May 10, 1775, with a mostly military agenda. This body would sit continuously from 1775 to 1781, when it adopted the title "The United States in Congress Assembled," and then continue in effect until the adoption of the United States Constitution. Between 1774 and 1789, this body, under both designations but best referred to simply as the Congress, was served by 342 individual delegates. In 1775, it comprised a who's who of the resistance elites: The Massachusetts Adamses; Ben Franklin and James Wilson from Pennsylvania; the Livingstons, John Jay, and Alexander Hamilton from New York; the South Carolina Rutledges; Connecticut's Roger Sherman; and Virginia's Richard Henry Lee, Washington, and later Jefferson. Joseph Galloway and other conservatives were missing. The Congress called for specialized "rifleman" units to be raised for the so-called "Boston Army," the core of a new Continental Army. George Washington was elected to be Commander in Chief. The North Carolina delegation arrived with the

"Mecklenburg County Resolutions," which advised the annulment of royal authority, at least in the short term, and while no copy of the "Resolutions" has been discovered, and they were not in fact presented to the Congress, their reported existence was a foreshadowing of independence. It is difficult to estimate who — or how many of the delegates and the population, for that matter — was thinking seriously of independence in the spring of 1775, but the actions of the New England militia had pushed the Congress into a full-blown military uprising. The Congress called for a budget to be raised proportionately from the 12 "confederated colonies" (Georgia did not send delegates until later in the year). Over 20,000 men were sought for the Continental Army, in addition to what could be drafted into local militias. In late May, the British appointed three major generals to assist Gage. Generals Sir William Howe, Sir Henry Clinton, and John Burgoyne were veterans of the Seven Years' War and were thought to be comfortable in the American environment. As the British Army reinforced its Boston garrison, the militias in the area reached about 10,000.

Bunker Hill

General Gage then exacerbated the crisis. He instituted martial law by fiat and charged all armed Americans as traitors. He offered pardons to any leaders who offered a renewed allegiance to the King, but made an exception of Samuel Adams and John Hancock. Neither was offered amnesty. Gage then decided to increase fortifications in Boston, but the local Committee of Public Safety tried to beat him to the punch by erecting its own fortification at Charlestown, on high ground overlooking Boston. Gage ordered an assault on the rebel position, and Generals Howe and Clinton led a series of frontal attacks on the 1,600 militiamen on Breed's Hill. The results were devastating for the British, who suffered casualties of over 1,000 from an attack force of about 2,400. The losses of officers in the assaults were higher proportionally than the losses among the rank and file, but the British did drive the Americans from Breed's and Bunker Hill and killed over 100 militiamen in the process. The American retreat from the site was hasty and desperate, and, while the British Army had been badly hurt, it had also shown its toughness and discipline. Still, the battle demonstrated that the British Army was not invincible. The experience had the effect of rallying the Continental Congress to even greater military resolve and, at the least, delayed any hope of reconciliation. Perhaps if Howe had pursued the retreating Americans, he might have scattered the New England militia. He did not, largely because his troops were exhausted. His victory was, in the end, a Pyrrhic one.

When George Washington reached Cambridge two weeks after Bunker Hill, he took command of about 14,000 militiamen. This throng, along with an impatient and angry population, made it clear to the British command that New England might not be recovered. Gage, who had never underestimated the problem in New England but who might have underestimated the tenacity of its people, put the military situation into sharp focus in the aftermath of Bunker Hill: "These People Shew a Spirit and Conduct against us they never shewed against the French.... you must proceed in earnest or give the Business up... The loss we have Sustained is greater than we can bear." This trenchant observation helps put the American position into perspective. The French had seldom, if ever, threatened Americans in their homes. The British were now doing so with arrogance that aroused passion in citizens who had been proud to be associated with the Empire only a few years earlier. To George Washington, however, the Continental Army's passions and prospects were not bright in the summer and fall of 1775. The majority of enlistments were up at the end of the year, and what Washington saw at Cambridge was an assemblage of farmers in traditional work clothes, including some in buckskin. Others were in the near universal long pullover shirt of wool or linen. Some were in tents and makeshift covers, and others were billeted in homes and in the Harvard dormitories. These were mostly infantrymen, and the absence of engineers and cavalry or experienced officers struck the orthodox Washington as his first problem. These men would have to be used as an American army, but, in July 1775, they were more a collection of provincial part-timers and militiamen. Their mood was good and echoed the *rage militaire* that Gage had noted, and the veterans of Bunker Hill, who had been involved in the brutal hand-to-hand fighting there, rounded out an enthusiastic gathering. The majority of the troops, however, were looking forward to going home at the end of the year. The pressing need to create a full-time army was made very clear by the way the militiamen at Cambridge appeared content to be in temporary service, when what was needed was a tougher and more conventional resistance to British arms.

The Olive Branch Petition

By the summer of 1775, the British had formally recognized that a state of war existed in Massachusetts. As they began to commit more military resources to America, the Congress in Philadelphia decided to make a last ditch overture to the King. The Olive Branch Petition of July 5, 1775 is a fascinating bit of historical confusion. John Dickinson polished the final draft and sent it to London in the hands of Richard Penn, a loyalist descendent of William Penn. The thrust of the overture was the familiar colonial appeal to reason and reconciliation, but, in this case, the King, when he heard of it, considered it to be another bit of insolence from what he considered an illegal, even treasonous gathering. The Petition repeated the formula of asking for American control of American affairs including taxation and local legislation while pledging allegiance to the King as the legitimate executive. It rejected any role for Parliament in the colonies, and appealed to George III to end military operations. The King refused to see Penn or the petition. To do so, it was thought, would be to recognize the Continental Congress, something that would tempt it to assume legitimacy. In fact, the Olive Branch Petition has an odd irrelevance about it, and raises questions about its sincerity. For the Continental Congress to say that it would pledge allegiance to the King while rejecting Parliament's authority to do anything in the colonies was a bit like asking the King to denounce Parliament. The weakness of the logic could not have escaped the notice of the sharp minds at Philadelphia, and leaves the impression that there was a public relations purpose in its drafting because Congress then stated that it was not interested in independence but would nevertheless continue to resist the current British policy in America. The *Declaration of the Causes and Necessities of Taking Up Arms*, written jointly by Thomas Jefferson and John Dickinson, was effectively an ultimatum and included a note on the possibility of foreign aid for the American cause. Although the Congress was denying any suggestion that its aim was independence, the design of the Olive Branch Petition, the predictable rejection of it, the military preparations, and the intransigence on both sides all pointed to a complete breakdown of the Empire in America.

While the Olive Branch Petition was on its way to an ignominious reception, the British commander in Canada, Sir Guy Carleton, was planning an invasion of New York and was raising Quebec militia to do it. Meanwhile, Congress hoped to repeat its partial successes of the spring in Canada. A force of about 1,000 men authorized by Congress and led first by General Philip Schuyler and then Brigadier General Richard Montgomery laid siege to St. John's (St. Jean), south of Montreal. It had been taken in the spring and then abandoned, but it fell again to the Americans in early November. Montgomery then occupied Montreal, and Carleton was chased to Quebec. Benedict Arnold, under Washington's orders, led an ambitious expedition from Cambridge through the rigors of the northern New England terrain and late fall temperatures to the heights opposite Quebec. The assault against Quebec was a disaster, and Montgomery, who had brought a few hundred Americans up from Montreal, was killed, and Arnold was wounded. Over half of the American force was killed, wounded, or taken prisoner. Arnold stayed in the area over the winter in a weak siege posture. The invasion of Canada was not over, but its days were numbered. The Continental Congress had used some strategic imagination in its northern campaigns but had failed to take the rebellion into French Canada.

The Expansion of the Conflict

The Canada excursion was a flawed strategy but did serve to underline the message that the rebels were serious, and, along with the shock of the Massachusetts encounters, it threw matters into the royal lap. Before the end of the year, Virginia's Royal Governor the Earl of Dunmore declared that the colony was under martial law. Given that Parliament had announced that the colonies were in a state of rebellion, Dunmore's declaration was a tactical one, aimed at Virginia's political leadership and driven by the offer of freedom to any slaves who abandoned their masters. There were close to 200,000 slaves in Virginia in 1775, and Dunmore shrewdly noted that Virginia's rebels were being organized and led by the planter class. A glance at the roles of Jefferson and Washington and the inflammatory tongue of Patrick Henry confirmed that. So the governor decided to strike at their interests by "freeing" the slaves in Virginia, in a profoundly ill-advised gambit. The edict had the reverse effect and drove the entire planter class closer to full support for the Continental Congress. In addition, Dunmore put together an African-American regiment to supplement the loyalist army he was raising from the Virginia population, but a rebel army of nearly 1,000 Virginian and North Carolina militiamen defeated Dunmore's loyalists and drove him from Norfolk on the coast. The town was completely destroyed and rendered useless as an operations center. The war had come to Virginia, flavored with social and racial issues to go with the politics. From the patriot perspective, the loyalist agenda in the Chesapeake had challenged the planters' slaveholding rights, and, while Jefferson and others might lament the institution as a blight on American character, the majority of southerners, planters, and farmers, rich and poor, were in no mood to contemplate the turning loose of the slave population. None of this suggested a benign or egalitarian racial attitude in British official policy or loyalist sentiment, but rather the political and military exigencies of the moment. The response from the rebels was a sharp reassertion of their rights as slaveholders and their defense of the slave societies of the south. The rebel planters saw the cynicism in Dunmore's tactic as well as its potential for calamity, and white non-slaveholders in Virginia saw the Dunmore policy as an affront to their own racial status.

When Congress reconvened in September 1775, it was joined by a Georgia delegation, and the thirteen contiguous American colonies were locked into what would be a permanent alliance. In November, the Congress learned that the Olive Branch Petition was dead. Moreover, although George III had refused to look at the petition, the House of Commons did see it and easily rejected it by a vote of 83-33. In Congress, meanwhile, military matters entered a new phase with the creation of a navy and a plan to establish two battalions of marines (a "battalion" denoted a combat unit of anywhere from 200 to 600 men). Between October and the end of 1775, four ships were commissioned by Congress. Within a few months, the colonists had created an army and navy for collective purposes. The apparent discrete nature of mainland British North American societies and the apparent disparity between say South Carolina and Connecticut dissolved as Britain persisted with its policies, and the colonial assemblies began to find common political affinities in the Continental Congress. All Americans, despite their various locations or cultural or economic differences were British, but that citizenship apparently meant nothing to colonists who had been attacked by their own senior government. The colonial assemblies' cooperation at Philadelphia was a first large step in redefining citizenship. As historian Edmund Morgan puts it, American nationalism was a product of the Revolution, and not the cause of it. The assemblies fused quickly into the Continental Congress because the British had betrayed the political arm of each colony and had violated the local agencies of citizenship.

Despite the colonies' cooperative mood, Congress was an unformed institution in 1775 and had not defined any clear objective for itself, short of dealing with the military situation. Congress cautiously opened a tentative diplomatic connection with other European powers through its aptly named "Committee of Secret Correspondence." At the end of 1775, the French gave informal permission for American ships to use French ports. There was a hint, too, that there might be some material aid. The message was sensibly vague but suggested that, if the military confrontation continued, arms might become available to the rebels. The Continental Army, the new navy, and the tens of thousands of colonial militiamen were so poorly equipped that, even with training, the absence of personal means for each combat soldier, that is a musket, ammunition, shoes, coats, and bedding, added up to terrible military liabilities. There would have to be a dependable supply of war materiel and an operational infrastructure for any reasonable hope in the war that was coming. If Britain committed its full military apparatus, the aspirations of the Continental Congress were doomed. With cooperation, will, and emergency procedures, the Congress and the individual colonies could certainly supply and equip a formal army and the various militias, but only to certain material limits, and then the weight of the Crown's military establishment would determine the course of any war. As early as the fall of 1775, Congress understood this, hence the early overtures to France, an old enemy, while it pleaded for commitments from the various colonies.

Thomas Paine and the Logic of Independence

By the winter of 1775-76, the decade-long war of words had become a real war of maneuver, strategy, hardship, and death — of passion, anger, and fear. During that winter, an Englishman managed to bring words back into the dispute. Thomas Paine (1737-1809) had arrived in Philadelphia in 1774 with an introductory letter from Benjamin Franklin just as the relationship between the colonies and Parliament was collapsing and the first Continental Congress was winding down. Paine, who was born a Quaker, was nearing 40 years old when he began writing articles for the *Pennsylvania Magazine*. His experiences as a corset maker, excise man, grocer, and schoolteacher had left him restless and vocal. The poverty he had witnessed and endured had shaped his political values. Also, he had read deeply and broadly into the political and scientific literature of the Enlightenment and had absorbed a great deal of history and theory. His passions intersected with the events of the 1770s. He fell in love with America's potential for revolutionary change and, on balance, was the most radical egalitarian in America. His later participation in the French Revolution and his books, *The Rights of Man* and *The Age of Reason* are sermons on his vision of social equality and testify to his republicanism and secular political theories. These works mark him as an important figure in modern political history. His ideas have been embraced by socialists and liberal democrats alike, but his political career began as a publicist for the rebel cause in America. On January 9, 1776, *Common Sense* was published in pamphlet form, but its length and structure mark it off as a book-length treatise. Paine cut through the seemingly endless debates on sovereignty and, in simple, straightforward prose, called for Americans to immediately declare independence. The moment had passed when reconciliation was possible, according to Paine, and the colonies' histories in any case showed that they and not the British Empire were the future model for mankind. Monarchy in the late eighteenth century was an anachronism, corrupt and illegitimate. The world had moved on, and America was in the vanguard of a movement for equal civil rights "for all of mankind" as he put it, in a politics devoid of privilege. The vivid language, referring to George III, for example, as the "Royal Brute," and the identification of a few simple truths made *Common Sense* a sensation and a guide. Paine's message was simple: independence was not a matter of choice but a necessity. Colonists, according to Paine, were by experience and right already independent, and Britain was redundant.

As sharp and clear as was the message in *Common Sense*, perhaps the most significant thing about it was its circulation. The estimate of 120,000 copies being sold is generally accepted, and the distribution of it and of its contents in print or by oral repetition suggests that it might have become familiar to a majority of the American population in 1776. In an era richly defined by pamphlet literature, *Common Sense* stands out because of the size of its readership and its impact. It was perhaps the most important political essay of the American Revolution because of its timing and language. Its originality lies in the stripping away of options or alternatives and in embellishing the American cause as a model for the world. Along with John Dickinson's *Letters From a Farmer* and Jefferson's *Summary View* dozens of other iterations had driven the debate. Perhaps Paine, as radical as his language seems, was largely punctuating dramatically and conclusively the end of the British Empire in the thirteen colonies and adding, more in hope than in prophecy, the "universal" mission of the revolutionaries. *Common Sense* and the Declaration of Independence a few months later were both calls to arms that had already been taken up. Paine's genius and lasting claim to a place in American history was in his identifying a political and moral reason for supporting a war that was already underway.

Paine and Propaganda

Common Sense was a milestone, but it needs to be seen also as part of a rich body of revolutionary political discourse. A great deal of that literature in the 1760s appeared to have been written by an intellectual minority for a literary minority. Was John Adams's use of the Latin *Novanglus* widely understood by the farmers of Massachusetts? Were Jefferson's references to "Tresilian and the other judges … in the reign of Richard the second" in *A Summary View* a readily acceptable analogy to a semi-literate farmer in Acton, Connecticut or to a backcountry settler with no education living in the southern highlands? Perhaps not, but Adams, writing as *Novanglus*, could use a phrase such as "a government of laws, and not of men," which he acknowledged to have borrowed from James Harrington's *Commonwealth of Oceana* (1656), that made sense to most colonists, most of whom did not know of Harrington. The phrase was later used in the Massachusetts State Constitution of 1780. Regardless of whether a person could read, that person would understand Adams's statement just as they would have an oral recitation of Jefferson's phrase from *A Summary View* that "Our Saxon ancestors held their lands, as they did their personal property, in absolute dominion." The steady stream, a torrent really, of letters, pamphlets, manifestos, acts, rebuttals, propositions, and resolutions that washed over America in the decades after 1763 could have been read in some form by no more than half of the colonial population. But readings were rebroadcast orally, and news and ideas circulated at church gatherings, in taverns, and in neighborhood gossip. The heated flow of words that accompanied the imperial dispute after the Seven Years' War reached audiences that had a long tradition of exposure to newspapers, pamphlets, and sermons, a tradition reaching back into the seventeenth century. There were about 37 weekly newspapers being printed in America when *Common Sense* was published, compared to one in 1704. About seven of those newspapers were "loyalist" or "neutral," and the total circulation of all journals was in the 3,500 range, a figure that should be contrasted with the 120,000 copies of *Common Sense* in circulation in 1776. Sermons, which throughout the colonies were used as moral, social, and cultural advice, were routinely published for reading and for repetition by word of mouth. Local laws were posted or read aloud for those unable to read, and a steady recording of the larger world beyond the parochial communities was available and understood throughout the eighteenth century. The use of *Cato's Letters* by Morris and Zenger in the 1730s in New York had indicated an audience for political history and theory. When the Stamp Act Resolutions had announced in 1765 that "the only representatives of the people...are persons...chosen...by themselves" and "all supplies to the crown [are] free gifts of the people," it was officially addressing its words to Parliament and the King and to the colonial assemblies, but we can be sure that any colonist who read or heard those words understood them in context and purpose.

What Paine did in 1776 intensified the severity of the situation by highlighting the inevitability of independence. He had an audience. Those who fomented rebellion were heading towards separation anyway, and, in fact, George III had already acknowledged this fact in his speech from the throne in October 1775. In December, the British had ceased all trade with the colonies. In this atmosphere, with the question of "what was to be done" ringing in the air, *Common Sense* simply stated the obvious in a rousing, unsentimental, and unequivocal way. The polemic is a great example of distillation and compression. Paine took a myriad of political theory and a millennium of history and produced a tract that was not only accessible but inspiring. It was neither entirely original nor an abstract departure from reality into theory; rather it placed the issue of separation in front of colonists as a *fait accompli*. It is Paine's plain language that makes *Common Sense* an important document. He writes, "Volumes have been written on the subject of the struggle between England and America. Men of all ranks have embarked in the controversy, from different motives, and with various designs: but all have been ineffectual, and the period of debate is closed. Arms, as the last resource, decide the contest; the appeal was the choice of the king, and the continent [America] hath accepted the challenge." After establishing separation as necessary, Paine attacked the colonists' propensity to waffle over the ultimate ends of their actions. The last remnants of connection with Britain, according to Paine, had been lost, and Americans "have been long led away by ancient prejudices, and [have] made sacrifices to superstition" by assuming that Britain at any time cared for the colonies. The "superstition," as Paine called it, was the colonists' misreading of their historical relationship with the Empire and their misplaced loyalty to a constitutionally illegitimate King. Parliament had wandered off into a collective tyranny, and only the colonists remained fixed on virtue, honesty, and natural equality. And Paine could be devastatingly blunt, of course, referring to George III as a "brute" and a "hardened sullen tempered Pharaoh." But, in his candor, he noted America's abilities and resources to wage war against the military might of Britain and to thrive in an open market: "I challenge the warmest advocate for reconciliation [including foot draggers and loyalists], to shew, a single advantage that this continent can reap [in trade] by being connected with Great Britain."

Paine's suggestion of a republican confederated state and his use of the term "the United States of America" were prescient. The Continental Congress, in fact, was very much like a "republican" federation already. Paine advocated a stronger, permanent union, but that was a matter for a future that Paine could not quite grasp. By lumping all Americans together in spirit, objectives, and character, Paine perhaps could not foresee the deeper divisions in American society that would require care and compromise after independence. The separatist cause of 1776 could not guarantee a common *national* cause down the road. Yet Paine sensed the need for deliberation and suggested that, if America did not create a united republic, then, even if Britain left, there would remain a potential for the former colonies of British North America, despite their natural virtues, to dissolve into several oligarchies. "Here then is the origin and rise of government; namely, a mode rendered necessary by the *inability of moral virtue to govern the world*; here too is the design and end of government, viz., Freedom and security" (emphasis added). Paine here anticipates the Declaration's "governments are instituted among men ... to secure [their natural rights]" and the thoughts of James Madison (1751-1836) about governments being designed both to accommodate and check human self-interest. He may have admired the virtues of Americans, but Paine was realist enough to see that they would need more than the effort or desire of an activist minority, or the obvious justice of their cause, to secure independence.

If Paine himself saw independence as inevitable, he was not sure his audience did. In one of the pamphlet's most obvious exaggerations, Paine made the claim that "I never met with a man either in England or America, who hath not confessed his opinion that a separation between the countries would take place at one time or another." Paine stretched his intuition here, and, if he was not lying, his research was flawed. The point is moot in the long run, but, in early 1776, the American population was split between those who saw independence coming and those who could hardly contemplate it. Paine was pushing rhetoric to the limit. He was a verbal dynamo, and, while the most refreshing quality of *Common Sense* is its common sense, it has an energy that propels the reader along. It is a brilliant identification of the issues and a stern warning against any backsliding or dilatoriness. John Adams's claim that "History will ascribe the Revolution to Thomas Paine ... without the pen of Paine, the sword of Washington would have been wielded in vain" is not entirely a conceit. The clarity of Paine's thesis affected the tone not only of the debates in the Continental Congress but of debate everywhere, as it filtered into every part of the continent.

The series of pamphlets Paine wrote after *Common Sense* and after the Declaration under the title of *The Crisis* ("these are the times that try men's souls") were distributed throughout the rank and file of the Continental Army and were as influential in sustaining the independence spirit as anything else he wrote. There can also be no doubt that, as the military situation deteriorated for the Continental Army in the spring of 1776 and as the Congress struggled with its options, Paine's *Common Sense* was on the minds and in some cases the lips of all who had committed to the patriot cause. Yet Paine is not as well regarded in America as he is in Britain. For example, he has survived in memory as a hero of the nineteenth-century laboring classes even though he was burned in effigy in England in 1793 over the *Rights of Man*. After independence, his reputation in America dimmed; he became active in French politics, wrote a lengthy deist polemic against scriptural literalness, and appeared too close to the French Revolution's radicalism to suit American political culture, even though Thomas Jefferson supported his return to America. In 1809, he died in opprobrium, impoverished and excluded, and John Adams, who had earlier praised Paine, in 1805 denounced him for the extremist politics and deism that Paine advocated in *The Age of Reason*. Theodore Roosevelt is alleged to have referred to Paine, a century after his death, as a "dirty little atheist," and the authoritative *Dictionary of American Biography* dismisses Paine as "something of a professional radical" whose works are more "arguments...than expositions" and who "was essentially a propagandist through whom the ideas of more original men were transmitted to the crowd." The same can be said of the majority of revolutionary propagandists, even the cherished founders.

War and the Second Continental Congress

Propaganda set a lofty tone for the war, but it had to be fought on the ground and by a mostly civilian army at that. In March 1776, the strategic Dorchester Heights in Boston was occupied by 2,000 Continentals and fortified with cannon and mortars from Ticonderoga. The hauling of artillery over dreadful terrain for about 250 miles in the fall of 1775 was a logistical marvel and speaks to the growing dedication of ordinary Americans to the cause and to the organizational abilities of young Colonel Henry Knox (1750-1806). It was an easy thing to instill something close to hatred among the New England population for the British occupation army. General Howe, who had replaced Gage, could not find the right conditions to attack Dorchester Heights and, realizing that he was in the midst of a large, armed, and hostile population, withdrew his troops and about 1,000 loyalist Americans and took them by sea to Halifax. The British had quickly abandoned New England as untenable. They also appeared to have abandoned the south in the spring of 1776. Patriot forces in North Carolina scattered a loyalist contingent and the British Army under General Clinton and General Cornwallis failed to wrest Charleston, South Carolina from the patriots. It would be two years before the British Army and the Royal Navy were back in the south in force. Not all military news was good news for the Congress. The tattered remains of the Continental Army in Canada made it back to Fort Ticonderoga in early July after being repelled by General Carleton's enlarged and revitalized force. The strategies for the northern theater of the war were set in these months, and the struggle for control of Lake Champlain had begun. Arnold and Carleton were each bent on naval construction and control of this crucial waterway. If an American army could assault Canada by this route, then the reverse was painfully obvious: the British could move south along the same route.

In the spring of 1776, the Continental Congress had reached a crossroads in its brief existence. Despite the fiery assurances of *Common Sense* and the British evacuation of Boston, it was faced with a British military command that was clearly bent on crushing the rebellion. Also, a majority of the American population may have been neutral, meaning it did not care about the crisis or was undecided, or was genuinely committed to the Crown's policies. If the patriot leadership in each colony and in Congress could not start to control events, then events would soon overwhelm the resistance movement. The problem at this point lay somewhat in the structure of the movement itself. The Continental Congress was really nothing more than a voluntary association. Its authority was derived almost entirely from the delegates who were bound in some ways to instructions from home. The Congress had no separate or independent authority to speak of. It had commissioned an army and navy, but the former was being reduced to a shell as enlistments and levies dried up. It could issue pronouncements and declarations, petitions, requests, and assessments, but it had only the authority and means granted to it by the colonies, and each colony could act unilaterally if it chose. Congress needed firmer objectives and a purpose that went beyond the obvious resistance to the British Army. It was quite clear that the colonies to the north, in Newfoundland, Nova Scotia, and Canada, and those in the Caribbean were not going to support the cause. North of New England, the scattered English populations were eventually too remote from the issues to be affected, and the French in Quebec could not be drawn into the constitutional nuances of New England politics. The small communities of white English elites of the West Indies had not cultivated either the political institutions or the environment of the kind that produced Samuel Adams, James Otis, John Dickinson, Thomas Jefferson, and scores of other revolutionary leaders or the political constituencies that supported them.

Time and events were pressing on the patriot cause. The Congress needed to do three things quickly if it were to succeed. First, it needed to have some sort of binding authority that went beyond a set of honorable agreements. The result was the Articles of Confederation, which, as modest as they were, did not appear in contractual form until 1777 and then were not fully ratified until 1781 when the war was winding down. The reluctance of the colonies to surrender any authority to a new and potentially autonomous legislature was obvious in the limitations placed on the Congress by the Articles. Second, the Congress needed to persuade its thirteen members to redefine their political identities. The colonies ("provinces" really, in the official charter language of the eighteenth century) were beginning to see themselves as "states," and the terminologies, as symbolic as the words were, seemed to be interchangeable in 1776. In

May, the delegates to Congress agreed to urge their assemblies to write independent constitutions as quickly as possible. By the end of 1776, eight of the state assemblies or conventions had begun or completed the process. Third, the Congress had to tie its military instrument to a firm political structure. There was no point in having a Continental Army if Congress could not support it without the hassles of collective agreements by the colonies. It could not fully engage the population with a policy of simply resisting and disclaiming British motives. A decisive mandate was needed, and, in April 1776, a North Carolina convention provided a start when it told its delegates to the Continental Congress to vote for a declaration of independence. Virginia advocated the same a month later.

The Declaration of Independence

In her study of the Declaration of Independence, historian Pauline Maier referred to it as "American Scripture." Elsewhere, Garry Wills claimed that the document was responsible for "inventing America." Carl Becker's graceful little book *The Declaration of Independence* (1922) stands out in the thousands of treatments accorded the Declaration. Becker takes the words and their editorial and intellectual provenance and considers their literary value and their cherished place in the canon of American political language in a meticulous reconstruction of the document's creation. Its phrases are virtually sung in lyrical cadences as in "all men are created equal" in their "unalienable rights" "to life, liberty" and, best of all, the "pursuit of happiness." The language proceeds to summarize a people in revolt over rights and freedoms. A famous invocation of this is Abraham Lincoln's speech of July 4, 1863 and, even more pointedly, his *Gettysburg Address* of December 1863 when he used the ringing phrase "our fathers brought forth ... a new nation, conceived in liberty." July 4 is America's national holiday, not June 21 (1788) when New Hampshire made the Constitution official by being the ninth state to ratify it, or March 4 (1789) when the first Congress of the United States of America convened. Why not April 19 (1775) when at Concord the "shots heard around the World" signaled the beginning of the war between the colonies and the Crown? The question is an important one because it tells us what Americans want their history to say to them. The Declaration of Independence was actually finished and submitted to and accepted by the Continental Congress on July 2, 1776 but did not become public for two days. As John Adams wrongly predicted in a letter to his wife Abigail, "The second day of July, 1776 will be celebrated from this time forward forevermore." The second day was pre-empted by the fourth day, which was recognized as the *official* day to celebrate by the early 1780s and which became, by the early decades of the nineteenth century, the most important secular holiday in the country. What Americans recognized then, as they do now, is a superb ideological and theoretical explanation of the need to separate. Whether or not that need had been demonstrated earlier is irrelevant. The position taken by the thirteen colonies in announcing their separation from Britain was a historic one, and the language fit the moment superbly.

On June 7, 1776, Richard Henry Lee, on behalf of the Virginia delegation, resolved that the "United Colonies," as he introduced them, "are, and of right, ought to be, free and independent States." Lee verbally translated "Colonies" to "States" in a single phrase. The word "state" here meant a functioning and independent political entity. Virginia would prove a devoted member of the Congress and an ally of Pennsylvania and Massachusetts, but "independent States" meant that Virginia was inclined to be a "nation" or a "country" in the modern sense within the rubric of the Congress, even if the ever-quotable Patrick Henry had earlier announced to the first Continental Congress, "I am not a Virginian but an American." Given his subsequent political career, it is not clear what he had in mind with the statement, because he sometimes put his Virginia interests ahead of those of the larger collective. Henry fought in the war, served as Governor of Virginia, feuded with Jefferson, opposed the move to disestablish the Anglican Church in Virginia, voted to compensate loyalists who had lost property, and, most important, condemned the United States Constitution as a "chameleon." Henry was already an American, but not a proponent of the nation state that emerged. That reminds us that independence in 1776 did not fully contemplate the federated constitutional union that is the United States. Congress was acting on behalf of the states' concerns and, on June 11, convened a high-powered committee to draw up a document to deal with Richard Henry Lee's Virginia proposal. This committee, comprising Jefferson, Franklin, John Adams, Robert Livingston of New York, and Roger Sherman (1721-93) of Connecticut, was formed but was ordered to do nothing until July 1. The thirty-three year old Jefferson was given the task of composition, and it was edited by the others. The document itself, "a call to arms already taken up," was seen mostly as part of Congress's business, albeit a somewhat more than routine part. Most of the signers of the Declaration did not mention it in their memoirs. On July 4, the document was distributed to the public and, specifically, to the Continental Army. Congress had voted on secession on June 11, but had delayed ratifying that resolution. Even the signing of the original document was not done until July 19, and six of the signers added their names after that date.

The Declaration is neither original in its theories and references, nor accurate in all its charges against the Crown. While it is stylish, clear, and gently persuasive, it would have been read as containing familiar claims, thoughts, and proposals. It is a brilliant political manifesto rather than political philosophy. It borrows from John Locke in a direct way and from the eighteenth-century Scottish moral and social philosophers, with references that would resonate with Jefferson's literate and learned readers. It also repeats language and concepts that had been made public for years, including some of Jefferson's own writings, and the list of 27 grievances against the King that had been accumulating and voiced since the Stamp Act Congress. The first part of the document echoes George Mason's Bill of Rights for Virginia of June 12. Jefferson and the others were aware of Mason's part in the creation of the Virginia Constitution that was issued on June 29. The Declaration was intentionally derivative, and, as Jefferson later made clear, the intent was to state familiar ideas. He was given the job because of his felicitous pen. Even at that, the Declaration is not simply the work of Jefferson or the committee so much as it is a summary of the great pamphlet literature of the preceding few years, within a framework of the politics of natural rights and the principles of representation and consent. Locke's *Second Treatise of Government* (1690), from which the principle of "rights" is taken, was over three quarters of a century old in 1776.

History would make the Declaration decisive only after the war had made independence possible. Of the 1,333 words in the text of the final draft, the most important to the political moment occur in the last paragraph:

> We, therefore, the representatives of the united States of America, in General Congress assembled, appealing to the Supreme Judge of the world for the rectitude of our intention, do, in the name and Authority of the good People of these Colonies, solemnly publish and declare, That these United Colonies are, and of Right ought to be Free and Independent States; that they are Absolved from all Allegiance to the British Crown.

Jefferson quotes Richard Henry Lee verbatim here and invokes "the good people of these colonies." It is debatable that a majority of the "good people" wanted what Jefferson said they did, but it would come to them anyway. Of particular note is the cancellation of allegiance to the King. The colonists had some time earlier ceased their obedience to Parliamentary authority.

In the end, the Declaration did find its way into the national canon as a kind of secular scripture and as a way of "inventing" America. Indeed, its universal themes of "all men are created equal" and "self-evident truths" have a cachet for Americans because the Declaration's use of the ideas turned out to accompany a successful war that was fought, ostensibly, to support those principles. The document was written to justify a specific act, but its language gives it a timeless quality, and the committee's expert paring down of what was already a distilled summary is a credit to the editorial talents of the group, especially those of Benjamin Franklin. Of Jefferson's draft, 86 changes were made and 480 words were removed, including what John Adams called a "vehement philippic against negro slavery" that Jefferson had touched on in his *A Summary View* of 1774, which stated that the "abolition of domestic slavery is the great object of desire in these colonies where it was unhappily introduced in their infant state...." At that time, Jefferson accused the King of refusing colonists' appeals to apply high duties on slaves that might have served to discourage their importation. In 1776, Jefferson went even further than charging the Crown with the responsibility for bringing African slaves to America; he accused the Monarch of shaping and maintaining the system of slavery:

> He has waged cruel war against human nature itself, violating it's [sic] most sacred rights of life and liberty in the persons of a distant people who never offended him, captivating and carrying them into slavery in another hemisphere ... and that this assemblage of horrors might want no fact of distinguished die, he is now exciting these very people to rise in arms

among us [a reference to Lord Dunmore's promise of freedom to slaves who would fight to defend British authority in Virginia] and to purchase that liberty of which he deprived them.

Jefferson here seems quite prepared to contradict fact because it was, after all, the very colonial ancestors to whom he ascribes the shaping of American society who wrote the original slave codes in the Chesapeake. These were the ones who greedily imported slaves into the booming tobacco economies of the eighteenth-century south. As noted, Jefferson's apparent preoccupation with the evils of slavery was at odds with the reality of southern needs and preferences. He clearly saw the contradiction between colonial culpability for slavery itself and the colonial rhetoric of charging the tyrant King with treating white Americans as "slaves." Jefferson saw slavery for what it was, a great blemish on the budding society, and he blamed the King for its success and character in America, for reasons that are both politically strategic and highly personal. Did committee members excise the anti-slavery tirade because it was embarrassing? Did they remove it because it would diminish the Declaration's "self-evident truths"? Was it redundant given the permanence in the south of the institution of slavery? In any case, the controversial passage was expunged.

The Declaration stands as a statement of purpose and wraps its logic in elevated political theory. It lists the irreconcilable differences between two peoples and two polities, and it declares the secession or independence of the colonies from Britain. It is propagandistic and aimed in varying degrees of focus at colonists, the Crown, the British population, and Europeans. It is a universal appeal, as indicated by the clause "a decent respect to the opinions of mankind," so it "let Facts be submitted to a candid world." It is polite but firm, and, at its heart, it attempts a syllogistic argument that makes independence necessary and irreversible, but also welcome, progressive, and missionary. The core of its argument, a single sequence at the start of the second paragraph, is a simple proposition:

[Premise 1] We hold these truths to be self-evident, that all men are created equal, that they are endowed by their Creator with certain unalienable Rights, that among these are Life, Liberty, and the pursuit of Happiness. —
[Premise 2] That to secure these rights, Governments are instituted among Men, deriving their just powers from the consent of the governed, —
[Conclusion] That whenever any Form of Government becomes destructive of these ends, it is the Right of the People to alter or to abolish it, and to institute new Government, laying its foundation on such principles, and organizing its powers in such Form, as to them shall seem most likely to effect their Safety and Happiness.

In other words, God creates "all men ... equal" and effectively leaves them in a "natural" state that assumes certain fundamental and "natural" rights. Those "unalienable" rights cannot be taken or given away. Mankind is left then to establish agencies (governments) to secure those God-given rights. Here, Jefferson assumes that man left to his own devices could not secure his life or freedom to act and needs formal political organization to do so. If Jefferson's premises are accepted, then the conclusion is compulsory. The King and his government have "become destructive" to the ends of civil government and have alienated the consent of the governed, so a new authority must be consented to and instituted in order that man's natural rights be "secure." A large and speculative theory of society is thus translated into a specific call for action by a specific group, rebelling Americans. And then there is the contentious "all men are created equal" clause, which has had a history that sometimes appears to be separate from the meaning of the Declaration as a whole. In 1776, it might have meant simply what Americans had been saying since the Stamp Act, that Americans were equal to all other "nations" or specifically that they were equal to Britons who happened to be in Britain. More likely, Jefferson and the committee intended it in its full natural law sense that people come into the world with equal rights. Then, it seems, only the *pursuit* of happiness is assured, not the realization of it. This view, and the reference to "Life, Liberty, and the pursuit of Happiness" (or the pursuit of "property" in John Locke's usage) was a fully developed theory in the English-speaking world. Locke's *Second Treatise* and Thomas Hobbes's *Leviathan* (1651) had discussed humans, as historian C.B. Macpherson puts it, in terms of their "possessive individualism." Governments, especially in Locke's thesis, being creatures of human design, should correspond to mankind's liberal (that is selfish and autonomous) nature. In that way, Locke's "The Ends of Civil Government" and "The Possibility of Resistance" sections from *The Second Treatise* inform the Declaration's claim that "Governments are instituted among Men...." Governments are intended to secure rights and optimize freedoms, and, when they do not, men are entitled to "to institute new Government." Taking a somewhat different approach, Hobbes saw the best government as a neutral but powerful instrument to restrain the excesses of possessive individualism. In doing so, governments would enhance the individual's security from the potential desires of other individuals. Hobbes's "Leviathan" was not subject to the consent of the ruled. Surely, however, if Hobbes, Locke, and Jefferson in their various ways believed that all men were "created" equal, the fact that men were not equal in condition or in opportunity tempers the Declaration's assumptions. It turns the proposition into an idealistic comment or renders the phrase worthless. That issue is made much more difficult for the present day reader who might wonder why women are excluded. We know that Jefferson, while deploring slavery, believed that African Americans were inferior. He supposed that they had not been created equal. Jefferson's views on civilization would also find native Americans less than equal, in birth or in condition. If we choose to see the Declaration as more than a comprehensive political *tour de force*, we are then left to puzzle over the abstract possibilities of its sentiments and to question its sincerity, logic, and accuracy. The Declaration was a formal announcement of the actual, and not simply the intended, independence of the "United Colonies" or, as the document boldly affirmed in upper case letters, "THE UNITED STATES OF AMERICA."

The Declaration is the work of skilled rhetoricians, and its structure conforms in many ways to the conventions of the age. After setting the case for independence in a universal theory of consensual government, the document moves to the specifics of the 27 violations of colonial rights (many of which had appeared in the Virginia Constitution of a few days earlier). Most of those are introduced by "He has," a reference to George III's culpability and a deliberate exclusion of Parliament in any of the charges. The litany of accusations includes the major grievances against standing armies, the Proclamation and the Quebec Act, the Coercive Acts, the taxing without representation, waging war against "His subjects" instead of protecting them, cutting off trade, appointing judges and other officials without the consent of the colonial assemblies, and so on. The final charge is a particularly provocative one: "He has excited domestic insurrections amongst us, and has endeavoured to bring on the inhabitants of our frontiers, the merciless Indian Savages." As with Jefferson's charge that the King and his predecessors had imposed slavery on the colonies, the charge here is a bit tenuous, as the frontier clashes with natives all along had been mostly the result of the encroachment of colonists into traditionally neutral territory from long before the Seven Years' War and the Proclamation of 1763. After listing the grievances, the Declaration seems to shrug, verbally, and announce that the need for actual representation, the case for natural rights, and the "Usurpations" of George III have confirmed the separation because George, or any "Prince" who becomes a "Tyrant, is unfit to be the ruler of a free people." Jefferson makes an ethical point when he states that Congress has not taken its decision lightly. When he notes that the King had been warned repeatedly of the callous behavior of Parliament and of the "patient sufferance" of the colonists, he is laying the blame for independence at George III's feet and dodging any suggestion that this is a "rebellion" or insurrection for illegitimate ends. In a vivid passage in the second paragraph, the Declaration notes,

> [M]ankind are more disposed to suffer, while evils are sufferable, than to right themselves by abolishing the forms to which they are accustomed. But when a long train of abuses and usurpations, pursuing invariably the same Object, evinces a design to reduce them under absolute Despotism, it is their right, it is their duty, to throw off such Government, and to provide new Guards for their future security.

As Paine had indicated, it was not the malevolent designs of a disloyal people but the British themselves who had determined the Empire's break up. That is a brilliant twist on the affair, but it should not obscure the careful wording of Jefferson's conclusion: "[A]ll political connection between ... [the former colonies] and the State of Great Britain is, and ought to be, totally dissolved; and that, as Free and Independent States, they have full Power to levy War, conclude Peace, contract Alliances, establish Commerce, and to do all other Acts and Things which Independent States may of right do." This appeal for international recognition would require military success, but the world had heard the call, and the signers' dramatic "pledge to each other our Lives, our Fortunes, and our sacred Honor."

The Declaration was an act of collective treason, and each signatory was subject to a capital charge. While its language was rich in feeling, it was still a "declaration" and not a reality. More than a century earlier, Thomas Hobbes had said that in politics "covenants without swords are mere words," and, in July 1776, words were mostly what the Continental Congress had. The British government did not accept American independence because it had been declared, so there would be no independence until it was won, in war. At this point, though, the Declaration had stolen a huge march on the disorganized loyalist community, which was now without a broadly acceptable alternative to either restoration of the Crown's authority and perhaps a more rigorous colonial administration or the unknown ends of independence. All along, the rhetoric of the pamphleteers, even Paine's treatise and Jefferson's apparently inescapable logic, had been open to dispute. To a loyalist, Paine was talking nonsense — there was nothing inevitable about separation — and Jefferson did not understand Parliament's legitimate role in America because he was driven by ambition. History has recorded the patriot rather than the loyalist thesis as the right one, but arms would decide the issue in the end. In the 1763 to 1776 period, however, words did declare a war of ideas, and a major battle in that war had been won with the Declaration of Independence.

1776: The Continental Congress and the Continental Army

The "sword" that Hobbes said was needed was the metaphorical power to enforce a covenant. Meanwhile, a more prosaic sword would be forged and wielded, largely by George Washington but not without the assistance of a military leadership that was perhaps latent in American society and that was only slowly and painfully refined as the war progressed. When Congress declared independence, a war had been going on for a year in a sporadic way, and, although the British Army had abandoned New England, its size and range in America remained formidable. Congress's ambitious expedition to Canada had failed, and, while loyalist forces in the Carolinas had been neutralized and pro-independence governments secured, it was difficult to see how the Declaration of Independence could be made to stick. The Congress knew that to leave the war to the local militias would result in a few localized triumphs but also in ultimate military and political fragmentation. As noted, Washington's optimism at Boston in July 1775 had disappeared by winter. The army in Massachusetts was not only an amateur and seasonal one but undisciplined and generally unpaid. The earlier stalemate around Boston had extended into the fall of 1775, and much of that army had melted away into the farm towns of New England. To be sure, there were Pennsylvania and Maryland riflemen in New England. One exceptional company of nearly 100 Virginia militiamen had marched 600 miles in three weeks to get to Cambridge, and not one member fell out. This discipline was maintained by Captain Daniel Morgan (1736-1802) who was later captured and released in the Quebec campaign. He went on to become a brigadier general in Washington's army. But Morgan was not present in July 1776, and neither was his company of riflemen. The British Army was gone and enthusiasm for war had softened in Massachusetts.

Congress managed to replace the "Boston Army" of 1775 and, by the end of 1776, had developed a formula for each state's military quota. Incentives such as enlistment bounties followed by decent and assured pay were needed if the army of 1775 and 1776, mostly militia, were to be converted into a regular force. In its first year, the delegates to Congress had held the colonies together by consistent liaison and had established the rudiments of an organized confederacy by creating a military wing and declaring independence. That military wing would have to be professional and committed if it were to compete with the British. Over the next few years, it is remarkable what the Congress did achieve as a voluntary collective. It waged a war, forged alliances, and negotiated treaties with European nations and with some native American nations; it created a post office, a currency, and a functioning bureaucracy, and it offered advice to states on writing constitutions. Its most important achievement was in helping to coordinate the war effort and in appointing key senior officers. On a political level, the Articles of Confederation can be said to be its finest achievement and the first formal national constitution. Although it took several years to get the Articles ratified, an indication of the hesitation in forming a federated state, they paved the way for the Constitution of 1787. What helped keep the enterprise going was the contribution of a wide representation of American political experience. A review of the names who served in the Congress between 1775 and 1789 reveals a galaxy of American social and political leadership. Each of the first five presidents of the United States of America served in the second Continental Congress, including Washington who was briefly a delegate before leaving to command its army. By one account, of the 342 men who served as delegates to the Congress, 134 also served in either the Continental Army or the militia.

The Political Structure of the Continental Congress

The term "the United States of America" had been coined even though no such political entity existed. Even under the Articles of Confederation, the states shared and often dictated the terms of political, diplomatic, and military administration, but a body of committed and intelligent representatives who controlled enough authority at home managed to transfer some of that power to Congress. The signers of the Declaration represented a cross-section of the patriot political intelligentsia, and, of the 56 signers, 29 were either full-time or part-time lawyers or judges. Another nine identified themselves as farmers, including some slaveholders. The given occupations of the signatories of the Declaration are as follows:

Lawyer 13, Lawyer-Farmer 1
Judge 11, Judge-Physician 1, Judge-Educator 1, Judge-Author 1, Judge-Merchant 1
Farmer 9
Merchant 9
Physician 3
Political Leader 1, Surveyor 1, Soldier 1, Printer-Publisher 1, Ironmaster 1, Educator 1

These were late colonial America's "middling" and "better" sorts, a revolutionary vanguard guiding the political agenda. The "farmers" here were not plowing a few acres and raising a few sheep; they were southern "planters" or commercial farmers, or even "gentlemen" farmers from the north. Few of the mass of Americans wrote polemical literature or served as representatives to the various corresponding committees or conventions, even as they voted to send representatives or otherwise endorsed the edicts of the first or second Continental Congress. Urban workers had taken part in the various riots and protests from the Stamp Act to the Boston Tea Party, and rural and backcountry folks had stood up against the British to the point where the subsistence farmers of Massachusetts had been politicized and then bloodied at Lexington-Concord and Boston in defiance of the Coercive Acts. The independence movement would be led by the older political leadership. The rest of the population, while it was imbibing revolutionary ideals, provided the cannon fodder.

Among an assembly of political leaders, the only person who gave his occupation as "political leader" was Samuel Adams, whose earlier brewing career had long ago been abandoned for a fixed role as revolutionary agitator. His rough and tumble and even tactless political behavior obscures the fact that he was an urban entrepreneur, in much the same way as was the more sober silversmith and artisan, Paul Revere. These were not members of a proletariat, if that term has any meaning in late eighteenth-century America, or "lower" sorts or even workers in the ordinary sense of that word. There were poor white people in eighteenth-century America, but there was not an oppressed peasant class, and no *sans culottes* as there were in the French Revolution, so that the distance between the mass of the population and the wordsmiths and political ideologues was not great by European standards. If the merchants, lawyers, and jurists defined the issues and dictated the actions, their ideas somehow found receptive minds in the general population. White Americans were not all equal in status, but a majority would ultimately believe that they shared equal rights. There was something modest about the use of terms such as "surveyor," "printer," or "educator." The printer in this case was Franklin, who added "publisher" to his professional identity. But Franklin was also one of the best known figures in America, as scientist, diplomat, politician, writer, bureaucrat, and traveler. He has since become the bourgeois American everyman, with his *Poor Richard's Almanac* homilies and witticisms, his frugal but creative fiscal habits, his technical (the Franklin stove) expertise and scientific (electrical experimentation) curiosity, his leanings to middlebrow culture (the lending library), and his apparent openness. He was also the typical revolutionary in a way, having moved from anglophile and imperialist to separatist. Franklin, like so many others in this era, seemed to be everywhere and involved in every issue. He dipped below the revolutionary horizon at times, by spending most of his later life in Europe, while the rest of the founders toiled at home with the frustrating political demands of independence. Still, Franklin embodies much of what Americans admire most about their culture. He was an eclectic and practical man whose life story, from Boston apprentice printer to Philadelphia burgher to the French court, remains the subject of frequent biographies. Franklin was both celebrity and revolutionary. He signed the Declaration, in fact helped compose it, because, like so many others of his station, he had a sense of obligation and believed independence was the only option for Americans.

The only full time "educator" identified among the signers was John Witherspoon (1723-94), a remarkable Scottish immigrant who, from his arrival in America in 1768 until his death, was front and center in the debate over sovereignty. He was a complex man whose calling was the clergy but whose life became one with politics and secular theories of social and political philosophy and action. Witherspoon had actually lived in the great hothouse of the Enlightenment, Edinburgh, and had communed with many of the great thinkers of the age. He came as principal of the College of New Jersey (Princeton) and served it well, even in the turbulent war years. In addition to his signing the Declaration, he spent a further six years in the Continental Congress and helped design the executive functions under the Articles of Confederation; he sat in the New Jersey legislature and in the New Jersey convention that ratified the Constitution. All the while, he was promoting the spread of the Presbyterian Church. Samuel Adams, Benjamin Franklin, and John Witherspoon are a varied trio of revolutionaries in their backgrounds, talents, and occupations, but they were, like Jefferson and a host of other leaders, a competent, respected, and ultimately decisive revolutionary force.

If political art and experience existed in the Continental Congress, there appeared to be less expertise at the military level. As noted, Congress's first formal military appointment had been Artemus Ward, at Boston in the aftermath of Lexington-Concord. Ward was a storekeeper, not a soldier, but he acquitted himself reasonably well. He was superseded by George Washington, and he resented that and eventually left the military. In the months after May 1775, Congress created a command hierarchy and a dozen generals to go with it. Among them were Charles Lee (1731-92), a professional soldier who had served with the British Army in America in the late 1750s, and the Irish-born Richard Montgomery, another veteran of the British Army who was killed in the Canada campaign of 1775. Horatio Gates (1729-1806) was another veteran of the British Army who settled in America to escape the "caste" system in England only to become a slaveholder in Virginia. He would eventually free his slaves after the war and move to New York. Most of the others were American born veterans of the French and Indian War. Nathanael Greene (1742-86) was a Rhode Islander whose ancestors had been in New England since the 1630s and who, next to Washington, was the most celebrated commander in the Continental Army. He ran an iron forge almost to the moment the war began and might be said to have been a "natural" soldier. Of those appointed in 1775, Greene was the most successful and the only one of the originals to serve for the duration. Gates and Lee had uneven and even disastrous careers mostly because of their personalities. The creation of a citizen army meant that a mostly civilian officer corps would command a completely civilian military effort. The military leadership of the independence movement in 1775-76 was not very impressive on paper, and, as enthusiasm waned and a major British military commitment seemed likely, independence was not a sure thing.

Conclusion

The most striking thing about the crisis of the British Empire in North America is how quickly the relationship between the colonies and the British government went from one of tension, dispute, and constitutional debate to war and separation. In the months between the fall of 1774 and the spring of 1776, the colonial population, through its political representation, had organized itself first to dispute the Coercive and Quebec Acts and then to arm itself and commit itself to an organized war of resistance against a King and Parliament whose policies were intractable. The patriot leadership itself became quite inflexible, and its appeals for reconciliation gave way in the space of months to outright rejection of anything short of a new and enhanced status for the colonies. The Continental Congress's Olive Branch Petition was the last overt appeal by the colonies. Paine's logical note that the time for reconciliation was past was an accurate assessment of the situation in the spring of 1776. While the issues had revealed a split in the colonies between loyalists and patriots, the respective numbers were not known in early 1776. What was clear was that, while the vast majority of colonists could not have contemplated independence before 1774, it seemed to be inevitable by the summer of 1776. The language and references in *Common Sense* and the Declaration of Independence were familiar to most colonists and provided a passionate rationale for a war that was underway. The Declaration was notable in the short term for the way it reflected the political sophistication of the Continental Congress, an organization considered treasonable by the Crown, and signaled the end of any hope of reconciliation. The great quality of the Declaration originates in its blending of the protests and appeals of a decade of debate and dispute, its superb use of rhetorical device, and its mix of practical and emotional references. That it has become the benchmark for defining American nationalism was a result of success in the war. Contemporaries recognized the gravity of what they had done, and the language in the Declaration was seen by patriots for what it was — ambitious, proud, and necessary. While there was talent to spare in Congress, the same could not be said for the army that was to represent it, and all the rhetoric in the world would not win independence. The bold announcements in *Common Sense* and the Declaration would require the addition of a supreme military effort. The British Army would demand it.

Suggested Reading

Robert A. Gross, *The Minutemen and Their World* (New York: Hill and Wang, 1976) is a vivid and original treatment of the rural society that made the armed rising at Lexington and Concord possible and effective. It can be read with profit along with David Hackett Fischer, *Paul Revere's Ride* (New York: Oxford University Press, 1994). The various intellectual sources of the Declaration of Independence are discussed in Garry Wills, *Inventing America: Jefferson's Declaration of Independence* (New York: Random House, 1978), a study that should be compared to the classic Carl Becker, *The Declaration of Independence: A Study in the History of Political Ideas* (1922; New York: Knopf, 1942) and to Pauline Maier, *American Scripture: Making the Declaration of*

Independence (New York: Knopf, 1997). The most recent edition of *Common Sense* is Thomas Paine, *Common Sense*, ed. Edward Larkin (Peterborough, ON: Broadview Press, 2004). A useful annotated edition of Locke's masterpiece is John Locke, *Two Treatises on Government*, ed. Peter Laslett (1690; Cambridge, England: Cambridge University Press, 1960). Bernard Bailyn, *The Ideological Origins of the American Revolution*, cited previously, is an excellent study of the ferment of ideas that preceded the Continental Congress's composition of the Declaration. For a lively discussion of the role of newspaper propaganda, see Bernard Bailyn and J.B. Hench, eds., *The Press and the American Revolution* (Worcester, MA: American Antiquarian Society, 1980). The emergence of a loyalist opposition to the independence movement is dealt with clearly and succinctly in William Nelson, *The American Tory* (New York: Oxford University Press, 1961), which remains the most convenient starting point for understanding this vital aspect of the Revolution. Another useful study, with commentary on the impact of loyalism on Canada is Christopher Moore, *The Loyalists: Revolution, Exile, Settlement* (Toronto: McClelland and Stewart, 1984). A contemporary loyalist view can be seen in Douglas Adair and John A. Schulz, eds., *Peter Oliver's Origin and Progress of the American Rebellion: A Tory View (1781)* (Stanford, CA: Stanford University Press, 1961). For pictorial images of this period, see http://classroom clipart.com and follow the links through History, United States, American Revolution.

CHAPTER FOUR
THE WAR FOR INDEPENDENCE

I am a constant Advocate for a regular Army, and the most masterly Discipline, because I know that without these We cannot reasonably hope to be a powerfull, a prosperous, or a free People, and therefore, I have been constantly labouring to obtain an handsome Encouragement for inlisting a permanent Body of Troops. But have not as yet prevailed, and indeed, I despair of ever Succeeding, unless the General [Washington], and the Officers from the Southward, Should convince Gentlemen here [Continental Congress in Philadelphia]; or unless two or three horrid Defeats, Should bring a more melancholy Conviction, which I expect and believe will one day or other be the Case.

— John Adams to Henry Knox, September 1776

We therefore still kept upon the parade in groups, venting our spleen at our country and government, then at our officers and then at ourselves for our imbecility in staying there and starving in detail for an ungrateful people who did not care what became of us, so they could enjoy themselves while we were keeping a cruel enemy from them.

— Continental Army Private Joseph Plumb Martin, reflecting on conditions in 1780. Quoted in James Kirby Martin and Mark Edward Lender, *A Respectable Army: The Military Origins of the Republic, 1763-1789* (Arlington Heights, IL: Harlan Davidson, 1982) viii

Time Line

1776	The British abandon Boston.
	The states begin writing constitutions.
1776-77	Campaigns in New York, New Jersey, and Pennsylvania.
	American defeats at Long Island and New York City.
	American victory at Trenton.
1777	American victory at Saratoga.
	The Articles of Confederation drawn up by Continental Congress.
1777-78	Continental Army winters at Valley Forge.
1778	French alliance with the Continental Congress.
	Carlisle Commission.
	The British leave Philadelphia.
1779	Spanish alliance with the Continental Congress.
1779-81	Intensive war in the south.

1781   The British surrender at Yorktown, Virginia.
           The Articles of Confederation ratified.
1782-83 Peace talks.
1783   Treaty of Paris recognizes American independence.

A Special Kind of War

After July 1776, a civil war was on between two parts of the Empire. It was also a civil war between two groups of Americans, patriots, who sought independence, and loyalists, who did not. It was also a "rebellion," a term frequently used by the British. Was it also, as the historian John Shy suggests, a war of "national liberation"? Writing in the 1970s, Shy compares the American revolutionary movement and war with the Vietnam War and the anti-imperialist thrust of the Vietnamese "war of national liberation." Shy notes parallels in the struggle between two domestic factions and the role of the outsider, in this case the United States, as a perceived colonial power struggling for the "hearts and minds" of the Vietnamese population, as Richard Nixon put it, perhaps borrowing from John Adams. In hindsight, Adams exaggerated the inevitability of revolutionary success when he said in 1818, "The Revolution was effected before the war commenced [and was] in the minds and hearts of the people." Well, many of the people to be sure, but perhaps not all "the people." In any case, there are similarities even down to the remarkable victory of outgunned peoples over powerful military establishments. The British could claim in 1775 and later that they were attempting to "liberate" the colonial population from a rebel minority, just as the United States claimed in its references to the Viet Cong 200 years later. But the analogy, while valid in some details and fashionable in the 1960s and 1970s, is tenuous. The major difference between the American war and the host of national wars of liberation and independence of the twentieth century is that the American colonists were really not "colonized" people as were the Indo-Chinese or for that matter contemporary African anti-imperialists. The Americans were, in fact, the colonizers. The members of the Continental Congress represented a colonial enterprise that by conquest and occupation had become de facto governors of a considerable part of North America. A frequent reference in the pamphlet literature of the 1760s and 1770s was to the fact that the colonists' predecessors had come to America and tamed the wilderness and its "savage" peoples and civilized it and improved it. The British countered with a theory that the Empire was a set of interdependent extensions of Britain, originated and nurtured by, and responsible to, the Crown. The notion of two levels of senior authority in the same system was anathema to the British government of 1776. Even in 1839, when Lord Durham suggested a form of limited self-government for Canada, Parliament was suspicious and hesitant. The British rejected the Olive Branch Petition and emphatically denounced the Declaration of Independence because they refused to acknowledge either's legitimacy. The language of dissent should have told them that the rebels in British North America had a clear sense of how their claims were rooted in history.

Yet one of the vexing questions regarding the American Revolution concerns the support for it among the colonists themselves from the Stamp Act crisis to the summer of the Declaration of Independence. We can never know for sure what percentage of the population was fully aware of the issues before the Coercive Acts, how those issues affected political consciousness, and how the escalating political dispute and organized armed conflict expanded the range of engagement and decision. Not even contemporaries could be sure because many silent Americans in all regions did not commit to either the loyalist or patriot camps. They equivocated and even switched, depending on the moment. John Adams's guess that at the time of the Declaration one third were for independence and one third were opposed to it, while one third were neutral, has to be seen in the light of his later observation that the revolution was in the "minds and hearts" of Americans before the war. Adams simply did not know. We can be sure that, at the end of the war, the entire white population, with minor exceptions, supported independence simply because it was a *fait accompli*. But during the war, majority support for independence was achieved fitfully, and, while British policy and behavior fueled the patriot cause, a major impetus to it came in the person of George Washington and, over time, in the political and military enterprise he represented.

George Washington

Among the patriots' greatest assets throughout the war were geography and demographics. After the spring of 1775, the British had the forbidding task to restore rule, by force, over a vast landscape of varied landforms and climate, populated by hostile or indifferent people. However, this impediment was offset by the inadequacies of American military preparation and organization. The juxtaposition of the formal military arm, the Continental Army, with local militias created difficulties in coordinating strategies. At the Continental Army command level, a number of senior officers contributed experience and passion and kept the campaigns going with skill, persuasion, and persistence. Nathanael Greene, Henry Knox, Daniel Morgan, Anthony Wayne, and Benedict Arnold were all instrumental in exploiting any American military success by politicizing it. Later in the war, the notorious Arnold unintentionally added a measure of drama to the cause when he defected to the British. His name became a pseudonym for treason. But Arnold had been a very competent and innovative general who had acquitted himself with distinction early in the war. The best of the American military leadership was Washington himself, and it is difficult to describe his contribution without lapsing into hyperbole. The war was a long one that violated some of the standards of eighteenth-century warfare by being formal and conventional at times, in various maneuvers and pitched battles between Continental troops and regular British Army forces, and unconventional at other times, as militia forces and smaller patriot units ambushed and harried British troops in more limited and irregular "fights." The so-called "war of posts," later defined as "guerrilla war," constantly harassed the British Army and its planning.

Washington does not have a great reputation as a thinker by the standards of the leading revolutionary theorists and pamphleteers, but he had sound practical talents, common sense, and, above all, a consistent moral view of his universe that reverberated through his relationship with soldiers, politicians, and civilians alike. When he was not tending to military matters, he could be impatient and aloof, but he maintained a level of dignity that impressed his contemporaries. He stayed in the field for the entire war and missed only a few days of duty because of illness. He and his major generals could lose battles, as they did at times with alarming frequency, but the army he held together won the war. Washington had enough political influence and was savvy enough in his dealings with Congress to overcome many of the inevitable problems of funding, supplies, and manpower. He maintained a command structure that worked over the long term. His most significant positive traits were his persistence and his ability to learn. He was a raw tactician at the outset but improved as the war went on. He seldom despaired for the cause and eventually became the Revolution's first icon, whose courage and devotion, and even his stately appearance, became intertwined with the political objectives of the Congress. If the American cause represented "liberty," "honor," "virtue," "patience," "forbearance," "consent," and "rights," then Washington was seen to embody those qualities in contrast to what Americans saw as the "tyranny," "corruption," and "enslavement" that defined Britain's "arbitrary" purposes in America. Washington projected American moral superiority. While Jefferson's words rang with principle and purpose, Washington's leadership in the war brought the words to life. He managed a military endeavor that often seemed too shaky to succeed. Turnover was high, and, of the twenty-nine major generals appointed to the Continental Army during the course of the war five were killed, two were dismissed, seven resigned before their terms were up, and one, Arnold, went over to the British. That instability was repeated at every level from field officers to common soldiers, and the continuity required for success was maintained in part by Washington's forbearance. After the *rage militaire* of 1775, as the emotional and physical commitment of Americans waxed and waned from enthusiasm to apathy, Washington persisted.

Participation

The citizen army needed to maintain a high rate of emotional commitment, material support, and participation. That was the most difficult task for Washington, the Congress, and the various states and their militias. After the deaths of Joseph Warren at Bunker Hill and Richard Montgomery at Quebec, they were slowly raised to martyrdom. The identification of the cause with "sacrifice" in the deaths of "heroes" lent an emotive spark to the war, but the death of an ordinary private could do the same thing for a village or parish. At other times, it could provoke a backlash over the loss of a son or husband or sibling or neighbor in a battle or campaign that had taken place hundreds of miles away. Depending on timing and circumstances, the war was intensively meaningful or irrelevant to different segments of the population. The propaganda machinery of sermons, speeches, and neighborly rumor and opinion, as well as the proximity of the British Army, kept the fact of the war alive in all localities. This resulted in an important American asset, the local militias. These often ephemeral units were maligned by the British for their uncouth deportment and their unconventional and therefore "cowardly" tactics. Washington himself did not trust their commitment to the larger cause and, in 1776, said that placing "any dependence upon militia, is, assuredly resting upon a broken staff." In their neighborhoods, however, the militias constantly hounded the British. As historian John Shy puts it, they were the "sand in the gears of the [British] pacification machinery." Geography and demographics imposed serious limitations on British strategies, and, while the scope of the war at times held back full and consistent American coordination, the British were subject to greater logistical problems.

There were an estimated two and half million people in the wartime states in the late 1770s, a half million of whom were slaves. If we assume a rough equivalency in sex ratios, there were about one million white males. Given what we know of age distribution, about 400,000 were eligible for service in the Continental Army or the local militias, using the standard 16 to 60 age range for adulthood. Clearly, there would be a limit to the number of fifty- and sixty-year-olds who could serve, as there would be for sixteen- to eighteen-year-olds. In fact, few forty-year-old men were found in the ranks. As we chip away at the numbers, the pool of eligible useful recruits in America decreases, and we might find that the authorities had about a 300,000 manpower pool to draw on at any time during the war (slightly fewer in the early stages and growing larger as the overall population rose). Even allowing for shifting allegiances, there were likely about 50,000 committed loyalists who were not available and either served in loyalist militias or in so-called "Provincial" regiments attached to the British Army. By assuming a pool of 250,000, the known figures for enlistments in the Continental Army and the estimates for militia service reveal a high rate of participation. In 1787, the Paymaster General for the Continental Army provided figures for enlistments. The numbers for militia enlistments are estimates from a variety of state sources.

Table 4.1: Estimated American Enlistments for Military Service

Estimates include multiple individual enlistments. The militia figures are less precise than the Continental Army numbers, but both sets are subject to the same qualification: the unknown number of individuals who enlisted for several successive short-term stints of service.

State	Continental Army	Militia
New Hampshire	12,497	4,000
Massachusetts	67,907	20,000
Rhode Island	5,908	4,000
Connecticut	31,939	9,000
New York	17,781	10,000
New Jersey	10,726	7,000
Pennsylvania	25,678	10,000

Delaware	2,386	1,000
Maryland	13,912	9,000
Virginia	26,678	30,000
North Carolina	7,263	13,000
South Carolina	6,417	20,000
Georgia	2,679	8,000
Totals:	231,771	145,000

Total: 376,771

Source: Francis B. Heitman, *Historical Register of Officers of the Continental Army* (1893; Washington, DC: Government Printing Office, 1914). Heitman notes that the figures need to allow for the inflation caused by multiple enlistments. See also Mark Mayo Boatner III, *Encyclopedia of the American Revolution* (New York: David McKay Company, 1974), 262-64.

With the numbers of estimated available males, those enlistment figures cannot be accepted at face value. The militia figures are estimates compiled by historians from a variety of sources, and their accuracy is doubtful. The Continental Army figures are reasonably reliable, but must be qualified. For a start, the numbers include multiple enlistments and so include the two or more times any individual would enlist. The militia figures are subject to the same caveat. The best estimates for actual, *individual participation* puts the figure at about 200,000 for both Army and militia service, as well as the smaller numbers involved in the navy and marine corps. Also, neither set of figures can say much about types or length of service. A militia enrolment might be for a few days, weeks, or months. Not all enlisted men saw action or even encountered the enemy. A sensible estimate would indicate that the number of individual Americans who "bore arms" in the war was about 100,000. The Continental Army in 1776 levied proportional quotas on the states for one-year enlistments and, in 1777, extended the demand to three years, but the quotas were never met. During each year of the war between 1776 and 1781, Congress called for about 80,000 Continental Army enlistments a year, based on a per capita commitment from the states; for example, Massachusetts and Virginia were each required to raise 15 "battalions" (in effect "regiments"), and Georgia was asked for one. These were in addition to the ability of the states to raise additional militia units. The Continental Army seldom reached half its requirements, and the militia enrolments were always irregular. Still, if we look at the ratio of individual enrolments to available manpower, the participation rates in this war are very high. Yet Washington never had an army in the field larger than about 17,000 Continentals and militia, and, in some of his major campaigns, he or his generals worked with about 4,000 to 5,000 men. The largest number of Continental soldiers in service at any time was about 35,000, reached in the fall of 1778. As an indication of the Continental Army's reduced role in the lower south, of the total military enlistments in Georgia and South Carolina, the militia participation, based on actual numbers of enlistments including multiple enlistments, was at least three to one over Continental service. By contrast, in Massachusetts, Continental Army numbers ran at a three to one ratio over militia service, reflecting a more efficient recruiting system and perhaps a greater commitment to longer-term service.

Assets and Liabilities

For all Washington's disdain of the militias, they were often Britain's greatest problem. In some cases, the farmer in April would be armed and in combat in July and back farming by September. Also, with a few exceptions, the Continental Army operated in friendly civilian territory while the British mostly did not, and, when they did, they could never be sure if the population was merely tolerating them until their departure. The other intangibles that favored the American cause were periodic bursts of enthusiasm and anger, an obvious homeland incentive, and the encouragement of families, neighbors, and friends. Yet, for all that, desertion rates were high. Sickness, including homesickness, ate away at the zeal of Continentals and militias alike. Quite often, what sustained Washington's army and the militia was local reaction to the British Army's attempts at pacification or recovery, and its arrogance and propensity to plunder, or at least to requisition materials. The British found that there was never really any hope of a complete recovery of the affections or loyalty of the entire population even if they could sustain an occupation in New York, parts of New Jersey and Pennsylvania, Rhode Island, and the lower south. The British could not win this war, but they persisted with it, and therein lay a sad irony. It was not that the British had no reasonable expectation for some success, but their overall political policy was tied to military strategies. In the end, it simply did not matter. Victory in New York, for example, would mean nothing, after all, if most of the rest of revolutionary America could not be conquered and recovered. After 1776, that should have been understood by Parliament and the King. General Gage had implied as much in 1775.

On the other hand, in addition to the problems of commitment, the war raised awkward questions about a national, that is, a "standing" American army. After 1776, women, who in many areas had encouraged the volunteering of their sons, *engagés*, and husbands in the first two years of the war, worried increasingly for the safety of their men and about the dereliction of male domestic responsibilities as they and their farms became neglected. There was constant pressure on soldiers of all ranks to return home and not re-enlist, a problem for local recruitment officers, clerks, and administrators in Congress, and, most of all, for Washington and his generals. When the drafts were sent out, pay and incentives had to be designated and hard money (specie) was scarce. The new currencies being released everywhere were often mistrusted. Congress began issuing paper currency in an attempt to stabilize values as much as possible, noting that comparison with the value of the pound sterling and metal coinage still measured any currency's worth. But Congress's money was no more than promissory notes or bills of credit, which became terribly devalued as the war went on and were eventually dismissed by the population with the derisory term "Continentals," the same term used by many to describe Washington's troops.

A set of legendary attributes has been ascribed to the revolutionary military generation. One older version of the legend is that the citizen soldier, fired with patriotism, justice, and fortitude was simply too much for the British. He had more natural talent than his highly trained but deferential counterpart in the British Army. His heritage made him less an automaton and more an inventive individual with spirit and imagination. He was used to firearms, so was a ready-made warrior. He lacked formal training, and in fact was difficult to train, but that was a sign of his flexibility and self-direction. The image of the free-spirited soldier taken directly from the days of the ever-ready Minuteman has been challenged in recent years by historians. The very qualities that were praised for bringing victory to the American cause can also be used to explain Washington's failure to end the war earlier. The alleged patriotism of Washington's army, while it was always there, has to be tempered by the facts of short-term service, high desertion rates, unpredictable behavior, familiarity and lack of respect for officers, and a tendency to quarrel with soldiers from other states (colonies). The alleged bravery of the Continental soldier has to be weighed against the number of times the ranks broke and ran. The individualism that made the soldier a creative fighter also made it difficult for him to be disciplined and organized for formal confrontations. The celebrated riflemen were only occasionally gathered in numbers large enough to encourage combat innovation and were useful mostly as sharpshooters and snipers. These men, drawn largely from the backcountry, were equipped with the so-called Pennsylvania rifle, a musket with a rifled interior barrel that helped propel a ball three times farther than the smoothbore musket could, and with more accuracy. The vast majority of Continental soldiers and militiamen were armed with smoothbore short-range flintlock muskets similar to the standard issue for European armies. Over 100,000 French-made Charleville smooth-bore muskets were distributed to Continental Army troops. This weapon was accurate to less than 100 yards and so required opposing infantry formations to come virtually face to face with each other. The bayonet was still an effective attachment and would remain so until the longer-range, rifled firearms of the later nineteenth century made them superfluous. According to textbook standards and eighteenth-century practice, British troops fired volleys and advanced in a series of ranks, with each rank pausing to reload while the rank behind discharged its load. These troops simply fired ahead and did not always choose targets. The Americans, it was said, did aim and fire and deliberately targeted officers, who were conveniently identified by their uniforms. This ran against European convention and appalled the British commanders. The number of British field officers who were killed at Bunker Hill, for example, shocked Gage. Was this approach by the freethinking Continental soldier effective? Massed intensive volleys could terrify half-trained American troops into fleeing, and the erratic if accurate fire of the Continentals often did not deter the British. The best-trained American soldiers in the early days of 1775-76 were artillery units and some cavalry squadrons. While the French supplied uniforms after 1778, there remained some variability in appearance among Continental Army units, depending on the soldier's home state. The basic staples for all troops, including the otherwise individually attired militias, were the haversack, blanket, and cocked hat. At times, the unkempt, loud, hard drinking, and mostly illiterate farm boys who swept through neighborhoods in Continental Army units were a nuisance to local civilians, but, for the most part, they were tolerated or respected.

Nevertheless, the stereotypes of the mindless British regular and wanton Hessian mercenary on one side and the clever, resourceful, politically motivated American volunteer on the other have some claim to reality. The militias were the repositories of that near mythical American character, and it was from within the militias, the "sand in the gears" of the British Army, that those individualistic attributes did contribute to the American success in the war. The Continental Army, though, held the British Army in check while the militia did its work, and the Continental Army took on the British Army in large set battles. The militias gave the British Army no rest and, at significant times, joined with the Continentals to inflict heavy losses on the enemy. Yet, without the Continental Army, it is difficult to see to whom the British might have surrendered at Yorktown in 1781 when they chose to quit. Throughout the conflict, the French and Spanish would certainly have had difficulty negotiating treaties and providing loans and supplies to a Continental Congress that had no armed wing, but which represented a myriad of occasional militias who were mostly bound to their neighborhoods. Washington's role was vital in military terms, to be sure, but his role also has to be judged as a political asset. His army, like the British regulars he would face, was dominated by the poorer, landless, and restless segments of society. Most of the recruits into Washington's army were landless, and perhaps two-thirds of them lacked a useful civilian skill. The average Continental Army private was younger than his British counterpart and lacked the experience and, in some cases, the camaraderie that went with membership in well-established combat regiments. The British Army was an institution, a miniature society in itself. The Continental Army was a formative, fluid organization that had to find its collective spirit over time.

The French Connection
One of the unquestioned patriot assets was France. Beginning with its promise of support in 1775, and the clandestine support it later gave, the French took a great interest in the war and eventually signed a formal diplomatic and military alliance with Congress in 1778. It was a cynical arrangement on both sides. For the French, the principle of "my enemy's enemy is my friend" helped it support independence and drive home a post-Seven Years' War revenge on Great Britain. For the Continental Congress, the French aid and then alliance made for a purely utilitarian relationship. At one level, the Americans feared that a treaty with France might come back to haunt them after independence if the French government decided it wanted to reapply itself in America. There was also the dicey issue of patriot collaboration with the *ancien régime* and the reverse problem of French absolutism aiding an assault on the institution of monarchy, even a British monarchy. The French were cautious, and the Comte de Vergennes, the French Foreign Minister, played a very cagey game for fear that the pro-American

tack could backfire. What if, in 1776 or 1777, the Continental Congress and Parliament reached a compromise and negotiated an end to the conflict? The British might then punish France for its interference. So, the French approach was to allow a trickle of private and informal aid in 1775 that gave way to a more conspicuous participation in 1776. Caron de Beaumarchais, the playwright, set up a company for the explicit purpose of trading military supplies, including medicines. Beaumarchais was one of a number of French thinkers, politicians, and artists who considered themselves genuine "friends" of America, and there was nothing cynical in their intentions. Before the formal treaties of 1778, French supplies reached America in increasing volume, using French West Indian ports for trans-shipment, while American ships were granted access to ports in France.

In 1776, hoping for French recognition, Congress had appointed a commission to Paris to test the Declaration's reception. Benjamin Franklin, Arthur Lee, and Silas Deane were to negotiate whatever aid, loans, and political support they could. While Lee and Deane annoyed the secretaries and officials, Franklin charmed the French court, the public, and the *philosophes*. As Edmund Burke noted, "Dr. Franklin has had a most extraordinary reception at Paris from all ranks of people." His genial behavior and sharp wit were ever in view, and the French loved his directness and wide-ranging conversation and saw in him a new phenomenon, an American genius. But Franklin's true genius in this case lay not in his folksy charm or keen scientific mind but in his shrewd political manipulation of Vergennes. French caution gave way under Franklin's threats to quit Paris for America or even for London leaving the French position up in the air. Vergennes's hesitations and fears of an armistice or American loss were overcome by a combination of Franklin's skilled diplomacy and the defeat of the British Army at Saratoga in late 1777. French aid then opened up, and supplied thousands of troops and tons of materiel. The European alliance went on to include Spain. The French navy grew in response to a new war with Britain and diverted precious Royal Navy resources to the Caribbean. For all that, it should be remembered that the first major decisive victory for the Americans at Saratoga occurred before the French formalized their support. In 1776, however, the war was only just beginning to take shape.

Parliament and the British Army

British liabilities in America began with the difficulty of blending political with military objectives. Also, the militias' behavior — sullen at times and enthusiastic at others, easily routed one day but tenacious the next, apparently loyalist but potentially pro-rebel, here today but gone tomorrow — confounded British strategy. Washington's army, which could suffer a series of terrible losses and embarrassments and then reappear in a ragged remnant to defeat the British, simply added to the British military uncertainty. That unpredictability made the prospects of the full recovery of America dim as the years went by, and the British Army was ground down in America by the scale of the war, the uncertain disposition of the population, and the difficulty in achieving a sustained series of decisive military triumphs. Still, the imposing resources of the Empire created fear in much of the American population, and the bravado of 1775 hardly disguised the American public's basic anxiety about the British Army's destructive potential. Colonial Americans may have stereotyped the common British soldier as a mindless "lobsterback," but they also remembered the way the British Army had defeated the French in Quebec. Britain's main advantages were daunting on paper, but its resources, experience, and reputation were subject to the realities of mismanagement, logistics, and confusion. A shifting political culture and agenda in Britain confounded military policy from the start. London often decided the strategies and even demanded certain tactical applications. Commanders were appointed for the wrong reasons, and calculations of the amount of force required were generally inadequate. The British ended up using about 50,000 regular troops and over 10,000 Provincial (loyalist) troops in organized regiments, an unknown number of loyalist militiamen, and 30,000 mostly German (the so called "Hessians") mercenaries in the American campaigns. The menacing behavior of Hessian troops in the field, even the very presence of "paid foreign" conquerors along with thousands of loyalist enlistees contributed to a widening disrespect for Britain and its American "Tory" lackeys. The Declaration of Independence listed the immoral use of Hessians as one of its 27 grievances, charging the King with using Germans to "compleat the works of death, desolation and tyranny ... with ... Cruelty & perfidy scarcely paralleled in the most barbarous ages." In the end, the troop strengths were not enough. Double the number might not have worked, although a more committed military build up in 1775 would certainly have changed the course of the war.

The British Army was professional and it was conservative. It drew its rank and file from the lower orders, from the unemployed or underemployed, from ex-prison inmates, vagabonds, runaway husbands, and an assortment of youths and apprentices escaping the drudgery of ordinary work. It was a last resort for steady employment for many. It was a volunteer force, strictly speaking, but some enlistments were coerced and terms of service were long. There are recorded instances of convicted felons, facing capital punishment, being spared the gallows by "volunteering" for the British Army in America. Functional literacy ran at about 35 per cent. While discipline was harsh in peace and war, the British soldier was well fed and clothed and decently paid by European standards. In fact, the British Army in America while campaigning was often accompanied by wives, mistresses, prostitutes ("drabs"), and even children. Women cooked and tended to the wounded and added a palpable social atmosphere to military campaigns. The soldiers who served in America were veterans, for the most part, with average service of nearly nine years and an average age in most regiments of about 29 years, a more mature age than we tend to think of in modern wars. The combat structure of the British Army was organized by regiment and company (about 500 and 50 men respectively), and the officer to "ranks" ratio was about one to ten. This was similar to the system adopted by the Continental Army, which assembled its regiments regionally. British Army officers purchased their commissions and many of the field officers were the young sons of gentry families.

The British approach to most combat situations was to combine cavalry and artillery with frontal attacks by rows or columns of infantry. As noted, the volley and charge approach was a European convention dictated by the limitations of the smooth-bore musket, the shock and terror produced by aggressive well-disciplined assault troops, the effective maneuvering of reserves, flanking tactics, and the relative strength and displacement of the enemy. Battles were usually decided in a matter of hours. Troops were precious commodities and only so much blood could be afforded, depending on objectives. There was a tendency to agree to end combat when the end appeared certain. In many of the eighteenth-century wars, in Europe and in America too, a single major battle was often enough to either end the war or at least suspend operations, as in the case of the Battle of Quebec in the French and Indian War. That would not be the case in the War for Independence. The terrain was not as forgiving as Europe's, and the patchy road network, trails in most cases, made conventional operations difficult. Lurking in the woods or farmyards might be a militia unit or a patriot sympathizer reporting to a large American force up the road and around the corner. The distances were formidable, and the climate often too cold or too hot for easy movement. The British infantryman carried a load of about 50 pounds of field equipment, including the musket, the standard issue "Brown Bess," which alone weighed over ten pounds. The British Army adapted somewhat to the unusual tactical demands of the American war by moving towards the use of light infantry units and more flexible combat formations, but, overall, it conducted a war more suited to the conventions of Europe. The scale of most battles was small by comparison with what would follow in nineteenth-century warfare, but the consequences of combat were deadly, and both sides in this war were subject to the same kinds of combat anxieties over the prospects of death or incapacity. Crude medical facilities and procedures meant that wounds and mental fatigue were not treated properly. The ordinance of the era, the small arms and artillery, and the assortment of lethal projectiles used in combat meant that many more soldiers were wounded in the field than were killed outright. Field artillery released a variety of missiles: ball, grapeshot, chain, and other metal fragments. Along with musket balls of a half inch or more caliber, those missiles could shatter bones, lodge in muscle, maim, disfigure and cripple, and leave the victim alive but vulnerable to neglect, hemorrhage, infections, sepsis, and amputations that usually complicated the condition and led to death. What killed the majority of combatants in most wars in history before the very recent past was the lack of medical remedy for injury and an absence of proper sanitation. The majority of military fatalities, on both sides, occurred away from the battlefield, in camps, and in transit. During the war, thousands of prisoners were taken by each side, and, while there were frequent exchanges and repatriations, many languished in prisons and expired there from wounds or diseases. The British kept many American prisoners offshore, in the notorious prison ships where significant numbers perished.

It would be unfair to blame the loss of the American colonies on the inadequacies of the British Army. It won most of the battles, which after all was its major function.

The military enterprise in America was undermined not by the Army's performance but by the poor planning and the political indecision that bedeviled British objectives from the start. General Gage's warnings were not so much ignored as they were misunderstood. In 1775 and the early months of 1776, Parliament was unclear what its military objectives should be. Not until 1778 did it realize that its approach was flawed. Up to that point, Britain was in a quandary about whether to prosecute the war to the utmost or to be firm in resolve but lenient towards civilians and hope for an early armistice. Did it need to subdue the population or woo it with a hope of isolating what it thought was a limited uprising? The key pockets of revolutionary fervor in 1776 spread and grew as the war went on. If the British pressed too hard, more of the population might be pushed into the rebel camp, but if they were too relaxed, that might be seen as weakness. The failure to develop pragmatic military objectives originated in Parliament's confusion and not with the military command in America. Parliament's administrative structure meant that each minister reported directly to the King, and the decisions made in Parliament, in the Commons or the Lords, had to clear the King's authority. Lord North was prime minister, but that meant technically that he was the first among a body of presumptive equals. He had influence in controlling Parliament but was not fully independent in the administration of policy. Lord North was officially First Lord of the Treasury and Chancellor of the Exchequer and so had great influence over finances, but the secretaries of state and especially the Secretary of State for the Colonies had principal roles in the direct planning and conduct of the war. Lord George Germain (later Viscount Sackville) held the latter post from 1775 to 1782 and was responsible for blending political and campaign strategy. For all the transport expertise of the Royal Navy, the coordination of political policy, military strategy, and the supply and distribution of resources often broke down. The use of some 30,000 Hessians during the war (not all of whom would be in America at any given time) added to Britain's battlefield abilities, but their very presence in America antagonized even the most indifferent in the general population and undermined British appeals to neutrals.

British efforts were further complicated by the huge material, financial, and manpower demands of the war. As early as 1776, the war promised to be expensive. Britain had long been a militarized state, and its rise to global prominence in the seventeenth and eighteenth centuries had created a grand military establishment. But the Atlantic Ocean, the geographical expanse of eastern North America, and, most important, the war's duration put an unprecedented strain on the nation's military agencies and budgets. One set of estimates notes that, in 1775, the British Army's regular contingent numbered about 48,000 officers and men worldwide, about 10,000 of whom were in America. The Royal Navy's strength was 16,000. In 1783, those figures had risen to 110,000 regular troops and 107,000 sailors (the annual average in the latter part of the war was about 80,000 sailors). The majority of the land force was committed to America and was bolstered by some 20,000 loyalist enlistments of which over 8,000 were in service in 1780-81. By 1783, the British had in operation over 600 naval craft of all types including nearly 100 ships of the line (heavily armed "battleships"). The Franco-American alliance in 1778 drove much of that expansion, including the raising of nearly 100,000 reservists in Britain on call for a possible French invasion. The French took the war to the Caribbean and stretched British naval resources. The East India Company maintained an army of some 64,000 that protected both its own and the Empire's interests in India, but costs were still incurred to deal with French naval threats. The British spent about 109 million pounds sterling on the American war, about 12.5 per cent of national income. This amazing expenditure doubled the national debt. As a proportion of the national income, the American War for Independence cost the British more than either the Seven Years' War or the French Revolutionary and Napoleonic wars.

Serious questions were raised in Britain about the Empire and Britain's wasteful policy in America. While the vast majority in Parliament supported the war, as did most of the engaged public, there were high profile opponents who contradicted the views of the King and the imperial hawks. Isaac Barré, the MP who had served in America during the Seven Years' War and who consistently opposed British taxation policies, was a friend of America. His support was acknowledged with the suitable renaming of Hutchinson, Massachusetts in 1776 as Barre, Massachusetts. Wilkes-Barre, in Pennsylvania, joined Barré's name with that of John Wilkes, who was perhaps the most conspicuous radical in England during the era of the Revolution, a champion of free speech and an opponent of royal prerogatives. Thomas Pownall (1722-1805) had spent a great deal of time in colonial America in a variety of capacities before returning to England, including a brief stint as Governor of Massachusetts during the Seven Years' War. Pownall was ahead of his time in advising the Crown that the colonies needed a separate status within the Empire, and wrote an impressive study on the issue in 1764, *The Administration of the Colonies*. He saw a federated Empire with specific authority residing in each part of it. He opposed the war as a waste of the Empire's resources and persisted in his case for giving the colonies more autonomy in order to keep them. Another voice in the wilderness was that of Josiah Tucker (1712-99), a Welsh-born clergyman and economist and a proponent of an imperial free market economy in which colonial interests were freed from Board of Trade control. Tucker balanced Parliament's political authority within the Empire with colonial economic rights based on the colonies' contribution to the Empire's prosperity.

Richard Price (1723-91), a prominent pro-American Welsh clergyman and philosopher, not only supported the American position on legislative, civil, and natural rights but later spoke in favor of the French Revolution, drawing the wrath of Edmund Burke who also attacked Thomas Paine on the same matter. Despite their differences, Price and Burke each saw the folly of Parliament's American policies and the utter futility of the war. While their letters of protest, treatises, and speeches were nugatory, they are worth noting for their predictions and for the evidence of serious, if minority opposition in Britain. In the prescient views of Pownall and Tucker, one can see another consequence of the Revolution that was shaped in the decades after independence: the development of a functionally autonomous set of colonies in Canada and the future maritime provinces that would lead to the Dominion of Canada in 1867. In the immediate aftermath of independence, the Revolution influenced the future shape of the British Empire. The loyalists, natives, and various French and British settlers in the remaining British territory in North America fought a version of their own war of independence against the American expansionists of 1812. One of the important consequences of the Revolutionary War was that, as it ended satisfactorily for the patriot rebels, it also laid the foundations for the creation of the Canadian nation state. In 1776, however, neither the British politicians nor the military command could see past immediate aims. A long war lay ahead for the antagonists.

The Campaigns of 1776

In the summer of 1776, after abandoning Boston and most of New England, British strategy called for the occupation of New York City. By August, General Sir William Howe had under his command 32,000 troops. With 150 transport vessels, he landed 20,000 men on Long Island, demonstrating what Britain could do with competent organization tied to superb resources. The British then proceeded to pound a smaller American force of about 5,000 at Brooklyn Heights, took General Sullivan prisoner, and chased the Continental Army forces into Manhattan. Some Americans were forced to surrender to German units under Howe as the British prepared to attack Manhattan. The Battle of Long Island was a disaster for the American cause, but it did not break Congress's will. The King had earlier appointed General Howe and his brother, Admiral Sir Richard Howe as "peace commissioners," and, with the Long Island victory in mind, the brothers convened an informal "peace conference" on Staten Island. Benjamin Franklin, John Adams, and Edward Rutledge of South Carolina were appointed by Congress and, after a cordial exchange, rejected both the British offer of amnesty for recanting Americans and a demand for a revocation of the Declaration. The British delegation had no authority to deal with any state or with Congress, and the desultory meeting spelled the end of any hope for a personalized diplomatic end to the conflict. The Staten Island demands by the Howe brothers followed the fixed position of the Crown and the lingering assumptions of the 1766 Declaratory Act, which had long ago become irrelevant.

The war continued, and, in the fall of 1776, it went in favor of the British. General Howe's superior numbers and tactical imagination disrupted American movement in the vicinity of Manhattan and led to the abandonment of New York City after a series of encounters between late September and November. A fire destroyed hundreds of buildings in the city, and the fate of thousands of Continental Army personnel remained in the balance while they resisted British assaults at Harlem. Eventually, nearly 3,000 American prisoners were taken at the flimsy and poorly managed Fort Washington at the northern end of the island. British General Cornwallis pried Nathanael Greene from Fort Lee, New Jersey. Greene then joined Washington to run across New Jersey while Cornwallis chased them. The loss of the prisoners and the

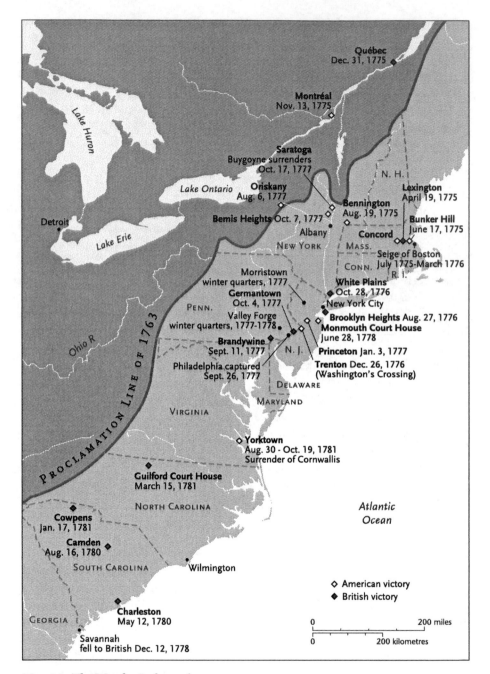

Map 4.1 The War for Independence

deaths and injuries to several hundred more men were bad enough, but the British had demonstrated their military abilities, and Washington's army was stunned and demoralized. During the battles in and around New York City, Nathan Hale, a Continental Army officer, was caught behind British lines in civilian clothes and executed without trial. His gallows statement, "I only regret that I have one life to lose for my country" would find its way into patriotic propaganda during the war and become one of the Revolution's great slogans. While he amplified the patriotic temperament of Washington's officers, he died at a moment of desperation for the American cause.

Meanwhile, to the north, at Valcour Bay on Lake Champlain, General Carleton's British fleet destroyed Benedict Arnold's American flotilla. Carleton then removed to Canada, leaving Crown Point and Ticonderoga to the Americans, who nevertheless were now quite vulnerable along the northern frontier. American prospects continued to decline. The major part of the Continental Army made its miserable way across New Jersey as winter approached. Hunger, cold, and depression accompanied them. The combination of disorder and cold compounded the losses on Long Island and in New York City by making hundreds of the survivors sick and useless. The normally phlegmatic Washington admitted privately that his troops had not behaved well, having been scattered and outfought by the British and Hessians. This was when Paine published his memorable "These are the times that try men's souls. The sunshine soldier and the sunshine patriot will, in this crisis, shrink from the service of their country; but he that stands it *now*, deserves the love and thanks of man and woman." Paine's "The American Crisis" was a timely call to arms but fell mostly on deaf ears. At the end of 1776, Washington worried that, if Congress could not raise a better, larger army in 1777, "the game will be pretty well up," as he put it in a famous private correspondence. Yet, as the drafts sputtered along, Washington found the permanent heart of the Continental Army that would be sustained over the next year or so by the hardiness of a committed core of officers and men, and then he got an unexpected reprieve. Howe decided to rest his army, and sent the bulk of it back to New York to winter quarters. He shunned the possibility of destroying the Continental Army in the middle Atlantic region. Howe may have thought that the American force was going to disintegrate, or that his plundering, rapacious troops would do harm to the British cause, or simply that his army needed rest and that there was no profit in stretching his supply lines into Pennsylvania.

Washington's Crossing of the Delaware

As Howe mused on the damage he had caused the Americans, an anxious Congress moved from Philadelphia to Baltimore and gave Washington a renewed authority to operate at will. Just before the year ended, the American army scored a great victory at Trenton. The spectacular success there did not end fears of an American collapse, but it certainly brightened the prospects for a reversal of the army's misfortunes. The attack on Trenton, New Jersey by Washington's army from the Pennsylvania side of the river is one of the war's most dramatic and tactically impressive events. Washington took

2,400 men across the Delaware River nine miles north of Trenton, on the evening of a bitter cold Christmas with ice crusting the water. He launched a two-pronged attack on a surprised Hessian garrison at Trenton and, in a sharp and vicious fight, routed them. The number of casualties was small given the hard house-to-house combat, but the Americans captured over 900 Hessians to parade later through the streets of Philadelphia. Washington's success attests to his tactical acumen and to the work of his spies who noted the casual demeanor of the garrison at Trenton. It also reflected desperation; he needed a victory of some kind to prevent the calamity that seemed to await the cause after the Long Island and New York to New Jersey debacles. Trenton was a wake-up call to American civilians and British military planners alike. The skeletal, dispirited army that Howe had earlier embarrassed recovered itself sufficiently to embarrass him.

The attack on Trenton has come down to most Americans subsumed in the image of "Washington's crossing." The valuable morale boost it gave to the patriot cause and the scare it gave General Howe are often obscured by the sentimental value of the crossing. As the pictorial celebration of the Revolution boomed after independence, it celebrated one image in particular, George Washington. Charles Peale painted about 60 portraits of Washington during and after the war, including seven "from life." John Trumbull's idealized reconstruction of the signing of the Declaration and his representations of the Hessian surrender at Trenton and Lord Cornwallis's surrender at Yorktown in 1781 are visual images stitched into the meaning of the Revolution for Americans. We are familiar with Copley's portrait of the relaxed and casually attired Paul Revere or Benjamin Franklin in a fur cap, and text books and montages show an array of celebratory images of the American struggle for independence, but the whole can be summarized in the great 1851 painting by Emmanuel Leutze, *Washington Crossing the Delaware*.

This massive painting, twelve by twenty feet, is a marvel of compression. Leutze managed in this image to portray the history of the war to that point. The poses are heroic, and not the least of the heroes is Washington himself standing tall and confident as he surveys the Jersey shore. Next to him is another future president, Lieutenant James Monroe, holding up a flag that did not exist in the winter of 1776, the stars and stripes. If any flag were present in the boat, it would have been Washington's command flag. The river is choked with ice, and the occupants comprise a sample of the valorous Americans who stormed Trenton that night: a Scot perhaps, some Gloucester fishermen, a wounded man, and some huddled but focused riflemen. There appears to be a woman in male winter garb, a note, perhaps, on the small but significant number of women who did disguise themselves as men in order to take part in combat. In the painting's distance are other boats all being rowed and steered by enthusiastic crews. The artist depicted the scene in daylight, even though the crossing took place in the dark. It is altogether a scene of lavish imagery. Imitations and then reproductions of this painting would find their way into countless homes in the United States in the nineteenth century. If there is a single image of the war that satisfies the national imagination, it is that one. But images notwithstanding, the victory at Trenton was a timely corrective to collapsing morale. Washington was able to address his ailing army and persuade many whose time was up at the end of the year to re-enlist. Two thousand Pennsylvania militiamen, seeing that the war had come to their state, arrived to boost his force's numbers. The army that had looked like it was disintegrating was still together. The sick, wounded, and uncommitted did leave, but about three quarters of Washington's army remained.

Burgoyne's Disaster

After the Delaware crossing, in early January 1777, the British attempted to engage Washington's main army of about 5,000 near Trenton. Washington outmaneuvered them, drove Lord Cornwallis back, and cleared the British Army from most of New Jersey. These successes reversed the disasters of late 1776 and seriously hampered British efforts to pacify New Jersey. The loyalists in the province were quieted, and, while Howe had not yet given up the goal of reinstalling royal government in the New Jersey-New York-Pennsylvania region, the odds were being stretched against him. On another level, the campaigns in New York and New Jersey had clarified an internal problem that had bothered Washington since his appointment in 1775. Charles Lee, the egotistical ex-British Army officer who had been appointed to the rank of major general in the Continental Army in the summer of 1775, was captured by the British during the New Jersey campaign. He was about to be prosecuted as a traitor when it was discovered that he had resigned from the British Army before the war. He was eventually released in 1778 and returned to the Americans, but his erratic behavior and the lingering suspicion that he was a double-dealer limited his career. Lee had created problems for Washington even before his capture and release. As a senior field commander, he had influence in Congress and had intrigued to challenge Washington's intention to make the Continental Army the Congress's main military arm. Lee was convinced that the war effort should revolve around a well-funded and better-equipped set of state militias. He opposed the concentration of resources in the Continental Army and envisioned a sustained series of small wars ending in a complete fragmentation of British military operations. The issue is an important one in that the charismatic and flamboyant Lee, the opposite in personality to Washington, had a valid point, in some measure. There was no way the British Army, even at its most effective, could triumph permanently over hundreds of militia units. On the other hand, the British could never be brought together to suffer a decisive loss. What Lee represented was an alternative military strategy that had huge political ramifications. His capture in late 1776 took him out of the decision-making process and left Washington's Continental agenda as the Congress's central policy. As 1776 rolled into 1777, the elimination of the Charles Lee option made Washington's centralized military strategy the only option for Congress.

In the spring of 1777, Congress made direct appeals to foreign nations for recognition and material aid. Envoys and commissioners were sent to Europe. The older Committee for Secret Correspondence was replaced with the more formal sounding

Committee for Foreign Affairs. American emissaries were soon stationed in Savoy, Tuscany, Vienna, and Berlin, in addition to the major French and Spanish commissions. Foreign officers were sought out by Congress to boost military efficiency. The program encouraged a young French aristocrat, the Marquis de Lafayette, to volunteer his services. He was made a major general in the summer of 1777. Neither he nor the Congress saw any anomaly in a hereditary aristocrat leading commoners against British aristocrats. Other European officers such as Thaddeus Kosciuszko, Johann de Kalb, Baron Von Steuben, and even the less successful Count Casimir Pulaski added depth and professionalism to the cause. By June of 1777, Congress had authorized a flag, an important representation of collective identity and a further politicization of the war. Language, action, and visual imagery were being bundled together, and the Continental Army was becoming an agency of political education. Wherever it went it installed its authority. In New Jersey, for example, and later in parts of the south, as it wrested control from the British Army, it was advertising the failed regime of George III and excoriating his agents and supporters in America. There could be no serious British political control in America except that which was maintained by military force in a few areas. As for civilian loyalist control, it too often was tenuous and subject to collapse as patriot militia or the Continental Army appeared. It is no conceit to say that the war began as an American defense of British liberties but, as it went on, began to broadcast a different political message and drew international attention. While the Continental Army continued to serve as a formal, regulated, and effective force and the militias continued to suppress loyalist (Tory) activity at the local level, the French remained neutral but favorable to the American cause. There was a growing cohesion to the American cause that emanated from a committed Congress.

With that in mind, Lord Germain approved a plan of coordinated operations that would isolate New England, occupy Philadelphia, consolidate British-loyalist control of New York, and step up the blockade of other ports. This plan, it was felt, would scatter Congress and its army, control major centers of politics and finance, and, most important, choke off New England's supply of men and materials to the war. The shutting down of the Massachusetts war effort alone would be a very serious blow to the American cause. Massachusetts supplied troops to the Continental Army at a rate double the average of the combined states. A cordon around New England would mean the end of Boston as a port of entry and generator of political propaganda. The British plan was ambitious and costly, but it further demonstrated the will of the King and the continued blind spot in the British view. Opposition to the war had begun to increase in Parliament, and many ministers were wary of the war's direction. The opposition spread as costs mounted and American resistance looked more durable. Could America be recovered, in part or in whole? The chief architect of the 1777 plan, Sir John Burgoyne, thought the latter, and was confident in the plan that called for his own army to move south from Canada to link up with another, smaller force from the west, from Oswego. With a force moving north from New York under General Howe, an effective blockade, a cord would be looped around New England. The scheme required up to 20,000 troops and mountains of materiel. It would involve long distances with the immense logistical impediments of uneven and heavily forested terrain that would force the army to carry enough food and armaments to do the job, which, it was thought, could be finished by the autumn. In June, Burgoyne left St. Jean with a force that included more than 7,000 regulars, including over 3,000 Hessians, a few hundred Canadians and loyalists, about 400 natives, and, according to one account, an additional 2,000 women. Burgoyne's personal baggage train consisted of thirty carts filled with tents, tables, dinnerware and dinner service, clothes, liquor, special foodstuffs, and servants. He would add a mistress to his personal entourage, en route.

Meanwhile, Howe received Germain's permission to move on Philadelphia. That led to an elaborate strategy wherein Howe split his Army, leaving 2,400 troops at Newport, Rhode Island and 4,700 regulars and 3,000 loyalist militia at New York. For a variety of reasons, mostly to avoid American resistance, Howe took an 11,000-strong army that included Hessians by sea from New York to the head of Chesapeake Bay, 50 miles from Philadelphia. Bad weather delayed the assault force, but, by September, Howe was in a position to tie up Washington's army and limit American abilities in the north as Burgoyne made his way south. The optimism was short lived; eventually, 17,000 Continentals and militia trapped and shattered Burgoyne's army in and around Saratoga, New York in a sensational upset that convinced the French that Britain could not suppress the rebellion. However, Howe managed to defeat Washington at Brandywine Creek and then again at Germantown, Pennsylvania. Those losses ominously echoed the 1776 Long Island and New York disasters, but Nathanael Greene led an effective retreat that limited their impact. The American army had not been destroyed, and Greene would go on to demonstrate, especially in the south, that, in this war, one could lose battle after battle and still succeed in wearing down the enemy. Still, Philadelphia was now in British hands, and Congress had relocated first to Lancaster and then to York, Pennsylvania. Washington's army was now a morose and scruffy ensemble that made its way into winter quarters at Valley Forge. Howe should have rejoiced at beating Washington again, but there was a question of its value. The largest city in America was now under British control, but the American army was still alive and in the vicinity. Burgoyne's loss in the north meant that another British strategy would have to be devised. It is easy to imagine the stress that the British field commanders felt over their repeated failure to comprehensively defeat what they saw as little more than an armed rabble. As winter approached, Washington's biggest job would be to hold the Continental Army together. The hibernation at Valley Forge tested that resolve. Strategically, the winter site lay between the British in Philadelphia and the Congress at York, and, although Howe's army in the city was only 20 miles away, he had no intention of attacking the Americans. He was emotionally and functionally easing himself out of the war because of the failure of the overall 1777 campaign. His victories in Pennsylvania meant little to him because of the Burgoyne fiasco. He moped in Philadelphia with his mistress and offered his formal resignation. He was replaced by Sir Henry Clinton in the spring of 1778.

Valley Forge

The American army that settled in at Valley Forge in December 1777 was ill clothed, hungry, weak, and vulnerable to exposure, depression, and infectious disease. But the winter of Valley Forge was important to the course of the war. It survives as one of the stock of legends that go with the Revolution. As the story goes, the hardships endured there revealed the tenacity of the Continental Army rank and file, and the army that emerged in the spring of 1778 was better than it had been in December, but not before the 10,000 complement had been reduced by about 2,500 deaths. The incompetence of the American supply system meant that the men at Valley Forge were undernourished and cold. Epidemics of influenza and other infections ("camp fevers," especially typhus) carried away hundreds of soldiers, as did the regular outbreaks of dysentery and cholera. There was some desertion but not as much as one might expect. At any time, hundreds of men were too weak to leave their huts. The shelters were constructed from the abundance of wood in the area, a source too of plentiful firewood and one of the reasons for the army's survival. Despite the hardships, the winter pause at Valley Forge produced two changes in military administration that had positive effects on the future of the American independence movement. The failure of the supply system prompted the dismissal of the Quartermaster General of the Army. His replacement was Nathanael Greene, who took the position on condition that he could remain a combat soldier. The graft and profiteering and the outright lack of expertise that had plagued the supplying of the American army began to diminish under Greene. In February 1778, an equally important event during the Valley Forge winter was the appointment of a former Prussian officer, Friedrich Wilhelm Augustus von Steuben.

Steuben was born into a military family and had known little outside military life. When he arrived in America, from France, he was carrying inflated credentials. He was not a serving officer and had never achieved the rank ascribed to him. Nevertheless, his contribution to the army at Valley Forge and thereafter was crucial in the recovery of American military fortunes. He devised a set of accessible drill programs that began with small groups who passed on the drills to other groups. By regularizing inspections and other formalities, Steuben helped pull the army out of its Valley Forge torpor and left instructions that stayed with the army to the end of the war. Steuben's drills were no doubt effective in the latter days of the war, but the immediate effect in the late winter and spring of 1778 was the arousal of a sense of purpose in the army. He was most certainly a character. His elaborate and colorful uniform stood in contrast to the shabby clothing of the troops he addressed and ordered about. He spoke only the English he picked up in camp, and a bit of French. His conflation of those with his native Prussian kept his translators amused. The men he trained, using subordinates, were not a rabble to begin with and were not a smoothly functioning military machine when they left Valley Forge in June of 1778, but they constituted a more efficient fighting force because of the friendly discipline that Steuben instilled. He had come to Washington as an unpaid volunteer, but his contributions were tangible enough that

Congress later appointed him Inspector General. He served with the army in the field thereafter and became a citizen of Pennsylvania in 1783 under its constitution. He retired to New York and became a citizen of that state in 1786. He was a friend of Alexander Hamilton (1755-1804), who, as Washington's *aide de camp*, had encouraged Steuben's appointment at Valley Forge. Hamilton helped get him established after the war. Stueben's place in the index of revolutionary military figures is secured, and Washington's imprimatur remains the most reliable comment on the value of his contributions.

In June 1778, Clinton decided to abandon Philadelphia and take Howe's old army to New York to defend against a rumored French naval attack. Washington left Valley Forge and caught up with Clinton's army. After some initial setbacks, in intense early summer heat at the battle of Monmouth, New Jersey, he defeated Clinton's force and sent it hurrying to New York City. At Monmouth, Washington's old rival Charles Lee, who had been released from British captivity, disobeyed orders and was court-martialed out of the army. He did not trouble Washington again. The young French officer, Lafayette, introduced himself to the Americans at Monmouth and would remain a great favorite. Washington pursued Clinton's army and took up a position at White Plains north of New York City. As Clinton's hasty retreat to New York showed, the French alliance had begun to influence British military strategy. Nevertheless, the first formal application of French force in America was a failure. In August of 1778, a French fleet planned a seaborne attack on the strategically important British garrison at Newport, Rhode Island while an American army under John Sullivan approached from the land side. A storm drove the French fleet away, and Sullivan withdrew after his attack faltered.

As a Franco-American alliance appeared likely after Saratoga, Lord North began to think of ways around the increasingly difficult military situation. In February, he presented a series of bills to the House of Commons, which passed them in March. These bills in sum suggested rescinding the Coercive Acts and proposed the wholesale repeals of many others. It was a dramatic and desperate gambit. One of the bills authorized a commission to negotiate the end of hostilities and the suspension of the Continental Congress. The Earl of Carlisle gave his name to the commission, and it petitioned Congress to debate Parliament's proposals. It was rejected outright. In fact, the Congress announced that it would only meet with the Carlisle Commission if the British Army was removed from all thirteen states and if Parliament recognized the independence of those states. The states had begun to identify their own terms, and reconciliation was definitely not in the cards. The commission tried to bribe some delegates to Congress and then, in a formal message, appealed directly to the people with a saber-rattling warning of an all out war of even greater magnitude than the current one. After seven months in America, in an obvious perfunctory role, the Carlisle Commission returned to England. It was doomed from the start because, by 1778, the situation had passed any point of reconciliation.

The Widening of the War

The Atlantic was the lifeline for both sides in the war. For the British, the sea lanes kept troops and materials moving between Britain and the West Indies, Nova Scotia and the open ports on the mainland of North America. For Congress, the shipping of weapons and clothing from Europe had to be secure, and, in the other direction, whatever goods, such as timber and tobacco, that could raise revenue in Europe had to be safeguarded. On the American side, until the formal French alliance and the later Spanish treaty, large-scale naval operations were not possible. Strictly speaking, the Continental Congress's Naval (Marine) Committee of 1775 never produced a substantial navy, but the authorizing of "privateers" acting in their own interests and against British shipping proved to be a useful contribution to the American war effort. The formal part of Congress's naval effort put more than 50 ships into service during the war, and state navies, operating in a similar way to state militias, commissioned about 40 more. One estimate has these warships capturing or disabling about 200 Royal Navy ships, mostly in single encounters. By one estimate, over a period of about six years, more than 1,000 American privateers with experienced and aggressive crews were commissioned, and, given the instant rewards of looting British merchant vessels, they captured some 600 British merchant ships of all types, about three times the number claimed by the Continental Navy. The latter was reduced to only a few effective warships by the end of the war with the French clearly taking up the slack. On balance, however, the British blockade was not seriously weakened, and British supply lines were not significantly impaired. The biggest transportation dilemma faced by Britain was coordinating strategy in London with conditions in America and thence to the supply administration in London. Under awkward organizational conditions, the administration had to provide the materials, men, horses, and instructions for application in campaigns such as Gage's in 1775, Howe's and Burgoyne's in 1776 and 1777, and Clinton's thereafter.

The war at sea was not a major issue until the French navy created problems for the British along the coast of North America, and in the West Indies especially, threatening British interests to the extent that vital British resources were diverted to that theater. The cost of the war ballooned. The splendid work of Admiral Sir George Rodney helped keep the British Caribbean safe, mostly, from French and later Spanish and Dutch activity. While there was no internal threat to the Empire in the West Indies, the war there should not be seen as a sideshow but as an intense and complex consequence of the European alliances with the Americans. It absorbed British manpower and naval resources through the entire conflict and especially during the last three years of the land war in North America. The naval conflict also produced at least one American hero, John Paul Jones (1747-92), the Scottish immigrant whose audacity in 1777 and 1778 took him on raids on the northwest coast of England and the coasts of western Scotland and Northern Ireland, where, although he did only minor material damage, he managed to convince some Britons of America's abilities and purpose. Jones, who was born John Paul but added the Jones as an alias to avoid a possible criminal charge, demonstrated his full potential in an encounter in 1779 with British warships. His skill and fortitude memorialized his own phrase "I have not yet begun to fight" when he was requested by the British to surrender. He was the war's only naval celebrity and was the sole Continental sailor to be awarded a gold medal.

As important as were naval operations, the war was decided on the ground in the rebelling colonies and in the frontier zone that ran from northern New York south to the Georgia backcountry. It even crossed the Appalachians and reached in a small way to the Mississippi. If the battles in the main theater of the war involved a few to several thousand men, the frontier battles and skirmishes counted their participants in the few hundreds and often less. The frontier war drew native populations directly into the conflict. When the war was over, native allies of the Crown confronted not only unrestrained white American migration but also deep American prejudices that linked natives to British reactionary politics and also condemned the alleged savagery of native warriors. The British, and in many cases organized loyalist units, were also charged with barbaric behavior on the frontier. Burgoyne had already blundered in that regard by apparently allowing his native allies to murder civilians, and Joseph Brant (born as Thayendanegea), a Mohawk veteran of the Seven Years' War, was alleged to have allowed his native troops to commit atrocities when he fought under St. Leger during the Burgoyne campaign. Here the record is not very clear, and Brant was lauded as a hero in exile after the war and had a town in Upper Canada named for him (Brantford, Ontario) where his statue strikes a graceful and heroic pose.

Allegations of atrocities went both ways. When the war was finally taken to the south in 1779 and 1780, accusations of terrorism and cruelty were made against patriot militia units. Earlier, the royal marauder Sir John Butler and his loyalists and natives, who were much feared on the northern New York-Pennsylvania frontier, wrought havoc on civilians and militiamen alike at the so-called Wyoming Valley massacre in July and the Cherry Valley massacre in November of 1778. Joseph Brant is alleged to have demanded the turning over of prisoners from the loyalist raider Butler so that his men could torture them. Again the words "indian" and "savage" were used interchangeably and remained synonymous for generations. It mattered not that many natives had supported and died for the revolutionary cause or that natives had been terrorized by Americans encroaching on disputed territory. In one of the war's most violent reprisals, George Rogers Clark of Kentucky led an expedition in the summer of 1778 against one of the most hated British officers in America, Colonel Henry Hamilton of Detroit. After a campaign that took him almost to the Mississippi, Clark managed to capture Hamilton and scatter his native associates. A year later, an American force broke up a combined loyalist-native army, again involving Joseph Brant, in the New York-Pennsylvania frontier region. It then turned toward Fort Niagara and terrorized Seneca and Cayuga towns along the way, destroying the natives' food supplies. The Americans stopped short of the Niagara frontier but had permanently weakened the Iroquois in the region. The residue of these affairs would linger, but, for the remainder of the war, the violence on the northern frontier would be amplified on the southern frontier after the British decided in the winter of 1778-79 to shift their priorities. The threat of Spanish entry into the war and their presence to the south and west of Georgia certainly influenced that decision, but so too did the prospect of support from southern and backcountry loyalists.

The War in the South

By the winter of 1778-79, the British were holding on to some strategic locations in America but had not yet settled anything. From Gage's failure in New England in 1775-76 to the Burgoyne disaster and the uncertain conditions in Pennsylvania and New Jersey, the successive large-scale military plans, mostly predicated on the principle of divide and conquer, had been foiled. The Continental Army was still in the field. States were moving to write their own constitutions. The French had vowed to help achieve American independence, but the efforts of the Carlisle Commission and British military persistence indicated that there was an expectation that America could be recovered in some form or another. There was no risk of insurrection in Canada, Nova Scotia, or the West Indies, and, late in 1778, General Clinton decided that all or parts of the south could be detached from Congressional control and restored to full British authority. By the time Spain formally entered the war on the American side in 1779, British resources were being severely stretched, and more opposition to the Germain and Clinton policies was showing up in Parliament and among increasingly overtaxed Britons. In spite of that, there were in 1779 and 1780 some very hopeful signs that a southern strategy would work.

Savannah, Georgia had fallen to an amphibious force of 3,500 British troops just before the end of 1778. By the beginning of summer 1779, British and loyalist forces had control of most of populated Georgia, and, despite setbacks when Washington sent in some Continental regiments, the British managed to secure enough of Georgia to establish a loyal government; it was the only one of the thirteen states that the British could count on as being recovered or restored. By most measurement criteria, 1779 was the most successful year for the British military in the entire war. But the tenacity and survival of the American army limited the effects of British triumphs. A confident Congress in early 1779 established a "peace committee" to negotiate conditions for ending the war. These included recognition of American independence and the settling of boundaries, the removal of all British troops and personnel from the territory, and navigation access to the Mississippi. Later that year, John Adams was appointed as peace commissioner in Paris and was joined by Thomas Jefferson, Benjamin Franklin, John Jay, and Henry Laurens in 1781. The commission's mandate was changed to simply having American independence and sovereignty recognized. It left the rest of the peace details to the discretion of the commissioners. At the same time, Russia refused to recognize the British blockade policy in Europe, and, while staying neutral, it began to use warships to protect its merchant fleets. In 1780, Britain declared war on Holland hoping to curtail Dutch West Indies trade with the American states. Beginning in September 1780, Russian and Austrian proposals for a negotiated peace were circulated through the courts of Europe. The War for Independence had expanded far beyond its origins and was eating away at British stamina.

As Britain became increasingly isolated in a hostile international environment, it pressed on in America with efforts to leverage a military advantage. Commander in Chief Henry Clinton decided in the summer of 1779 to leave New York and wage war in the Hudson Valley, hoping to prevent the building there of permanent American forts, and also to campaign along the northern shoreline of Long Island Sound and ease into New England. Some Connecticut towns were burned and local populations were frightened, but nothing of value accrued to the British. Clinton was appalled at the excesses of the British raiders and noted the public's outcry against the British barbarism of waging war on civilians. While the British were engaged in these ultimately wasteful diversions, Major Henry "Light Horse Harry" Lee (1756-1818), a dashing symbol of Continental Army bravura, managed to clear the last of the British garrisons from New Jersey. By the time Clinton resumed his New York headquarters, there was not much left of British military ambition north of Virginia, except for the garrison at Newport, Rhode Island. The promise of success in the south, however, beckoned Clinton. He soon applied most of his resources there in what would turn out to be the last attempt to salvage some of the American Empire. It began well. A joint Franco-American attempt to recapture Savannah failed in the fall of 1779 with heavy losses. British optimism was boosted further in May 1780 when Charleston, South Carolina fell to Clinton's large army of nearly 15,000. Clinton had now abandoned Rhode Island in order to transfer resources to the South Carolina campaign. For Washington and the Congress, the grave mood over losing Charleston was magnified when it was learned that Clinton had captured over 5,000 Americans. By any measurement, the triumph at Charleston was, after five years of war, Britain's greatest military success. Clinton deluded himself into thinking that South Carolina could join Georgia as a liberated state, but the war continued with increased bitterness. Even after the calamity of Charleston and the loss of what would be a medium-sized American army, there was no sign of Congress or the Continental Army abandoning South Carolina to the British. Again, the British could win a battle — in this case two, if one includes the defense of Savannah — and seem to be no further ahead in their recovery strategy. So long as the Continental Army remained in the south, the British Army was faced with a dilemma. When it was forced to deal with regular American troops in formal confrontations, it was obliged to use troops that otherwise might have controlled the countryside. Patriot militia began to enter the picture in the south in very impressive ways.

The hoped for upsurge in loyalist military support did not materialize on the scale needed by the British, and the new commander in the south, Lord Cornwallis, suffered the consequences. At the same time, a savage civil war erupted in the area from the Virginia Piedmont to the Georgia boundary and into the eastern slopes of the southern Appalachians. Old political, class, and religious antagonisms that went back into the colonial period erupted in the guise of patriot or loyalist support. In some cases, minor family feuds or residential and settlement antagonisms sparked murderous behavior under the rubric of war. The militia war in the south became one of intimidation, revenge, and cruelty. While the British Army, the organized militias, and the Continental Army moved around the south in 1780 and 1781, feeling each other out, striking at each other, and generally conducting low intensity conventional war, the hundreds of independent militia units, identifying themselves either with the King or with Congress struggled with each other. One explanation for this civil war was that the British presented a brake on local authority that, in places like the Carolinas and Virginia, was historically in the hands of local oligarchs. But the British were often slow to enlist loyalist militia to their operations because they did not trust them to stay loyal or to otherwise fulfill their obligations. The most loyal Americans, in the eyes of the British, were the thousands who enlisted in the many loyalist provincial regiments over the course of the war.

The early signs of British success in the re-conquest of Georgia and the apparent control of South Carolina continued into 1780. In August at Camden, South Carolina, Washington's southern Continentals suffered a massive defeat at the hands of Cornwallis. The attempt to capture a British supply base there turned into a disaster, and many of the under-equipped and unprepared American Continentals and militia were shocked by the resiliency of the British and the devastating impact of Colonel Banastre Tarleton's British dragoons. One estimate indicates 800 to 900 deaths at Camden, a much higher than normal battlefield count. Another 1,000 Americans were captured. The only setback suffered by the British at this time was at King's Mountain where a loyalist force of 1,200 was routed by a similar sized force of mostly backcountry militia riflemen whose marksmanship and combat prowess was on full display. Still, the war was not going well for Congress. There were problems with the Continental Army in Pennsylvania. In conditions that were worse than those at Valley Forge, Washington's wintering army of 1779-80 survived in rags and with paltry food rations. Some Connecticut troops threatened mutiny in the spring, demanding food and back pay. In fact, a full-blown mutiny did occur later among Pennsylvanian troops in the Continental Army in January 1781. It was ended by Washington's personal intervention. These incidents were the result of graft and incompetence, despite earlier reforms to the requisition and supply system, and provisioning the troops was exacerbated by the collapsing value of the Continental currency. While the army held together, it did so in spite of civilian corruption and indifference. Some historians have noted that, in the crucial period of the southern theater of war, much of the American population eased away from their earlier concerns, thinking that the war's end was imminent. Participation levels dropped as most of the north appeared free of the British. Even the French expressed alarm over the decline of local enthusiasm, as they began to pour men, ships, and materiel into America. Farms and families started to demand the return of soldiers for work. The war's casualty tolls reached into most communities as death, injury, and disappearance hit home. Returning troops, on leave or after their service, brought home negative reports of the conditions they faced, and the war began to lose some of its high purpose, even for the willing. Soldiers also brought infectious diseases home with them, and reports of epidemics in some localities underline some of the more unpleasant costs to a part-time army of civilians.

Yorktown

After the disaster at Camden, Gates was replaced by Nathanael Greene. The one-time presumptive rival to George Washington was now broken. Charles Lee's caustic remark to Gates after the latter's victory at Saratoga in 1777, "beware your Northern laurels do not change to Southern willows," now seemed brilliantly prophetic. Greene was certainly a more competent commander than Gates, but he was also less concerned with personal status than with the execution of his office and the preparation and security of his troops. In the summer of 1781, Greene exercised his great talent of gaining in strength and strategic advantage even while appearing to be losing. With General Daniel Morgan and "Light Horse Harry" Lee conducting a mixture of guerrilla and conventional maneuvers, the Americans won a sharp battle at Cowpens. Cornwallis then moved into North Carolina and all the way to the Virginia border where he stopped and returned south. Greene was then reinforced. With an army of 4,500, he took on Cornwallis in a conventional battle and lost, although he inflicted enough damage to the British that Cornwallis decided to withdraw and await seaborne reinforcements at Wilmington, North Carolina. Greene invaded South Carolina, and although he lost some small engagements, his supporting units, including Harry Lee's cavalry, began to clear the South Carolina countryside of organized British and loyalist units. By the fall of 1781, Cornwallis's early triumphs had given way to frustration. His army controlled only the Charleston region of South Carolina. The British still held Georgia, but that was beginning to look like a consolation prize. Cornwallis decided to move into Virginia to attack Washington's and Greene's assembly points and storage facilities, thus starving the American army in the Carolinas. The British left Wilmington and marched unrestrained into Virginia where they were reinforced to about 7,500. These numbers were enough to terrorize Virginia. The enterprising Tarleton almost seized Governor Thomas Jefferson at Charlottesville. But the scattered American resources in Virginia were pulled together by Lafayette and Steuben, and these two foreign-born patriots and their veterans halted the Cornwallis campaign and drove him to the sea at Yorktown at the mouth of Chesapeake Bay. The fate of Cornwallis was to be the fate of the British Empire in the thirteen states.

Earlier in the summer of 1780, the French had landed 5,000 men at Newport, Rhode Island. Washington had planned to use his army and the French under the Comte de Rochambeau to attack New York, which, along with Charleston, was the last serious British-controlled major center in America. The plan failed because Newport had been blockaded by the British soon after Rochambeau's arrival. The French general did manage to meet Washington in Connecticut in May 1781. The difficulties of an attack on New York were obvious, so, with the assurances of support from the French naval commander de Grasse for a campaign in the Chesapeake, the Franco-American combined force feigned a move on New York City and then headed south into Virginia. In August, de Grasse's fleet and 3,000 French troops arrived off Yorktown, and, after a brief encounter with a smaller British fleet, began a blockade. When the British ships took off for New York for repairs, the way was opened for de Grasse to sail up to the head of Chesapeake Bay, there to begin transporting the Washington-Rochambeau army to Yorktown. By the end of September, the combined Franco-American army was nearing 18,000 in number. It began pounding Yorktown with heavy siege artillery. The allied force was more than double the strength of the Yorktown defense, which was now hopelessly backed up to the sea without apparent relief. Cornwallis was foiled by weather from escaping across the York River, and his counterattacks failed. By the middle of October 1781, his army was surrounded and under heavy bombardment.

At the end of the month, Clinton started out for Yorktown with a fleet of transports and 7,000 reinforcements. He turned back to New York when he learned that Cornwallis had surrendered his entire army. The latter was one of the more competent British generals in the war, and a successful administrator later in India and Ireland, but his name will always be associated with the Yorktown climax to the war. On October 20th, he began a long letter to Clinton with a stark fact: "Sir, I have the mortification to inform your Excellency that I have been forced to give up the posts of York and Gloucester, and to surrender the troops under my command, by capitulation on the 19th inst. as prisoners of war to the combined forces of America and France." Washington's moment had arrived. The formal surrender of Cornwallis himself and the ritualistic laying down of arms by some 8,000 British soldiers was indeed a sign of "The World Turned Upside Down," the name of the popular tune played by the British bandsmen as they marched out as captives. The French stood aside in a gesture of respect and let the Americans accept Cornwallis's formal surrender. The British commander had wanted what he thought was a more respectable act of handing the terms over to the French. As was the case so often during the war, the British did not quite understand how they could lose to Americans. Washington was less impressed with formality than with the need to finish off the rest of the war. He wanted to attack New York immediately, but de Grasse had to get his fleet back to the West Indies and Rochambeau's army was left to winter in Virginia. Washington then took most of his army north to reinforce the armed cordon around New York City. There was an unmistakable finality in the sight of a potent imperial army being escorted to safety by an army that was still underpaid, underfed, and mostly poorly clothed. The men who chased Cornwallis to Yorktown were anything but neat in their appearance, and any images of American rank and file in crisp uniforms in this war need to be taken lightly. At Yorktown, the best uniforms were worn by the French.

The End of the War
While the war was being decided in the south during the 1779 to 1781 period, it had not gone away elsewhere. One of the least important of its outcomes was Benedict

Arnold's defection in September 1780, an event that had no direct influence on the military outcome but that made a great symbolic statement. Arnold's military expectations for advancement and status in the Continental Army had never been realized, and his peevish responses to apparent snubs had caused him to seek better terms with the British as early as 1779. There is no doubt that Arnold's ambitions and need for money had influenced his surreptitious behavior, and his personality was such that, after being passed over for promotion, he harbored a spiteful dislike for Washington. He had begun betraying his cause in 1779 by giving information to Sir Henry Clinton about Washington's movements. In 1780, he was given command of West Point, a key American fortress in upper New York. There he negotiated a payment for his services to the British and, through a liaison (Henry Clinton's adjutant Major John Andre), agreed to reveal the defense arrangements at West Point. Andre changed into civilian clothes on his way back to the British lines. He was captured by militiamen who found the evidence of the betrayal on him, and, according to the protocols of war that distinguished between military activity in uniform and out of it, he was hanged as a spy. Arnold fled and did service in the British Army at a senior level. His talents, which he had demonstrated on behalf of Congress earlier, were used by the British in the last years of the war in Connecticut and Virginia. His story is melodramatic, and its place in the history of the Revolution is overblown, but the treason became a signpost on the way to patriotic orthodoxy, and Arnold's name and deed became a byword for betrayal.

Before the showdown at Yorktown, the Continental Congress had begun to face up to its deplorable financial condition. One of the spurs to currency reform and budgeting was the ratification of the Articles of Confederation late in the winter of 1780-81. As noted, the Articles were a giant step forward for the states' collective management, administration, and governance in Congress. It had taken a year (1776-77) to agree on the Articles and nearly five years more to ratify them. The Articles were essentially a treaty or pact or "league" that promised a "perpetual union" but that emphatically confirmed each state's ultimate sovereignty. The confederacy the Articles created, called The United States of America, had no executive or independent taxing powers, so was rather a loose political confederation for the purposes of waging war and negotiating peace. Ratification of the Articles meant that the Continental Congress could operate by a code of agreed to rules and standards. In one very significant way, the Congress began to prepare for the future by establishing a department of finance. Its first superintendent was Robert Morris (1734-1806) of Pennsylvania.

The English-born Morris was a late convert to the revolutionary movement and did not fully commit to it until after 1775, when he became a delegate to the Continental Congress. Even then, he hesitated to sign the Declaration and was one of those who waited until August 1776 to do so. Thereafter, he was as important as any political figure in advancing the patriot cause. He was both a financier and a merchant, and his skills and contacts helped in getting material support for Congress. As superintendent of finances, he laid out a sensible program of fiscal reform that cut through the chaos of state and collective funding of the war. He organized loans from the Dutch and French governments and established a way of retiring debts incurred at various inflationary values of the money Congress had issued. The disparity between the battered American paper bills and concrete values, such as the British pound sterling or specie (gold and silver), was effectively reduced. Between 1775 and 1780, Congress had authorized 37 currency releases, which had driven inflation from a paper to specie exchange ratio of 1.5 to 1 to one of nearly 150 to 1. This inflation required the adjustment of the money in circulation to the real economic assets of the states, individually or in concert. He established a "national" system that helped regulate the circulation and exchange of promissory notes, bills of credit, and devalued "Continentals" (the currency circulated by Congress). He led the insolvent Congress to a deficit financing approach that was a manageable alternative to the looming utter chaos. Morris was a delegate to the Constitutional Convention of 1787. He supported strong centralized government after independence but declined to take the position of Secretary of the Treasury in Washington's first cabinet in 1789, a position that fell to Alexander Hamilton. The final note on Morris is an ironic one; this aggressive financial theorist and organizer lost his own fortune in land speculation, spent three years in debtors' prison, and died broke. Yet, he remains an important figure in the development of modern federal political economy. His preliminary policies of 1781 paved the way for the more orderly and effective fiscal policies developed later by the United States.

In the early months of 1782, the full impact of Britain's naval losses in the West Indies to the French and on land in Virginia to the Franco-American armies hit home. The last British commander in the war was Sir Guy Carleton who replaced Henry Clinton. He was charged with winding down British military operations. Support for Lord North's aggressive policies had been steadily declining, and the loss at Yorktown ended his lengthy ministry. The House of Commons voted against any further military activity in America, and Lord North was replaced as prime minister by the Marquess of Rockingham, who also had a long-running role in the American Revolution. He had been the minister responsible for the repeal of the Stamp Act in 1766 and would be front and center as the negotiations to end the war began. He died as the talks got underway and was succeeded by the Earl of Shelburne. The British moved with an alacrity that belied their often confused and contradictory war strategies. Yorktown seemed to stimulate action to end the conflict as quickly and as smoothly as possible. John Adams had secured Dutch recognition of American independence and a substantial loan to boot. There was a plethora of technical issues to deal with, but the combined talents of John Adams, Franklin, John Jay, and Henry Laurens made sure that the potential for French and Spanish demands on Congress would be minimal. The talks were complicated by the permutations involved in separate agreements between each of the belligerents. For example, Britain and France had issues to settle that were distinct from the American issues. The proposals set forth by the American delegation were largely the basis for the formal treaty that was eventually formalized. Franklin had earlier wanted to annex Canada but dropped what was more a provocation than a practical possibility. The "articles of peace" were signed on November 30, 1782 and went into effect on January 20, 1783. The chief provisions of the treaty were as follows:

- The independence of the thirteen states was to be recognized and respected by Britain.
- Borders were to be established at the 31st parallel north of Florida respecting Spain's acquisition of the Floridas. The Maine-Nova Scotia boundary was established and a line at the 45th parallel that ran west through the Great Lakes to Lake Superior. Most significant was the boundary line that was acknowledged in the middle of the Mississippi River that identified all the area east of Spanish Louisiana to the Atlantic as United States territory.
- Fishing rights were guaranteed to the United States in the waters off Newfoundland and Nova Scotia, as was the freedom to dry and cure fish on the coastlines of Nova Scotia, the Magdalene Islands, and Labrador.
- Debts owed by Britons to Americans, and vice versa, were to be honored.
- Loyalist political and property rights were to be restored by the Continental Congress.
- All fighting was to cease immediately, and all British Army and Navy personnel were to be removed "with all convenient speed."

The French Foreign Minister Vergennes was reported to have disapproved of British "generosity" in its concessions to the Americans, but, because he wanted a speedy resolution, he was persuaded, again by Franklin, to accept the terms. The Treaty was signed by the various delegates in September 1783, the date usually cited as the formal end of the war. It was ratified by Congress on January 14, 1784. The United States were independent.

Conclusion
American independence was achieved through war, and the war itself helped to define the Revolution. Heroes emerged, such as Washington, Greene, and Jones, whose actions and persistence came to identify American virtues and an image of the composite patriot. On the other side, villains would include Arnold, Burgoyne, the frontier natives, and the Hessians. More important, the composite loyalist was also a villain who came to vividly represent the antithesis of the noble cause. These images have endured. If the war was a triumph for the American people, whose commitment ranged from enthusiasm to indifference to opposition, it was a triumph guaranteed by a hard core of leaders and warriors, in Congress and in the military, from Washington to the common soldier. Diplomacy helped, as did the changeable and often inadequate British policies. At a certain point, perhaps as early as the Stamp Act, British political authority in the thirteen colonies had been jeopardized. But it was the war that created the United States, not the Stamp Act riots nor the Declaration of Independence. The British, it can be argued, not only started the war but shaped its direction. Their 1774-75

initiatives got away from them, and the humiliation at Yorktown surely was the very last thing on the mind of George III and his ministers when they committed Britain to suppressing the 1775 insurrection. Also, the human cost of the war could not have been foreseen.

The total number of Americans who died in the war is open to wide debate. Many estimates put the battle deaths at between 4,400 and 4,600, but the meticulous research of Howard Peckham in *The Toll of Independence: Engagements and Battle Casualties of the American Revolution* (Chicago: Chicago University Press, 1974) has come up with the following figures: In 1,331 military engagements on land and 215 at sea, Peckham records 6,824 battle deaths (p. 130). His other estimates include "Died in Camp" — 10,000 — and "Prisoners who died" — 8,500 — for an estimate of "Probable deaths in service" of 25,324. Where one might expect more precise figures for the British armed forces, the data are scattered and difficult to estimate but are probably similar to the numbers of American deaths. It is likely that there were about 25,000 British deaths including regular British troops and sailors, Germans, loyalists, and native allies. It must be stressed that the British Army underwent many of the same hardships as Washington's army. Disease, inferior medical care, cold, and isolation depleted British Army ranks and chewed at that army's resolve as surely as it did that of the American army. The ratio of battle deaths ("killed in action") to engagements is small, and, for what was at stake, the numbers pale in comparison to what was to come. Within a generation, the French Revolutionary and Napoleonic wars saw armies of 100,000 and more confronting each other in Europe in a single encounter. In fact, Napoleon invaded Russia in 1812 with a vast European army estimated at about 600,000 men, and, at the Battle of Borodino in the same year, there were 108,000 casualties, over half of whom were fatalities. By the time the weapons and transportation systems of war had been mechanized in the Crimean War and American Civil War, killing rates would reach levels that would have been unfathomable to George Washington. At Gettysburg in July 1863, as many Americans died on the battlefield in three days of fighting as were killed in combat during the entire course of the War for Independence. What is most significant about the war is not necessarily the scale of combat or even the nature of the fighting, which was mostly localized, shifting, and often dirty, angry, tiring, and emotional. Rather the length of the war and the great geographical scope of it were important. It was a marathon of sorts, and thus an endurance test. It stretched, episodically, from Quebec to Florida and from the Atlantic to the trans-Appalachian west. No part of the former thirteen colonies was spared the war's military or political impact. Because of this war, a new political institution was created, the Continental Congress under the Articles of Confederation.

Suggested Reading

There is a vast literature on the War for Independence. Among the best overviews are Jeremy Black, *War for America: The Fight for Independence, 1775-1783* (Stroud, England: Alan Sutton, 1991) and Stephen Conway, *The War of American Independence, 1775-*

1783 (London: Edward Arnold, 1995). Conway's bibliography is very good. Piers Mackesy, *The War for America, 1775-1783* (Cambridge, MA: Harvard University Press, 1965) is rich in detail and, after 40 years, is still the standard for general studies of the war and its wider international scope; as the title and time frame suggests, Eric Robson, *The American Revolution in its Political and Military Aspects, 1763-1783* (1955; Hamden, CT: Archon Books, 1965) ties the earlier political debate to the eventual war. Howard H. Peckham, *The War for Independence: A Military History* (Chicago: The University of Chicago Press, 1970) is a briskly written short introduction. Specific themes are dealt with in James Kirby Martin and Mark Edward Lender, *A Respectable Army: The Military Origins of the Republic, 1763-1789* (Arlington Heights, IL: Harlan Davidson, 1982); E. Wayne Carp, *To Starve the Army at Pleasure: Continental Army Administration and American Political Culture, 1775-1783* (Chapel Hill: The University of North Carolina Press, 1984); and Charles Royster, *A Revolutionary People at War: The Continental Army and American Character, 1775-1783* (Chapel Hill: The University of North Carolina Press, 1979). John Shy, *A People Numerous and Armed: Reflections on the Military Struggle for American Independence*, rev. ed. (Ann Arbor: University of Michigan Press, 1990) is a stimulating compilation of the author's essays. David Hackett Fischer, *Washington's Crossing* (New York: Oxford University Press, 2004) shows how rich results can be achieved when a fine scholar applies his talents to an account of a single incident. Leutze's painting is at www.metmuseum.org/explore/gw/el_gw.htm.

The British perspective can be found in both Mackesey, *The War for America*, and Robson, *The American Revolution*, cited above, and in Sylvia R. Frey, *The British Soldier in America: A Social History of Military Life in the Revolutionary Period* (Austin, TX: University of Texas Press, 1981); Lawrence Stone, ed., *An Imperial State at War: Britain from 1689-1815* (London: Routledge, 1994); and Neil Longley York, *Turning the World Upside Down: The War of American Independence and the Problem of Empire* (Westport CT: Praeger, 2003). Of statistical note is Edward Curtis, *The Organization of the British Army in the American Revolution* (New Haven: Yale University Press, 1926). J.W. Fortesque, *The War of Independence: The British Army in North America, 1775-1783* (1911; London: Greenhill Books, 2001) stands up well after nearly a century. On the impact of the war on natives, see Colin G. Calloway, *The American Revolution in Indian Country* (Cambridge University Press, 1995). The war in the Caribbean is handled with clarity in Andrew Jackson O'Shaughnessy, *An Empire Divided: The American and the British Caribbean* (Philadelphia: University of Pennsylvania Press, 2000). James Kirby Martin, *Ordinary Courage: The Revolutionary War Adventures of Joseph Plumb Martin*, 2nd ed. (Naugatuck, CT: Brandywine Press, 1999) is a lively example of the impressions of an American soldier. The British opposition to the war is discussed in Jerome Reich, *British Friends of the American Revolution* (Armonk, NY: M.E. Sharpe, 1998).

CHAPTER FIVE
THE PROBLEMS OF INDEPENDENCE, 1783-1787

His Britannic Majesty acknowledges the said United States, viz. New Hampshire, Massachusetts Bay, Rhode Island and Providence Plantations, Connecticut, New York, New Jersey, Pennsylvania, Delaware, Maryland, Virginia, North Carolina, South Carolina, and Georgia, to be free sovereign and independent States; that he treats with them as such, and for himself, and heirs and successors, relinquishes all claims to the Government, propriety and territorial rights of the same, and every part thereof.

— Treaty of Paris, 1783, Article I

Time Line

1775-89	Increased western migrations.
1781-83	State land claims concessions.
1783	The Treaty of Paris.
	The independent states.
1784, 1785, and 1787	The Northwest Ordinances.
1786	Shays's rebellion in Massachusetts.
	Virginia Statute of Religious Freedom.
1787	The Annapolis Convention.
	The Constitutional Convention in Philadelphia.

Postwar Adjustments

What did independence mean to Americans in 1783? We know what it meant to most of the generation's political and intellectual leaders and to the host of memoirists and correspondents who left copious records of their impressions. But what did the mass of the population think? What did the end of the war mean to New England farmers, southern backwoodsmen, slaves, natives, or the 50 per cent of the population that was female, most of whom were locked into the rituals and cycles of agricultural subsistence? What did it mean to those substantial numbers who had avoided military service during the war or the neutrals or quiet loyalists who had avoided identifying their interests or the 5,000 or so free African Americans who served in the Continental Army? Wars seldom if ever end in predictable ways. The Revolutionary War began as an untidy and localized rebellion by a committed minority for the redress of political rights but grew first into an anti-imperial war and then into a global conflict. It expanded from a clash of competing authorities into a separatist movement and, ultimately, into a new political entity. Although the war began as a protest *against* political change, it resulted in sweeping political changes. Canada and the British West Indies were affected by the territorial limits of American independence, and the war had also sparked changes in short-term relations between France and Great Britain. The end of the war presented Americans with ill-defined political sovereignty. The meaning of independence for the majority of the population, the "many," was different from what it meant to the "few," who were the older elites and the political, economic, and political leadership that had managed the war and defined its purpose. The novelty of independence required adjustments and experimentation.

Western Land Claims

Historians have long stressed the localism that prevailed in British America in the eighteenth century. From John Adams and George Washington to every other New England or Virginia farmer, locality defined one's immediate social and political attachments. Yes, there was an Empire, but it was a benign one, distant and comforting. There were provincial governments, but the town or parish or plantation was where authority and political relations were expressed. Localism was not unique to Americans, but they enjoyed a level of local political autonomy that was not available to most. The degree of centralized state authority present in the lives of rural populations in Britain, France, Russia, or China in the eighteenth century is open to question, but it was likely higher in those places than it was in pre-industrial America. In Britain and France, the national governments had for some time controlled the politics of local communities. Few colonial Americans, on the other hand, had experienced the full weight of Parliament until after the Seven Years' War. Resistance and the War for Independence brought Americans together as it removed the older state apparatus of the Empire. The war opened up the south to New England farmers in the Continental Army just as it exposed New Yorkers to Carolinians and Pennsylvanians to New Hampshire farm boys who hadn't strayed far before their enlistments. It had been obvious to the colonial elites that they were part of a provincial English culture in America, but the war brought Washington into contact with Alexander Hamilton of New York in a common cause. It did the same for John Adams and Thomas Jefferson and for various permutations of political and military leaders in and out of the Continental Congress. The duration and comprehensive nature of the war expanded the cultural and political horizons of most Americans, and, even as it saved their colonial neighborhoods, the war linked them under a formal, if limited, contractual political instrument, the Articles of Confederation.

The Articles of Confederation were the first formal definition of an American union when they were ratified in 1781. They turned the unwritten agreements of 1774 and 1775 into a contractual obligation, in the words of the Articles, a "perpetual union." If the Declaration of Independence had pledged the "lives" and "honor" of Americans to the cause of separation, the Articles formally bound the governments of the states to a federated "league" or system. When Richard Henry Lee raised the issue of independence in June 1776, he also proposed a stronger form of government for the Congress. The first articulated model for the formal union of the states had been written, mostly by John Dickinson, by July 12, 1776, in the immediate afterglow of the Declaration of Independence. After more than a year of occasional debate, the 13 Articles of Confederation were adopted and sent to the states by a unanimous vote in Congress in November 1777 in the month after the victory at Saratoga. Yet the treaty was not ratified by all the states until March 1781, largely because of Maryland's objections.

The issue of western land claims had been raised by the Articles after pressure from states with no charter claims to the west. The process was sometimes bitter and always difficult, but, in the end, it was felt that no state could benefit so long as *all* states made concessions. By surrendering their claims, the states freed the land to Congress on behalf of the whole. Maryland was the last holdout, but, when it saw that Virginia was finally prepared to forego its land claims, it agreed to ratify the Articles just as the war was winding down. The process took over a decade and indicates the tenacity of the states in defense of what they saw as their sovereign rights to the west. Delaware, Maryland, New Jersey, Pennsylvania, and Rhode Island made no claims, but the others did, claiming rights that went back to the charter period. The claims were as follows:

- Virginia had the largest claim, consisting of more than half the territory acquired at the Treaty of Paris. The state claimed all the land from the Ohio River north to beyond the western edge of Lake Superior and land south of the Ohio River in what would become Kentucky. When Virginia announced in 1781 that it would cede the land, Maryland signed the Articles of Confederation and made them official. Virginia also claimed Kentucky until 1792, when the latter was granted statehood. By 1786, the state had surrendered its claim to the rest.
- Massachusetts claimed a large east-west territory that ran all the way from Lake Erie to the Mississippi, and it disputed Virginia's claim to the same land. It also claimed the area that had been declared an independent state, Vermont, and part of western New York between Lake Erie and Lake Ontario. Those claims were relinquished in 1784-86.
- New York had disputed the territories claimed by Massachusetts but deferred to Congress.
- Connecticut disputed land with Virginia in the northwest but conceded the claim to Congress in exchange for a piece of that territory directly south of Lake Erie.
- New Hampshire was in dispute with Massachusetts and New York over Vermont.
- North Carolina claimed a contiguous strip from the Appalachians to the Mississippi, which was not disputed by any other state. It abandoned the claim in 1790.
- South Carolina claimed a narrow strip from its western border to the Mississippi and ceded it in 1787.

- Georgia, like North Carolina and Virginia, simply claimed everything west of its colonial boundaries to the Mississippi, and did not cede that land officially until 1802. The extreme southern section of its claim was disputed by both the United States and Spain.

In addition to the hold up over land claims, there were other objections to the Articles that showed the novelty of the agreement's design. Some delegates thought that too much power was centralized while others thought the Articles too weak. The fact that the states had effectively surrendered any future claims to territory meant that any additional territory gained from independence would be governed collectively. This was the first significant sign of a territorial redefinition of the "united states."

The Articles of Confederation

The official title of the agreement was "The Articles of Confederation and Perpetual Union between the States of [and all thirteen rebelling states were named]," and the first of the 13 articles stated that "The stile of this confederacy shall be 'The United States of America,'" a name used in the Declaration and elsewhere that would stick from this point on. In Article Three, the treaty is defined as "a firm league of friendship [of the states] for their common defence, the security of their liberties and their mutual and general welfare." Because the Articles lasted only seven years, their value has been depreciated, and contemporaries and historians have argued that the movement to create the Constitution of the United States was encouraged by the failure of the Articles to deal with the demands of independence. This is a fallacious view because it assumes that the Articles were intended as a national template, which they were not meant to be, especially if we take national as defining a nation state. Indeed, the Articles were no more than the legal or contractual expression of the second Continental Congress and reflected the state-based politics of the independence movement. The delegates had not developed a model for the large federated republic because they had not envisioned one in the late 1770s. Also, the United States Constitution did not follow as simply a corrective to the "weaknesses" and "failures" of the Articles. Rather, another movement had emerged from the war, a movement to take independence to a national level. The Articles were a wartime measure, but peace brought with it different demands and a more acute need for long-term security. In any case, the creation of the United States was a slowly developing process and had always been pushed by competing ideas and interests and by changing circumstances. The Articles must be understood as part of a continuous political readjustment that began in the 1760s and continued well into the nineteenth century.

Indeed, the Articles contained two features that marked a great step towards what can be considered a functioning decentralized confederation. First, the potential acquisition of western territory by the Continental Congress gave that body a geographical identity, and when Britain turned over the territory from the Appalachians to the Mississippi, it did so to the authority of the Continental Congress under the

Map 5.1 The United States in 1783, with State land concessions, 1782-1802

Articles of Confederation. When the Congress dealt with that collective space in the 1780s, it assumed that *independent* states would be created there. Another original feature of the Articles was in Article Four, which ran as follows:

> The better to secure and perpetuate mutual friendship and intercourse among the people of the different states in this union, the free inhabitants of each of these states, paupers, vagabonds and fugitives from justice excepted, shall be entitled to all the privileges and immunities of free citizens in the several states; and the people of each State shall have free ingress and regress to and from any other State, and shall enjoy therein all the privileges of trade and commerce, subject to the same duties, impositions, and restrictions as the inhabitants thereof respectively; provided that such restrictions shall not extend so far as to prevent the removal of property, imported into any... other State of which the owner is an inhabitant; provided also that no imposition, duties, or restriction shall be laid by any State on the property of the United States, or either of them.
>
> If any person guilty of, or charged with, treason, felony, or other high misdemeanor in any State, shall flee from justice and be found in any of the United States, he shall, upon demand of the governor or executive power of the State from which he fled, be delivered up and removed to the State having jurisdiction of his offence.
>
> Full faith and credit shall be given in each of these States to the record, acts, and judicial proceedings of the courts and magistrates of every other State.

This was a clear start to defining American citizenship. It excluded slaves and restricted the idle poor and fugitives from justice, but, in the absence of a national court system, it sought to guarantee the legal rights of any one from any state who moved or was temporarily in another state, and it sanctioned a freedom to trade throughout the union. It suggested that the legal status of a white New Yorker was the same as the legal status of a white Virginian, wherever they happened to be. At a more fundamental level, however, there were deliberate limits to any centralized power in the Articles as can be seen below, where they are compared with the United States Constitution:

Table 5.1: Main Features of the Articles of Confederation

Articles, 1777 (Ratified 1781)	*United States Constitution, 1787* (Ratified 1788 and effective 1789)
Each state, large or small, with one vote in the Continental Congress	States represented according to population in the United States House of Representatives and equally by state in the United States Senate
Congress not empowered to levy or collect taxes	Congress given the power to levy and collect taxes

Congress could not regulate foreign or interstate commerce. It could "mediate" between states, declare war, and make treaties.	United States Congress given the power to regulate foreign and interstate commerce.
No provision for an executive to enforce the acts of the Congress.	Presidential system
No provision for a federal judiciary (court system).	A national system of federal courts and a national Supreme Court
The Articles could be amended only by unanimous consent.	The US Constitution could be amended by a two-thirds majority in both houses of Congress and ratification by three quarters of the states.
A two-thirds majority in the Congress needed to pass laws.	A simple majority in both houses needed to pass laws, and a two-thirds majority if the act was vetoed by the President.

This brief comparison reveals the differences between a federation in which *each* of the various components (the states in this case) retains a brake on centralized authority and a system in which a central government exercises overriding power in most matters, on paper at least. The keys here are the government's ability under the United States Constitution to tax on its own initiative, the power to regulate interstate and foreign commerce and the creation of an executive with the money and legal means to enforce the law. There were limits to those powers, but clearly the Constitution represented a new kind of authority, one that transferred authority from a states-based system to the federated but centralized republican nation state. In 1783, such a mechanism was not fully understood or contemplated. Only the states, as independent republics, had gone so far as to write fully sovereign constitutions.

State Constitutions

In 1775, the Continental Congress had instructed its members to declare their grievances in the form of individual colonial protests against British policy. A revolutionary convention in New Hampshire composed a "constitution" in late 1775 and passed it on January 5, 1776. That document has been seen as the first state constitution of the Revolution, but, because it still stated the hope of reconciliation with the Crown, it fell short of declaring a fully independent form of republican government. In fact, it is a good example of the lingering hope of reconciliation and notes in its preamble that, because Governor Wentworth and the Council had left suddenly, the people needed a code of laws to secure good government. Its authors go so far as to plead that "we neaver [sic] sought to throw off our dependence upon Great Britain but felt happy under her protection.... And we shall rejoice if such a reconciliation between us and our parent State can be effected as shall be approved by the CONTINENTAL CON-GRESS, in whose prudence and wisdom we confide." That appeal to reason also appeared in the South Carolina constitution in late March 1776, which said in part "until an accommodation of the unhappy differences between Great Britain and America can be obtained, (an event which, though traduced and treated as rebels, we earnestly desire,) some mode should be established by common consent, and for the good of the people, the origin and end of all governments, for regulating the internal polity of this colony." On March 19, 1778, a new South Carolina Constitution repealed the earlier one and in the preamble declared the state's sovereignty: "Whereas the con-stitution and a form of government agreed to [on March 26, 1776] *was temporary only*.... [be] it therefore constituted and enacted ... [t]hat the style of this country be hereafter the State of South Carolina" (emphasis added). That was typical of what poured forth after the Declaration of Independence when Congress urged the states to write independent constitutions.

Within a year, all the states had written independent constitutions, and the states of Connecticut and Rhode Island simply took their charters and omitted the sovereign references to the Crown. Massachusetts took until 1780 after a popular convention approved its constitution. This first wave of constitution making was certainly the work of rebellious and committed political minorities, but the speed of the change tes-tifies to the superb organizational skills and tactics of the revolutionary cadres in the early months of the war. Keeping in mind the fact that the Declaration of Independence was a manifesto and not a constitution, as we understand that term, the revolutionary Virginia assembly had adopted a constitution a week before the Declaration was fin-ished, and its preamble anticipated the language of the Declaration. The Virginia dec-laration begins with a statement that individual civil rights were the "basis and foundation of government." It then makes the natural rights claim "[t]hat all men are by nature equally free and independent, and have certain inherent rights, of which, when they enter into a state of society, they cannot, by any compact, deprive or divest their posterity, namely, the enjoyment of life and liberty, with the means of acquiring and possessing property, and pursuing and obtaining happiness and safety." As with the Declaration of Independence the "inherent rights" of all "equally free" men were not applicable to slaves.

Unlike the other constitutions that preceded the Declaration, the Virginia Constitution of June 29, 1776 had abruptly ended the colony's nebulous status in Britain's dissolving Empire in America and anticipated the state constitutions that fol-lowed. It was a formal political and legal definition of sovereignty and a fully articu-lated design for government, down to defining voter eligibility and the appointment of state officials. Certainly there would be no confusing the state constitutions with the Articles of Confederation; all power lay with the former. The Virginia Constitution introduced a valuable feature to American politics by including in the document a "declaration of rights" that guaranteed citizenship and clear civil rights for all citizens. It enjoined the State of Virginia's government to defend and advance those rights. Americans were certainly familiar with the listing of "rights" from the precedent of the 1689 British Bill of Rights. The latter had been intended to curb royal excesses in the wake of the Glorious Revolution but was far from expressing a republican world view. The Virginia Constitution, however, did just that, and its insistence on legislative, representative sovereignty is a clear and forceful rejection of legalized hereditary rule of any kind. The Virginia Constitution states that "the common benefit, protection, and security of the people, nation or community" is the principal function of government. It separates the law-making function from the executive and each of those from a judiciary. It imitates, in a sense, the idealized form of colonial governments but removes the supreme authority of the Monarch and effectively lodges that authority in a written constitution. It is instructive to compare the Virginia "declaration of rights" with the first ten amendments of the United States Constitution, the 1791 "Bill of Rights." The guarantees of freedom of speech and assembly, equal protection and due process of law, trial by jury, the sanctity of property, and the right to have an armed militia were originally the prerogatives of the individual states. When such "civil rights" were omitted from the 1787 United States Constitution, the states soon insisted on their inclusion. In fact, the man who framed the Virginia code, George Mason, was a delegate to the Constitutional Convention and refused to sign off on it until it included a formal bill of rights. Thus, Virginia had declared itself an independent nation a few days before the formal collective Declaration of Independence and 12 years before the Constitution of the United States was written and ratified.

The Republican Structure of State Governments

The later state constitutions shared much with Virginia's. While some states initially retained the old habit of referring to themselves as a "colony," there was no doubt that each constitution was a statement of and a model for political autonomy. There are some interesting differences among them, but each incorporates basic republican values and mechanisms. In other words, there were no allowances made for hereditary titles or executive privilege. The main organizational features of the state governments were as follows:

The Electorate: The qualifications for voting in state elections were close to the colonial requirements but were relaxed in some jurisdictions. Even in those areas where the franchise was limited, there was room for its expansion in the way the various constitutions were designed. New England offered clear routes to voting rights, and New Hampshire, for example, had a very low threshold of tax assessment for eligibility. The traditional pre-revolutionary formula for representation in New England was continued in the various state constitutions. The town was the fount of actual representation, and, in New England, the towns' electorates chose people to represent the town in the legislatures. In Pennsylvania, the sons of freeholders (mostly farmers with title to even small holdings) were eligible to vote, perhaps the first sign of a shift away from property or wealth as a criterion for participation. In the south, the restrictions were more exclusionary, and Virginia, for example, required the ownership of 25 acres of worked ("settled") land or 500 acres of any kind of land. Most states would eventually recognize taxable assets (personalty) as a criterion for voting rather than the older, strictly land based (realty) eligibility.

Legislative design and authority: The usual legislative format was the bicameral system, drawn from two kinds of representation, a popular "lower house" representing locality and an "upper" house representing statewide interests. Here the principle was a clear check on too much popular control of the legislature as envisioned in the single chamber or unicameral system — the feared rule of the many, "mobocracy." The committees that drew up the constitutions were generally drawn from community leaders who, in some cases, feared the effects of a complete leveling of political representation. The identification of a socio-economic divide in revolutionary culture can be seen in the way the bicameral system was promoted. There were two exceptions to this model, in Pennsylvania, where a single legislative assembly was established, and in New Hampshire's preliminary model, which had a single assembly from which an executive council was drawn. The amount of authority vested in the legislatures was significant. In eight states, the executive was elected by the legislature, and, in nine states, all money bills had to originate in the lower (popular) house. Six states allowed the legislature to share in the executive's administration appointments.

Executive office: The Revolution had raised the specter of the corrupt leader, the despot or tyrant, so in the late 1770s, with a war being waged against a despot, it was natural that the states would limit the power of the executive while retaining it for administrative purposes. Massachusetts was the only state that gave considerable powers to the governor's office. Nine of the states restricted the governor's term to one year. Nine of the states denied the governor the older privilege of vetoing bills, and several states limited their governor's eligibility for multiple re-election. In that respect, the states and the Articles of Confederation shared an apprehension of strong executives. The Articles, as noted, had made no provision for one. The United States Constitution, by comparison, was designed with a relatively strong executive office.

Office holding: The property requirements for holding office varied greatly, from a minimal level that encouraged some upward political mobility in some of the New England states to prohibitive wealth requirements in the south. The Governor of South Carolina needed to have 10,000 pounds sterling in landed assets to be eligible. That excluded all but a handful of South Carolinians. North Carolina, on the other hand, had a 2,000 pounds sterling requirement. In New Jersey and Maryland, each candidate to the upper chamber needed 1,000 pounds sterling in property value or 500 pounds sterling for eligibility for the lower house. The references in those early constitutions had not moved away from using British currency denominations and values because of the pound sterling's continued reliability in the currency chaos that prevailed.

Frequency of elections: This had been a contentious issue for the colonial assemblies. The aftermath of the Zenger affair in New York in 1734-35 had demonstrated the growing concern of assemblies and electorates about the arbitrariness of governors and councils regarding elections. State constitutions were sensitive to the issue, and all but South Carolina demanded annual elections for their lower houses and elections every two to four years for the elected upper houses.

Bills of rights: Many of the constitutions contained a direct and separate declaration of civil rights in their drafts, and all of them contained language that took the meaning and design of government in the direction of civil rights. After all, the air had been dense with the language of liberty and rights for over a decade. The general thrust of the "freedoms" announced by the various constitutions included specific references to freedom of worship and religious affiliation. Still, women were not given voting rights, and only one state, Massachusetts, while not specifying an immediate end to slavery, appeared to open the door to its abolition.

For all the regional variation among the thirteen states, their constitutions were similar. The key features were drawn from what revolutionary Americans had experienced or desired in the late colonial era: a balanced system with checks on each branch of government and access and representation that reflected the social, economic, and cultural characteristics of each society. Even when some of the constitutions were modified or enlarged, the controls over representation and voting qualifications were maintained. The states retained control over their voting procedures and state office-holding qualifications even after the adoption of the United States Constitution. In the scramble to create independent sovereignties, a new political entity appeared, Vermont. The ownership of part of this crucial territory, wedged between western New Hampshire and northern New York, was disputed by these neighboring states and also by Massachusetts because of muddled boundaries. A small population had been fixed in Vermont since the 1720s. Its people wrote a constitution in the summer of 1777, and, when it was rewritten in 1786, it included an immediate ban on slavery. After New York officially relinquished its claim to the territory in 1790, Vermont applied for admission to the union and became the fourteenth state in 1791.

Slavery
The military use of African Americans in the War for Independence was the result of

simple manpower needs and not in any way a route to the liberation of slaves or even to respect for freed African Americans. The best estimate of the number of African Americans who served in the Continental Army is 5,000, most of whom were free. The British, for their part, employed many more African Americans. They freed many more when they had the chance, as a wartime strategy, but it is unlikely that African American soldiers were active in the British ranks during the war. They were used mostly for general labor (as "pioneers"), cooking, transportation help, carpentry, tailoring, and the myriad of supporting chores required by eighteenth-century armies. For the most part, the African American population, including the less than 10 per cent who were free, had not been drawn into the Revolution as participants. By 1780, as the war was nearing its end, the slave population in America was well over half a million. That staggering figure helps explain why the Revolution would confirm rather than remove slavery. Each of the 500,000 slaves was a financial asset, a "labor producing commodity." There was still value in the slave as property even if the economy was in shambles and the monetary value of slaves had declined in some areas. Slaves also denoted social and political status to their owners. What made slavery endure was the simple cultural imperative of race relations. The labor systems, class relations, legal definitions and sanctions, and the economic rationale for slavery were all suffused with attitudes of paternalism at one end of the spectrum of white authority and contempt and even pity at the other end. As the Revolution passed over the slave population, it was passing over an increasingly American-born population. Even as large numbers of slaves continued to be imported, the term "African American" as a cultural and ethnic reference became even more ironic in this era.

African Americans were lodged in a peculiarly American system of bondage. The reinforcing mechanisms of the slaves' material dependency, concepts of biological inferiority, and the persistent social and emotional degradation of blacks, repeated through generations, had strengthened the white view of African Americans as a debased people. Colonial America had stitched permanent race-based slavery into its fabric as much as it had sewn in the language of "liberty" and "rights" and "consent." When Samuel Johnson, the great English writer and wit, asked James Boswell the now famous rhetorical question — "How is it that we hear the loudest yelps for liberty among the drivers of negroes?" — he was being clever and critical at the same time. But Johnson's witty sarcasm answers its own question. The concepts of "liberty" or "freedom" were not available to slaves because their condition already denied them the "unalienable rights" that were assumed for whites. The status of the slave was not changed by the Revolution, despite the efforts of some to ease their consciences. They and the others who spoke out against slavery in pamphlets, letters, and conventions were helpless to limit let alone end the practice. The tiny abolitionist movement led in part by an active Quaker leadership was likewise stifled in its efforts to end slavery. Slavery did bother American revolutionary figures, but not enough of them and not to a sufficient extent to end it. The ending of the slave trade would be negotiable, but slavery itself was not.

The ultimate measure of the failure of revolutionary rhetoric and ideology to end slavery in America lies in the United States Constitution, which sanctioned it as a protected institution. The adoption of the Constitution as the nation's framework for sovereignty, rights, and citizenship was not possible without the guarantee of slaveholders' rights. In fact, the Articles of Confederation at one point had to wrestle with the feelings of a majority of delegates who wanted to specify that no African Americans, free or otherwise, should be allowed to bear arms for the Congress during the war. The recruitment clause was eventually left color-blind. At one point, Washington himself saw the benefits of enlisting African Americans, and Nathanael Greene praised their abilities and performance under arms. Alexander Hamilton wrote an anxious appeal for slaves to be drafted into the army in South Carolina in 1779, to little effect. The number of African Americans who bore arms for independence is small but is a very generous proportion of the population of free African Americans available to the army. The southern fears of slave insurrection, dating from the Cato Conspiracy, Stono Rebellion, and Charleston Conspiracy of 1739-40, were a constant brake on any easing of control. But northern apprehensions were also manifest in the paranoia of the New York City riots of 1741 that resulted in the execution of 31 African Americans, including 13 who were burned alive, and the hanging of four white "conspirators." Even recruiting whites in the south was made difficult because of the need to keep as many as possible white males at home to keep slaves in check. Thus, the contribution to independence of the African American population was buried in the record, and was systematically and conspicuously reduced. The African Americans who did see action fought with as much verve and commitment as did the whites in the Continental Army, but received no rewards for it. By the end of the war, the slave population in the Chesapeake constituted nearly 40 per cent of the area's population, a figure that generally applied in the plantation states. Some regions in the far south had black majorities, such as the South Carolina and Georgia Tidewater where a mixed African and African American population constituted over 50 per cent of the whole. Slaves on larger plantations were assigned specific tasks (the so-called "task system") in specialized areas of production and plantation maintenance. The number of southern landholders who owned slaves varied from state to state and regionally within states. It was generally about 25 per cent overall, but there were higher proportions of slaveholders in the Tidewater regions than farther inland. In a counterintuitive way, while the majority of slaveholders owned fewer than 20 slaves, the majority of slaves lived in units of more than 20. It is a notable feature of the southern plantocracy that it was not a monolithic economic class, given variations in landholding, slaveholding, and income levels. Much of the political and economic power in the south resided in a small group whose members owned hundreds of slaves.

Slavery and Sectionalism

The division between the slave states of the south and the free states of the north began in earnest during the Revolution, so that, by the start of the Civil War in 1861, of the original thirteen states, seven were free and six were slave states. All had begun their independence as slave states. The northern states gave up slavery by choice, but in the most reluctant and cumbersome ways. Those original southern states never gave up slavery but had it removed by force in 1865. Although it is often assumed, plausibly, that, in the flush of independence, the northern tier of states eliminated slavery by constitutional or legislative will, that was far from the case. Only 10 per cent of American slaves were in the four New England States, Pennsylvania, New Jersey, and New York. The highest number of African Americans in the north was in New York, amounting to about 21,000 in 1780. The majority of those were slaves. The lowest number was New Hampshire's few hundred. Few slaveholders in the north had more than one or two slaves, but, whether on the docks or streets of Boston, New York or Newport or here and there in nearby fields, these were still master-slave relationships. The need for slave labor in the north was slight, and the slow process of emancipation is a telling example of the depth of the region's racism.

The only jurisdiction that banned slavery in its constitution was Vermont. Otherwise, in the original states' constitutions, only Massachusetts used language that hinted, but only hinted, at the possibility of abolition. Any legalized end to slavery in the north required action, and some of the action came from African Americans who appealed to revolutionary sentiment and the constant repetition of the language of egalitarianism. Quock Walker became one of revolutionary America's most famous slaves when he was freed following a convoluted set of legal actions and a charge of assault against Walker's owner in 1781. A Massachusetts judge interpreted the Massachusetts Constitution's "all men are born free and equal" as meaning that "slavery is…effectively abolished" and that "the idea of slavery is inconsistent with our own conduct and Constitution; and there can be no such thing as [an involuntary] perpetual servitude of a rational creature," except "forfeited by some criminal conduct." Quock Walker walked away free. Alas, Massachusetts did not ban the importation of slaves until 1788, and the Walker precedent was ignored or rejected elsewhere in the north. In every northern jurisdiction, complete emancipation was achieved slowly and for all the publicity generated by Walker's case, there was little legislative or judicial replication of it.

Slaves pressed everywhere for freedom and were usually unsuccessful. Even before the Walker case, a group of 19 slaves petitioned the New Hampshire legislature for their freedom. They appealed to the language of the Declaration and the New Hampshire Bill of Rights but were rejected anyway. The names given to some of the petitioners by their owners, in typical classical reference, sadly contrast with their status. Nero Brewster, Pharaoh Rogers, Seneca Hall, Cato Newmarch and Caesar Gerrish were among the appellants. It is certain that the irony of naming slaves after classical thinkers like Seneca and Cato and rulers such as Nero, Caesar, and Pharaoh was not lost on the magistrates, who rejected their passionate appeals. In Pennsylvania, the Quaker community had begun to rid itself of its slaves early in the war and was the only coherent body of whites in all the colonies that advocated complete abolition of slavery. The French Huguenot immigrant Anthony Benezet (1713-84), who converted to Quakerism, was an early advocate of abolition and, at one time, ran a school for slave children in his home. His pamphlet attacks on slavery reached abolitionists on both sides of the Atlantic. He and the Quaker minister John Woolman, who died in 1772, were models of anti-slavery zeal in the late colonial period and among the few genuine abolitionists to emerge in the eighteenth century, but their influence in America was limited mostly to the few Quakers who pressured merchants, planters, and legislators in the 1780s. Pennsylvania's most celebrated citizen was Benjamin Franklin. He was not a Quaker and owned domestic slaves. Yet he took a leading role in the state's civil rights issues in the 1780s and became president of an organization with the comprehensive title of the Pennsylvania Society for Promoting the Abolition of Slavery, and the Relief of Free Negroes Unlawfully Held in Bondage. Pennsylvania, which in some ways appeared to be the most politically progressive state, was nevertheless slow to free the slaves who remained there after the voluntary emancipations by slaveholders. In 1780, it passed a law to end slavery by stages. Gradualism became the most common approach everywhere in the north. It usually entailed the freeing of all slaves born after a certain date. According to New Jersey's abolition code of 1804, for example, a male slave could not be freed until he was 25 or a female until she was 21. New York and New Jersey were especially slow to act. New York did not end slavery until 1817 when it forbade its residents to own slaves. Then, many owners did not free their slaves but simply sold them to southerners; but, throughout the north, as African Americans were slowly emancipated, they were usually socially segregated from whites. The following chart indicates the slow process of freedom in the middle-Atlantic states:

Table 5.2: Mid-Atlantic Slave Populations, 1790-1850

(Brackets indicate slaves as percentage of total African American population)

	1790 (%)	1800 (%)	1810 (%)	1820 (%)	1830	1840	1850
NY	21,324 (80)	20,343 (62)	15,017 (38)	10,088 (26)	75	4	0
NJ	11,423 (81)	12,422 (73)	10,851 (57)	7,557 (38)	2,254	674	236
PA	3,737 (37)	1,706 (11)	795 (3.5)	211 (0.7)	403	64	0

Source: Simeon F. Moss, "The Persistence of Slavery in a Free State, (1686-1866)," *Journal of Negro History*, 35 (1950): 311. See also Table 8.2 below.

The only states to abolish slavery in their constitutions were Vermont (in 1777, 1786, and 1791, when it was admitted to the union) and, under the terms of the Northwest Ordinance of 1787, Ohio (1803), Indiana (1816), and Illinois (1818). The Walker case in Massachusetts indicated that the state constitution could be interpreted as forbidding slavery, without being specific, and New Hampshire's abolition process resulted from a similar interpretation of that state's revised 1783 constitutions. Technically, however, slavery was not forbidden directly by law until 1857, even though New Hampshire became more liberal than most in its treatment of its black population.

The numbers of African Americans in New Hampshire was minuscule. The other states to ban slavery did so with gradualist legislation: Pennsylvania, 1780; Rhode Island, 1784; Connecticut, 1784 and 1797; New York, 1799 and 1817; and New Jersey, 1804.

Nothing comparable happened in the slave societies of the south. The universal principles of the Declaration, the states' bills of rights, the philosophical ruminations and moral anxiety of people like Jefferson, and countless other pronouncements of a new political world order were not enough to dislodge the institution of slavery in the south. Even the southern agreement in the 1787 federal constitutional debates to seek a moratorium on the "execrable" importation of slaves into the United States was a condemnation of a barbaric trade practice and not an indictment of slavery itself. In the south, even if the moral or ideological will had existed to end slavery, the institution and the attitudes of white southerners were too deeply set. When colonists had proclaimed their liberties in the 1760s or in the Declaration, they did not have slaves in mind, and, by the time the war was over, the status quo had been maintained in the south. Even if, for the time being, slavery had been merely modified in the north, a line had been drawn between a fixed southern institution and a receding and doomed northern variant of it.

The Loyalists

In his brief study, *The American Tory*, the historian William Nelson aptly summarized the loyalists' fate this way: "The Loyalists in the American Revolution suffered a most abject kind of political failure, losing not only their argument, their war, and their place in American society, but even their proper place in history." Thomas Hutchinson's ally Peter Oliver, from his refuge near London in 1781, composed a fast-paced loyalist version of the "rebellion" entitled *The Origin and Progress of the American Rebellion*. It is a scathing reproach of his fellow Bostonians and their *disloyalties*. It is a valuable alternative perspective on the events of 1774 to 1776, but, in light of the outcome of the "rebellion," it appears wrong-headed and reactionary. As informative and logical as it is, it is a loser's view, as William Nelson aptly puts it. The accepted early account of the Revolution was the patriotic *History of the American Revolution* (1789) by David Ramsay, who, as early as 1778, had delivered a rousing Fourth of July oration.

Yet Oliver's account retains a plaintive immediacy and reveals the genuine fears of Boston's loyalists as their world came tumbling down. The loyalists have been portrayed as either misguided conservatives who foolishly resisted the inevitability of the republican cause or as traitorous agents of a repressive Britain. But they were Americans after all, who had chosen the wrong side in the conflict. In 1763, all Americans were loyalists, but, within a generation, the measurement shifted from loyalty to the Crown to loyalty to the independence movement. The sheer force of the movement overwhelmed the loyalist alternative as early as the rejection of Joseph Galloway's plan and Thomas Hutchinson's exile in 1774. Thereafter, loyalists failed to coordinate any logical political alternative to the Declaration of Independence, but a very substantial minority of Americans persisted in rejecting independence and the republican cause right to the end of the war, and in exile thereafter. In April 1783, an estimated 7,000 loyalists left New York in advance of the evacuation of the British Army from America. Those loyalists were among the last of the estimated 80,000 to 100,000 who left during and immediately after the war. The figures identify only those who could arrange it, many of them under the protection of the British Army. Many more thousands stayed behind and either converted to republicanism or swallowed their opinions and quietly merged into the new political landscape.

Who were the loyalists? They could be found in every state, in varying numbers and with varying impact on events. The best estimates of their social and economic backgrounds include most royal officeholders; lawyers with Crown work; some provincial politicians such as Galloway; northern Anglicans; many recent British, Irish, Scottish, and Palatine immigrants (remembering the great many exceptions including Thomas Paine and John Paul Jones); tenant farmers, mostly in New York; large numbers of frontier settlers; some merchant enclaves, in Newport, New York, and Philadelphia, for example; and part of the Quaker population. There were concentrations of loyalists on Long Island and near New York City; in the Mohawk Valley of New York; in Newport, Rhode Island; in parts of New Jersey; and even in the cradle of resistance, Massachusetts. The British could count on support in the frontier regions of New York, Pennsylvania, Virginia, North Carolina, South Carolina, and Georgia. Those identified as active loyalists were not the only Americans who opposed the independence movement. There was a more passive population of dissenters, those who did not openly support the British Army but who sympathized with the Crown because a) they feared the potential disorder of the patriot cause or b) because they had older and ongoing problems with the patriot leadership in their neighborhoods. In other words, there was a great deal of opposition to the Revolution that was not necessarily a clear sign of pro-British sentiment. The weaker and more threatened those groups became, the more they depended on the British Army. The consequence of that, especially in the south, was an ugly partisan war of violence and terror.

In November 1777, the Continental Congress advised the states to confiscate the property of all known loyalists. Some states had already begun to do so, and most state governments had written acts requiring known loyalists to take a test of loyalty *not* to the Crown but to the new state authorities. Loyalists were barred from the professions, dismissed from public office, and, in some states, disenfranchised even before the Congress began to act. Nine states passed acts to exile local leaders who were active loyalists. The inflammatory charge of "Tory" became a way of adding contempt to the identity of suspected British sympathizers. In many areas, the day-to-day tension in local communities was perhaps the most visible, constant, and confusing aspect of the war. Benedict Arnold's treason came too late in the war to serve as an example of the extremes of opposition to independence. His betrayal was more the result of opportunism than of ideology. For most of the war, suspected loyalists were seen as potentially capable of betrayal, or of spying, and were always subject to harassment by local militia or committees of citizens, acting as an informal police force. The loyalists were doomed from the start if the British could not win the war. Those who went into exile were as American in their heritage as any who stayed, but they did not, and likely could not, either offer an alternative to the revolutionary leadership or, in the end, influence the course of the war. They did retain their British citizenship and took it to Britain, the West Indies, Nova Scotia, and Canada. In the latter case, along with the French, they helped sow the seeds of a continental alternative to the United States: British North America and its independent successor, today's Canada. After the war, over 4,000 of the loyalist refugees made claims for property compensation, and, in 1790, the British Parliament agreed to an aggregate settlement of over three million pounds sterling.

Religion and Independence

Christian Americans were emphatically Protestants. They went to war in the ringing words of the Declaration to achieve their "equal station to which the Laws of Nature and of Nature's God entitle them." The otherwise secular republic that emerged from the overthrow of the Empire would be sanctioned by a Protestant imperative. The subsequent emphasis on the separation of church and state meant that Americans could associate the Revolution with Christian purpose but leave the church out of the political, ideological, and legalized management of the republic. Before the Seven Years' War, the Great Awakening had weakened the local authority of church leaders while advancing a more visible mass commitment to the Christian faith. The Revolution in many ways advanced faith-based Protestantism and periodic "awakenings" and revivals became part of the nation's social character. Nominally, the majority of committed Americans, before and during the Revolution, belonged to either the Congregationalist Church in New England, the Anglican Church in the Chesapeake and middle states, or the Presbyterian Church in Pennsylvania and the backcountry. A plethora of smaller and very active sects arose in the heady social and political atmosphere of eighteenth-century America. The growth in Baptist and Lutheran affiliations attested to the new nation's cultural pluralism. Smaller numbers of Catholics and Jews (the latter an important group in Newport, Rhode Island, for example) were found among America's kaleidoscopic array of independent churches. The number of churches, meeting houses, and separate congregations had doubled between 1750 and the war and was likely in the neighborhood of 3,000. Most colonies had supported an established church sponsored by taxes, for example, the Anglican Church in Virginia or the Congregational Church in Massachusetts. The established churches were tied to the civil government insofar as they were supported by tithes (taxes to support the church's operation). The rhetorical thrust of liberty and freedom of thought that had been generated for political purposes would inevitably find its way into religious matters, and orthodoxies would not survive intact. While there had never been a possibility of a trans-colonial single ecclesiastical establishment, the individual state establishments themselves were dealt a deathblow by the Revolution's emphasis on freedom of speech and thought.

In Virginia, the movement to disestablish the Anglican Church was begun with

Jefferson's draft in 1777. It was eventually pushed by James Madison in 1785 and adopted in 1786. For Jefferson, it was one of the three achievements he wished to be remembered for, the others being the writing of the Declaration of Independence and the founding of the University of Virginia. Jefferson's *Bill for Establishing Religious Freedom* contains the following passage: "[N]o man shall be compelled to frequent or support any religious worship, place or ministry whatsoever, nor shall be enforced, restrained, molested, or burthened in his body or goods, nor shall otherwise suffer, on account of religious opinions or belief; but...all men shall be free to profess, and by argument to maintain, their opinions in matters of religions, and...the same shall in no wise diminish, enlarge, or effect their civil capacities." Beginning in 1777, the various states followed that path to disestablishment, even though it was 1818 before Connecticut enacted a similar law and 1833 before Massachusetts followed suit. Americans would carry their religious values with them as they poured into the west after independence. One's religious preferences were guaranteed by laws that kept the state from enforcing a single church organization or theology on anyone. Freedom of religion in America became part of the broader emphasis on freedom of conscience and opinion. Independent America was and would remain an aggressively Christian culture while it accommodated a pluralistic aggregation of churches and sects. The remarkable outcome of disestablishment was the increased influence of religion in social, political, and cultural affairs. The myriad new sects and the independence of large denominations meant that there would be a permanent religious context for public life, and cycles of revivals would continue to have an impact on social values in America long after the Revolution.

The West

Independence not only presented Americans with new political systems and language; the transition from Monarch and Empire to a loose confederation of republican states also brought with it enormous territorial acquisitions. The treaty of 1783 more than doubled the land mass available to the states. In 1803, United States territory doubled again with the Louisiana Purchase, and, within a generation, the former colonies had forged a new empire of their own. They controlled a geographical area from the Atlantic to the Rocky Mountains that was larger than continental Europe. All the land ceded by the British in 1783 was habitable, and most of it was more fertile than the overworked fields of New England or Virginia. It was the promised land of the revolutionary generation. Benjamin Franklin had earlier declared that the west would accommodate America's future millions for centuries. It promised the realization of Jefferson's dream of a pure and grand agrarian republic. American national identity began with a western outlook projected by the east's formative institutions of government and order.

Americans had spilled into the trans-Appalachian west before the Revolution, but the trickle of settlers into the upper Ohio in the 1740s and 1750s after a stall in the 1760s became a stream after 1775 and then a river after 1783. By 1810, nearly one million

Americans were living west of the Appalachians, and one-third of the increase in the American population between 1790 and 1810 had occurred there. This early rush of internal migration began a long, steady, and mostly unrestrained westward movement. A century after the first United States census, Frederick Jackson Turner suggested that the 1890 census revealed the closing of the American frontier and the completion of a decisive phase in the creation of American civilization. His thesis was that the frontier had shaped American institutions, values, and identity. The frontier had offered an escape valve and had encouraged a continuous renewal of the democratic impulses that had come with independence. Whether or not the "Turner Thesis" is a workable model for the development of American democracy in the nineteenth century, there can be no doubt that the process of pushing the frontier across the entire continent began in earnest in the revolutionary era. From the crowded farms of New England all the way to Georgia, settlers began to cross into the upper and lower Ohio country in huge numbers. The most attractive initial destinations were Kentucky and Tennessee. There the migration consisted of not just nuclear families, hauling their meager belongings over mountain trails in makeshift carts, but of slaveholders too, who took thousands of Virginia slaves with them into the west. Later, the areas north of the Ohio River (the future states of Ohio, Indiana, and Illinois) would take in hundreds of thousands of farm-bound settlers. The opening of the trans-Appalachian west meant that land development companies flourished. The old Ohio Company of the 1740s was succeeded by the Tennessee Company, the New England Company, and many others that negotiated land deals with Congress and encouraged the needy and the ambitious to cross the Appalachians. For some, the west proved lucrative, right from the start. John Carter, a Virginian, had settled in the western reaches of North Carolina before the war. When he died in 1781, he was one of the largest landholders west of the Alleghenies. His son, Landon Carter, went so far as to join the movement to create the state of "Franklin" in the early 1780s out of parts of Tennessee and the far western edge of Virginia. The movement petered out by 1787 but shows how the west was perceived by the ambitious migrants of all classes who crossed the mountains.

The appropriately named "Transylvania Company" was formed in 1775 and, with a land treaty with the Cherokees, sent Daniel Boone (1734-1820) to establish a community in Kentucky. Boone's early exploits soon became a mainstay of frontier folklore. To this day, his name conjures up an almost mythical reverence for an imagined American prototype: the semi-literate, resourceful trailblazer of the early frontier. Franklin, Washington, and Jefferson notwithstanding, Boone may well be the first popular international celebrity to emerge from revolutionary America. James Fenimore Cooper's fictional hero "Leatherstocking" shares much of his personality with the Boone legend. Cooper himself was a product of a New York frontier community that, in the early republic, sought to exalt the colonial ethic while embracing American independence. It was Boone, however, that became the quintessential embodiment of the exotic American frontiersman. Lord Byron's epic satire *Don Juan* (1823) has seven effusive stanzas devoted to his legend. Boone was an adventurer and wilderness explorer, but he was not the first to cross to Kentucky through the storied Cumberland Gap via the Wilderness Road. While much of his history is exaggerated or apocryphal, his life does read like a composite of the American settlement experience in the revolutionary era. He was born in Pennsylvania farm country during the Great Awakening and, with his parents, moved with many thousands of migrants to North Carolina in the early 1750s. He fought with Braddock's doomed expedition of 1755 and showed courage and verve in escaping the aftermath of the defeat. Twenty years later, he was captured and adopted by the Shawnee in Kentucky. He escaped and roamed the eastern and western sides of the Appalachians before ending up farther west than even he might have imagined. He was a crack shot and a fearless warrior, completely at home in the wilderness, but also sociable and civic minded, retaining some of the values of his Quaker origins. He was known as a fearless "Indian fighter," when that was considered a virtue, but he maintained a respect for native culture. While much of Boone's restlessness was caused by poor real estate decisions and money problems, he was a larger than life character in an exciting new environment, the American west. He spent his final days in Missouri just as it became the first state on the western side of the Mississippi. It is interesting to compare two of independent America's most enduring images: the dignified, almost stoical and always reliable "father" image of George Washington, the first national hero (and until Lincoln the most celebrated political figure in America) and the image of folk hero Boone, the epitome of the other side of the American coin of personal exceptionality. Boone's cult status and the legend of his personal endeavors should not obscure what he represents. From his birthplace in the settled regions of one of the original colonies to his death 86 years later west of the Mississippi, Boone traces the flow of American development throughout the entire period of the Revolution. His reputation, stripped of the inevitable hagiography, should remind us that hundreds of thousands of Americans followed his lead. A great many of them saw in his life and disposition a mirror of their own.

The West and Native Resistance

During the war, various states had made treaties with natives in anticipation of claiming their western charter boundaries. In 1776, Congress and some of the states had issued land grants as bounties (enlistment incentives) to Continental Army officers, ordinary soldiers who signed up for the duration, and to British Army deserters who served in the Continental Army. As the Continental Congress and its successor, the United States Congress, as well as the various states dealt with the complexities of competing territorial claims and the need for compromise, many native groups who had signed treaties with say, Virginia or Pennsylvania, found themselves without any legal recourse to collective ownership. White settlements in Kentucky and Tennessee were poised to declare their own independence. The early settlements in Kentucky caused the Virginia Assembly to claim certain areas as counties. The Articles of Confederation were helpless to deal with the complex land issues that arose during the war in the west. With independence, the situation stabilized largely because the last of the major state boundary disputes were settled. But, as the population grew in the west, the need to regulate it became a major problem for Congress in the 1780s. Inevitably, the thousands of white settlers who headed for the west threatened the security and integrity of the local native societies. A generation before 1783, the natives of eastern North America had coexisted in a tripartite white world of French, Spanish, and British administrations competing with each other. Time and relentless attrition had left the native populations east of the Appalachians in a sorry condition. From the 1750s to the end of the War for Independence, the lives of frontier native peoples had been in constant flux as wars and diplomacy changed the older imperial borders. With the removal within a generation of both the French and English, the natives west of the Appalachians had only the new independent American governments and the pent-up population of white settlers to deal with. As Americans surged into the west, the natives' worlds were about to take another turn for the worse.

The Treaty of Paris of 1783 confirmed the west (at least to the Mississippi) as American territory but did nothing to protect or accommodate the resident native population. The protective British policies in the Proclamation of 1763 and the Quebec Act of 1774 should be compared with the Articles of Confederation and the state constitutions. The latter ignored natives in defining citizenship. As slavery was being constitutionally defined as permanent and slaves were specifically denied citizenship, natives also found themselves excluded. They had little military or political utility and were viewed as impediments rather than assets in the trade and economic development of the west. Natives had emerged from the war with many of the earlier stereotypes of their social and cultural worth further denigrated. It is worth remembering that, in the final draft of the Declaration of Independence, Jefferson had been persuaded to remove his attack on George III for imposing the "cruel" institution of the slave trade and slavery on benevolent colonials. However, the committee did leave in the final draft Jefferson's charge that "[the King] has endeavoured to bring on the inhabitants of our frontiers, the merciless Indian Savages, whose known rule of warfare, is an undistinguished destruction of all ages, sexes and conditions." Here Jefferson was playing on the anecdotal prejudices of his audience. The reference to native savagery in the Declaration was not original. But it was appropriate propaganda in 1776. At the end of the war, natives had been routinely lumped with loyalists and Hessians as enemies of American independence. With few exceptions, the native peoples on the frontier and beyond had supported the British in the war. These peoples were now left to deal with the Americans. As early as 1776, Congress had endeavored to keep many of the frontier native groups neutral, and treaties remained in place in some areas of the south. These would be ignored and abandoned as white land hunger pressed against native culture and society. The war's end created a double blow to the native populations of the older frontier and then in the west. First, and perhaps most important, the natives' usefulness as allies and economic agents was gone. Second, the long-standing prejudices about native culture had been inflated by the war. The dynamics of white encroachment included violence, disorder, and ultimately conquest and submission.

It is possible that 100,000 native peoples inhabited the region from the Appalachians to the Mississippi in the 1780s. The exact figure is unknown and, as with much of the conjecture on native demography, is subject to regular revision. We can be sure that the region represented a great variety of cultural traditions and societies, but the historical relationships between native societies and even between native peoples and earlier European and white American cultures were under severe threat. In the social geography he wrote in the 1780s, *Notes of the State of Virginia*, Jefferson listed over fifty "tribes" in the region between the Appalachians and the Mississippi. He attempted to list native populations for the entire region. What is important in Jefferson's *Notes* on "Aborigines" is his poignant comment on the fates of the tribes who had welcomed the English to Virginia in 1607: "Very little can now be discovered of the subsequent histories of these tribes severally.... There remain of the *Mattaponies* three or four men only, and they have more Negro than Indian blood in them. They have lost their language, have reduced themselves, by voluntary sales to about fifty acres of land.... The older [Pamunkies] ... preserve their language to a small degree, which are the last vestiges on earth as far as we know, of the Powhatan language." To put that into perspective, in 1624, John Smith had estimated a population of about 8,000 in the Powhatan Confederacy. Jefferson's grim observations can stand for the experiences of the majority of native groups in the areas eventually occupied by whites. Over time, the same fate would befall the members of the fifty or more tribes Jefferson had noted in the 1780s as living in "United States territory." The founding of Detroit in 1701 had led to a permanent European presence in what the French considered "Illinois Country," a huge area that had linked French Canada to the Gulf of Mexico. To the south and father west, the Spanish had for generations operated settlements and missions. Those natives were familiar with Europeans but were ill prepared for the American onslaught. The sad fact is that, in the older Appalachian settlements, the natives had long-running relations with the English, and, in northern New England, the Abenakis had been engaged in the frontier politics of the French. Also, to the west and south of that area, the great Iroquois confederation — the Cayuga, Mohawk, Oneida, Onondaga, and Seneca peoples — had served as a buffer for the British. When their long-serving intermediary Sir William Johnson died in 1774, his son Sir John replaced him. The elder Johnson and the Iroquois had been crucial in campaigns against the French in the Seven Years' War. The younger Johnson had remained loyal to the Crown during the War for Independence, so, along with many in the Iroquois League, he went to Canada.

The Iroquois culture confounded white Americans because it appeared to observers to present two social and behavioral extremes. On the one hand, the Iroquois had well-developed political institutions and practices that approached some of the representational ideals of American revolutionary theorists. They also practiced a refined form of domestic ethics, caring for children and the needy, and had a well-developed communal integrity that was peaceful and spiritual. On the other hand, the Iroquois' military reputation fit Jefferson's generalized Declaration comments. The Iroquois were "cruel" and did not seem to discriminate between whites, natives, women, children, combatants, or non-combatants, but appeared to enjoy torturing all prisoners. It was the negative side of the Iroquois duality that Americans chose to see as the natives' chief moral feature. While some Americans understood the complexities and ambiguities of native life and even admired native cultures, most did not. The charge of barbarism echoed a long and bloody history of white and native relations that went back as far as the initial contact. The war had exaggerated the stereotypes, but the association of natives with the British was an additional smear on native culture. As Burgoyne's campaign of 1777 had shown, a few incidents, such as the murder of Jane McCrae by native allies, became typical examples of native cruelty, savagery, and deceit. The infamous Henry Hamilton, for example, was assumed to have encouraged scalping by his native troops during the war in the west. He was known as the "Hair Buyer," and, while there are doubts about the accuracy of that reputation, at some point he likely did pay for scalps. In any case, the practice went both ways. New Hampshire adopted a scaled bounty system offering various sums for native scalps depending on the victim's gender and age. The minimum age was twelve. Even those natives who had supported the patriot cause — the Oneida in some cases, the Tuscarora, and tribes throughout western Massachusetts and in the northern Maine and Nova Scotia borderland — fared poorly in the war's aftermath. They were not legally or socially rewarded in any way. The famous Stockbridge natives had fought with valor but without benefit.

To Americans, natives fused into one conceptual mass, and, in some cases, the flow of militant and armed settlers forced many native groups to consolidate. Settlers in large numbers encountered Tuscarora and Cherokee societies along with Choctaw, Creek, Chickasaw, and Muskogee and Seminole peoples during and after the war. The Cherokee, in particular, had impressed colonists in the south with their sophisticated social and political organization even as violence and war had colored relations throughout the eighteenth century. After 1775, white settlers often moved around these groups, surrounding them and pinching into their territories. Farther west, when ordinary Americans came into contact with the Shawnee, Miami, Ottawa, Fox, Sauk, and others, they displayed little recognition of native territorial or cultural rights. The period between the War for Independence and the War of 1812 was characterized by the absence of consistent government policies for native affairs. By the time the federal government did intervene in the protection of native lands and peoples, in the second decade of the nineteenth century, the entire region was a full extension of the American republic. The white to native population ratio was more than 10 to 1. Spontaneous and sometimes organized violence accompanied the American wave into the west, and decimation was the result. As the historian Colin Calloway puts it so succinctly, "By the nineteenth century, Indian country was envisioned as a place beyond the Mississippi.... The United States looked forward to a future without Indians. The Indians' participation in the Revolution guaranteed their exclusion from the new world born out of the Revolution; their determination to survive as Indians guaranteed their ultimate extinction [in the eyes of white republican America]." As Calloway also notes, "Indian peoples had other ideas," and the fractured native societies did survive. Today there are about two and a half million Americans who claim native ancestry and the numbers are growing. There is now also a successful movement underway to recover cultures, languages, religions, and identities. The trend to extinction that quickened throughout the nineteenth century was halted and is now being reversed.

Families and the Persistence of Rural Life

It is both cliché and fact that, in the era of the American Revolution, the family was the glue that held the community in place. It was also the first stage of a politics that expanded to the wider community and beyond. Independence did not change the structure of the family or relationships within families. At all economic and cultural levels, the war preserved the family structures of late colonial America. While the end of the war left thousands of families without sons and husbands, it also brought a resumption of traditional domestic organization and rhythms. The flow of families searching for land could now move beyond the older backcountry onto the rich soils of the Ohio Valley; the landless sons of crowded towns in New England could marry and move west. Slaveholding families with money for land and additional slaves could install their offspring in the southwest all the way to the Mississippi. The merchants of the port cities could resume their trade and domestic patterns in a more secure political atmosphere even in the postwar depression. The image of Daniel Boone should not obscure the fact that the trailblazers in a very real way were entire families. The Kentucky and Tennessee settlements were extensions of the plantation and farm societies directly on the eastern side of the Appalachians. To the north, New Englanders and others arrived in the upper Ohio Valley for the most part as young families. A substantial number of traders, speculators, and adventurers headed west too, but the first major expansion of the republic was made by families. The Northwest Ordinances of 1784, 1785, and 1787 calculated the distribution of land north of the Ohio River to accommodate the tens of thousands of farm families who would settle there.

Some forms of land tenure were retained from the colonial era, and some were changed in the transition to independence. In most of colonial New England and the middle colonies, the practice of partible inheritance had encouraged economic equilibrium, with the small family farm operating as the mechanism for social continuity. The original deeds of lands in those places had been sufficient to last for a few generations through the subdivision of holdings for sons' inheritances. That had often meant that young men were in thrall to their fathers until the father decided to part with enough land for the son to consider marriage. Over time, as estates diminished in size, the prospects of inheriting even 20 acres of arable land disappeared for many in eastern and southern New England, the Delaware Valley, Long Island, and elsewhere on the eastern seaboard. More landless men in these areas meant delayed marriage or no marriage at all. Thus, the early social impact of the Revolution was the opportunity for family growth and development. People could marry younger and find subsistence in the west. While partible inheritance had shaped the development of family size and function in most of the northern colonies, the southern colonies had retained the

English system of primogeniture and entail. That meant that *only* the eldest son was legally entitled to inherit a father's estate and was then obliged to keep the estate intact. Younger sons were compelled to move farther into the interior of the colony to farm on land that was often less than satisfactory. Georgia eliminated legalized primogeniture in 1777, followed by North Carolina in 1784, Virginia in 1785, Maryland and New York in 1786, and South Carolina in 1791. Rhode Island kept the system until 1798. In the rest of New England and Pennsylvania, where partible inheritance practices had prevailed, the eldest son had been entitled to a double share of the deeded land, but that was ended with independence.

White Americans remained tied to the land in either nuclear or extended family groups and in traditionally integrated ways. Husbands, wives, and children performed agricultural tasks, in concert in some cases and separately, by function, in others. Male children did what they could, according to their age, as did girls whose exclusion from the inheritance laws led them as they reached puberty to marry young or go into domestic service on larger farms until marriage. While no subsistence or small farm was completely self-sustaining, either in the original thirteen states or on the growing new frontier, there was a remarkable degree of economic competence in the family economic structure. The new field and crop techniques advanced by Jared Elliot and others and the introduction of better plows and implements began to reform the agricultural practices of American farmers, but the family remained dependent on what it could grow and manufacture at home. Women in this small-scale rural environment have been seen as the guardians of the hearth, the bearers and nurturers of the children, and the cooks, bakers, spinners, seamstresses, and gardeners. That much is accurate, but women also helped with plowing and harvesting, and the division of labor was not as clear as we imagine. Men did some weaving, gardening, and cider making and worked with their children and wives in the myriad of chores that sustained these tiny commonwealths from season to season. The family farm dominated most rural landscapes, but it was not the only agricultural setting. Some conventional farms in the north were large enough and produced enough to require the use of female servants and field labor. Most white families in the south were located on small farms and lived within nuclear family units, but the plantation culture produced a different kind of family dynamic, one in which labor was provided by slaves. Slave families continued to exist by the grace of masters, in a precarious way, always subject to sale and separation. The larger plantations of the Chesapeake and the south were more like small multiracial societies. Gender, labor, and authority were functionally segregated, and the role of the white male was supervisory and that of the white female, domestic. Appalachian families could be functionally nuclear at one level and bound to larger kinship groups at another. Traditional native family structure crumbled as waves of white migration swept over tribal lands. White Americans, by and large, remained morally nourished by land, farming, and family self-sufficiency into the early nineteenth century. As patriarchal as it was in law, the pre-industrial family balanced economic function much more evenly than would be the case later in the more specialized work environments of the nineteenth century that arose away from the older household environment, especially those that converted craftsmen and urban artisans to wage earners. Even then, however, farming dominated American life for most of the nineteenth century.

For the majority of Americans, the family farm and the deed that went with it represented traditional economic security, just as both had in the colonial period. The early national west, however, often promised more for the future than it offered in the present. The grind of breaking land for crops or finding pasture, the fluctuating markets, rural isolation, and limited finances presented a lifetime of hardships for settlers. First generation habitations were generally crude, small, and crowded. For most, debt was inevitable, for equipment, seed, and breeding stock. Winters were as harsh in Ohio and Indiana as they had been in New England and Pennsylvania, and even harsher in some areas. The soils were generally superior to what remained in the east, and the amount of arable land seemed limitless, but the west was no "promised land" for the many families who, through incompetence, misfortune, poor or erratic markets, and transportation problems, did little more than survive. All of America, including the west, was a less salubrious place in the early decades of the nineteenth century than it had been. The demographic historian Herbert Klein notes that life expectancy in America declined in the early nineteenth century. It was generally lower than it had been before the Revolution and, as the nineteenth century unfolded, was lower in some parts of the United States than it was in parts of northwestern Europe. Mortality rates in America rose, no doubt encouraged by increased population densities in the east, some early urbanization, and the periodic outbreaks of cholera, typhoid, and infectious diseases. Women still averaged seven births and even more pregnancies. While we must speculate, given the absence of data, it is likely that infant mortality was high where exhaustion, poor nutrition, weak or no sanitation, and isolation worked against comfort and safety in pregnancies and births. The toll on the farm women of the west was great. As Klein notes, natural increase in the United States population was relatively high at the beginning of the century, at nearly 3 per cent a year, but declined thereafter. While the falling birth rate explains part of the decline, the higher mortality rates at all levels contributed to it. Klein makes the point that without large-scale immigration, especially after 1820, the United States population would have been about 25 per cent smaller than it was in 1860. Jefferson and others had envisioned a happy agrarian republic of fat, virtuous farmers, but that was not fully realized in the early national period. In addition to the sheer physical impediments to joining the republic of "yeomen," farmers struggled in an unreliable economic climate. The postwar economy slowly rebounded from depression in the early part of the century, but its benefits were unevenly distributed. Embargoes, the War of 1812, and a more aggressive capitalist behavior, while benefiting some, punished others.

Women and Independence
Historians have attempted for some time to explain the Revolution's effects, if any, on

the status of women. What they have found is that, at the legal and political levels, not much changed. Women had taken part in the War for Independence in very direct ways, in all the supporting roles that mothers and wives could provide. Women imbibed the passion and moral thrust of the Revolution and provided material support with homespun and ancillary help, especially to the militias. At the local level, the war was sustained by women and children who often kept farms and households together when men were absent performing military service. When we consider that fewer than 50 per cent of women were sufficiently literate to leave any record behind and that only a small minority of those women actually did so, then their impressions of the war and of female sentiment cannot be taken as a general guide. While the same caveats must be made for the mass of males, we know from constitutions and laws, tax lists, military lists, deeds, wills, and land titles what even the inarticulate males' statuses were, even though few lower class Americans left records of their experiences and views. Historian Mary Beth Norton's influential studies, *Liberty's Daughters* and *Founding Mothers and Fathers*, make a good case for a rising female consciousness associated with the resistance movement, the war and the new age of republican virtue, equality, and progress. Women's associations and collectives pressed their cases for inclusion into male-controlled politics, but the efforts of middle-class and upper-class women to take part in what was a transitional era were usually incomplete or more likely unsuccessful in the wake of independence. As Norton puts it, "[A]n educated woman in 1800 had only a modicum more control over her destiny than her uneducated grandmother had had in 1750: she could, if she wished, teach school for a few years before marriage, decide not to marry at all, choose a husband without consulting her parents, or raise her children in accordance with republican principles. But she could not, realistically, aspire to leave the feminine sphere altogether." Given the trends in the American economy, an *uneducated* woman would have had even less reason to thank the Revolution.

Norton's point, however, is a good one so far as it goes. She and sister historian Linda Kerber and a generation of students of the subject have identified a large population of literate, opinionated, and politicized women in this era. Eventually, the rhetoric of 1776 required an intellectual leadership of women to carry it across gender lines, but it would take a long time to develop. John Adams's wise and articulate wife Abigail has left for posterity a set of lively and provocative thoughts. It can be assumed that she represented the sentiments of at least some of her class when she noted in her oft-quoted advice to her husband in the spring of 1776, "In the new code of laws which I suppose it will be necessary for you to make I desire you would remember the ladies and be more generous and favorable to them than your ancestors." The shrewd Abigail was perhaps anticipating a new definition of political rights, but she was most likely exercising her wit. She is endlessly quotable and convincing, and sardonically played with the contradictions in the revolutionary proclamations of the 1770s. In the way that slaves were to be excluded from the natural rights claimed for "all men," she notes that women too are outside the substantive application of the Declaration. In another letter to her husband John, a month after the Declaration was signed, she announced, "Whilst you are proclaiming peace and good will to men, emancipating all nations, you insist upon retaining an absolute power over your wives." The Revolution raised the issue of gender equality in a way that was new, and it did sow the seeds of a later push for women's rights. Abigail Adams's sharp criticisms seem remarkably close to the proto-feminist movements of the 1830s and 1840s and to the *Declaration of Sentiments and Resolutions* (patterned deliberately on the Declaration of Independence) issued by the Women's Rights Convention at Seneca Falls, New York in 1848. The actual Declaration, however, and the various state constitutions, the Articles of Confederation, and the United States Constitution (1787) were all silent on women, unlike on slaves and natives. The citizenship of white women was implicitly acknowledged (presumably by not denying it), but the voting and legal exclusions continued. The era revealed the intellectual talents of women like Mercy Otis Warren (1728-1814), the sister of James Otis, whose intelligence, literary skills, and patriotism were expressed brilliantly in a variety of dramatic satires and poems. Her *History*, published in 1805, deserves a bigger audience today than it generally gets. But Adams, Warren, and other writers were exceptions to most, who complied with the more restrained role of women. As Linda Kerber puts it, the Revolution would leave women, middle-class women at any rate, in an "ambiguous relationship between motherhood and citizenship." However citizenship was defined for women in independent America, the great mass of women continued in their roles of gender-specific work and childrearing, while other educated or middle-class women would have to fight for equal rights for women. Among the social values that survived independence was the assumed place of women in society, in politics, and under the law. It is worth noting that the most influential feminist political tract of the period did not come from America but was the Englishwoman Mary Wollstonecraft's *A Vindication of the Rights of Woman* of 1792. Wollstonecraft had earlier published an attack on slavery and poverty in *A Vindication of the Rights of Man* in support of the radical purposes of the French Revolution. America did not produce a Mary Wollstonecraft.

The Political Limits of Independence

The war had removed the superstructure of the Empire and replaced it with a makeshift set of institutions and a great deal of space. It had also left a depressed set of economies, a debased currency, and a voluntary confederation with too many political uncertainties. As early as 1781 and the fall of Yorktown, some leading political figures had urged a review of the Articles of Confederation to endow the confederation with a more coherent administrative authority. Independence had been achieved, but could it be protected and secured? The British had maintained a series of forts and trading networks on the fringes of what was, technically, the northwest boundary of American territory, where it ran into the vastness of British North America in the western regions of the Great Lakes. Those forts were an affront to American autonomy. In addition, the British controlled the Atlantic and the world's major trade routes, and, for all that the

French had been vital allies in the American cause, there was no assurance that the entente could be maintained if the French decided to exercise their own trade preferences and leave the American economy further isolated. A generation of Americans had grown up with the Continental Congress and the Continental Army as political reality, but their roles were now passé in many ways, and the Revolution had still to run its course. The war had bound the majority of Americans together across the spectrum of class and locality, but how durable was that bond? Peace raised an unexpected question. Could the common cause of the war be sustained? One common attachment that most Americans shared lay in their affection for George Washington. What he represented would be as important in peace as it had been in war.

Henry ("Light-Horse Harry") Lee's famous eulogy for Washington in 1799 is an indication not only of the public's veneration of Washington but also of Washington's very real contribution to American politics in the 1780s. Lee (not to be confused with Richard Henry Lee) composed the resolution to the House of Representatives that was addressed "to the memory of the Man, first in war, first in peace, and first in the hearts of his fellow citizens." Here was America's first recognizable statesman and the embodiment of American citizenship. Washington had led the Americans to victory in the war, and, while the glamorous Lafayette; the subtle Nathanael Greene; the martyrs Warren, Montgomery, and Nathan Hale; and the brave rank and file were memorialized and celebrated, Washington's image had been superimposed on the meaning of independence. That much is obvious in Lee's resolution, but its full significance is in the words "first in peace, and first in the hearts" of Americans. The theoretical proposals of Alexander Hamilton, the debates on independence among the revolutionary leaders and in state legislatures, and Thomas Jefferson's leadership on the question of western development were all crucial in the way independence was reshaped in the first few years after Yorktown. James Madison's role in the making of the Constitution and its ratification were indispensable to the nation's birth, but Washington's presence as the automatic presiding officer at the Constitutional Convention in 1787 gave the process the necessary cachet it would need to advance. Washington's approval of change *after* the war is the reason Lee could claim him as being "first in peace."

As early as 1783, Washington exhibited his reputation in a showdown with Continental Army officers at Newburgh, New York before the Army was officially disbanded. The event, sometimes referred to as the "Newburgh Conspiracy," was a test of the role of civil government in the United States. In January of 1783, a group of officers from Newburgh sent a "memorial" to Congress requesting settlement of their promised food and clothing allowances, pensions, and back pay. The major complaint resulted from a report that Congress was ignoring pensions, a very important consideration for the officer corps. On the advice of an anonymous motion passed through the camp urging determined pressure on Congress, the officers first requested and then demanded that Congress settle the issue by legislation. The officers were on sound ethical grounds, but their aggressive tone seemed to defy civil authority. They informed Congress in Philadelphia that unless its demands were met, the Army would not disband. Washington blunted the movement briefly with an announcement that was deliberately misrepresented by some officers as supporting their actions. On March 15, Washington then appeared in person and denounced the officers' decision to put their own interest above that of the civilian authority. Because of his reputation, his personal intervention worked; if their beloved Commander in Chief supported the authority of Congress, how could they not? Their continued defiance of Congress would then stand as an unthinkable repudiation of Washington himself. The officers quickly recanted and resolved to show respect for Congress. While there is evidence of a plot (even General Horatio Gates was implicated along with a group that wished to disgrace Congress and push for a stronger central government) there was likely little possibility of a military coup. Rather, the Newburgh Conspiracy was an attempt to manipulate Congress. Its historical significance lies in Washington's endorsement of the supremacy of civilian government in military matters. The issue of a standing army would arise later, but Congress and most Americans saw no sense in the retention of a full-time army after the war was over. Congress did issue generous officers pensions but only after the contrition of the officers at Newburgh. Washington had shown that he could be "first in peace." The Continental Army was disbanded a few months later.

Financial Problems

Because it suited the states, for a few years after 1783, the Articles of Confederation survived, largely with the help and good will of most of the delegates. There were doubts, however, about Congress's ability to secure the peace. John Adams's attempts by negotiation to get the British to abandon their forts in the west went nowhere. Britain insisted on compensation for loyalist property losses, but the various states insisted on their rights to the appropriations. Congress also tried to integrate American trade into the larger world economy. Some concessions were made by the British to accommodate American trade, but, by the middle of the 1780s, the states were running a trade deficit with Britain of four to one, and, while that ratio closed to two to one, the value of American exports declined. Trade volume with the Dutch and French was improving, but America's best markets were British. The trade imbalance depleted America's hard money reserves, and the Congress remained dependent on requisitions from the states. The latter had been fiscally unreliable in wartime, but, after 1783, their payments shrunk to about 20 per cent of requests. The Congress could barely conduct the limited mandate it had. At the beginning of 1785, the British made it clear that they could not enter into firm trade treaties with Congress so long as any single state could render any accord "ineffectual." The states' desire for autonomy was now hampering economies. Some leaders had begun to advocate revisions of the Articles. The most important early proposal was to allow Congress to act unilaterally in matters of commerce, thus obviating the need to appeal to every state government to negotiate even the simplest agreement. The proposal was rejected, and the depression continued. Independence had been achieved at a huge financial cost. Economic historians have estimated that American per capita income declined by 46 per cent between 1774 and 1790, and, while it slowly and erratically recovered, it was still 14 per cent below the 1774 standard in 1805.

When Robert Morris stepped down as Superintendent of Finance in 1783, he was replaced by a board that managed to keep the stretched finances of Congress in order. Morris deserves more attention than he usually gets in the historical record; he was crucial in devising mechanisms for financing the war, and like others, such as Franklin, he arranged loans in Europe. He went into personal debt to help pay for the demobilization costs of the Continental Army and pressed Congress to start minting its own coins to prevent the loss of hard currency (specie). The war had shown Morris and others that a sound currency was essential to a stable economy. Americans had been using any specie they could find as monetary exchange both before and during the war. As far back as anyone could remember, Spanish, French, and Dutch as well as British hard currency had circulated in the colonies and revolutionary states. The most common coins were Spanish pistoles and doubloons. The western Atlantic did as much trade in Spanish dollars, "pieces of eight" and "doubloons," as in any other national currency largely because of Spain's mining of large supplies of gold and silver in the seventeenth and eighteenth centuries. In the colonies, the various jurisdictions had long circulated "bills of credit" loosely tied to the British sterling system of pounds, shillings, and pence. These bills were unstable but had represented as much as 75 per cent of monetary exchange in the states and led to a steady devaluation of Congress's notes ("Continentals"). Huge debt loads were created in the states. While the Articles of Confederation had authorized Congress to regulate the money supply and assess each state its portion of the collective requisition, the system was chaotic and dangerous. Issuing bills for redemption was fine, but the values were never stable. Morris and astute merchants and investors could always measure the relative or exchange value between a Massachusetts shilling, a Spanish doubloon, and the British shilling coin, but they could not control the fluctuation in exchange. A single standard was needed for America, but it was slow in coming. Morris took the initial step, and Jefferson continued with it. By 1786, a system was beginning to emerge. The decimal system was adopted, and a unit called the dollar, derived from the German word "taler," was decreed. The larger denominations, fives and tens, were to be issued in gold and single dollars in silver. By 1792, the United States Congress had established a national currency based on those specifications.

Despite the limits to American influence in Europe, John Adams at the British court and Franklin and Jefferson in France provided the appearance, at least, of formal diplomacy. Franklin, in particular, enhanced America's image as he had done in the past. The Philadelphia polymath entertained the French with his manner, his learning and, as ever, was refreshingly sociable and likeable. Jefferson's intellect and refinements made another kind of impression on the French, a respect for American political acuity and cultural depth. In London, Adams had the most difficult task of trying to appease British doubts about the Continental Congress's fragile authority. Although he stuck it out for four years and was joined by Abigail, his achievements were slight even as he kept the British engaged. In the meantime, while Congress managed to establish more trading agreements with Prussia, its relations with Spain soured. The Spanish refused to agree to American access to the lower Mississippi, thus closing a potential outlet for American goods from the west into the Atlantic via the Gulf of Mexico. John Jay (1745-1829) and the Spanish minister Don Diego de Gardoqui negotiated for months and in the end gave up when Congress indicated that it could not muster the two-thirds majority it needed to sign a treaty on boundary issues. That failure underlined Congress's limitations in foreign affairs. Similarly, an attempt to get a treaty with Morocco for access to North African ports fell through but was successfully revived in the 1790s by the new national government. American ships began to round Cape Horn and were active in the Pacific. Some trade deals with Chinese interests resulted, but trade was generally hampered by the hodgepodge of various state interventions. Ad hoc and confused practices bedeviled American merchants as states leveraged their trade laws for advantage. In 1785, for example, Massachusetts banned exports to Britain carried in British ships. Other states followed, raising duties to protect local economies and the shipping industry. The wayward trends in trade and diplomacy were met with disdain by the British who noted that it was becoming difficult to deal with thirteen authorities. The Massachusetts legislature was encouraged then to make a formal call to revise the Articles of Confederation, but the state delegates to Congress did not bring it up. Nevertheless, a problem with the Articles had been clearly identified.

In domestic matters, some cooperation and solidarity was achieved. The surrender of state claims to western lands was a healthy sign in peeling away the obstacles to interstate harmony. An agreement on navigation rights in the Chesapeake between Maryland, Virginia, and Pennsylvania in 1785 augured well for more interstate collaboration. The Congress served as a clearing-house for these state-based initiatives. The Continental Congress had moved to New York, and, in the meantime, plans had been made for a new and permanent location. By 1786, however, wherever one looked, the economy was suffering as the volume of trade declined along with incomes and property values. The states' retention of fiscal, trade, and judicial controls had led to thirteen mostly incompetent small economies. Charles Pinckney (1757-1824) of South Carolina proposed a revision of the Articles in August of 1786 to grant Congress more legislative and judicial control over interstate and foreign affairs and to strengthen the means to assess and collect the Congress's requisitions from the states. The proposals failed simply because amendments to the Articles of Confederation required unanimous approval. In this case, New Jersey balked, but it might have been any other single state or group of states. Nevertheless, an earlier plan to discuss interstate commerce, scheduled for Annapolis, Maryland, went ahead in September 1786. This was a propitious meeting, although only five states showed up and the host, Maryland, failed to send delegates. Among the handful of delegates were John Dickinson, the former Pennsylvanian and prominent revolutionary who was then living in Delaware, and

Alexander Hamilton, Washington's former military assistant, a rising force in New York politics, and a vigorous advocate of a general government with independent authority. Hamilton drafted a call to the states to meet in Philadelphia the following spring to "render the constitution [the Articles of Confederation] of the Federal Government adequate to the exigencies of the union." Congress took months to consider it, but eventually agreed to the Philadelphia convention. The notice from Congress was unequivocal; the meeting to be held in May of 1787 was for "the sole and express purpose of revising the Articles of Confederation and reporting to Congress and the several legislatures such alterations and provisions therein."

Shays's Rebellion

While the west beckoned, many prospective New England migrants were not in a financial position to heed the call. By 1786, in the local gathering places, taverns, town meetings, and churches in central and western Massachusetts, poverty had replaced independence as the chief topic of discussion as beleaguered farmers saw their livelihoods disappearing in mounting debt loads and meager prospects for relief. Several hundred of the state's farmers were bankrupt, and thousands more were close to it, ground into debt by depressed markets, underemployment, and rising taxes. A textbook clash of debtors and creditors loomed. Many creditors themselves were in debt and showed no patience with the insolvent farmers who had petitioned the Massachusetts government to devalue the currency so that debts could be repaid more easily. In the spring of 1786, farmers had failed to get a moratorium on foreclosures. A town meeting in Worcester and a larger rally at nearby Hatfield confirmed the farmers' solidarity and the degree of discontent. Once again, the farmers appealed to the government to issue paper money and reduce taxes. They complained about the lawyers who harassed them on behalf of creditors and about a state Senate that clearly supported creditor interests. No violence was advocated, but mobs interrupted court proceedings anyway. Governor Bowdoin sent some 600 militia to Springfield to secure the court there, but a force of 500 angry farmers managed to close it. An insurrection was underway, and, by September, it was being led by Daniel Shays (1747-1825), an impoverished former Continental Army captain. The arsenal at Springfield in western Massachusetts became a target for the insurgents. Congress was alarmed enough to authorize Henry Knox, the former bookseller turned Continental Army general who was then the War Secretary, to raise an army of 1,300 men in New England on the public relations premise of dealing with natives. That force was in fact poised to step into Massachusetts's unhappy state of affairs.

By December, Shays was at the head of 1,200 men and set to join up with another insurgent army led by Luke Day. Bowdoin called for 4,400 militiamen to put down the rebellion. He ended up with about three-quarters of that number, and, while the uprising collapsed in eastern Massachusetts, it grew stronger in the west, throwing the state into panic. Shays intended a *coup d'état* by seizing the arsenal, arming an even larger rebel force, and bringing down the government. The state militia was led by General

Benjamin Lincoln, who had a varied war record and had served briefly as Secretary of War. On January 24, 1787, Shays attacked the arsenal and was repulsed by artillery. Shays had proceeded thinking he had Luke Day's support. Lincoln then arrived and chased the late arriving Day into New Hampshire and the hapless Shays into Vermont, capturing 150 of his men and, by the end of February, scattering the rest. The great drama resulted in only a few deaths, and the leaders were eventually pardoned for their treason. Later in 1787, Massachusetts relaxed some of its tax laws and amended the list of materials that could not be recovered for debt. Eventually, some Shaysites made it into the legislature in a vindication of their ideological position, but what gives Shays a permanent place in history was the impact the rebellion had on the minds of the delegates as they made their way to the Constitutional Convention in May 1787.

The Northwest Ordinances

The most important legacy of the Articles of Confederation occurred in the final months of their existence. As the delegates sweated through the convention in Philadelphia in July 1787, Congress passed the Northwest Ordinance, a law that provided for orderly government in the west. The entire region north of the Ohio River and west of the Appalachians running all the way to the western limits of American territory was included in the Ordinance. As settlers made their way into the northwest after 1787, they would enter lands that were destined to become states. The Ordinance capped a series of surveys, plans, and proposals that had begun in the wake of western land concessions. As the territory became a formal extension of the states *collectively* under the Articles of Confederation, the Congress had assumed full jurisdiction over it. The Northwest Ordinance was eventually and silently absorbed into the United States Constitution, which was being composed even as the Ordinance was passed.

The 1787 Ordinance followed two earlier designs, and the three together set out a western settlement policy of considerable detail. The first step was the Territorial Ordinance of 1784, the work of a committee headed by Jefferson. It recommended that the entire area north of the Ohio be subdivided into a series of administrative units that would later be joined to the confederated states east of the Appalachians. Jefferson's proposal that slavery be banned in the area after 1800 was rejected, but a start was made on ensuring that, as the United States spread westward, it would avoid what the British had done in America. There would be colonists to the west, but there would be no "colonies" in the west, rather a series of states with completely equal status under the Articles of Confederation. There was a provision in this ordinance for the careful subdivision of lands for settlement. In a fanciful separate note, Jefferson proposed the creation of fourteen new states in the entire north to south range of the territory and all the way to the Mississippi. He went so far as to name ten of them: Sylvania, Michigania, Cherronesus, Assenisipia, Metropotamia, Illinoia, Saratoga, Washington, Polypotamia, and Pelisipia. His appreciation of the historical significance of Saratoga and Washington is noteworthy. The Land Ordinance of 1785 adjusted and refined the 1784 proposal. The geometrical design of allotting land moved with

Americans on to the western plains beyond the Mississippi. It was later adopted by Canada for its prairie settlements in the late nineteenth century. The plan called for a symmetrical series of sections of one square mile (640 acres) each, collected into townships of 36 sections. One section in each township was reserved for public education purposes. Settled land was then defined as "Range, Township, Section," and later, for example, as being "west of the first principal meridian [approximately following a line of longitude]." A piece of land might be described simply as "S.W. $^{1}/_{4}$ of sect. 32, T 4 S., R 5 W." This was the way Abraham Lincoln's parents' 160-acre farm in Illinois, a quarter of a square mile (the "$^{1}/_{4}$ of sect. 32" in the deed), was identified in 1816. Land was purchased and sold in parcels of those divisions, and, as noted, even the single section could later be subdivided into half and quarter sections to accommodate family farms. This grid allowed for a sensible and symmetrical settlement pattern, and the distribution of the land seemed favorable to speculators and settlers alike. Congress intelligently assigned the formal surveying of the territory to a consortium of state surveyors who established the first set of ranges in the upper Ohio.

The culmination of this process was the act of July 1787. While it was intended initially to refine the 1784 Ordinance and include the distribution variables of 1785, it went a great deal further. First, it confined itself to the territory north of the Ohio, so, when it banned slavery from the entire region, it tacitly left the territories south of the Ohio open to slavery. It took the 1784 divisions, reduced them to five new territories, and specified the number of inhabitants necessary for statehood. There are six clauses in the Ordinance as follows:

1. A guarantee of freedom of religion.
2. A guarantee of property rights and due process of law, including very clear provisions for protecting the rights of the accused in any legal case.
3. A provision to protect the "property, rights and liberty" of the natives in the region, except in "just and proper wars authorized by Congress."
4. A formal declaration of the permanent equal status within the union of any states created in the region: "the States which may be formed.... shall forever remain a part of the confederacy ... subject to the Articles of Confederation, *and to alterations therein as shall be constitutionally made*." (Emphasis added.)
5. The provision for a minimum of three and a maximum of five new states in the territory that would eventually include the states of Ohio, Indiana, and Illinois in the initial phase of organization, with Michigan and then Wisconsin later. They would be admitted when their populations each reached 60,000 and when a suitable state constitution had been submitted for approval to Congress. The Ordinance was very precise on the geographical boundaries of the potential states.
6. A ban on slavery in the region. The potent phrase "There shall be neither slavery nor involuntary servitude in the said territory" indicates why this would be a "Northwest Ordinance" and why there was no serious effort to create a doctrine for settlement of the area south of the Ohio River.

The Ordinance ensured that nineteenth-century America would develop in its inevitable westward direction as two distinct zones or "sections." The traditional north-south axis of late colonial America, would become two east to west axes defined by slavery. As for the natives who inhabited the western lands, their property and freedoms were ostensibly protected, but could be set aside in the case of wars "authorized" by Congress. In the case of informal clashes between the swarms of whites who moved west and the natives they encountered, Congress would inevitably favor the whites.

Conclusion

American independence was achieved by a long and bitter war, fought for the most part within the inhabited parts of the former colonies. As throngs of families began to move west, native people, who had been drawn into the war mostly on the British side, were repaid by being marginalized by the peace. The loyalists in the population, worn down by the war, were deprived of property and citizenship. The war's length had engaged women at every level, but their contributions did not result in improved legal or political status and, at the level of work and political roles, nothing of consequence changed for them. Socially, there were no immediate benefits for poorer Americans, but, if they could find their way into the west, they had prospects, even if nothing was guaranteed. Large continuous migration began in the 1780s. The potential for economic exploitation went west in the form of planters in the south and land speculators in the north. There would be no freeing of the slaves in the south, where the great majority lived, and a sporadic and often reluctant emancipation in the north. Free African Americans were still subject to the moral and economic discriminations that had existed before the war, even where there was clear evidence of their contributions to the war effort. Despite the war's length and its strident rhetoric, the abolitionist movement was weak and utterly helpless in the south. Politically, the war produced a set of republican institutions and ideas. The Articles of Confederation were adopted after considerable delay and proved to be the basis of a federal order, even if they were largely ineffectual in confirming America's international status or economic viability. The war had removed a powerful imperial sovereignty and replaced it with a loose federation of small republics. Shays's Rebellion vividly illustrated the fragility of the new order, and the movement to tighten up the confederation, already underway, was given impetus by it. Yet for all the problems and disappointments of the era, the seeds of security and growth were demonstrated in the emergence of a republican vanguard most commonly associated with Washington and other "national" figures. The projected development of the west, stipulated in the Northwest Ordinance, pointed the way to a systematic expansion of republican culture. Nevertheless, in 1787, despite the energy and optimism inspired by the war and independence and regardless of the accompanying grandstanding, America was still not fully realized as a nation. It was not a fully coherent union, nor was it yet a political democracy.

Suggested Reading

The period between independence and the Constitution was christened "the critical period" by the historian John Fiske in 1899. The concept has stuck. A superb discussion on the period is Merrill Jensen, *A New Nation: A History of the United States During the Confederation, 1781-1789* (1950; Boston: Northeastern University Press, 1981); see the same author's *The Articles of Confederation* (1940; Madison: The University of Wisconsin Press, 1966). Jensen's interpretations should be bolstered by Jack N. Rakove, *The Beginnings of National Politics: An Interpretive History of the Continental Congress* (New York: Knopf, 1979); Richard Hofstadter, "The Founding Fathers: An Age of Realism" in *The American Political Tradition and the Men Who Made It* (1948; New York: Vintage, 1973) is a useful comment on political exigency. On the same theme of insecurity and exigency, Shays's Rebellion attracts a great deal of scholarly attention, and the most recent analysis of the event is Leonard Richards, *Shays's Rebellion: The American Revolution's Final Battle* (Philadelphia: University of Pennsylvania Press, 2002).

On the effects of independence on slaves and free blacks see Ira Berlin, *Many Thousands Gone: The First Two Centuries of Slavery in North America* (Cambridge, MA: Harvard University Press, 1998); Philip S. Foner, *Blacks in the American Revolution* (Westport, CT: Greenwood Press, 1976); and Duncan J. McLeod, *Slavery, Race, and the American Revolution* (London: Cambridge University Press, 1974).

An excellent introduction to the roles and fates of various classes of women (including native and African American women) is Carol Berkin, *Revolutionary Mothers: Women in the Struggle for America's Independence* (New York: Hill and Wang, 2005). See also Linda K. Kerber, *Women of the Republic, Intellect and Ideology in Revolutionary America* (Chapel Hill: The University of North Carolina Press, 1980); Mary Beth Norton, *Liberty's Daughters: The Revolutionary Experience of American Women, 1750-1800* (1980; Boston: Little, Brown and Company, 1996); and Laurel Thatcher Ulrich, *A Midwife's Tale: The Life of Martha Ballard Based on her Diary* (New York: Vintage, 1991). On the west and the frontier, see Reginald Horsman, *The Frontier in the Formative Years, 1783-1815* (New York: Holt Rinehart and Winston, 1970); Henry Nash Smith, *Virgin Land: The American West as Symbol and Myth* (Cambridge, MA: Harvard University Press, 1950); and Malcolm J. Rohrbough, *The Trans-Appalachian Frontier: Peoples, Societies, and Institutions, 1775-1850* (New York: Oxford University Press, 1978), which notes a continuous process of frontier development and change over the many decades of western migration after independence. On economic developments, see A. Barton Hepburn, *A History of Currency in the United States*, rev. ed. (New York: The MacMillan Company, 1924), and John McCusker and Russell Menard, *The Economy of British America, 1607-1789* (Chapel Hill, NC: The University of North Carolina Press, 1985). On the impact on natives, see Colin G. Calloway, *The American Revolution in Indian Country* (Cambridge: Cambridge University Press, 1995). David Waldstreicher, *In the Midst of Perpetual Fetes: The Making of American Nationalism 1776-1820* (Chapel Hill: University of North Carolina Press, 1997) notes the stirring of a "national" consciousness.

CHAPTER SIX

THE CONSTITUTION, RATIFICATION, AND THE FIRST PARTY SYSTEM

A form of government that is not the result of a long sequence of shared experiences, efforts, and endeavors can never take root.
> — Napoleon Bonaparte, 1803, as quoted by J.C. Herold, *The Mind of Napoleon* (1955)

Time Line

1787	Constitutional Convention.
	The United States Constitution (September 1787).
1787-88	The ratification of the Constitution.
	Federalist Papers.
1789	First United States Congress, controlled by Federalist Party.
	The French Revolution began.
1790	Hamilton's economic proposals.
1791	First ten amendments to the Constitution (The Bill of Rights) were adopted.
	The First Bank of the United States was chartered.
	Vermont admitted to the union as the 14th state.
1792	Kentucky admitted to the union as the 15th state.
	Washington re-elected to the presidency.
1794	Eli Whitney's "Cotton Gin" patent.

The Making of a National Politics

The convention to revise the Articles ran from May to September of 1787 and stands as one of the most invigorating events in American political history. It had been endorsed by Congress in February 1787 and given impetus by the Shays crisis in Massachusetts. The prospects for more civil insurrection had frightened many in Congress and even more in the various state legislatures. But even without Shays, there was going to have to be a substantial revision or even replacement of the Articles. Alexander Hamilton and James Madison were leading advocates of reform. Hamilton had urged a strengthening of Congress's ability to act for the whole without having to consult the whole. Pinckney and others, including the Massachusetts government, had wanted Congress to have more control over interstate and foreign affairs, even before Shays. There had been complaints of the impotency of Congress and the Articles since before the war's end, and, despite the various achievements of the Continental Congress, the confederation seemed adrift. At Annapolis the previous fall, Hamilton had been adamant in calling for a meeting to reform the Articles and end the "embarrassments which characterize...national affairs, foreign and domestic." Hamilton had used the term "national" and so had others, but he was using it in a way that made him one of what historian Jack Greene termed "hard core nationalists." If the Articles of Confederation had been seen by a majority of leaders as concluding the Revolution, others saw completion only in the creation of a fully developed nation state. Hamilton was one of those. So was James Madison, the 37-year-old veteran of Virginia politics who had helped frame the Virginia Constitution as a 25-year-old. He had sat in the Continental Congress before his 30th birthday. Madison was not a very forceful public speaker but wrote with great confidence and effect. A month before the Philadelphia convention was to meet, he denounced the states for their behavior and condemned the Articles of Confederation for being incapable of "coercion" in making the states comply with their obligations.

In a stunning attack on the enfeebled system as it stood in the spring of 1787, Madison called for an end of the Articles and their replacement with a national government with authority over the states. This was truly revolutionary, and it marked a new definition for independence. Madison's essay *Vices of the Political System of the United States* was both a catalogue of current ills and a prescription for reform. Its logic is simple: the states had not lived up to their pledges in ratifying the Articles, and the Articles did not have the teeth to make useful laws nor to enforce the few it did make. Madison makes the case for dissolving the Articles as follows:

> As far as the union of the States is to be regarded as a league of sovereign powers [which it was, according to its own definition], and not as a political Constitution by virtue of which they are become one sovereign power, so far it seems to follow from the doctrine of compacts that a breach of any of the articles of the Confederation by any of the parties to it, absolves the other parties from their respective Obligations, and gives them a right if they chuse to exert it, of dissolving the Union altogether.

Madison was fully aware that the Articles had been deliberately designed with that provision in place. The "compact" was an "agreement" only and not a transfer of power from state to Congress. Madison saw it as folly to continue the arrangement. His essay begins with a torrid assault on the states' short-sighted behavior, and attacks their lack of ethics. Madison noted that the states had never met their financial obligations (the "requisitions") to the collective interest; the states had violated Congress's authority by making treaties with natives and with each other; they had circumvented Congress's efforts to rationalize its foreign affairs and had violated the 1783 treaties with France and Holland; they were actually competing with each other and restricting other states' trade and monetary freedoms; and they had displayed "perverseness" in refusing to collaborate on a variety of commercial opportunities. Madison believed that the apparent inability of the states to defend their own interests against internal revolt was obvious (an allusion to Shays perhaps). Also, they had never put the Articles directly to the people for ratification but had left the matter solely to the legislatures, and states had made such a volume of laws in such a short space of time that many were contradictory within their own bounds as well as uncoordinated with the laws of other states with similar interests. Besides, he argued, state laws were often transient and "mutable," subject to change at the whim of legislatures.

Madison then summarized his complaints by questioning the competence of state legislative majorities, which often failed to satisfy "the fundamental Principle of Republican Government." He supposed that, in a small jurisdiction such as a state, there was no way to check the personal ambitions of politicians. It would be naïve, said Madison, to suppose that the "public good" could govern politics in these small selfish legislatures, and a larger more varied republic would at least help offset these deficiencies. But his best rationale for change was in his assessment of the wayward and selfish interests of unchecked individual ambition and liberty. In a passage, the theme of which would appear a year later in *The Federalist* (no. 10), Madison noted that "a still more fatal if not more frequent cause [of republican incompetence and failure], lies among the people themselves. All civilized societies are divided into different interests and factions, as they happen to be creditors or debtors — rich or poor — husbandmen, merchants or manufacturers — members of different religious sects — followers of different political leaders — inhabitants of different districts — owners of different kinds of property &c &c." Those "interests" appear to Madison to be natural and inevitable in the structures of republics, but psychology also informed Madison's theory of selfishness. He agreed with the seventeenth-century English theorists of natural man and with the eighteenth-century Scottish thinker David Hume, who saw "human nature" as the defining feature of societies. To turn what he saw as social habits into the public good, Madison came up with a trenchant idea drawn from the perceived dangers of "notorious factions & oppressions...in corporate towns limited as the opportunities are, and in little republics when uncontrolled by apprehensions of external danger." Madison saw that if there was "an enlargement of the sphere" there was less possibility of any faction or concert of factions forming a majority to oppress the rest. A larger republic was superior to the smaller because the larger "Society," as he puts it, "becomes broken into a greater variety of interests, of pursuits of passions, which check each other." Madison concludes with a memorable summation:

> The great desideratum in Government is such a modification of the sovereignty as will render it sufficiently neutral between the different interests and factions, to controul one part of the society from invading the rights of another, and at the same time sufficiently controuled itself, from setting up an interest adverse to that of the whole Society.... As a limited monarchy tempers the evils of an absolute one; so an extensive Republic meliorates the administration of a small Republic.

Madison went to Philadelphia with a firm idea of what American politics needed.

The Meeting in Philadelphia

The Constitutional Convention, as it would come to be known, contained all the ingredients of high political drama. The confused foreign affairs, the cantankerous interstate differences that continued despite the agreements on western land conces- sions, the economic depression, the specter of more Shays-like troubles — in fact, the tendency to disunion — all seemed like a repudiation of the Declaration of Independence and the exuberance of 1775-76. It did not matter that Madison blamed the problems of the independent states on the narrow ambitions and wilful self-interests of individ- uals, factions, or state legislatures; it was clear to many that a renewed union had to be devised. The political theorizing that marked every stage of the Revolution would be brought to bear on real issues. The United States Constitution would mark an original American example of meshing theory with experience and need, as had the Stamp Act resolutions and the Declaration of Independence in the recent past.

Still, the Convention began inauspiciously. On May 14, the formal date for the meeting, only two delegations were in attendance, those of Pennsylvania, the hosts, and Virginia, their neighbors. A quorum of seven states was achieved by May 25. The debates began in earnest at that point, and George Washington was chosen to preside over the proceedings. By the time the convention got down to business, it was clear to most del- egates that there would be no simple tinkering with the Articles of Confederation; they would have to be replaced. The objective at Philadelphia was immediately understood to be to preserve the republican qualities of the state constitutions and find a mecha- nism to hold them together under a design that effectively created an aggregate authority, something the Articles had failed to do because they had left *all* final author- ity with the states. A federation could not work if it relied on the whims or self-interest of its component members. The chief problem thus confronting the delegates was to find a way to give the confederation more power to act decisively for the whole, while the states retained their own clearly defined local prerogatives.

The United States Constitution emerged after only four months of proposals, debate, compromise, and design. It stands as a remarkable achievement, but the docu- ment is not entirely original. It draws its premises and mechanisms from an array of state and Articles precedents and strikes a republican tone in its descriptions of repre- sentation, rights, and balances. In its institutional design, it reflects American political experiences and is less an invention than a derivation of existing political models and ideas. What is original is the way it amends or shapes its models and precedents to cre- ate an entirely new force in American history, a political sovereignty that appeared to be superior to the various sovereignties that had created it.

The delegates to the Convention included only eight of the signers of the Declaration of Independence. Thomas Jefferson and John Adams were in Europe and did not attend, but other significant older political figures did. John Dickinson, James Wilson, Robert Morris, Roger Sherman, George Mason, William Livingston, and Elbridge Gerry were only a few of the luminaries in attendance. Alexander Hamilton and James Madison had already shaped the debate at Philadelphia, and the Convention was given prestige with the addition of George Washington and the aging, venerated Ben Franklin as delegates. Some nominees refused the appointments and were replaced. Twelve states nominated a total of 65 delegates to the Convention. Rhode Island ignored it. Ten of the nominees did not attend, and, of the 55 who did, not all attended on a regular basis. Sixteen delegates failed to sign the document when it was finished. The remaining 39, including the presiding officer George Washington and secretary William Jackson, signed it on September 17, 1787. The average delegate was a professional, middle-class, college-trained lawyer. More than half the delegates had college degrees, a few of them more than one. Several, including Washington and Franklin, had honorary doctorates. There was a broad distribution of age: four delegates were still in their twenties, 14 in their thirties, 23 in their forties, and 14 men were over fifty years old. Franklin, at age eighty-one, was the eldest by fifteen years. What the group had in abundance was intellectual credibility, political experience, and an array of opinions. A secretary had been assigned, but no minutes were taken and what we know of the debates we get mostly from the observations of James Madison whose notes left a sparkling record that was not published until 1840.

The delegates, despite their obvious need to satisfy their respective states' interests while still coming up with a stronger federal agreement, were all concerned with the difficulty in designing a single system that could accommodate the political needs and assumptions of large states, small states, slave states, and free states. Could any system be designed to embrace such a diversity of social, political, and economic environments? In fact, the delegates had to come to terms with Madison's basic premise: that small republics, that is, the states, were fallible in their own right. What the Convention revealed was not so much a bold experimentation in nation building as a "bundle of compromises" that sought to settle the concerns of all the states in terms of their respective "advantages" and "disadvantages." In other words, what advantages would state A get by this or that formula, against what advantages state B might get? Put another way, the delegates were being invited to give up the advantages of their autonomy in order to prevent the disadvantages of their autonomy. The key obstacles to accord were revealed in two early proposals, the so-called "Virginia Plan" of union of May and the "New Jersey Plan" of June.

The Constitutional Debates

On May 29, Edmund Randolph of Virginia proposed a complete rejection of the Articles. His "Virginia Plan" was transparently favorable to big states. For example, Virginia's total population (including slaves) was 11 times larger than that of Delaware and 10 times the size of the absent Rhode Island, and its white population was second only to Pennsylvania's. Virginia was also the richest state and felt that any plan that gave each state an equal vote on requisitions or taxes, or trade regulations, was unacceptable to it and to other large and wealthier states. The proposal was largely the work of James Madison. It envisioned a bicameral legislature with a lower house elected by the eligible population in each state and an upper house elected by the representatives in the lower house. The executive and federal judges would be elected by both houses. A council drawn from the executive and justices would then have veto power over acts of the legislature. The scheme went even further by advocating that the national legislature should have the power to veto certain acts of *state* legislatures. This plan was a clear case for power resting in the principle of representation by population in a way that did not separate the various governmental powers (lawmaking, administration, judicial) by constituency but by a process that repeated the same majority through every branch of government. The national government would then be in the hands of three or four of the largest states in concert. Madison had prepared a model that fit his theory of the benefits of a large republic; even the proposed veto on state legislation had been seen by Madison not as an intrusion into the rights of individuals at the state level but as a way of having the larger authority ensure that states, as small republics, did not violate individual or any other category of political or legal rights. Regardless of the Virginia delegation's purposes, the plan was unacceptable to small states, and went much further in its proposed national authority than many delegates had expected. To many, the Virginia proposals looked very threatening to states' interests, and, by lodging so much authority with a federal government, they seemed to go too far towards a centralized, British-style system. On June 15, William Patterson of New Jersey countered with a plan that served the interests of the smaller states at the expense of the larger states and also limited the authority of the national government.

Patterson's "New Jersey Plan" was conservative in that it consisted of nine resolutions that retained the main features and language of the Articles of Confederation but gave the new government the power to regulate commerce and tax in its own right. Then, Patterson's plan turned the Virginia Plan on its head by rejecting the representation by population formula and advocating that the bicameral legislature would have each house composed of equal representation of the states. It called for a plural executive and a supreme court drawn from the legislative houses. If the small states had balked at the Virginia proposal for its obvious smothering of their interests, then Patterson's plan was clearly unacceptable to the big states for the same reasons. The delegates were coming round to the idea that only a fully national government would hold the union together and that reforming the Articles of Confederation, even according to the New Jersey Plan, was not the answer to America's problems. The Constitution that emerged in September 1787 was the result of compromises, concessions, and exhaustive debates. It was a great learning experience for the delegates, who had come to the convention in various stages of knowledge, preparation, and theoretical background. It demonstrated a lively and at times deeply committed engagement of ideas, projections, and fears. The debates were marked by sincerity and respect for procedure. Every possible scenario was considered, and history, necessity, and urgency were dealt with in open discussion. After the two major plans had been digested, the convention retained the Virginia Plan as its point of departure.

Madison and Hamilton stood out at the convention. The former had come prepared to advance his large republic model, but Hamilton, on the other hand, had reduced his own approach to the simple demand for a very strong central government. At Philadelphia, he came across as an elitist and Anglophile. He had an honest and outspoken disdain for mass or popular politics, and, in one of his most quoted utterances, he announced in June that

> All communities divide themselves into the few and the many. The first are the rich and the well born, the other the mass of the people.... The people are turbulent and changing; they seldom judge or determine right. Give therefore to the first a distinct, permanent share in Government. They will check the unsteadiness of the second, and as they cannot receive any advantage by a change, they therefore will ever maintain good government.

That anti-egalitarian remark was less inflammatory than his observation that "the British government forms the best model the world ever produced... [it] has for its object public strength and individual security." This struck contemporaries as a very peculiar example of what Americans might want in their new nation. Hamilton, however, was a *bona fide* patriot and as vigorous a nationalist as any who attended the Convention. What he meant was that Britain's strong *centralized* government encouraged efficiency in international policy, economics, and internal stability. Hamilton's very aggressive pronouncements were harbingers of a debate that would survive the Convention, the question of how power was best applied, and to what ends. Hamilton's use of the "few" and the "many" was not what Madison had in mind when he talked about factions and interests; he viewed American society as a nuanced congeries of classes and interests and never accepted the sharp division that Hamilton had applied. They would eventually become opponents in government because, while Madison sought a strong government to advance the rights of all interest groups, Hamilton wanted a central authority strong enough to contain the "unsteady" behavior of the masses. Hamilton's leanings would also clash with Jefferson's disdain for class divisions. Writing to Virginia Federalist Edward Carrington from Paris earlier in 1787, Jefferson had criticized European models of government and "the general prey of the rich on the poor." In a letter to Madison written during the Convention, Jefferson made a statement that has long been seen as his agrarian credo: "I think our governments will remain virtuous for many centuries; as long as they are chiefly agricultural; and this will be as long as there shall be vacant lands in any part of America. When they get piled upon one another in large cities, as in Europe, they will become corrupt as in Europe."

Shays's Rebellion was fresh in the minds of the delegates and inspired occasional rumors of similar disturbances elsewhere. But the most heated and difficult questions were about structures and mechanisms of government. What political model would make a federal system most readily acceptable, one principally shaped on the basis of representation by population or one in which states were equally represented at every level of the national government? Another question concerned the degree of power that could be lodged in this new institution. It needed to be sufficient to overcome the grave limitations of the Articles but should not entirely nullify individual state sovereignty. Madison's assumptions were being proven right by the delegates' factious, self-interested, and jealous arguments. The debates at the Constitutional Convention were lively and intelligent, but they also confirmed Madison's apprehensions. Not only were classes, groups, and individuals self-interested, but the states, as a collection of entities, were themselves factious. Virginia wanted the best deal for itself, as did each state. How each was to sell its needs to the rest in a package turned out to be both the problem and, in the end, the solution to America's crisis of union. For any state to accept a Constitution along the lines of the Virginia Plan meant being assured that whatever that state gave up was given up by every other state and that what each gave up was in fact a contribution to a national sovereignty. In June, as the discussions ebbed and flowed, Roger Sherman offered the "Connecticut Compromise," but it was rejected. In early July, it was submitted again.

The Great Compromise
Sherman's revolutionary credentials are outstanding, and he was well known going into the Philadelphia meetings. He has the distinction of being the only person to sign all four documents: the Continental Association of 1774, the Declaration of Independence, the Articles of Confederation, and the Constitution of the United States. He later served in the United States House of Representatives and the Senate. His proposal to break the Convention deadlock pivoted on balancing the concerns of the big and the small states. The Connecticut proposal, in very broad structural terms, called for a lower house based on representation by population and an upper house based on the equal representation of the states. The proposal went through a series of reviews. On July 12, the Convention agreed to the three-fifths principle that allowed states to apply their slave populations at three-fifths for the purposes of representation in the lower house. The term "slave" does not appear in the Constitution; slaves are referred to as "other persons." The notorious apportionment concession was made to appease the Virginia Plan advocates who had insisted on a straightforward representation by population. The concession increased Virginia's representation in the lower house by about 25 per cent over what it would have been with a whites-only formula. The three-fifths concession could also be used for tax apportionment. First, the slave population as property would mean that a slave state would be taxed for federal revenue purposes at a three-fifths higher rate than it would with a solely white apportionment. The northern states acceded to the slave states' cynical use of the slave to enhance representation and as property. In fact, the three-fifths fraction was arrived at by compromise. Northern states wanted the slave population to be counted for direct tax apportionment at 100 per cent, and southern delegates wanted the slave population to be counted at 100 per cent for representational apportionment in the House. In legal and moral terms, the slave remained *no*-fifths of a person. Sherman and other northern delegates accepted the representational adjustment as a way of assuring union. In a way, the three-fifths principle underscored the broad-based acceptance of a racially

explicit double standard, and, rather than see the states hive off into regional collectives, delegates saw the drive to a complete union of the thirteen states as more important than any equal rights attack on slavery.

The Sherman proposals sparked a great debate. When at last they were approved, a committee drew up a set of 23 resolutions as the basis for the Constitution. The material was given to the Convention on August 6, 1787 and debated for the next five weeks. Specifics were articulated, rephrased, adjusted, or amended, and, by early September, something approaching a final draft was apparent. On September 10, the Convention debated the matter for the last time and handed over its draft to a small committee that refined the language and organized the various clauses. The final document contained seven articles and was subdivided into sections and paragraphs. The uniquely named Gouverneur Morris (1752-1816) of New York refined it, overcoming his own disapproval of the document's tendency to blunt the power of elites. It was then examined by all in attendance before the 39 signed it on September 17. Of the 42 delegates in attendance, the three who declined were Elbridge Gerry of Massachusetts and the Virginians, Edmund Randolph, who had presented the Virginia Plan, and the redoubtable George Mason.

From Sherman's framework, a remarkably concise document emerged. The results of the final few weeks of debate show the distance the Convention had come from its early days. The Constitution clearly converted the limited power of the Articles into a new, separate, and superior agency. But the Constitution made careful concessions to the naysayers who feared a despotic centralism. Structurally, the terms of elected officials were fixed but staggered to keep the system moving and never to have the entire government replaced in one election. Representatives were elected for two-year terms, senators to six-year terms with one-third being elected every two years, and the executive branch was to be elected every four years. The new Congress was given specific authority to regulate trade across state boundaries and to tax independently. While no list of civil rights was included in the draft (these would come with the first ten amendments, the "Bill of Rights" in 1791), there were protections included for individual security. So-called "Bills of Attainder" were banned, meaning that the legislative branch could not pass laws or punishments of a specific nature against a group or individual, or otherwise act in the place of a court. The Constitution also banned the passing of retroactive (*ex post facto*) laws. The Constitution included a clause that permitted the importation of slaves for another twenty years, assuming that the trade would be banned at that point. Here again the issue of slavery revealed a sectional division in the nation. The three-fifths clause, the protection of slave importation, and another clause that allowed slaveholders to recover their runaway slaves (property) in slave-free states lodged the institution firmly in the Constitution. The owning of slaves was now a constitutionally protected right.

The Constitution: Adoption and Ratification
The Constitution was sent by George Washington to the states on September 28. It was

offered in a format familiar to Americans, as a set of specific articles in the manner of the state constitutions and the Articles of Confederation. The preamble to the Constitution, while not formally a functioning part of the document, has been invoked from time to time as its basic principle. It credits the "people" and not the states with the responsibility for legitimizing the Constitution: "We the People of the United States, in Order to form a more perfect Union, establish justice, insure domestic Tranquility, provide for the common defence, promote the general Welfare, and secure the Blessings of Liberty to ourselves and our Posterity, do ordain and establish this Constitution for the United States of America." The personal pronouns used in the Constitution include "they," "persons," and "others," for example, but also "he," "his," and "him," but no direct feminine usage. This omission tacitly acknowledges the formal exclusion of females from political participation. A full version of the 1787 Constitution is included in this text as an appendix. It can be summarized in outline, as follows:

Article I. Legislative authority: This, the longest Article in the Constitution, contains 10 sections and 54 paragraphs. It specifies the design and roles of the House of Representatives and the Senate, the methods of electing members and the terms of their service, how laws are made, and the checks on each branch by the other. Any bill passing the Senate would have to pass the House and vice versa. A simple majority was required to pass bills. The Senate was given authority in foreign affairs, treaties, trade relations, and declarations of war. The House had taxing and fiscal powers. This provision echoes the 1765 Stamp Act principles of popular elected control over taxation and lays down a mechanism, including biennial elections, for a broad-based check on government budgets. The states had earlier introduced this formula in their state constitutions. The legislature (the Congress) was not allowed to administer the laws it made.

Article II. Executive authority: The executive (the president) was empowered to administer the law. This was a clear separation of power. The president could veto bills, but that veto could be overturned by a two-thirds majority in the Congress. Conditions of behavior were included, and bound the president to abide by the constitutional stipulations of the office. As was the case with all elected and appointed officials, the president could be removed from office for violating those terms. The president could choose officers (the cabinet) to administer the law, but those officers had to be vetted by Congress (the so-called "advice and consent" procedure). The president had to be American-born and over 35 years old. As the head of state, the president was seen to be above regional or special interests.

Article III. The judiciary: The provision for a national court was a singular achievement of the Constitutional process. The Court was designed to adjudicate on matters within the purview of the federal government and ensure the legal rights of citizens. As with cabinet members, judges were selected by the executive branch and vetted by both houses of Congress. The judges were appointed "on good behavior." They could be removed by impeachment and trial, as could all elected officials, for violating their oaths of office. Article III also allowed for a Supreme Court, a court of final appeal.

Article IV. Residual powers: These were the separate, relative, local, and residual powers retained by each state. This Article retains much of what the Articles of Confederation had said about citizenship and its transferability. It enjoins each state to respect the laws of other states. It refers indirectly to Shays's uprising by promising to intervene when requested to quash "domestic violence," and it guarantees republican governments in each state and protects each from foreign invasion. The article also incorporates the Northwest Ordinance and the rights of the national government to administer territories of the United States.

Article V. Methods of amendment: One of the limitations of the Articles of Confederation was the need for unanimity for amendment. Here, a two-thirds majority in both houses or a request by two-thirds of the state legislatures would be sufficient to amend the Constitution after the amendment was approved by three-quarters of the states.

Article VI. The supremacy of the Constitution: The new government assumed the debts that the "Confederation" had incurred. State judges had to recognize that the laws and treaties made by the United States under the Constitution were to be "the supreme law of the land." Article VI also emphasized the need for and sanctity of the oath of allegiance to the Constitution and added a clear prohibition on any religious test as a precondition for office holding.

Article VII. Ratification: The method of ratification stated that the approval of nine state conventions would be "sufficient for the Establishment of this Constitution," which was dated September 17, 1787, "the Twelfth" year of "the Independence of the United States of America [assuming independence as a fact as of 1776]."

The Constitution of 1787 was predicated on the principles of the *rule of law* and *republicanism*, in that the law defined citizenship and legitimacy and the people were sovereign. The Constitution was careful to abolish monarchical and hereditary rights and privileges. *Checks* were applied to legislative and executive power, which *balanced* rather than neutralized the powers in each branch of government. The functions and responsibilities of the executive and Congress were distinct from each other. The Court was seen as outside the law making and administrative realm but would inevitably play a major role in interpreting the constitutional law. There were practical reasons for this model of the *separation of powers*, but the framers were also familiar with theoretical versions of it such as Locke's 1690 treatise and French political philosopher Baron de Montesquieu's 1748 thesis, *The Spirit of the Laws*.

By controlling elections, the states retained an important leverage in determining representation. The bicameral legislature appeared at first glance to represent two constituencies. The Senate members would be elected or chosen by the state legislatures while the House would consist of popularly elected representatives chosen by the people in districts within state boundaries. No congressional district crossed or straddled state boundaries. For example, Massachusetts's eight representatives in the first United States House of Representatives came as representatives of districts within the state, while the two senators were chosen in a statewide method, presumably to represent the state's distinct interests in Congress. The president was not elected directly by the voters but, according to Article II, by a number of "electors," who were appointed or elected by each state, the exact number corresponding to the total number of representatives and senators in each state. In the case of Massachusetts, for example, that would amount to ten electors for the first presidential election, being the sum of eight representatives and two senators. Delaware was the first state to ratify the Constitution, and did so by unanimous vote in December of 1787. The Constitution had stipulated a nine-state requirement for the Constitution to be operational "between the States so ratifying the Same," and, as the list below shows, the number of states required to enact the Constitution was reached in June 1788.

Table 6.1: Ratification of the United States Constitution

State	Date Ratified	Vote, for and against
Delaware	December 7, 1787	30-0
Pennsylvania	December 12, 1787	46-23
New Jersey	December 18, 1787	39-0
Georgia	January 2, 1788	26-0
Connecticut	January 9, 1788	128-40
Massachusetts	February 6, 1788	187-168
Maryland	April 28, 1788	63-11
South Carolina	May 23, 1788	149-73
New Hampshire	June 21, 1788	57-47
Virginia	June 26, 1788	89-79
New York	July 26, 1788	30-27
*North Carolina	November 21, 1789	194-77
*Rhode Island	May 29, 1790	34-32

*North Carolina and Rhode Island did not ratify the Constitution until after the first United States Congress had met.

Sources: Richard B. Morris and Jeffery B. Morris, eds., *The Encyclopedia of American History,* 7th ed. (New York: HarperCollins, 1996), 133-135. David J. Siemers, *Ratifying the Republic: Antifederalists and Federalists in Constitutional Time* (Stanford, CA: Stanford University Press, 2002). Siemers offers slightly different dates for Georgia and Maryland.

The Continental Congress declared that the Constitution was to be effective after the first Wednesday of March 1789. This happened to be March 4. After the first Congress had met in session, the remaining states ratified the Constitution. North Carolina on November 21, 1789 voted to adopt the Constitution by a 194-77 margin, having rejected it on August 4, 1788 by a vote of 84-184. The main concern was the perceived need to include a Bill of Rights. Rhode Island agreed to the Constitution on May 29, 1790 by a vote of 34-32, and, even after over two years of hesitation, its ratification vote was the closest of any. The attempt to put together a convention in 1788 had been rejected by a strong rural movement opposed to centralized power, and it took two years to overcome that opposition. There, as elsewhere, the promise of a package of civil rights was what swayed the vote. Vermont became the 14th state after a convention ratified the Constitution on January 10, 1791, and it was admitted by an act of Congress on February 19, 1791 to be effective on March 4. Vermont was the first state to be admitted under the provisions of Section 3 of Article IV.

North Carolina and Rhode Island were not alone in having difficulty accepting the Constitution. The Massachusetts convention had barely approved it in April 1788, and by summer, only one of the four largest states had ratified it. Pennsylvania had accepted it by a two to one margin, but the vote revealed an organized rural opposition. On June 21, 1788, however, New Hampshire became the ninth state to ratify and technically formalized the nation's existence. Two vital states were missing, Virginia and New York. In Virginia, the radical Richard Henry Lee (the "Sam Adams of Virginia") rejected it. He had been instrumental in persuading Virginians to cede their western claims after the war for the sake of the Confederation, but, in a sharp riposte, he repeated in 1788 what he had been thinking for years: "It will be considered, I believe, as a most extraordinary epoch in the history of mankind, that in a few years there should be so essential a change in the minds of men. 'Tis really astonishing that the same people, who have just emerged from a long and cruel war in defence of liberty, should now agree to fix an elective despotism upon themselves and their posterity." In opposing the Constitution, the radical had become a conservative.

The Federalist Papers

Lee wanted a "Bill of Rights," as did many others, and every ratifying state suggested some change, inevitably to do with individual rights and protections. Over 80 proposals came in with the ratifications, and these were eventually distilled into the first 10 amendments to the Constitution. A greater problem arose for the advocates of the Constitution with initial tentative support for ratification in New York and Virginia. These two large and strategic states were crucial to any successful union, so, in New York, an aggressive advertising campaign to sell the Constitution was begun in October 1787 and continued to May 1788. It resulted in a splendid body of 85 letters or essays that, taken together, come as close as anything in revolutionary America to original political theory. The first 77 of the essays carried the pseudonym "Publius" and were gathered together in 1788 with an additional eight essays to form *The Federalist: A*

Collection of Essays Written in Favour of the New Constitution ... In Two Volumes (New York, 1788). Like so many other political dissertations, these 85 essays reveal much about their time, place, and occasion but can also be read today with profit for the timeless insights into modern pluralistic society. John Jay wrote five of the papers, Hamilton 51, and Madison 26. Three were written by Hamilton and Madison together. The sheer elegance of the prose and the measured tone of the arguments convey a comprehensive explanation of both republican ideology and the proposed structure of the United States government. *The Federalist* is unalloyed propaganda aimed at a New York audience; but it is unsurpassed as a general exposition of American constitutionalism. It also gave its name to a political party or movement. The lower case "f" federalists, those who favored a strong federal nation state became the upper case "F" Federalists.

The *Federalist* can be read as a long multi-layered rumination on republicanism that, in many ways, harkens back to Madison's *Vices of the Political System of the United States*. It rests on the argument that the United States government under the Constitution would combine "stability and energy in government, with the inviolable attention due to liberty and the republican form." The series begins with Hamilton's celebration of independence, but also warns of the weakness of the Articles to maintain it, and ends in number 85 with Hamilton's passionate statements: "A NATION without a NATIONAL GOVERNMENT is, in my view, an awful spectacle. The establishment of a Constitution, in a time of profound peace, by the voluntary consent of a whole people, is a PRODIGY, to the completion of which I look forward with trembling anxiety." Madison, however, moves *The Federalist* from a set of editorials to a thesis on the advantages of balanced interests. Madison claims that the Constitution itself could not preserve the union or secure people's safety because the "security of civil rights" cannot be found in charters or appeals to humanity but only in "the multiplicity of interests" that characterize a free society. In a lovely phrase, Madison leaves the subject in his readers' hands with his gentle suggestion that "[t]his view of the subject must particularly recommend a proper federal system to all sincere and considerate friends of Republican government."

By amending and adapting earlier theories of liberal individualism, Madison pushed his idea of the stabilizing tendencies of competing interest. Thomas Hobbes, in the wake of the English Civil Wars, had argued for a fixed and permanent authority (his 1651 *Leviathan*) to ensure both individual security and opportunity. As he put it, "covenants [compacts, agreements], without the sword, are but words" and so, if "men live without a common power to keep them all in awe, they are in that condition which is called war; and such a war, as is of every man, against every man," with inevitable chaos, civil war, and anarchy. Hobbes's solution to mankind's natural possessive tendencies was the inviolable monarch or the neutral disinterested authority, which, not unlike Hamilton's elite "few," had nothing to gain by exercising all the power. Hobbes had written in the fiery atmosphere of revolutionary seventeenth-century England and saw the possibility of social collapse without a restraining force to prevent it. The other great English theorist of natural rights who was widely read in America was John Locke whose *Second Treatise* was written during the Glorious Revolution in England. It is a conspicuous presence in the Declaration of Independence and in scores of revolutionary pamphlets and state constitutions.

Hobbes and Locke are original and trenchant observers of individualism and faction, but Madison's thoughts on the subject, when applied to an actual case, demand our attention. Madison's proposals take older notions of natural rights and give them a fresh American flavor. In one of the most celebrated passages in American political theory, he writes the following in *The Federalist* (no. 10): "By a faction I understand a number of citizen, whether amounting to a majority or minority of the whole, who are united and actuated by some common impulse of passion, or of interest, adverse to the rights of other citizens, or to the permanent and aggregate interests of the community...." In the spirit of Hobbes, he makes the observation that "[no] man is allowed to be a judge in his own cause...." He then offers a disarmingly negative view of mankind and announces that the "latent causes of faction are... sown in the nature of man." Madison then suggests that faction can be limited either by "removing its causes" or "controlling its effects." The causes can only be removed by denying man his liberty — the origin of self-interest and faction — indeed, by eliminating the laws of nature. In other words, Madison describes faction as inevitable but manageable, controllable, given the right political system — and that system, for Madison, is a large republic. Earlier, in *Vices*, Madison had said that pluralistic republics could do a better job of optimizing individual rights than a monarchy could. For Madison, neither a monarchy nor an eighteenth-century notion of democracy could secure the body politic. In *The Federalist*, he compares democracy unfavorably with a republic in his discussion of political freedom and stability. His use of the word "democracy" is different from our present-day usage. He writes this in *The Federalist* (no. 10):

> [I]t may be concluded that a pure democracy, by which I mean a society consisting of a small number of citizens, who assemble and administer the government in person, can admit of no cure for the mischiefs of faction.... [I]n almost every case... there is nothing to check the inducements to sacrifice the weaker party or an obnoxious individual. Hence it is that such democracies have ever been spectacles of turbulence and contention; have ever been found incompatible with personal security for the rights of property; and have in general been as short in their lives as they have been violent in their deaths. Theoretic politicians, who have patronized this species of government, have erroneously supposed that by reducing mankind to a perfect equality in their political rights, they would at the same time be perfectly equalized and assimilated in their possessions, their opinions, and their passions.

To a present-day reader, this might appear oddly as a totalitarian's definition of democracy. Madison is clearly describing his fear of disorder, "turbulence and contention," and a system "incompatible with personal security" and protection of property. He makes the fascinating point that small republics tend to the same vices as democracies.

Madison's formula derives from his quite basic premise that smaller communities promote and are thus susceptible to tyranny, and the democracy he describes, perhaps
inevitable in some states, is not the best successor to the monarchy that Americans had
recently dismissed. Madison offers no contemporary or historical examples of the
flawed democracies or small republics he disdains, or of his preferred large republic,
but his proposals are not wholly abstract. One can find any number of intellectual
sources, from the Greeks and Romans to the French and British Enlightenment
thinkers in the pamphlets, manifestoes, and constitutions that flowed from Americans
in the revolutionary period; but it is well that we remember the empirical reality of the
founders. As well as being well read in history, Madison was a sharp analyst of the
political behavior he had observed in peace and war in America.

A Bill of Rights

The moment the New Hampshire ratification was confirmed, the old Congress began
to prepare for its own extinction. It met for the last time in early October, after having
set the dates for the elections to the first United States Congress. The location of the
first Congress was New York City, but the old Congress closed by acknowledging the
future site of the federal capital in what would be called the District of Columbia. As
the writing, ratification, and impending application of the Constitution went ahead,
the debates, letters, conventions, and pamphlets revealed a contentious "antifederalist"
opposition to the "federalist" proponents of the Constitution. Madison could sing the
praises of a large mechanistic republic. Others could condemn it as Richard Henry Lee
had in 1787, by reversing Madison's logic and claiming that the large republic, with its
"general government, far removed from the people" and with a constant turnover in
representation, could not enforce its laws efficiently except with "a multitude of officers and military force." Without these, Lee noted, the laws would be neglected and
"lead to anarchy and confusion" and a necessary "military execution of laws" that
would accompany a "despotic government." In other words, Americans would be tyr-
annizing Americans as the British had before 1776. In 1788, another Virginian, Patrick
Henry, added his respected voice to Lee's charge of "elective despotism" and warned of
the inevitable abuse that would accompany the new government. Words like "despotism" and "monarchical" peppered the opposition's language. While the doleful or
alarmed dissenters simply dismissed the entire Constitution and its purpose, there was
a cautious but no less serious opposition to it as it stood from many of its supporters
who objected to the absence of a written guarantee of civil rights. In a letter to
Madison from Paris in December 1788, Thomas Jefferson approved much of the content of the Constitution. However, he expressed a problem with the "*omission* of a bill
of rights providing clearly and without the aid of sophisms for freedom of religion,
freedom of the press, protection against standing armies, by law restriction against
monopolies, the eternal and unremitting force of the habeas corpus laws, and trials by
jury in all matters of fact triable by the laws of the land and not by the law of Nations"
(emphasis added). The Constitution would stay and a Bill of Rights would come, but

lines had been drawn. They would harden into the first party system in the United States, one that would thrive even after the Bill of Rights was adopted. Then, it was not so much a question of the type of government that came with the Constitution, but rather *how* and by *whom* government would be used. The Bill of Rights can be seen as a triumph for antifederalist ideals, and so it was, but it also suited federalists such as Hamilton. He welcomed the amendments as a way of further distancing the central government from state authority by making the United States the protector of individual rights and thus centralizing the civil functions of government. After its adoption, Madison moved almost immediately from a federalist position on the Constitution to an antifederalist position. He saw the Bill of Rights as a brake on the powers of the federal government.

Yet if the Bill of Rights arose from suspicions concerning big government's potential for tyranny and if it appealed to centralists like Hamilton on the basis of excluding states from civil rights authority, it also added a fascinating twist to the Constitution's purpose. The earlier lists of civil rights demands had been reduced to 12 proposals, two of which were rejected. The remaining 10 were attached to the Constitution in 1791. When they were ratified in December 1791, the Constitution, and thus the government of the United States, was technically responsible for protecting citizens *from* the very governments they would elect. As it was being ratified in 1788-89, the politely worded preamble to the Bill of Rights scarcely veiled the serious concerns over the Constitution: "The Conventions of a number of the States, having at the time of their adopting the Constitution, expressed a desire, *in order to prevent misconstruction or abuse of its powers*, that further declaratory and restrictive clauses should be added: And as extending the ground of public confidence in the Government, will best ensure the beneficent ends of its institution [emphasis added]." Taken together, the Bill of Rights is set up to protect the individual from arbitrary interference. It ensures freedom of speech and religion and the right to peaceful assembly; the right to a jury trial; equal protection under the law as an affirmation of common citizenship rights; due process in legal matters, meaning that arrests, charges, and incarcerations had to be made public; freedom from unreasonable expropriation; and rights to privacy and one's person. Because the Constitution had included a federal court, the civil rights that were now welded to the Constitution would have an agency for their testing and application.

Partisan Politics

The lower case terms "federalist" and "antifederalist," used as adjectives, gave way to the upper case formal party designations of Federalist and Antifederalist. The divisions revealed a myriad of ideological, social, and regional interests. Madison's "latent" cause of faction appeared early. As an experiment in republicanism, the new government encouraged the kinds of factions Madison had foreseen. Could the system deflect or absorb the excesses of faction? The complex political sociology of the United States had survived the war and the peace. The Revolution had not leveled American society;

it had removed monarchy and replaced it with a republic, but it had not done away with regional, cultural, social, or economic divisions. The ideological positions of the two rival political groups embodied the developing political cultures in the new nation.

The Federalist position derived from the belief that the United States government should be used to lead and educate the people. It was predicated on the principle of political deference:

- Government should encourage a balanced and diversified economic order and the systems to go with it to encourage national economic self-sufficiency.
- The national government should actively promote financial investments in industry, commerce, and trade.
- Law should favor debtor interests.
- The government of the United States should emphasize national issues and promote strong executive leadership.
- Federalists generally distrusted the people's collective capacity to govern efficiently, and they believed that the best government was that of natural elites.
- The Federalist program was based on the theory that the nation could be made secure and its economy would thrive if economic investment, capital accumulation, and centralized politics were combined in politics.

The Antifederalist position was based on the theory that governments were established to reflect the will of the people at large and to end or prevent further privileges in the republic:

- Government should encourage and facilitate a predominantly agrarian economic order of widespread freehold agriculture leading to an even distribution of wealth.
- The federal government should encourage an agricultural economy free of industry, urbanism, and organized finance.
- Laws should favor creditor interests.
- Antifederalists distrusted centralized government and trusted local prerogative as the means to political and economic stability.
- There was a tacit belief in the social harmony and perfectibility of individual morals if the agrarian model were used to underpin the republican framework.
- The nation could thrive, economically, by expanding the existing agrarian order through simple geographic extension.

According to the Federalists, the economy would stagnate if it did not embrace financial, commercial, and even industrial innovation, all of which required concentrations of investment. Thus, the Federalist leadership was looking to its own interests as it touched on the changing economic realities of the era. The Antifederalists had a different view of the universe. The Federalist position, they claimed, promoted class divisions and inequality. Here the Antifederalists slid around the inequalities in the class and race-based plantation culture that they had fit into their agrarian model. But the Federalist system seemed to replicate what many opponents saw as the growing European problem of industry and urbanization, and the older European system of privilege, elitism, and tyranny. Republican virtue, what would come to be seen in part as Jefferson's "agrarian vision," could only be achieved by an emphasis on popular politics, manifested at the local level, with the vast majority of Americans looking after themselves on their own farms. To each side, the other looked to be moving away, even backwards, from the Revolution's potential. For Federalists, decentralization was an invitation to political fragmentation and economic underdevelopment. For Antifederalists, centralized authority and the use of government to promote specific economic doctrines was a malevolent attack on republican virtue. The partisan debate is a useful example of mutually exclusive perceptions. The word "freedom" had been bandied about in the revolutionary era, from the first protests against British imperial policies to the meaning of the war and to the debates on the Constitution. The use of "freedom" was and remains an emotive tool in American political debate. In the America of the 1790s, the formative parties applied the word to describe two quite different "freedoms."

When Virginia ratified the Constitution the Federalists had no trouble in persuading the ostensibly non-partisan and reluctant Washington to stand for the presidency. He tried to reconcile the parties by appointing Thomas Jefferson as secretary of state, with responsibilities for foreign affairs, and Alexander Hamilton as secretary of the treasury, to administer federal finances. Given their respective talents, those were practical choices, and they reflected Washington's sincere desire for balance. Jefferson's views had already linked him to the Antifederalist position, while Hamilton had become the leading Federalist. John Adams had recently returned from Europe and had finished a distant second to Washington in the presidential race and so was made vice president under the terms of the Constitution. The electors (69 in total and chosen by the states) each cast two votes, each giving one to Washington for president and the second vote to other candidates as a way of electing the vice president. The procedure was changed with the twelfth Amendment in 1804, which required vice presidential candidates be listed *with* the presidential candidate.

James Madison chose to run for Congress but barely succeeded in getting a seat in the first House of Representatives because of opposition from Patrick Henry, who was suspicious of Madison's apparent Federalist leanings. In the House, Madison acted decisively in getting the Bill of Rights through Congress and then to ratification by the states, demonstrating an important feature of the Constitution; it could be changed by its own mechanisms. By the end of the first Congress, Madison had begun to define a party preference. His break with the Hamilton Federalists was underway by the time the second Congress met in 1790.

The number and method of distribution of seats in the first House of Representatives had been specified in the Constitution. Because Rhode Island and North Carolina had not yet ratified, they were not included in the first meetings, but, by the end of the first Congress with all 13 states represented, there were 64 representatives and 26 senators. With the three-fifths clause in effect, Virginia had 10 of the 64 seats in the House, Maryland 6, and North Carolina and South Carolina 5 each, numbers that gave the southern bloc, with Delaware and Georgia, a very significant representation in terms of their white populations. Of those members who indicated a political affiliation, the House had a Federalist majority of 38 to 26. When the Senate was filled out, there were 18 identified Federalists and 8 Antifederalists and a notable continuity: 16 of the 26 senators had served in the old Congress. Nearly half of the representatives had served under the Articles of Confederation. Representatives and senators were slow to attend the first Congress, a quorum was not achieved until early April, and Washington was not installed as president until the end of the month. In addition to a Bill of Rights, the first Congress accomplished a great deal. It installed a cabinet by creating four departments, including State, Treasury, War, and Postmaster General. The federal Judiciary Act of 1789 took the provision laid out in Article III of the Constitution and created a Supreme Court. It appointed the first chief justice of the United States, John Jay, and added the office of attorney general. It also provided for federal district and circuit courts.

Alexander Hamilton and the National Economy

Hamilton's first major initiative as secretary of the treasury led to the first in a series of bitter disputes between the parties. In the first Congress these were better understood as the "Administration" party (the Federalists) and the "Opposition" party (the Antifederalists). Hamilton reported that the old confederation had bequeathed a massive debt to the United States. The French, Dutch, and others were owed nearly $12 million by the federal government. The domestic portion of the debt was $40 million, owed to a variety of creditors. The states owed $25 million to another set of creditors. Hamilton's formula was to repay the debt at par when much of it had been made in depreciated currencies and stocks. He also proposed that the federal government assume most of the state debts. Hamilton reasoned that putting the nation's finances in some kind of order would demonstrate to the world a national responsibility and, at the same time, appease the nation's commercial and wealthy classes — the creditors — who were largely in the Federalist camp. Most in Congress and the public generally accepted the retirement of the foreign debt, but opposition to the domestic debt assumption scheme was immediate and hostile, largely because the repayment at par created winners and losers. The New England states, being the largest creditors, favored assumption while the southern states for the most part wanted other mechanisms to retire their debts. They saw the federal government's scheme as a way to begin taxing the states to recover the debt it was now assuming. To pay off 1778 depreciated dollars at 1790 values would profit those who held the debt, that is, the wealthy. Madison and the Virginians, some of whom were wealthy in taxable assets, land, and slaves but fiscally indebted, led the opposition to debt assumption and defeated the bill in the House by a narrow vote. Hamilton's drive and single mindedness had, however, made him a power in the administration. He managed to get a compromise agreement on the assumption issue by persuading northerners to agree to the situating of the national capital on the Potomac on the Virginia border, on land earlier negotiated by the old Congress. Madison was outmaneuvered by Hamilton. At a dinner party arranged by Jefferson, Madison agreed to Hamilton's deal even though the latter had already negotiated a compromise with other congressmen. While the bill went through Congress, Hamilton had revealed a deep gap between the government and the opposition. Patrick Henry and the Virginia Antifederalists protested, correctly, that the Hamiltonian scheme favored moneyed interests and punished the agricultural sector. It was pointed out that the Constitution did not authorize debt assumption. It did not seem to prohibit it either, but Hamilton was nevertheless perturbed by the prospect of attacks on the Constitution and attempts to limit its application. By early 1791, a rancorous political debate was underway.

The first report on the national system of debt and credit was followed by Hamilton's contentious design for the Bank of the United States. It was not the first government-authorized bank in revolutionary America. The Bank of North America of 1781 had been chartered by the Continental Congress under the direction of Robert Morris in an effort to stabilize government finances. State banks had been chartered by Massachusetts and New York in 1784. But Hamilton's bank, which envisioned a steady source of money for investors and speculators, was especially galling to the Antifederalists because it called on the national government to provide 20 per cent of the Bank's initial $10 million capitalization. Public money was to be used as a pool from which the rich could borrow. Opposition was fierce and took the "strict constructionist" view of the Constitution, which sought an explicit clause on matters of legislative innovation. When Washington asked his opinion, Jefferson attacked the bill on the grounds that the Constitution did not specifically allow Congress to create a national bank. Shrewdly, Hamilton replied that neither did the Constitution forbid it and invoked the argument of "implied powers." His "loose constructionist" view assumed that because the Constitution gave the federal government the right to tax and the responsibility to regulate trade, it allowed for the creation of the Bank as a means to those ends. The Bank was part of Hamilton's overall design for the future economic development of the United States. The rational retirement of debt and the means to produce government revenues were joined to an institution that was designed to provide funds for investors and capitalists. The bill required a 20-year charter and passed through Congress because of the Federalist majority. The Bank was headquartered in Philadelphia with eight branches in other cities. Washington apparently had doubts about its value and legality but felt that he needed to respect Hamilton's position as secretary of the treasury.

The first sitting of the new government set the tone for the politics of the 1790s, a decade of emotional and sometimes bitter personal and partisan rivalries that saw the hardening of the positions of the parties and the straining of the older revolutionary solidarity. The decade began with the passing of one of the most formidable of American personalities. Benjamin Franklin, who had spent so many of his later years in Europe, died at the age of 84 in Philadelphia in 1790. One of the largest gatherings in America to that time, an estimated 20,000 people, attended his funeral parade. We can only guess at what Franklin might have brought to the cantankerous politics of the decade, but the dignified Washington strove to rise above the fray while other leading founders became embroiled in the hot political atmosphere. Jefferson and Adams would have a falling out and Madison and Hamilton would go their separate ways. Control of government and therefore control of the national agenda was at stake. In both national and international affairs, the decade turned out to be one of the most tumultuous in American history.

The New Economics

Hamilton's reports echoed the social and economic changes that marked the 1790s everywhere in the western world. One of them, his *Report of a Uniform System for the Disposition of the Lands* of 1790-91, recommended scrapping the settlement design of the 1785 Land Ordinance and opening the west to a less rigid formula that would allow speculators even more opportunity than they currently had to carve up the new agricultural lands. The policy was not adopted, but its design shows clearly Hamilton's capitalistic logic. The market revolution had found its way to America even before the Revolution and had been evident in some of the colonial merchants' most aggressive protests. Adam Smith's *Wealth of Nations* was published in the same year as the Declaration of Independence, and the liberal temper of both those publications dove-tailed in the new economics. America would remain a predominantly agrarian society for generations, but the economy began to diversify in the 1790s, and Jefferson's night-mare vision of industry and urbanism would soon mesh with the nation's agricultural expansion. Hamilton's *Report on Manufactures* of 1791 is a sophisticated example of contemporary theories of political economy. Adam Smith had articulated the break with older economic axioms with his theorizing on the happy outcomes of open markets of supply and demand. The Italian, Cesare Beccaria, and later Thomas Malthus and David Ricardo in England, also identified what Hamilton saw: the need to adapt political organization to a firm set of economic ideas that were suited to the industrial, technological and transportation changes occurring in the late eighteenth and early nineteenth centuries. The *Report on Manufactures* is a way into Hamilton's world view. It lays out a series of means and policies to begin the process of bringing the United States into the nineteenth century by designing tariffs and incentives, and federal support for a transportation infrastructure. The principles of free trade and competition required, paradoxically, some market control and protectionism, as American tariffs, British Corn Laws, and Napoleon's "Continental system" all proved. Hamilton encouraged "bounties" for agriculture as well as manufacturing, but his overall scheme was to broaden the American economy to make it stronger, more progressive and flexible, and ultimately competitive with Europe's. As with his fiscal and tax programs, Hamilton was trying to prepare America to be self-sufficient and engaged in the global economy at the same time. None of the recommendations in the *Report on Manufactures* was enacted as federal law, but much of it was applied at the state level.

Among the laws passed by the first Congress was the patent law of 1790. While many of the early patents were simply improvements on older processes or products, a string of technological innovations resulted from the 1790 act. Eli Whitney (1765-1825), an inquisitive graduate of Yale who was familiar with all manner of mechanical crafts, patented his cotton gin in 1794. On a visit to the south, he had observed an improvised device for separating the seeds from the staple in picked cotton and went on to perfect a practical model that revolutionized the cotton economy. The gin (an abbreviation of "engine") mechanically combed the seed from the fiber of the boll. What had taken many slaves many hours could now be done with one slave who could clean 50 pounds of cotton a day using Whitney's machine. The consequences can hardly be overstated; it led to larger investments in cotton cultivation and helped push the plantation system into the southwest all the way to the Mississippi by the first third of the nineteenth century. Whitney's industrial activities were not limited to the cotton gin. He later devised machinery for making precision parts for firearms and advanced one of the great innovations in manufacturing, the production of interchangeable parts. He manufactured firearms for the federal government after 1798 based on that technology. Whitney was not alone in reshaping the American industrial landscape. In 1789, Englishman Samuel Slater (1768-1835), the "Arkwright of America," arrived in New England and, with some American partners, opened the first of a series of textile mills, building the machinery from his own plans. The British at this time forbade the export of designs and skilled textile workers, so Slater secretly left England after memorizing Richard Arkwright's models. The water power that ran the first machines in Rhode Island later gave way to steam power and transformed the economy of southern New England. Slater's mills began drawing cotton directly from the south. His mills also changed the social profile of southern New England. Whole towns became mill towns, and families were sometimes employed in units. He later expanded his textile revolution to include woolen as well as cotton mills. By the early nineteenth century, New England was home to a factory class and a rising dependence on wage labor. In fact, as cotton became an increasingly popular fabric, Francis Lowell and Patrick Jackson in 1814 established America's first fully integrated textile factory at Waltham, Massachusetts (the "Waltham System"). There, every part of the manufacturing process from raw cotton to cloth was contained in a single integrated factory. The activities of the textile innovators are indicative of a flood of industrial, agricultural, and technical improvements that accompanied the birth of the United States. If Hamilton's *Report on Manufactures* had gone unattended at the national level, the states and private entrepreneurs had marched ahead with investments and developments attracted by the lure of manufacturing. Massachusetts used incentive grants to attract business. Samuel Slater and his partners and the many enterprisers who followed were beneficiaries of state help.

Other entrepreneurs were given monopoly licenses to build turnpikes and bridges and even some small canal systems. The enthusiasm for these kinds of projects was contagious. George Washington, for example, had involved himself as early as 1785 in the Potomac Company, which proposed to open a water route to the west by river and canal connections. However, the era of major canal construction was still some way off. It would be inspired by the Erie Canal, begun in 1817 and completed in 1825 by a consortium of private and public interests. It linked New York City with the Great Lakes and was a triumph of engineering while it revolutionized economic and transportation development in the north. The opening of the Philadelphia to Lancaster Turnpike in 1794 was a great success and sparked a boom in road construction. The old Wilderness Road to the west was extended by the Knoxville Road and helped move even more people into the lower Ohio Valley. A road from Knoxville to Nashville made transportation and settlement easier in Tennessee. By 1810, some 300 corporations had been chartered in the United States as monopolies to operate turnpikes and collect tolls. By then, the Cumberland or National Road had been improved by engineering and construction standards from the coast into the Ohio Valley. Along with main transportation routes, a series of post roads began to crisscross the country as postal service expanded. But of all the changes wrought by investment and development, the real estate boom was perhaps the most significant. Land companies attracted both investors and settlement. As Kentucky and Tennessee grew, so too did western New York and Pennsylvania, and the Ohio territory became a magnet for northern migrants. The potential for transportation on the Great Lakes encouraged the surveying of Cleveland as a port in 1796. At the same time, despite the south to north cotton fields to mills connection, the distinct economies in each section pointed west as separate, parallel communities. The Mason and Dixon Line, the simple surveyors' colonial demarcation of the boundary between Pennsylvania and Maryland, was moving west, and, before long, the Ohio River became the western geographical marker for the north-south boundary.

Slavery and Republicanism

The Constitution and the Bill of Rights informed the political ethics of the early 1790s, as did the glow of the Enlightenment, where reason, knowledge, and truth came together. But as reason defined a set of political, civil, and human rights and freedoms, it also limited their application. Slavery survived the Revolution and the light of reason because rational minds saw no practical way to end it. The free inventive minds that accepted the doctrines of laissez faire could ignore Adam Smith's arguments about slavery's inefficiency while the technologists such as Eli Whitney and Samuel Slater indirectly enhanced the rationale for bonded labor. Slavery was preserved and extended because of rationalized racism, pure and simple. Several generations of race relations in the slave societies of the south ensured its survival. In 1787, Thomas Jefferson had published *Notes on the State of Virginia*. He had written it in 1781, while governor of Virginia, as a private response to a series of "queries" from a French diplomat. It was published anonymously in 1785 while Jefferson was in Paris. It is suffused with Jefferson's opinions, elaborations, and editorials and is a sophisticated history and gazetteer of the state. Amidst the descriptions of climate, topography, political and religious institutions, and land tenure, Jefferson discusses natives and African Americans. His discussions of natives have an anthropological and often condescending tone yet, in some ways, are respectful. His observations on the "black" or "negro," on the other hand, are more complex, negative, and rueful.

Jefferson's reflections in *Notes* are personal. In his overview of "negro" characteristics, Jefferson denies that African Americans are as biologically or "morally" advanced as whites. He states that they appeared to be brave because they were not smart enough to know danger. They were more sexually primitive. He adds that "their griefs are transient" and that their habits, culture and outlook are simple, dull, and apparently arrested. Jefferson thus ascribes the inferior abilities of the "negro" to nature, but acknowledges the debased institutional situation of the slave and comes close to confirming their inferiority to whites in a sociological way. In a compelling passage, Jefferson says, "I advance it therefore as a suspicion only, that the blacks, whether a distinct race or made distinct by time or circumstances are inferior to the whites in the endowments both of body and mind." He questions the morality of the slave institution and sadly notes the difficulty in freeing slaves — not because of slavery's injustice but because slaves, being inferior, are unable to function as free men and must be protected from the opprobrium and ostracism of whites. Jefferson concludes that only a removal of African Americans from America would make emancipation work. He changed his emphasis from time to time. As secretary of state, he appointed Benjamin Banneker, a free-born African American, to survey the proposed capital site of the District of Columbia. He praised Banneker's talents and, in a letter to him in 1791, hoped he would serve as an example to the world that African Americans could raise themselves to higher levels:

> No body wishes more than I do to see such proofs as you exhibit, that nature has given our black brethren, talents equal to those of the other colors of men, and that the appearance of a want of them is owing merely to the degraded condition of their existence, both in Africa and America. I can add ... that no body wishes more ardently to see a good system commenced for raising the condition of their body & mind to what it ought to be, as fast as the imbecility of their present existence, and other circumstances which cannot be neglected, will admit.

Earlier, Benjamin Franklin had echoed similar sentiments in the wake of Pennsylvania's gradual emancipation law, and he was very clear on the role of slavery, rather than race, as the cause of the plight of the free African American:

> The unhappy man, who has long been treated as a brute animal, too frequently sinks beneath the common standard of the human species. The galling chains, that bind his body, do also

fetter his intellectual faculties, and impair the social affections of his heart. Accustomed to move like a mere machine, by the will of his master, reflection is suspended; he has not the power of choice; and reason and conscience have but little influence over his conduct, because he is chiefly governed by the passion of fear. He is poor and friendless; perhaps worn out by extreme labour, age, and disease.

As for Jefferson, he praised Banneker as representing the potential of his "whole Colour," but in the *Notes* he had belittled the achievements of African American poets and writers as being mediocre at best and even then as exceptions to the rule. There is no reason to believe that his praise for Banneker was not tempered by the same considerations. Other African Americans of superior intellect and abilities would succeed Banneker and one need only think of Frederick Douglass in the nineteenth century and W.E.B. Du Bois in the twentieth century as latter day Bannekers whose great talents were measured by Americans against their color. As for Jefferson and most of his generation, and indeed for Abraham Lincoln three generations later, slavery might be deplorable, but the collective inferiority of black people, however that inferiority was planted, was obvious.

Conclusion

The United States began with an apparently moderate group of attendees to the opening of Congress in the spring of 1789. These elected representatives could not ignore the rancor of the debates that had preceded the Constitution, the animosity of the ratifying process, or the looming question of what this new thing was, this national government. The Constitution seemed to have been designed with sensitivity to the states, but it also revealed problems, the main one being the potential uses of the power that had been lodged with the new government. If the old Continental Congress, the "Confederation" as many called it, had appeared to be a union without power, the Constitution appeared to some to present a power that promised only disunion. The debates that had split the political community led to the unplanned emergence of serious political parties. Federalists and Antifederalists stood for two distinct views of the Constitution, but the Bill of Rights was accepted by both as respectively advancing the federal government's authority, in the case of the Federalists, or retarding it, in the view of the Antifederalists. The first great partisan issue after the United States Congress had convened was the Hamiltonian fiscal plan and its apparent embellishment of centralized power. As Washington's first term ended, the gloves were off, and partisan vitriol dominated political life in the 1790s. With a national economy taking shape, economic development was spurred by a variety of enterprises including a tentative start to manufacturing industries in textiles and machinery. Slavery had been included in the Constitution and slaveholders' rights were as secure as any other civil rights under the Bill of Rights. Slaves were given two new roles in the new republic: the total slave population could be counted as a three-fifths addition to the white population for representational purposes, and their labor would lift the southern economy into the cotton boom. The new transportation links to the west suggested that the north-south cultural divide of the eighteenth century would go west in the nineteenth.

Suggested Reading

The best single study of the political history of the United States between the Declaration of Independence and the Constitution is Gordon S. Wood, *The Creation of the American Republic, 1776-1787* (Chapel Hill: University of North Carolina Press, 1969); This long and articulate study is in its fourth decade as a starting point for understanding the politics of the era. Also recommended are Stanley Elkins and Eric McKitrick, *The Founding Fathers: Young Men of the Revolution* (Washington: Service Center for Teachers of History, 1962); Lance Banning, *The Sacred Fire of Liberty: James Madison and the Founding of the Federal Republic* (Ithaca, NY: Cornell University Press, 1995); Jack N. Rakove, *Original Meanings: Politics and Ideas in the Making of the Constitution* (New York: Knopf, 1996); and David J. Siemers, *Ratifying the Republic: Antifederalists and Federalists in Constitutional Time* (Stanford, CA: Stanford University Press, 2002). This chapter has referred to Thomas Hobbes's and John Locke's influences on the political ideas of the founders. C.B. Macpherson, *The Political Theory of Possessive Individualism: Hobbes to Locke* (Oxford: Clarendon Press, 1962) is a clearly stated analysis of their thought. See also Frank M. Coleman, *Hobbes and America: Exploring the Constitutional Foundations* (Toronto: University of Toronto Press, 1977), and Thomas Hobbes, *Leviathan* (1651), ed. C.B. Macpherson (Harmondsworth, England: Penguin, 1968). No study of the Constitution is complete without James Madison, Alexander Hamilton, and John Jay, *The Federalist Papers* (1787-88), ed. Isaac Kramnick (New York: The Penguin Group, 1987). Michael Kammen, *A Machine that would go of Itself* (New York: Knopf, 1986) is an imaginative inquiry into the Constitution's durability, and Akhil Reed Amar, *America's Constitution: A Biography* (New York: Random House, 2005) is a recent and engaging study of the political complexities of the Constitution.

CHAPTER SEVEN
THE POLITICS OF THE FEDERALIST ERA

In America there are factions, but no conspiracies.
> — Alexis de Tocqueville, *Democracy in America* (1835)

Time Line

1793	Outbreak of war in Europe.
1794	The Whiskey Rebellion.
	Jay's Treaty.
1795	The 11th Amendment (federal judicial powers).
1796	John Adams elected as president.
	Tennessee admitted as the 16th state.
1797	The XYZ Affair.
1798	The Alien and Sedition Acts.
1798-99	Kentucky and Virginia Resolutions.
1800	The election of Jefferson as president.

Parties

In May 1792, Alexander Hamilton wrote to a Federalist ally that "Mr. Madison cooperating with Mr. Jefferson is at the head of a faction decidedly hostile to me and my administration [as secretary of the treasury], and actuated by views in my judgment subversive to the principles of good government and dangerous to the union, peace and happiness of the Country." Madison and Hamilton had parted ways but the Madison-Jefferson alliance would last until Jefferson's death in 1826. Throughout 1792, Hamilton and Jefferson sparred in a series of published articles that worried Washington, who deplored the rivalry. In the months just before the December 1792 presidential election, Jefferson indicated his intention to retire from cabinet. Even though he had joined with Federalists to persuade Washington to serve again as president, he showed increasing antipathy toward the Federalists and to Hamilton in particular. The first party system had begun to crystallize and, by the end of Washington's second term, would dominate national politics. In the 1792 election, Washington again won easily, and John Adams was retained as vice president. The Federalists controlled both houses of Congress throughout the 1790s with the exception of the 1792-94 House of Representatives when the Antifederalists held 57 of the 105 seats. The majority of the politically active population was still committed to the Federalist agenda, and while Washington exercised his own version of non-partisan statecraft, Hamilton continued to shape the political agenda and had become, in the eyes of his opponents, *l'eminence grise*, the real power in the federal administration.

Modern political parties serve as legislative brokers. They work especially well in parliamentary systems, for example, and, by the late eighteenth century, were firmly established in Britain. The system evolved from the earlier practice of getting control of the legislative body, usually by a "faction" or a majority or an influential group, favored by the monarch, and offset by a concerted opposition. The process can be seen on a simple level as a contest for power between "ins" and "outs" or between a legislative majority and a minority serving interests in the wider community. Control of Parliament required support from the electorate, and the crude origins of what we would consider political parties emerged, as private citizens organized themselves to promote their interests through a representative political party. The looser and shifting party affiliations of the early modern period, particularly in the way they developed in Britain, became more important as electorates expanded. Today, parties are the engines of political operation, funding, ideologies, and agendas. Revolutionary Americans were no strangers to party politics. When Madison and others spoke of "faction," they referred to organized interest groups, parties, and a tradition that could be found in the colonial disputes between pro-governor and pro-assembly groups or in the ethnic and religious factions in Pennsylvania, for example. In the 1760s and 1770s, patriot and loyalist factions had settled into informal party organizations until the war had ended the loyalist role.

The Federalist and Antifederalist identities emerged when politics became national. The wartime Continental Congress and various state governments had divided on a variety of issues that were often fluid and simply indicated differences of opinions on specific issues. An ideological divide had emerged in the aftermath of the war, and the fight over the Constitution had confirmed the partisan nature of politics, especially at the national level. When Antifederalists began to refer to themselves as "Republicans" after Jefferson left Washington's cabinet, the Federalists in Congress and in the press added the derisory adjective "Democratic" to the name and it stuck. It was intended as a slander to tie Jefferson's group and their politics to the mob rule identified with the French Revolution. But the term eventually lost the stigma the Federalists intended, and "democratic" lost its negative denotation. The party, like the Federalists, began to function outside Congress. The "Democratic" societies that began organizing in rural districts and on the frontier appealed to small farmers, shopkeepers, westerners, and some planters, and these societies became core constituencies for the Democratic Republicans. The Federalists had already established a national constituency that tended to commercial and financial interests and to a broader conservative stratum in the general population. New England became the hub of Federalist strength.

The first national election had been delayed into early 1789. Thereafter, elections for the House were held every two years in even years, beginning in the fall of 1790. Because the term for elected senators was six years, and to ensure some continuity in that body, one-third of senatorial terms ended every two years. Presidential elections were held every four years with every second House election. Elections were, and still are, held in the fall of even years and inaugurations completed in the early spring of the odd year following. Thus a congressmen (representative), a president, or a senator who was elected in November took office in the following March (now in January).

Table 7.1: Party Distribution in Congress, 1789-1820

Congress	Year	House* Majority Party	House* Principal Minority Party	Senate* Majority Party	Senate* Principal Minority Party	President Party and President*
1st	1789-91	Ad-38	Op-26	Ad-17	Op-9	F (Washington)
2nd	1791-93	F-37	DR-33	F-16	DR-13	F (Washington)
3rd	1793-95	DR-57	F-48	F-17	DR-13	F (Washington)
4th	1795-97	F-54	DR-52	F-19	DR-13	F (Washington)
5th	1797-99	F-58	DR-48	F-20	DR-12	F (John Adams)
6th	1799-1801	F-64	DR-42	F-19	DR-13	F (John Adams)
7th	1801-03	DR-69	F-36	DR-18	F-13	DR (Jefferson)
8th	1803-05	DR-102	F-39	DR-25	F-9	DR (Jefferson)
9th	1805-07	DR-116	F-25	DR-27	F-7	DR (Jefferson)
10th	1807-09	DR-118	F-24	DR-28	F-6	DR (Jefferson)
11th	1809-11	DR-94	F-48	DR-28	F-6	DR (Madison)
12th	1811-13	DR-108	F-36	DR-30	F-6	DR (Madison)
13th	1813-15	DR-112	F-68	DR-27	F-9	DR (Madison)
14th	1815-17	DR-117	F-65	DR-25	F-11	DR (Madison)
15th	1817-19	DR-141	F-42	DR-34	F-10	DR (Monroe)
16th	1819-21	DR-156	F-27	DR-35	F-7	DR (Monroe)

*Abbreviations: DR=Democratic Republican. F=Federalist. Ad=Administration. Op=Opposition.

Source: US Bureau of the Census, *Historical Statistics of the United States: Colonial Times to 1970* (Washington: Bureau of the Census, 1975), Part 2, Series Y, p. 1084.

The Whiskey Rebellion, Politics, and the Press

In December of 1790, in his second report on the public credit, Hamilton asked Congress for an excise tax on distilled liquors produced in the United States to augment the revenues produced by duties on imported table luxuries such as tea, coffee, wine, and liquor. Once passed, the "whiskey tax," as it came to be known, aroused opposition, not simply from the commercial producers but from thousands of private, individual, and mostly amateur distillers, especially those in the backcountry of North

Carolina and western Pennsylvania. The opposition was somewhat reminiscent of the Stamp Act protests in that the tax was questioned on constitutional grounds. This time, however, the government's presumptive right to apply an internal excise was denounced. The measure struck a nerve where "stills" were an accepted part of the culture. In the summer of 1793, a convention in Pittsburgh drew up resolutions to legally block the collection of the tax. The Swiss immigrant Albert Gallatin (1761-1849), who went on to an illustrious career as a congressman, a long-serving cabinet member, a diplomat, and an ethnographer, took a major role in the affair. As a member of the Pennsylvania legislature, he had pushed for a wider franchise and lower economic qualifications for political representation. Gallatin was drawn to the national Democratic Republican cause. He had been elected to the United States Senate in 1792, only to be denied his seat because he did not meet the constitutional requirement of being a citizen for at least nine years. The federal government rejected the declarations of the Pittsburgh meeting, and Washington promised to enforce the act. In the summer of 1794, the rumbling discontent and refusal to pay the excise had grown into what the government saw as an insurrection on the scale of Shays's Rebellion of 1786. The heart of the defiance was in western Pennsylvania. After fruitless negotiations, the protesters refused to disperse and Washington finally settled on military intervention. An army of over 12,000 militiamen from four states, led by Light Horse Harry Lee, a staunch Federalist, scattered the insurrectionists without bloodshed. Hamilton accompanied the army, as did Washington himself for most of the way, making him the only sitting president to take the field with troops. The Militia Act of 1793 had been created to cope with native resistance in the northwest, but it made a major debut in the suppression of a potentially dangerous attack on federal authority by American citizens. The so-called "Whiskey Rebellion" showed the teeth of the Federalist administration and Washington's personal concerns with civil order, but it paved the way for an upsurge in Democratic Republican party support. When linked to Jefferson's resignation from cabinet, it revealed serious opposition to the Federalists at the highest level of government and more broadly, with the populace.

Meanwhile, three states were added to the union in the 1790s: Vermont in 1791, Kentucky in 1792, and Tennessee in 1796. The latter two wrote provisions for slavery into their constitutions while Vermont banned slavery even before its admission. Eight states permitted slavery, and eight had either ended it or were in the process of gradual eradication. The sectional balance in the Senate was now even. Some issues in the first few Congresses revealed a regional bias on national debt and credit initiatives, but the most contentious debates of the day continued to be about the role of the federal government and the limits, if any, of its authority. At times, the debate dealt with straightforward fiscal policies, but there was a broadly ideological undercurrent in dealing with any fiscal matter. The Hamilton-Jefferson rivalry was not only about getting control of government; each faction sought to apply one of two conflicting visions of the future. The literature this feud produced was as energetic and as poised as any of the pamphlet literature of the pre-war era. It was often personal and at times poisonous. If

The Federalist had laid down a model of measured and sophisticated debate over the necessity of a federal Constitution and the government that went with it, the political literature of the 1790s, while debating the government's mandate, often focused on individual reputation and behavior. Early tracts such as the *Federalist Gazette of the United States* (1789) and the opposition's *National Gazette* (1791) spelled out the respective positions of the two parties, and created a boom in the publications industry. There had been a long tradition of editorial politics in the colonies, and John Peter Zenger's *New York Weekly Journal* of the 1730s is the best remembered of a lively and persistent newspaper culture. In the era of the 1760s and early 1770s, newspapers were as vital as pamphlets in circulating opinion as well as news. By 1775, there were an estimated 37 newspapers in America, including at least one daily. Most of those newspapers had been politically motivated. Twenty-three of them can be identified as patriot and seven as loyalist.

After the war, the language and style of journalism became vituperative, and parti sanship tore at the union. Between 1790 and 1800, the number of newspapers in the United States grew from about 90 (including 8 daily newspapers) to about 230. Newspapers had short lives, and it is estimated that as many as 450 may have been started during the decade. One estimate shows that, of the 1,634 newspapers that appeared in the period between 1704 (when the first regular one was published in Boston) and 1820, only 4 lasted 40 or more years. The censoring of newspapers had always been around but became difficult after the first amendment to the Constitution encouraged a wide-open approach to political opposition and propaganda. Political parties and individuals used the newspapers of the 1790s and beyond to smear their opponents with *ad hominem* attacks while challenging government intentions such as the whiskey tax legislation. Newspapers and their widening circulation aggravated the political split that was taking shape.

Foreign Affairs and the French Revolution

If parties dominated national politics in a way that neither the Constitution nor the ratifying conventions had foreseen, the rivalries also spilled over into international affairs. While Congress stewed and newspapers defamed rival politicians, France had changed the course of European and world history following the overthrow of the monarchy in 1789 and the complete collapse of the *ancien régime* in Europe's largest nation. Britain resumed its military and diplomatic confrontation with France, but it faced a different kind of France, an explosive and popularly controlled state bent on radicalizing the politics of Europe and threatening not only British interests but the status quo all over the continent. For the second time in a generation, Britain would be engaged in a counter-revolutionary war and, by 1793, had joined with other European nations in the First Coalition against France. A twenty-year series of large-scale and lethal European wars was under way, which would result in the reshaping of international relations and the global balance of power. The French revolutionary spirit was driven by a nationalistic fervor that had been only partially realized among Americans during their war with the British. The following *levée en masse* (conscription) issued by the National Convention (the revolutionary French government) in August 1793 indicates the radical tone of the French Revolution:

> From this moment until our enemies have been driven from the territory of the Republic, all Frenchmen are *permanently* requisitioned for military service. Young men will go forth to battle; married men will forge weapons and transport munitions; women will make tents and clothing; children will make bandages from old linen; and old men will be brought to the public squares to arouse the courage of the soldiers, while preaching the unity of the Republic and hatred against Kings [emphasis added].

In America, the French Revolution appeared to the Federalists as radicalized chaos and catastrophe for Christianity and order, but many Democratic Republicans chose to see it as a triumph of the popular will over despotism, so, if the Federalists were pro-British then the Democratic Republicans would favor the French. Even as the excesses of the French Revolution revealed its darker and quirkier side, its capricious politics, and, most important, the hysteria of the "Terror," most Democratic Republicans continued to support it as openly as the Federalists condemned it.

In a significant way, the French Revolution's impact on the United States looms as large as or larger than any direct influence the American Revolution might have had on France. It created a greater problem for Americans than any question of its morality and ideology. Over the next two decades, the European wars, and especially their British and French phases, exerted enormous influence on American trade, foreign policy, national security, and domestic politics. The first example of the latter occurred in the summer of 1793 when the revolutionary Girondist government sent Edmond Genet to the United States to negotiate trade and seek American recognition of *La République*. In a most extraordinary display of tactlessness, Genet secured four privateers to attack British merchant shipping in American waters. Washington and Hamilton were predictably appalled by Genet's indiscretion, and even Secretary of State Jefferson, who was in part responsible for him, refused to condone the Frenchman's folly. The so-called "Citizen Genet affair" was an embarrassment to be sure, and it pushed Washington closer to Hamilton for advice on European matters. The president reversed his earlier recognition of the French Republic. By then, Genet had outstayed his welcome. The moderate Girondists had been driven from power, and the Terror had begun in earnest. Genet's extradition, and likely his head, was sought by the new extremist Jacobin government. To his credit, President Washington refused to comply, and Genet stayed in the United States and took up citizenship. But the gulf between Jeffersonians and Hamiltonians had widened. Jefferson resigned from cabinet, as promised, in December 1793.

Washington's Departure

George Washington had publicly sought the middle ground in international relations, and, in an effort to avoid being drawn into the messy affairs of Europe, Congress passed an act in 1794 forbidding Americans from serving in foreign governments and banning armed vessels from using American ports. Nevertheless, the parties drifted into a neo-colonial mentality by being dragged into debates over which of the European powers would best benefit American interests, or rather which side would do less harm. The treaty with Britain of 1794, Jay's Treaty, was the first major international agreement negotiated by the United States. Its results confirmed the weakness of the American government in international relations. John Jay, a major figure in the postwar period in many roles, was then the chief justice of the United States and led the negotiations for the United States. The major issues were tied to the British forts in the northwest and to outstanding loyalist debts. While the British appeared to be using the forts to leverage repayment of loyalist debt, they also wanted to protect their fur-trading interests in what was American territory. British strategy also called for a native buffer against American settlement, a position that angered westbound Americans. What must count as a calculated humiliation were British orders in council (the equivalent of a cabinet decision) in 1793 that declared that American vessels were subject to seizure and American crews liable for impressment into the British navy. The order derived from British irritation with the flow of deserters who left the British service for better pay and conditions on American ships.

That order stayed in place for the better part of 20 years. It ate away at Anglo-American relations and contributed to the coming of war in 1812. For the most part, in the 1790s the United States was impotent. It had trade agreements with France, and these complicated the Federalist desire to maintain trade with Britain. Hamilton understood that government revenues required the continuation of British trade. The duties alone from British imports helped sustain the United States Treasury. The treaty that emerged, while acceptable to Hamilton, was seen by the Democratic Republicans as an insult. The British promised to close the western forts but did nothing to amend their native alliances. While they permitted Americans access to West Indies and East Indies ports, they attached severe restrictions. The British agreed to compensate for naval seizures. They agreed to discuss boundary disputes in the northeast but insisted on and won an agreement to settle outstanding British claims for colonial debts. Southern states, who owed most to the British and who had sought compensation for slaves "stolen" by the British during the war, were enraged; the Federalists lost some southern support. The Senate approved Jay's Treaty while Washington, who was not entirely happy with it, nevertheless capitulated, much to the delight of Hamilton.

Hamilton left the cabinet in early 1795 and renewed his journalistic and public debate with Jefferson. The United States negotiated a satisfactory treaty with Spain that recognized American boundary claims in the southwest. It allowed American navigation on the Mississippi and the use of the port of New Orleans. Still, American relations with Britain and France were strained, and, when Washington declined to run for a third term in 1796, he left with a warning to avoid permanent alliances with foreign powers, advising that only "temporary alliances for ... emergencies" were acceptable if

America was to prosper. Washington noted his abhorrence of the party system but lauded the principle of public credit. The speech was written with Hamilton's participation. The departure of Washington was a moment for national contemplation. The acknowledged "father" of the nation had left office as he had entered it, mediating, and pleading with Americans to avoid debilitating internal ideological squabbles. In a way, America had moved beyond the easy optimism of Washington's first term and had entered a phase of deeply antagonistic competition for political power. The first few years of the nation state had revealed a paradox: a sometimes angry and always aggressively partisan interpretation of the Constitution but also a respect for it and a desire to maintain it. The *interpretation* of the Constitution and not its presence says a lot about American political identity. The next two elections revealed the Constitution's vitality and status: political factions could and would be accommodated *within* the broad republican structure of the Constitution. From the Stamp Act Congress to the first United States Congress, an interesting conservatism had emerged. The new nation had not veered off into chaos or counterrevolution. In the workings of the Constitution, Americans had found truth in the phrase *medio tutissimus ibis*, that is, "you will travel safest in a middle course." The elections of 1796 and 1800 were tests of that consensus, and demonstrated that, in the hurly-burly of the Federalist-Democratic Republican rifts, the dramatic rhetoric of party politics did not shatter the union but rather showed that it might be maintained with debate and compromise.

The Crisis of the Federalist Party
The first party system did not last long. Despite the bitter and personalized contests for power, and the difficulties of adjusting to new economic realities, the separate visions of Hamilton and Jefferson did not result in civil war or secession. In repelling Shays's uprising and the Whiskey Rebellion, force was used, but those were exceptions to the law and order that dominated public affairs. Even in the open west, only natives seemed exempt from the search for peace and order among the swarming settlers. The Constitution had been secured and respected. James Lowell Russell had a point when in 1888 he reflected on the Constitution as a "machine that would go of itself." Madison had seen that it could be a self-correcting instrument applied not only to the everyday interests and ambitions of the states and the pluralistic culture of America but also at the grander level of national policy. The elections of 1796 and 1800 were tests of the nation's political stability. The electoral majority still lay with the Federalists, whose control of government seemed secure and was affirmed in the election of 1796. There were two Federalist candidates for the presidency, John Adams and Thomas Pinckney (1750-1828) of South Carolina, who together received 130 Electoral College votes. The two Democratic Republicans, Thomas Jefferson and Aaron Burr (1756-1836) of New York, together received 98 votes. But Jefferson with 68 had polled the second highest number of votes after Adams, who had 71. Thus, by finishing ahead of Pinckney, the vice president was to be Jefferson, a member of the opposition. An unforeseen Constitutional anomaly had appeared.

The national political community of the 1790s was an intimate one. While politicians remained committed to local and state affairs, they came to know each other very well at the national level. Jefferson and Adams, despite their divergent views on government, were committed to the nation and to the Constitution. They were friendly and respectful and discussed their differences openly. Nevertheless, Jefferson found himself in an awkward position in 1796-97. The government was still in Federalist hands, and Hamilton's economic and international agendas were still in place. The office of the vice president was a difficult one; the holder had little authority except for what personal influence he might have on the president. But it was not Jefferson who ran afoul of the Federalist majority but Adams himself. The president was eager to keep the United States as neutral as possible in the Anglo-French conflict, but, in December, the French revolutionary government refused to receive Charles Cotesworth Pinckney (1746-1825), the brother of the presidential candidate Thomas Pinckney, as the United States minister to France. The French were naturally opposed to Jay's Treaty, which was, even to the neutral observer, favorable to Britain at France's expense. Pinckney, the Federalist, was unacceptable to the French. Adams, seeking to restore some diplomatic balance, sent a commission to France to try to get an agreement on trade and diplomatic relations. The results of the negotiations turned out to be more damaging to the Federalists than Jay's Treaty.

What became known as the "XYZ Affair" underscored America's international insignificance. In the fall of 1797, the American delegation of Federalists Charles Cotesworth Pinckney and John Marshall (1755-1835) and Democratic Republican Elbridge Gerry arrived in Paris. In a show of overt disdain for the Americans, the French foreign minister Talleyrand had three emissaries (identified as X, Y, and Z in the reports) attempt to bribe the Americans to negotiate a treaty favorable to France. The news shocked Federalists and Democratic Republicans alike and confirmed the degree to which partisan politics had taken over American public life. A group of angry Federalists demanded a declaration of war against France. Adams wisely declined to act but ordered a beefing up of the military, and Congress agreed to the creation of the Department of the Navy as a formal cabinet office. George Washington was enlisted in the summer of 1798 to command a coordinated national defense, with Hamilton as his second in command. The alliance with France was ended by a unilateral decision of Congress, and, while Adams insisted that France would have to start any conflict between the two nations, an undeclared war did take place at sea. In a series of brief encounters, American and French warships engaged each other sporadically between the fall of 1798 and the winter of 1799-1800. Adams persisted with his policy of reconciliation and continued his attempts to settle with France peacefully. Another commission was sent to France, after Talleyrand gave assurances of respectful treatment. It managed to secure a set of accords that recognized the rights of each to conduct foreign relations with other nations. The Americans succeeded in canceling the 1778 treaty of defense that had brought France into the War for Independence. This was no small matter. The French revolutionary regime had been using that treaty to bully the United States. Adams had exercised some diplomatic skill in dealing with France, but the Federalist Party was split. The aggressive pro-war faction of Hamilton and cabinet members Timothy Pickering (1745-1829) and James McHenry indicated that they had no confidence in Adams, who ended up dismissing both men from his cabinet in the spring of 1800. Adams was inclined to be moderate in foreign affairs, but he lacked the support that politicians of all stripes had extended to the heroic Washington. Moreover, party rivalries had intensified. The Federalists in Adams's cabinet and in Congress, in a combined effort to curb rising Democratic Republican popularity, began to override Adams's authority.

The Alien and Sedition Acts

Adams then faced the greatest crisis of his tenure. In the midst of the tense relations with France, Congress passed four acts in June and July of 1798 that are known collectively as the Alien and Sedition Acts. The consequences were devastating. Not only did the reaction to them bring into question the extent of federal authority under the Constitution, but it resulted in a diminution of Federalist Party power and support. By the time the smoke cleared, the Constitution had been exonerated in many minds as being not a threat to civil liberties but rather a brake on the abuse of national power. The acts turned out to be a terrible mistake made by an overconfident but misinformed Federalist Congress, and Adams, by signing them into law, committed a fatal political misjudgment. The imbroglio with France had created an atmosphere of confusion and xenophobia in the Federalist ranks. "Foreigners" in the United States were assumed to support the Democratic Republicans. The Citizen Genet affair of 1793 had been an embarrassment for Democratic Republicans, as Jefferson had indicated, and it had left Federalists confirmed in their suspicions of French intentions in America. The quasi-war and the insulting French treatment of American statesmen in the XYZ Affair had made France, and somewhat illogically, most immigrants, a threat to American security. The four acts that comprise the Alien and Sedition Acts were as follows:

Naturalization Act: This repealed the 1795 Act that had set a five-year residence requirement for citizenship. The new legislation set the residence requirement at fourteen years.

Alien Act: The act allowed the president to deport any "alien" suspected of plotting against the government or perceived to be a threat to peace and order.

Alien Enemies Act: In the event of a war, the president was given the power to order the arrest or deportation of enemy citizens.

Sedition Act: This act sought to censor opposition, in particular the Democratic Republican press. It allowed for fines and imprisonment for publishing attacks on the government or its officers. Obstruction of government officials was also considered sedition.

Of the four, the Sedition Act was the most controversial, and the prosecution of Democratic Republican publishers or printers under the act was obviously politically motivated. The law was formally attacked by the Virginia and Kentucky state legislatures because it violated the first amendment, the "freedom of speech" clause. Jefferson, who, it must be remembered, was the vice president, drafted the Kentucky Resolution anonymously, and James Madison wrote the one for Virginia. The Kentucky Resolution of November 16, 1798 was a straightforward repudiation of what it called the federal government's assumption of "undelegated powers," that is, powers not specified in the Constitution. The resolution argued that the Constitution was a "compact" between the states and did not indicate a disappearance of the states as the formative agents. The resolution argued that, in regards to "aliens," the states retained the authority over them and that the federal government was assuming "undelegated" powers in specifically targeting them. The logic points the way to a "states' rights" theory of federalism:

> Resolved, that the several States composing the United States of America, are not united on the principle of unlimited submission to their General Government; but that by a compact under the style and title of a Constitution of the United States and of amendments thereto, they constituted a General Government for special purposes, — delegated to that government certain definite powers, reserving, each State to itself, the residuary mass of right to their own self-government; and that whensoever the General Government assumes undelegated powers, its acts are unauthoritative, void, and of no force.

That terse paragraph prefaced a long and careful dissection of the acts. The statement invokes the first amendment and, in a telling conclusion, warns the federal government not to assume all the powers formerly held by the states. The Kentucky Resolutions were more heated than Virginia's, but both manifestos were unequivocal and intended for audiences far beyond the nominal boundaries of the two states. Kentucky and Virginia insisted on their allegiance to the union, but Jefferson and Madison had struck a blow against Federalist policy. Federalists were aroused, and several northern Federalist states denounced the resolutions, arguing that the federal government *alone* should interpret the Constitution. That inspired a second Kentucky Resolution, a year after the first one, raising the possibility of state secession.

In the midst of the controversies, George Washington died peacefully on December 14, 1799, while national political debate descended rapidly into intolerance.

The Election of 1800
John Adams was the most important victim of the Alien and Sedition Acts. Throughout his presidency, he had tried to straddle the political fence, while the press, the public, and the rising star of the Democratic Republican Party had drawn him into controversies over French policies and practices. Jefferson had used the Democratic Republican Party to openly criticize the Adams administration. As Adams's first term

drew to a close, it was clear that Jefferson and the Democratic Republicans would attack the Federalists over the Alien and Sedition Acts and the Federalists' attempts to raise federal taxes on property to pay for possible war expenditures. The increased British harassment of American shipping also helped to undermine Federalist power. Jefferson broke with tradition and not only campaigned on his own behalf but challenged the man whom he had served as vice president. In a distinctly unpleasant campaign, he attacked Adams directly. This inspired the wise and forceful Abigail Adams to issue a private scolding of Jefferson in a series of letters that were as strongly worded as any newspaper attacks on him, although by that time the majority of press opinion favored the Democratic Republicans. As Washington's successor, Adams should have kept the office, but Jefferson and Aaron Burr each received 73 electoral votes. Adams won 65, the second Federalist candidate, Charles Cotesworth Pinckney, 64, and another Federalist John Jay received 1 vote. The practice in the first three presidential elections had been for the electors to vote for the man and to split the two votes each elector had to indicate a choice for president and for vice president. In 1800, the electors had voted along strict party lines. The vote for Jay, for example, is an anomaly and most properly sits with Pinckney. The election summarized the 1790s political climate in the clear separation of the Democratic Republican and Federalist parties in electoral terms and the growth of a sectional alignment along party lines. Jefferson received no votes from New England and won only 20 of the 37 votes from the four middle states. The rest came from the slave south. Much has been made of the obvious benefits Jefferson received from the three-fifths clause. The electoral numbers in the five southern states and the new slave states of Kentucky and Tennessee had been inflated by the three-fifths calculation so that the 53 electors in those seven states would have been reduced to about 40 according to the white population. But Jefferson was not alone in benefiting. After 1800, southerners held a balance of power in Congress for some time. They dominated the Supreme Court and the presidency for much of the period up to the Civil War. This occurred even as the successor to the Democratic Republican Party, the Democratic Party with northern and southern branches, became a national force after the election of Andrew Jackson in 1828. In 1800, however, the Democratic Republican Party was a largely southern force that was ready to dominate national politics and eventually squeeze the Federalist Party out of existence.

In a very real sense, the 1800 election for the presidency was decided not by the public or the electors but by the efforts of Alexander Hamilton in a remarkable demonstration of political influence made possible by Article II, section 1, paragraph 3 of the 1787 Constitution, which read in part:

> The person having the greatest Number of [electoral] Votes shall be the President, if such Number be a Majority of the whole Number of Electors appointed; and if there be more than one who have such a Majority, and have an equal Number of Votes, then the House of Representatives shall immediately choose by Ballot one of them for President; and if no

Person have a Majority, then from the five highest on the List the said House shall in like Manner chuse the President. But in chusing the President, the Votes shall be taken by States, the Representation from each State having one Vote.

This clause is a good example of the checks and balance format of the Constitution in the role it gives to congressmen in presidential ties and in the case where no majority is reached. It invites partisanship, no doubt, but avoids the need of electoral run offs, as occurs in other later presidential systems throughout the world. In the 1800 election, the issue was thrown into the House by the tie between Jefferson and Burr, who shared a majority of the votes. Given the original intent of the method for electing the president, the runner-up according to the votes would become vice president. The electors in 1800 had voted for a Jefferson-Burr ticket but had split their votes evenly. This threw the issue on to the floor of the House. Hamilton had fought hard to prevent Jefferson from winning, but, with Adams, was now the runner-up. The Federalists in the House supported Burr, but Hamilton saw Jefferson as more acceptable given his apparent commitment to national interests. Moreover, Hamilton disliked Burr personally and had been quite public in his invective. However, the Federalist caucus's resistance to Jefferson complicated the issue. Hamilton eventually broke down the resistance, but it took 36 ballots to get the majority of the states to agree. On February 17, 1801, over two months after the election, ten states voted Jefferson into office. Burr became vice president, as had been expected in the first place. The election and Hamilton's role immediately jeopardized the Federalists' future as a national political force, but Hamilton was proved right in his assessment of Jefferson. In his inaugural speech, Jefferson used the memorable phrase "we are all republicans — we are all federalists" to assuage the Federalists' fears that Democratic Republicans were unsuited to national government.

Jefferson believed his administration could retain what its members saw as useful in the Federalist economic program while advancing their own agrarian policies. Jefferson saw the need to blend the two party protocols "with courage and confidence" to "pursue our own federal and republican principles, our attachment to our union and representative government." He lauded America's uniqueness by reminding the country that Americans were not only separated from Europe and the old ways by an ocean to the east but also poised to expand the virtues of the republic to the endless west. Jefferson announced his own version of isolationism with the phrase "peace, commerce, and honest friendship with all nations, entangling alliances with none." The imbroglios with Britain and France had made an impact to be sure, but Jefferson was echoing Washington's earlier call to a foreign policy that stressed no binding, formal alliances. Indeed, Jefferson's phrase "entangling alliances with none" is often mistakenly ascribed to Washington, who had warned against "permanent alliances" in his farewell address in 1796. The common thread here was the concept of a vast continental empire tied to the preservation and expansion of an American cultural, social, and political "exceptionalism." In the speech, the intellectually cosmopolitan Jefferson became downright parochial, and his verbal flourishes exalting the nation's destiny appear now as quite insular. Americans, according to Jefferson in 1801, were

> Kindly separated by nature and a wide ocean from the exterminating havoc of one quarter of the globe; too high-minded to endure the degradations of others; possessing a chosen country, with room enough for our descendants to the thousandth and thousandth generation; entertaining a due sense of our equal right to the use of our own faculties, to the acquisitions of our own industry, to honor and confidence from our fellow-citizens, resulting not from birth but from our actions and their sense of them; enlightened by a benign religion, professed, indeed, and practiced in various forms, yet all of them including honesty, truth, temperance, gratitude, and the love of man; acknowledging and adoring an overruling Providence, which by all its dispensations proves that it delights in the happiness of man here and his greater happiness hereafter — with all these blessings, what more is necessary to make us a happy and prosperous people? Still one thing, fellow-citizens — a wise and frugal Government, which shall restrain men from injuring one another, shall leave them otherwise free to regulate their own pursuits of industry and improvement, and shall not take from the mouth of labor the bread it has earned. This is the sum of good government, and this is necessary to close the circle of our felicities.

An original American credo informs that passage, and Jefferson brings several of his personal beliefs into it, but what shapes the message is not ambition but optimism. Like so many other historians, Richard Hofstadter struggled to make sense of Jefferson's ambivalences, moods, contradictions, indecisiveness, and even aloofness, but he found a consistency in Jefferson's belief that man was perfectible in the right circumstances, and that America offered those circumstances. Hofstadter compares the moral universe of Jefferson favorably with Hamilton's. As he puts it,

> Men like Hamilton could argue that manufactures ought to be promoted because they would enable the nation to use the labor of women and children 'many of them at a tender age' [for profit, presumably], but Jefferson was outraged at such a view of humanity. Hamilton schemed to get the children into factories; Jefferson planned school systems. While Hamilton valued institutions and abstractions, Jefferson valued people and found no wealth more important than life … and the 'pursuit of happiness.'

Nineteenth-century America would fulfill Hamilton's labor theories, but Americans would endorse, in spirit anyway, Jefferson's idealistic views as being closer to their national values.

John Adams's Farewell

Jefferson's complexities have created a varied historical judgment of him. He has been venerated for his role in bringing the republic to life and helping secure it but otherwise denigrated for his apparently enigmatic personality, and even for the contradictions in his presidential policies. His rival in the 1800 election, John Adams, is as important a founder as Jefferson, but he does not arouse the interest of Americans in the way that Hamilton and Jefferson do. Adams, the temperate, thoughtful, and intelligent revolutionary, whose credentials are as impressive as any of the major figures of the era, was no Washington. In the 1800 election, he would not achieve the public reverence of Washington or Jefferson. In fact, a recent poll by historians had Washington and Jefferson in the top five of importance among presidents while Adams ranked 14th. Both Madison and James Monroe, the presidents who succeeded Jefferson, ranked higher than Adams. Yet Adams, for 35 years — from the time he published his brilliant essay on the Stamp Act, *A Dissertation on the Canon and Feudal Law*, until he left for Braintree to a quiet Massachusetts retirement — had been in the forefront of public affairs. He had spent ten years as a diplomat in Europe and had helped define the Revolution in his writings, behavior, and energetic service. Still, his place among the founders falls short of Washington's leadership, Franklin's versatility, Jefferson's association with the Declaration, Madison's with the Constitution, and Hamilton's inventiveness and single-mindedness. Adams was the intellectual equal of any of his contemporaries, his writings as original and deep as any of the period, and his political values as patriotic and nationalistic as any. As his diary reveals, he was a socially conservative man who disdained frivolity and appeared at times to be so focused and controlled as to be stubborn. His personal discipline and intellectual habits can be seen in a note in his diary, written when he was 25 years old:

I began [Alexander] Popes Homer, last Saturday Night was a Week, and last Night, which was Monday night I finished it. Thus I found that in seven days I could have easily read the 6 Volumes, Notes, Preface, Essays, that on Homer, and that on Homers Battles and that on the funeral Games of Homer and Virgil &c. Therefore I will be bound that in 6 months I would conquer him in Greek, and make myself able to translate every Line in him elegantly.

In the end, the brilliant and vital Adams was defeated by politics, and yet, as the historian Joseph Ellis has recently noted, he and his fellow luminaries were bound together in the great republican project as "brothers" of a kind, and their disputes do not negate their consensual objectives. They and a great many other "founders" are properly understood as a nationalist collective who saw in the republic the fulfillment of America's past and the prospects for its future. Jefferson's victory in 1800 represented a genuinely peaceful transfer of power and was a sign that the nation had survived a great test. It was the last straw for John Adams and, as the Jeffersonian era was ushered in, he quietly departed for his Quincy Braintree home. While Adams regretted the election loss, he was more hurt and alienated by Hamilton's essay, *Letter Concerning the Public Conduct and Character of John Adams*, which he deemed to be an unnecessary and unfair criticism.

Jefferson's Republic

In a reference that crept into the American view of the world, a Pennsylvania miller named Thomas Lea suggested to the French traveler La Rochefoucauld-Liancourt that America in the 1790s had begun to define itself in contrast to the "decrepitude" of Europe. America was the future, as the miller and Jefferson himself had suggested, and its people the most free. And what was this Europe? In 1889, Henry Adams, the great grandson of John Adams, who had quoted the miller in his voluminous study of the presidencies of Jefferson and Madison, concluded, sardonically, that in 1800 decrepit Europe was actually

> on the verge of an outburst of genius. Goethe and Schiller, Mozart and Haydn, Kant and Fichte, Cavendish and Herschel were making way for Walter Scott, Wordsworth, and Shelley, Heine and Balzac, Beethoven and Hegel, Oersted and Cuvier, great physicists, biologists, geologists, chemists, mathematicians, metaphysicians and historians by the score.... investigators, reformers, scholars and philosophers swarmed, and the influence of enlightenment ... was working with an energy such as the world had never before conceived.

The brilliant Henry Adams was right, of course, but he also allowed that America's virtues lay elsewhere, in its open institutions, its opportunities and budding egalitarianism. It had more modern political flair than did Europe, and, if its culture, intellect, and art were not as original or refined, it was beginning to develop the "higher" forms of thought and culture. Meanwhile, Europe was wracked by wars of an increasingly destructive scale. It was class bound and unhealthy, and Americans could rightly identify their national virtues by simply noting what Americans were *not*; they were not European. That was borne out with the creation of specifically American repositories for the artifacts and documents of the American past. The founding of the Massachusetts Historical Society in 1791, the federal Library of Congress in 1800, the New York Historical Society in 1804, and the American Antiquarian Society in 1812 were important milestones in the creation of a national history that would predate independence. The Massachusetts and New York endeavors were originally national in their purpose, but, as the Library of Congress established its own national mandate, the various state repositories gradually focused on their own specific histories.

Jefferson's America was also actively Christian. The end of tax-supported Christian establishments had encouraged more not less religious activity at the local and personal level. The variety of modes and thought that had been developing for decades continued apace into the 1780s and 1790s and then into the nineteenth century. Baptists, Methodists, and even Catholics established networks and interstate organizations while smaller sects flourished everywhere. As an indication of the social transformation of some aspects of American life, a Catholic newspaper enjoyed a short-lived existence in Boston in 1789, and a permanent Catholic church was built there in 1803. In the early nineteenth century, several specialized theological schools were established along the east coast. The older Anglican (Church of England) establishment had given way to an American Episcopal Church. Deism was embraced by a growing number of Americans at the turn of the century, despite the surge in faith-based religion. Deism, as propagated during the Enlightenment and popularly broadcast by Paine's *Age of Reason*, added a lively dimension to religious behavior and controversy. It suggested that God was present in nature, in human morality, rather than in divine revelation. Jefferson's reference to "nature's God" in the Declaration suggests a deist leaning. But more conventional forms of Christian practices were also undergoing great changes.

By 1820, Unitarianism, with its emphasis on God (the Unitarian) as opposed to the older Trinitarian approach to worship and theology, had begun to exert its influence in Massachusetts. As a liberal alternative to the older Congregational establishment, it became a powerful moral and intellectual force as the century wore on. African American churches, mostly Baptist, had begun to organize during the Revolution and grew tremendously in numbers and participation during the first decades of the republic. Pietistic and Evangelical churches appeared everywhere in this period, but the most significant affirmations of Christianity's character in the early republic were the great revivals. They were similar to those of the earlier Great Awakening and occurred mostly on the frontier in the 1790s and again in the 1820s. From the large well-organized aggregations such as the Baptists and Congregationalists to the hundreds of small and sometimes exotic and radical sects, religion permeated American life in every way and reflected the nation's pluralism and mobility. The "religion of the heart," the faith over reason approach to Christian belief, was increasingly embraced by the masses. On the frontier and elsewhere, good works and hard work as moral imperatives to religious life began to erode the more fatalistic Calvinism and Presbyterianism of the past.

As Jefferson went to his inauguration in March 1801, he added an important corollary to the tone of his inaugural speech. He eschewed the formal carriage ride and ceremony that had attended Washington and Adams. Over time, a great deal of pomp has been restored to the inauguration, but, in 1801, Jefferson was making a point about his ideals. He walked in plain dress and hairstyle as if to emphasize his small "r" republicanism. The walk he took was in the new "federal" capital town of Washington that would eventually be coextensive with the District of Columbia, on land ceded by Virginia and Maryland. It was a sorry bit of habitation, located in a swampy, hot, and raw piece of land by the Potomac River. It has since become a city of national secular shrines, but, in the early republic, the unfinished federal district reflected the newness of the United States. Like the Constitution, its location was a compromise. Philadelphia was as strategically located as the new district, but that site would have favored Pennsylvania. A new capital for a new nation in neutral territory seemed appropriate. Beyond the settled east lay what all Americans saw as wilderness and dreams. But Americans had another image to reflect their achievements. It was manifest in a neoclassical approach to architecture, nomenclature, style, and simile. In the following decades, towns were named Rome, Ithaca, Troy, Cincinnati, Cairo (often pronounced Kay-row in America), and Athens, and public buildings assumed aspects of Greco-Roman design or "Georgian," style, mostly in rococo versions. Jefferson's Monticello or the national Capitol became visual American symbols. The "republic" would have a "senate" as in ancient Rome, and so on. George Washington had already been linked to the great Roman general Cincinnatus, who had fought the good fight and laid down his sword to take up the plow in peace. Then, in the first decade of the nineteenth century, Mason (Parson) Weems published two remarkable semi-fictional biographies of the "father of the nation." The titles alone convey the powerful image that Washington was to have as the moral foundation to the Revolution: *A History of the Life and Death, Virtues and Exploits, of General George Washington* (1800) and *The Life of George Washington, with Curious Anecdotes Laudable to Himself and Exemplary to his Countrymen* (1807). Weems invented the story of Washington's "I cannot tell a lie" regarding the chopping down of a cherry tree when he was a youth, and likewise made up a set of moral tales around sketched outlines. Washington was already a legend, but Weems helped to mythologize him. Chief Justice John Marshall also got into the act and published a multi-volume biography of Washington. At the same time, the prolific patriot historian David Ramsay published his *Life of George Washington*, a more conventional hagiographical book. It toned down Weems's exultations and inventions and is better remembered than Marshall's effort, but still leaves a larger than life Washington to represent a distinctive American kind of virtue: "his talent... was more solid than showy."

These celebrations reflected a growing national awareness that translated into American names for places. Countless towns, counties, streets, and squares bear the names Washington, Jefferson, Adams, Madison, and Franklin, and the trend would continue with Monroe and Jackson and Lincoln, and beyond. Those names, originally British, have become singularly American. The word "Columbia" became synonymous with "America" and with the distinctiveness of the new nation. Ohio's new capital would be in Columbus, and South Carolina would relocate its business to Columbia. In 1792, on a voyage that included North America's west coast and China, the New England trader and explorer Robert Gray saw the mouth of a great river and called it the Columbia, after his vessel. In an interesting comment on republican values, many of the new state capitals were placed in smaller communities away from the major cities, as in Harrisburg, Pennsylvania and Albany, New York. As the nation moved west, this trend continued in many of the new states. Was a capital located in Baton Rouge or Jefferson City less vulnerable to political corruption than a capital in New Orleans or Saint Louis? It seemed so to republican idealists. As to place names, there was an ongoing affection for original native definitions, even as natives themselves were disappearing from the landscape. The euphonious Massachusetts and Mississippi and the composite Indiana were part of an historically deliberate retention of native words for places. Americans had been practical in identifying geographical features such as the Great Lakes, and later in the naming of the Great Plains or the Rocky Mountains. The European imprint on North America was retained in the Dutch Harlem and Bowery, in the French Detroit, Louisiana, Vermont, and Maine, or in Spanish Florida. On another level, there was no movement to replace the thousands of British place names used in the settlement of the older colonies, and the Hudson River, New Hampshire, Boston, New York, Charleston and even the more recent Pittsburgh remained. That rich mélange of place names became "American" as time went by. In other ways, the separation from Britain was being completed with a new currency and a cluster of new national symbols, including the widespread use of George Washington's image and the appearance of the stars and stripes and the eagle as American logos. American linguistic usage, spelling and pronunciation of the English language had been developing for decades, and the process was hurried along after independence. Parades and other celebrations had accompanied the ratification of the Constitution, but, by the 1790s, it was the fourth of July that achieved the status of a national holiday in most parts of the country. Indeed, on July 4, 1794, even the inmates of the Boston workhouse were allowed to join the festivities, and the house was "Vacant by reason of the North American Independency."

Conclusion

The decade of the 1790s ranks high among the decisive eras in American political history. The first challenge of the decade was to run what was still an ill-defined federation. The Federalist political majority and its chief architect and promoter, Alexander Hamilton put in place a series of public funding and economic mechanisms that shaped the politics of the decade. As taxes and banking came increasingly under federal control, states' rights and agrarian opposition coalesced into the Antifederalist and the Democratic Republican movements. Federalist government taxing policies and the Whiskey Rebellion encouraged support for the Democratic Republican Party. By the 1796 election, political parties were a fixture. Economically, the advance of cotton culture in the south corresponded to the early development of a textile industry in New England. But agrarianism dominated American society. The magnet of the west created two new states, Kentucky and Tennessee, to go with Vermont in the northeast. Another phase began in Americans' intense commitment to Christianity and the nation's ubiquitous Christian pluralism. The distance between the church and government institutions widened, although politicians would need to demonstrate a definable Christian temperament. Washington's retirement in 1796 coincided with difficult international relations and growing factionalism at home. From the debates over Jay's Treaty to the XYZ Affair to the Alien and Sedition Acts, America appeared enfeebled by European power politics and by the pressures on America to support either France or Britain in the conflicts each waged with the other. As Adams's star dipped in the confusion of foreign affairs and domestic rancor, the Democratic Republican star rose under the leadership of Jefferson. The election of 1800 is a major event in American history, not the least because it demonstrated a political stability that seemed absent at times in the 1790s. Hamilton and Jefferson made a significant mark on the nation's future in that election, and, while Jefferson's later claim that it represented "a revolution" is an exaggeration, it did confirm the strength of the Constitution and allowed Americans to celebrate their republican innovations.

Suggested Reading

The most comprehensive history of the explosive 1790s is Stanley Elkins and Eric McKitrick, *The Age of Federalism* (New York: Oxford University Press, 1993). This large, detailed, and impeccably researched study can serve as an introduction to the era and an interpretative guide, and as a reference point for further study. A shorter, older overview of the decade is John C. Miller, *The Federalist Era, 1789-1801* (New York: Harper and Row, 1960). The literature on the personalized, partisan, and often angry politics of the age is huge, but start with Joseph Ellis, *Founding Brothers: The Revolutionary Generation* (New York: Vintage, 2000); Noble E. Cunningham Jr., *Jefferson vs. Hamilton: Confrontations that Shaped a Nation* (Boston: Bedford/St. Martin's, 2000); and Richard Hofstadter, *The Idea of a Party System: The Rise of Legitimate Opposition in the United States, 1780-1840* (Berkeley, CA: University of California Press, 1969). The biographical literature on the founders indicates a continued scholarly engagement with the personal and ideological rivalries during the first decade of the nation's existence. The crucial role of the press is studied in Carol Sue Humphrey, *The Press of the Young Republic, 1783-1833* (Westport, CT: Greenwood Press, 1996) and Jeffrey L. Pasley, *"The Tyranny of Printers": Newspaper Politics in the Early American Republic* (Charlottesville: University Press of Virginia, 2001). On American economic problems, see John E. Crowley, *The Privileges of Independence: Neomercantilism and the American Revolution* (Baltimore: Johns Hopkins Press, 1993). R.R. Palmer, *The World of the French Revolution* (New York: Harper and Row, 1971) is a clear-headed introduction of the way the French Revolution shook up world affairs.

CHAPTER EIGHT

JEFFERSON, MADISON, AND THE EXPANDING REPUBLIC

Once they were a happy race. Now they are made miserable by the white people, who are never contented but are always encroaching.

> — Tecumseh (1768-1813) Shawnee chief and diplomat, at Vincennes, Indiana Territory, August 1810

Time Line

1801	Jefferson's Inauguration.
1803	*Marbury versus Madison.*
	The Louisiana Purchase.
1804	The 12th Amendment (the method of choosing a vice president).
	Jefferson's re-election.
1807-08	The Embargo Acts.
1808	Madison elected as president.
1811	Battle of Tippecanoe.

The Judiciary Act of 1801 and the "Midnight Appointments"

John Adams lost the November 1800 election but remained president until March 4, 1801. The transition period allows for interesting behavior. Adams used the interlude and his impending departure to make some personal appointments to government, one of which was especially important. Adams had to replace John Jay who declined to serve again as chief justice of the United States Supreme Court. In January 1801, Adams nominated John Marshall of Virginia. Marshall, a war veteran and Federalist, had served for the final few months of Adams's term as his attorney general. It turned out to be a very auspicious choice. Marshall was appointed and served for thirty-four years as chief justice. He established the Court's pedigree and its role in the management of the Constitution. But another of Adams's decisions created problems. In February of 1801, Congress passed the Judiciary Act, a reasonable and not unpopular law that reduced the Supreme Court to five sitting justices. It created 16 circuit court judges and added numerous marshals, clerks, and lawyers to the system. The expanded circuit court and the plethora of officials to go with it allowed Adams to make some ill-considered last-minute appointments of Federalist friends and associates. This was tantamount to interference with the preferences of Jefferson's new administration, which immediately attacked the Judiciary Act and stalled some of the appointments.

Early in 1802, Jefferson managed to get the Senate to repeal the Act of 1801. A new act was in place by April 1802 that restored the Supreme Court's membership to six, limited the number of circuit courts to six and, most important, established a fixed annual term for meetings of the Supreme Court.

Marbury versus Madison

Jefferson's reaction to the 1801 Judiciary Act signaled his concern over the Court's partisan makeup. The entire system was dominated by Federalist appointees, and Adams's so-called "midnight appointments" were intended to entrench even more Federalist influence in the federal judiciary. Among those who had not been formally commissioned when Jefferson took office was William Marbury, the new justice of the peace for the District of Columbia. Marbury applied for his commission and, at Jefferson's urging, was turned down by the new secretary of state, James Madison. Marbury turned to the courts for redress, arguing that his appointment was legal and should be confirmed. He was joined in his appeal by three other Federalists in the same predicament. Marbury seemed to have an ironclad case. Section 13 of the 1789 Judiciary Act said that the Court could issue writs to confirm appointments such as the one Marbury had received. In other words, Marbury seemed to have the law on his side. But the Court turned down Marbury's request for a writ of *mandamus* ("order"), stating that the law requiring the Court to issue administrative appointments was unconstitutional. John Marshall, who wrote the majority decision, was in no mood to create a problem between the Court and Jefferson's government. While Adams had acted according to the law, and Marbury was right to appeal to the terms of the 1789 Judiciary Act, Marshall knew that, if he upheld Marbury's claim, Jefferson would ignore the Court, persist with a denial of Marbury's appointment, and thereby undermine the Court's status and usefulness. So, while Marshall allowed that Marbury had a case under the law, and by doing so took a dig at Jefferson, he also noted that the 1789 Act violated the Constitution. It was a subtle and intelligent decision that enhanced the Court's role in American political life but in a curiously contradictory way. While the Constitution forbids the Court to take part in either the making or execution of law, it now had assumed the job of testing whether an act of Congress or a presidential action was allowed under the Constitution. In other words, the Court did have a role in determining law. As Marshall wrote at the end of the decision to reject Marbury, "Thus, the particular phraseology of the constitution of the United States confirms and strengthens the principle, supposed to be essential to all written constitutions, that a law repugnant to the constitution is void; and that courts, as well as other departments [of government] are bound by that instrument." The Court would guard against "repugnant" laws by what came to be known as "judicial review." The next time the Court voided a law was in 1857 when, in the Dred Scott decision, it stated that the Missouri Act of 1821(banning slavery north of latitude 36°30' north) was unconstitutional. The precedent was *Marbury versus Madison*. Marshall's first major contribution to American legal standards was in determining how the Constitution set the parameters of legislative authority.

The Louisiana Purchase

By 1803, the leading edge of white settlement had moved considerably west of the Appalachians. To the south, Kentucky and Tennessee had earlier been admitted as states while Ohio to the north became the seventeenth state in 1803. The territory west of the Mississippi was nominally Spanish, but it had been formally but quietly ceded to France in early 1801 at Napoleon's urging. Jefferson knew of it and became alarmed because, while Spain presented no threat to the United States, Napoleonic France did. American shippers paid a so-called "right of deposit" fee for use of the port of New Orleans, and Jefferson declared that, if the French did occupy the city, the United States might have to "marry" itself to Britain for political and naval assistance. This illogical idea was relayed to Robert Livingston, the United States representative in Paris, and matched by an instruction to Livingston to negotiate a guarantee of the use of the port of New Orleans or to purchase or lease land at the mouth of the Mississippi. In the spring of 1803, Jefferson sent James Monroe to Paris as senior minister with instructions to offer $2 million or, if necessary, up to $10 million for the purchase of New Orleans and West Florida. The Americans' trepidations vanished when it was learned that, even before serious negotiations began, Napoleon decided to sell all of Louisiana, a vast tract that ran from the Gulf of Mexico and the Mississippi River to the Rocky Mountains. France's decision was not so perverse. The wars had eaten away at France's manpower, financial, and material resources. In addition, in a stunning end to a long, costly insurrection, the great Caribbean colony of Saint-Domingue (Haiti) was lost to France. It became a republic of former slaves in 1804, the only jurisdiction in the Americas where slavery was ended by the slaves themselves.

So, Louisiana was for sale. France's Foreign Minister Talleyrand asked Robert Livingston for a price, and the French Finance Minister Barbé-Marbois closed the deal with Monroe and Livingston on May 2, 1803. The cession was officially dated April 30, when 828,000 square miles of territory was turned over to American control. The price was stated in French francs and amounted to roughly $15 million, of which $11,250,000 was for the territory and the remainder for outstanding American debts now assumed by the United States government. There were some indeterminate boundary matters where the Louisiana territory's limits met remaining Spanish territory in West Florida and Texas in the south and British claims in the north. The bizarre process had resulted in a doubling of the territory of the United States. It also created doubts about the constitutionality of the purchase because Monroe and Livingston had not been authorized by Congress to buy all of Louisiana. Jefferson accepted the deal, although he had previously viewed the Constitution in strict or narrow "constructionist" terms, that is, "literally," and worried that the purchase was not allowed by the Constitution. Federalists reversed their earlier flexible interpretation of the Constitution's language and questioned the administration's authority to simply acquire territory without reference to Congress or the Constitution. Jefferson acted quickly to impress American claims on the territory. With the approval of Congress, he authorized an expedition to the west, across the Louisiana Purchase, to be led by Meriwether Lewis and William

Clark. The exploration was designed to establish good relations with natives and examine the feasibility of settlement and transportation and the prospects for trade in the far west. It was well timed, as agents of the British fur trading companies had already traveled overland to the Pacific. Alexander Mackenzie had reached the Pacific in 1793. Simon Fraser and David Thompson reached the Pacific in 1808 and 1811 respectively, via the eponymous Fraser and Thompson Rivers of today's British Columbia. Ironically, Mackenzie and Fraser were the sons of American loyalists and had ended up in Canada as children because of the war. Lewis and Clark spent two years getting to the Pacific. They wintered with the Mandan people in the far north of the Purchase and crossed the Rockies near the headwaters of the Missouri River. They reached the mouth of the Columbia River in late 1805. In what is now Idaho, they benefited from the services of a young Shoshone woman, Sacagawea. As their translator and liaison with the local natives, Sacagawea proved crucial in getting the expedition through the mountains to the Pacific. In late 1806, after a three-year absence, they returned to St. Louis and the Mississippi River, having opened the way to a future American empire. They charted a passage to the far west and figuratively planted the American flag en route. They made a record of the climate, topography, and peoples along the way, and noted the prospects for trade and settlement. The journal kept by Clark is a rich account of the odyssey. Among its many revelations are Clark's comments on depopulation in native communities devastated by smallpox in advance of the expedition. The microbial assault on native populations that had been going on for three centuries was running ahead of the American empire, which was now headed beyond the northwestern limits of the Louisiana territory to establish an American presence on the Pacific from the landward side. The British had already done so through Mackenzie. British naval explorers such as James Cook and George Vancouver and Spanish sailors such as Alejandro Malaspina had already charted the waters off the northwest coast. While Lewis and Clark were busy on the Pacific coast, Zebulon Pike was charting passes through the Rockies in the south, in present-day Colorado. The first conspicuous steps towards a continental empire had been made by the United States. Within thirty years, a call for colonial independence from Great Britain had been translated into a thinly populated republic of immense geographical scope.

Jefferson the Realist

Thomas Jefferson had demonstrated willingness to compromise on some Federalist policies, mostly by retaining the Hamiltonian economic framework. But, in other matters, he exhibited a sharp partisan approach to politics that belied the "we are all republicans — we are all federalists" platitude. The attack on the Federalist 1801 Judiciary Act and on William Marbury's appointment had shown Jefferson's potential for hard-nosed party politics. With a majority in Congress, he chipped away at some of the Federalist program. His secretary of the treasury, Albert Gallatin, introduced a tighter budgetary approach to government, reducing the national debt and eliminating most internal taxes, which in turn reduced the budgets for the military. Over Jefferson's two terms as president, the national debt was cut by over a third, only to rise again because of embargoes and the War of 1812. In 1802, Jefferson also oversaw the creation of the national military academy at the scene of Benedict Arnold's treason, West Point. He confronted the so-called Barbary States along the North African coast. The British had paid "tributes" or bribes to the pirates who preyed on shipping in the Mediterranean, and the United States had continued to do the same under Washington and Adams. When Tripoli raised the costs of the tributes in 1801 and declared war against the United States, Jefferson responded by sending warships to the Barbary Coast. The action created another American hero in the person of Lieutenant Stephen Decatur who destroyed a former American frigate that had been taken by the Tripolitans. The treaty of 1805 that ended the war met United States demands and was a symbolic as well as practical triumph. The other Barbary States, Morocco, Algiers, and Tunis, continued to collect tributes for another decade. At home, Jefferson's party hounded the Federalists with vigor. Under the Constitution, any officer, elected or appointed, who is shown to be in breach of the oath of office can be removed by process of impeachment and trial. In 1804, John Pickering, a Federalist federal district judge in New Hampshire was impeached (that is, charged) by the House of Representatives. He was tried and found guilty by the Senate and discharged from the bench, for patently partisan reasons. The Democratic Republican Congress showed no compassion for Pickering who was clearly mentally unbalanced and hardly responsible for the crimes with which he was charged. However, when Samuel Chase of Maryland, an associate judge on the Supreme Court, was charged with "bias," he was acquitted in a Senate trial presided over with fairness by Vice President Burr. That decision curbed what appeared to be a campaign against judges not in government favor.

Still, Federalist support continued to be regionalized. The Louisiana Purchase intensified Federalist fears of a permanent Jeffersonian policy against northeastern commercial interests, and New Englanders were increasingly alienated by emerging western and agrarian power in national affairs. There was even talk of secession in New England during 1803-04. Timothy Pickering, an old revolutionary and cabinet member under Adams, was interested in a "Northern Confederacy" as a way out of what he and many in New England and New York considered a growing Democratic Republican Party bias. The term "Essex Junto" was applied to this group, an imitation of the term applied in 1778 to opponents of the proposed Massachusetts Constitution. Pickering was a strident Francophobe and a devout Hamiltonian. His abrasive behavior had led Adams to dismiss him in 1800, and his continued extremism led ultimately to his isolation. As the Pickering movement lost its way, other dynamic figures appeared in the heady political atmosphere.

The mercurial Aaron Burr was one of the most colorful characters to emerge from the revolutionary era and a dynamic force in the early republic's political life. Long before the 1800 election, he had demonstrated a flair for excess, including a history of disruptive behavior in New York politics. His military service, financial speculations, political service, political scheming, social life, and generally flamboyant nature have

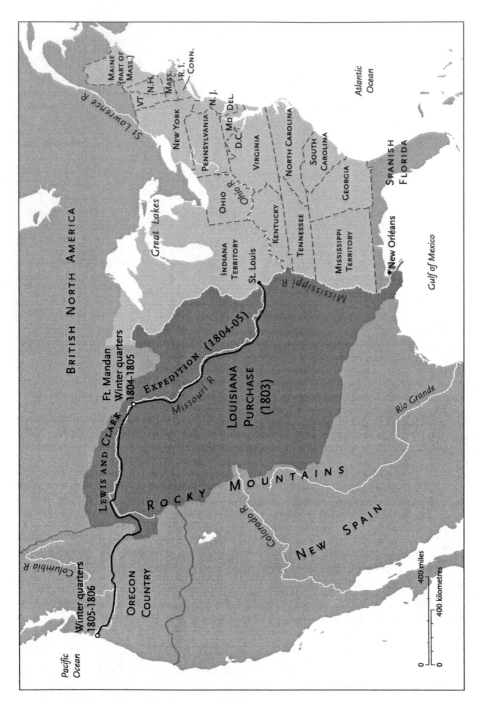

Map 8.1 The Louisiana Purchase, 1803

left him in the American imagination as a fascinating, if unsteady and even flawed, personality. Burr went on after 1804 to become embroiled in questionable political activities involving western schemers and a plan to provoke a border incident with Spain. He was tried for treason in 1807 but acquitted on a technicality. In 1808, he fled the United States, accused of conspiracy, treason, and homicide. He was never convicted of any serious offence. He seems to have been obsessed with Spanish territory, although it is not clear that he actually wanted to set up an independent state in Mexico, as was suggested, or even entice some of the western states to secede. He spent four years in Europe making brazen overtures to the British and French about prying Spain away from its North American holdings. He returned to New York in 1812 to practice law completing a series of dramas and misadventures all cloaked in his imperishable ego. Burr's permanent place in the popular imagination, however, derives from a single event, his duel with Alexander Hamilton in July 1804.

The death of Hamilton at the hands of Aaron Burr highlights the personalized politics of the period. Burr and Hamilton had been at each other's throats for years, and one is reminded of the way in which Hamilton created enemies as well as friends in the most intense way. Burr was clearly provoked beyond mere hostility when, in the run up to the New York gubernatorial race of 1804, Hamilton allegedly referred to him as "dangerous" and "not to be trusted with the reins of government." That slander probably led to the challenge to Hamilton to settle the matter of "honor." The duel, which took place on the New Jersey side of the Hudson River, is wrapped in legend and speculation. Did Hamilton fire first and deliberately miss, as was often the way to satisfy the aggrieved party, and did Burr then ignore the protocol and shoot to kill? Hamilton was gone and with him went the anchor of the Federalist Party. If the Party had been in decline before 1804, it was spent as a national force after that. Hamilton's role in pushing for the Constitution and getting it ratified and in designing Washington's first term policies helped shape the new republic. He was the architect of the first official national economic policy, and he controlled the Federalist caucus for much of the 1790s. He curbed his own party members' threat to the union by plumping for Jefferson in 1800 and then thwarted a Federalist secessionist impulse in the north in 1804. Alexander Hamilton remains one of the most important political figures in American history, yet he left behind no body of memorable patriotic *bon mots* and no striking visual images, as did other leading founders. He was blunt and prejudiced, and, if he were not truly anti-agrarian and anti-democratic, he appeared often to be both. He made enemies, but was above all a nationalist and an optimistic one. He was perhaps the most powerful man in America in the first generation of its political life.

Jefferson's Second Term

The American electoral process was opening itself to broader participation. In 1792, 9 of the 15 states chose their electors in their respective legislatures. By 1804, only 6 of the 17 did so, while the others opened the system to the entire voting population. Of the 176 electors nation wide, only 53 were chosen by legislatures and the rest by popular vote. The trend to more openness in the choosing of electors was well underway. It would continue into the 1820s as new states adopted the popular vote to determine electors and older states converted to that method.

Table 8.1: Methods of Choosing Electors, 1804*

State (17 in 1804)	Number of Electors	How Chosen
Connecticut	9	Legislature chose electors
Delaware	3	Legislature chose electors
Georgia	6	Legislature chose electors
Kentucky	8	Popular vote by district
Maryland	11	Popular vote by district
Massachusetts	19	Popular vote (statewide)
New Hampshire	7	Popular vote (statewide)
New Jersey	8	Popular vote (statewide)
New York	19	Legislature chose electors
North Carolina	14	Popular vote by district
Ohio	4	Popular vote, state at large
Pennsylvania	20	Popular vote (statewide)
Rhode Island	4	Popular vote (statewide)
South Carolina	10	Legislature chose electors
Tennessee	5	Popular vote, by district
Vermont	6	Legislature chose electors
Virginia	24	Popular vote (statewide)
Total (in 1804)	176 (derived from the total number of Congressmen and Senators)	

*Methods of selection changed over time in each jurisdiction.

Sources: Arthur Schlesinger, Jr., ed., *History of American Presidential Elections, 1789-1968* (New York: McGraw-Hill, 1971), 1: 164; Michael Dubin, *United States Presidential Elections, 1788-1860: The Official Results by County and State* (Jefferson, NC: McFarland and Company, 2002), xii, 12-14.

The Federalists chose Charles Cotesworth Pinckney of South Carolina in 1804. Jefferson was re-elected easily, and, even in the New England Federalist hotbed, he won four of the five states. George Clinton of New York became vice president under the terms of the Twelfth Amendment, and, while the Federalists had not gone away, there were signs that the Democratic Republican Party was becoming the nation's political broker. The United States was a farmer's republic, but the economy was increasingly diverse in the way Hamilton had intended. Industry and commerce were firmly in place, while the expanding agricultural frontier developed as a rough and tumble zone of raw rural and riverside settlements. Western growth was accompanied by transportation innovation as trails became roads and waterways became highways. Robert Fulton, who had spent much of his productive life in Europe, returned to the United States in 1805 with practical demonstrations of steamboat technology. Steam engines had been around for a generation but came into their own in transportation and manufacturing in the first part of the nineteenth century.

Medical schools and science programs appeared in American universities, as engaged citizens pushed for improvements in public welfare. The great Philadelphia yellow fever epidemic of 1793, the worst infectious disease epidemic in American urban history, was blamed by Dr. Benjamin Rush (1745-1813) and others on a lack of public hygiene even though mosquitoes caused it. While Rush and his fellow administrators erred in their initial judgment of the sources of yellow fever, their initiatives advanced public awareness of the need for better sewer systems and monitored water supplies. It is as well, too, that a start was made on understanding hygiene, diet, and epidemiology. As the northeastern United States grew, population densities increased. Mobility, periodic economic recession, poorer nutrition, and the infectious diseases circulated by demobilized troops during the War of 1812 all contributed to an overall decline in health standards. At the same time, universities began to refine a home-grown scientific, medical, and technological infrastructure. The tireless Rush must be considered a pioneer of medical science in America. He contributed to the growing interest in the causes and treatment of mental illnesses. On another level, he was an active politician who signed the Declaration and served in the military, going so far as to criticize Washington's abilities. Rush was active in Pennsylvania's ratification of the Constitution. He is an example of the public spirit, energy, and individual versatility that marked the mood of the early national period. Several public state universities were established in the early nineteenth century, including Jefferson's cherished University of Virginia. Still, most higher education continued to be offered in private colleges. There were some early attempts at free elementary education in some of the older cities, but no comprehensive program of public education was developed even though the benefits of literacy were being extolled. At the same time, a wave of what historians have called "republican virtue" swept through towns and cities. The mostly middle-class activists sought to demonstrate their civic responsibilities in volunteer associations. They aimed to improve literacy and manners among the poor and to form groups to combat illegitimacy, homelessness, poverty, and orphan care, all in league with formal institutional control. In New England, for example, before the Revolution, only about 42 "charitable societies" had been organized. Another 36 were created during the War for Independence, but, by 1817, nearly 1,500 had emerged. In concert with the rise in charitable voluntarism, there was a trend in some urban communities to deal more scientifically with the poor, the handicapped, and the socially and criminally deviant by establishing more efficient workhouses, prisons, and asylums.

· The American economy was also influenced by more theoretical and technocratic approaches and began to diversify in a manner that pleased Hamiltonians, even as Jefferson's agrarian vision was unfolding in the west. For example, as the cotton economy grew, it adapted to the industrial, technological, and managerial innovations of the age. The politically mobile Trench Coxe (1755-1824), a "neutral" during the war and a Federalist who defected to the Jeffersonians, was one of the early republic's keenest political economists. While he is remembered chiefly for his interpretation of the Second Amendment's "right to bear arms" clause (he argued that it supported the individual's right to be armed), he was in his time a great booster of economic innovation. Although he operated in the shadow of Hamilton's broader theories and is less well known than Eli Whitney regarding cotton production, his theories of textile technology, tied to his advocacy of slave labor, earned him a great reputation in his time. He represented a growing respect for scientific authority in economics, industrial organization, trade, and work. Slave labor was central to Coxe's model for cotton production. While the average American plantation was small by Caribbean or Brazilian standards, American plantations in the lower south adopted the "task system," where slaves were assigned specific jobs (tasks) that, when completed, allowed the slave to take time off from the normal daily schedule. Trusted slaves were given minor supervisory roles and a pecking order was created ranging from field work ("gang labor") to positions as house slaves and craftsmen. The cotton revolution, and that is what it became, is demonstrated in a simple statistic: in 1790, the United States produced 1,000 bales of cotton; in 1820, it produced 335,000 bales. Whitney's innovation and Coxe's programs would have been for naught without the abundance of rich soils in humid environments and the availability of a huge labor force. The cotton boom meant that the major beneficiaries of the first wave of American market capitalism were not northern or western merchants, investors, or manufacturers but the planters at the top of the southern wealth pyramid. The bulk of the cotton was for export and, before the Embargo Act of 1807, constituted 22 per cent of the value of American exports and, after the War of 1812, almost 40 per cent. The major effect on the slave population was that the plantation setting became more closed and disciplined even as health and material conditions improved. The segregation of free African Americans continued. Stricter controls (white overseers and runaway slave patrols) reflected planter paranoia following the Haiti uprising. The major effect on the south's overall economy and social structure was to lock it into a static rural and conservative ethos.

In foreign affairs, the United States continued to be drawn into the wars that plagued Europe. In the year of the Louisiana Purchase, Napoleon resumed his European ambitions and applied strict interdictions against American trade with Britain, ignoring American claims of neutrality. In 1804 and 1805, the British applied a systematic reform of their trade practices for the West Indies to prevent neutrals, mainly Americans, from trading with the Spanish and French islands. The staples coming from the French Caribbean were important to Napoleon's armies. American ships had overcome British prohibitions against neutral trading with the principle of the "broken voyage."

This practice had ships picking up a cargo in Martinique, for example, unloading it at an American port and then loading it again for shipment to Europe. The British Admiralty had condoned the practice in test cases in 1799 and 1800, and American shipping had benefited. But in 1805, a British judge ruled that those American ships had to show that the shipper's intention was in fact to terminate the voyage in America. The judge declared that American ships were now subject to search and confiscation if they could not prove the validity of their final cargo destination as an American port. The so-called "*Essex* decision," taking its name from the seizure of the American ship, the *Essex*, effectively ended the "broken voyage" practice. The Royal Navy began a vigorous program of impounding American cargoes and impressing American seaman while insulting American esteem by ignoring Secretary of State Madison's complaints. An angry Congress passed a non-importation act against a series of goods that could be produced in the United States or imported from countries other than Britain. Jefferson was cautious and suggested that Congress delay the act's implementation. In 1805, Britain won a great naval victory over the French at Trafalgar, and its subsequent blockade of the French coastline provoked the French into declaring illegal any American trade with Britain. The United States was once again being bullied by both great powers.

In 1807, the British further embarrassed the Jefferson administration by rejecting a treaty proposal that would have ended impressments and reopened the West Indies trade. The American treaty delegation, led by James Monroe and William Pinkney (not to be confused with the South Carolina Pinckneys), was obliged to sign a watered down version of the American position. Jefferson did not bother to offer the treaty to the Senate for approval but pressed his European envoys to negotiate further. Throughout 1807, the British and the French each sought to control trade to the disadvantage of the other, and American ships were essentially barred from the European market. The British insisted on foreign, that is, American ships clearing British ports and paying duties before they could clear the British blockade to land in Europe. Napoleon declared in the so-called "Milan Decree" that any ship that had been cleared by the British would be seized; American ships would then become British ships as far as the French were concerned. British aggression, more than French retaliation, provoked the Jefferson government to action. In June 1807, the British frigate *Leopard* stopped the American frigate *Chesapeake* off the Virginia coast to look for British deserters. The Americans refused the British boarding request, and the *Leopard* opened fire, killing three Americans and wounding many others. The declaration by Jefferson ordering British warships out of American territorial waters has a rather plaintive quality; what were British warships doing there in the first place, violating the territorial integrity of the United States? The British responded to Jefferson's order by mocking it. They took an even harder line on the impressment of British subjects who might be on American vessels so that it took until 1811 to get compensation from the British for the *Chesapeake* incident.

The Embargo Acts

Meanwhile, the 1806 Non-Importation Act failed to convince the British to take seriously the United States' complaints and protests. So, over the winter of 1807-08, Jefferson pressed ahead with even more ambitious economic sanctions, and Congress passed a series of Embargo Acts in December 1807 and January 1808. His assumption was that the world, and in particular France and Britain, needed to trade with the United States. The acts were designed to create material shortages in Europe. American shipping was stalled, and, while the acts allowed "foreign" ships to land goods in America, they were prohibited from taking cargoes away from American ports. Jefferson hoped in vain that the interdiction of trade would force Britain and France to respect American rights. Although the Democratic Republican Congress passed the acts with substantial majorities, they aroused public opposition at home and were met with indifference in Europe. Some American traders defied Jefferson and resorted to the kind of smuggling that had snubbed British authority in the 1760s and 1770s. The irony should not have been lost on Jefferson, especially as the British encouraged and helped effect the smuggling of trade goods between Canada and the United States. The British economy suffered little or not at all. It shifted to markets in Latin America and defeated Jefferson's purpose. Napoleon added insult to injury with a decree ordering the confiscation of American vessels in French, Italian, and some Baltic ports on the pretence that American registered vessels were really British vessels in disguise with false papers. One estimate suggests that these confiscations cost American shipping some $10 million.

New England merchants smarted from the collapse of some of their overseas business. Even though northeastern industries benefited from the absence of imported shoes, textiles, and other manufactured goods, there was widespread opposition to the embargoes that helped revive Federalist fortunes in the short term. They made gains in state elections in 1808. To effect compliance with the embargoes, Congress passed the Enforcement Act in January 1809, but New Englanders challenged it as unconstitutional. Some states refused to provide enforcement officers, and, in Connecticut, there was talk of nullification that echoed the states' rights tone of the Virginia and Kentucky Resolutions of 1798-99. In a reversal of their previous stance, Federalists protested a federal law on the basis of states' rights theory. It was in a losing cause because the Supreme Court in an unrelated case confirmed the supremacy of national over state law, and, in 1808, the constitutionality of embargoes was upheld by a federal court in Massachusetts. Despite the legality of the acts, both parties in Congress were at best lukewarm to them, and the embargo doctrine was eaten away by widespread dissent. In early 1809, the acts were repealed and replaced by another law that excluded only British and French importations. In the end, the embargo episode, in its failed objectives, was a low point in Jefferson's presidency. Yet, for all its frustrations, the government of the United States had behaved with purpose and had risked much to assert an economic and political defiance of the big powers. But the embargo remained a contentious issue during the 1808 election.

On January 1, 1808, the legal importation of slaves into the United States ceased. Article I, Section 9 of the Constitution had blocked any congressional action on slave imports for twenty years. Before the moratorium was up in 1808, Jefferson suggested that Congress forbid the trade and, in 1807, signed the prohibition into law and added penalties for violation. It had been assumed all along that the twenty-year grace was just that, a period for the south to adjust to the long-term inevitability of the end of slave importation. The demand for slaves had grown as the rich lands of the old south-west were exploited in the first two decades of the new century, but the politics of sectionalism, which were evident in 1787 and which had created the compromise of the three-fifths clause in the Constitution, meant that the northern tier of states would not accept a steady importation of slaves. The cost of field slaves thus rose steadily after the 1790s, from an average of approximately $300 in the 1790s to about $600 in 1820. By 1860, the average price for a healthy young male field hand was between $1,200 and $1,800. Those costs also added to the asset base of the south as the traffic in human commodities flourished with the end of slave importation. Slaves were hired out from one owner to another at a profit as the cotton economy grew. The internal trafficking in slaves boomed, with the older Tidewater areas, especially, supplying slaves to the southwest. Young second or third generation Chesapeake slaves would be found several hundred miles away in Mississippi or Alabama Territory.

The Election of Madison

At the end of his second term the 61-year-old Jefferson, in spite of his clear majority of national popular and congressional support, decided to follow Washington's lead and not seek a third term. Madison appeared to be the logical successor to Jefferson, but there was some congressional and public opposition to his nomination. Jefferson had touted Madison as a successor, but, as early as 1805, Federalist antipathies and Democratic Republican rivals had objected to his apparent coronation. Today, Madison is known as one of the chief architects of the Constitution. In 1808, however, he was better known for his historic break with Hamilton, for helping to shape the first party system, and for being Jefferson's partner. He had supported a states' rights position with the Virginia Resolutions but was otherwise a strong nationalist, even a centralist. His record in Congress as a Virginia representative and in Jefferson's cabinets indicated a continued regional and partisan mentality. In other words, he was in the ebb and flow of political identity and ideas that marked the era. The recharged Federalists mounted a strong campaign to regain the presidency and nominated South Carolinian Charles Cotesworth Pinckney for 1808. Then, when the Democratic Republican nomination process began, two factions contested Madison's candidacy. One was led by another Virginian, John Randolph (1773-1833), who was no relation to Edmund Randolph of the Constitutional Convention. John Randolph was motivated more by an antifederalist philosophy than by any devotion to Jefferson. He had already identified himself as a "Quid," a Latin term meaning "what," which was intended in the political language of the day to mean individualistic, non-conforming, and troubling to the party machinery in and out of Congress. Randolph supported James Monroe for the presidency, but the latter withdrew from the race in deference to his loyalty to the party and to Jefferson and Madison. A second Democratic Republican Party faction emerged in the northeast, largely in reaction to Jefferson's (and therefore Madison's) foreign policy. It nominated George Clinton of New York as a vice presidential candidate. With Monroe's withdrawal, Madison won the election with 122 of the 175 electoral votes. But New Hampshire, Massachusetts, Connecticut, Rhode Island, and Delaware all gave their votes to the southern Federalist Pinckney. New York gave 6 of its 19 votes for president to its own George Clinton, who was easily elected to the vice presidency. As for James Monroe, he later returned to the fray, and, when he was elected in 1816, he completed the "Virginia dynasty" that held the presidency from 1800 to 1824. If one counts Washington's two terms, Virginia slaveholders held the office for 32 of the nation's first 36 years.

The troubled and ultimately marginalized John Randolph was the least of Madison's troubles. The Federalist Party was still alive and restless and had made gains in Congress. Internal debate within the Democratic Republican Party continued, as did the most serious issue of the day, foreign affairs. Madison inherited one of Jefferson's last deeds, the signing of another Non-Importation Act in March 1809. It had repealed the Embargo Acts by opening up trade with the world while continuing to exclude France and Britain. In a gross misunderstanding, the British minister in America, David Erskine, indicated that Britain was ready to drop its own prohibition on "neutral" trade, which would free the United States from interference. In April 1809, Madison went so far as to announce a resumption of trade with Britain, but, a month later, British Foreign Minister George Canning nullified Erskine's deal, and Madison was forced to recant and resume the non-importation of British goods. Confusion, backtracking, and more trade interference hurt Madison's reputation in the first few months of his administration, but even more trouble lay ahead. In the spring of 1810, Congress passed "Macon's Bill" (named for Representative Nathaniel Macon of North Carolina), which empowered the president to reopen trade with the belligerents after the impending expiry of the Non-Importation Act of 1809. The bill was an invitation to France and Britain to resume trade and respect American neutrality. It was simply another tack in what appeared to be an endless charade of negotiations, agreements, posturing, and disappointments. Macon's bill was conciliatory but allowed the president to resume non-importation if the big powers did not ease their interferences with American trading. At that point, Napoleon entered the picture with a deception that caught Madison off guard for the second time in his early tenure. Napoleon suggested that, if the Americans maintained a no-trade policy with Britain, the French would accept a resumption of trade with the United States. Madison jumped at the promise and ordered the conditional prohibition of trade with Britain. Napoleon, meanwhile, had ordered the retroactive sequestering of United States vessels in French ports. He had fooled the Americans again. The British, taking Madison at his word, retained their aggressive policy against United States commerce for another year and went so far as to blockade New York. The British had effective control of the world's major sea routes. Napoleon, having caused some serious mischief in Anglo-American relations, such as they were, turned his attention to his European empire during 1811 and 1812. He eventually headed east to Moscow with dreams of Russian conquest and left Britain alone to intimidate the United States. By the time Napoleon invaded Russia, the United States and Great Britain would be at war.

Western Growth and Regional Politics

At home, expansion continued into the west, and, even if the embargoes, blockades, and failed diplomacies threatened agricultural prosperity, Americans marched optimistically westward in droves. Immigration from Europe during the first 30 years of the republic was steady and added about a quarter of a million people to the 1820 population. Between 1800 and 1819, six new states were added to the union: Ohio (1803), Indiana (1816), and Illinois (1818) were created out of the 1787 Northwest Ordinance. Louisiana (1812) consisted of the extreme southern portion of the Louisiana Purchase and, with Mississippi (1817) and Alabama (1819), constituted three more slave states that had formed in areas with a long experience of slavery. Natives and Africans had been enslaved in the region under Spanish rule since the early eighteenth century. In 1819, the Senate balance of slave and non-slave states settled at 11 each in a way that was increasingly important to southern interests because the white population of the non-slave states had begun to outstrip that of the south. Even the three-fifths count for slave populations could not match the increased northern representation in the House of Representatives, which by 1808 was in the majority. The backdrop to this was the astonishing growth in western population, which by 1810 had reached over one million. In a predictable burst, it passed two million by 1820, accounting for roughly 20 per cent of the nation's population and swamping the native population in the process. In 1810, the United States annexed the region around New Orleans and West Florida, the strip of territory to the immediate east of Orleans Territory. The rest of West Florida that ran east from the 1810 annexation was seized during the War of 1812. The so-called East Florida panhandle and the whole of the Florida territory were ceded by Spain in 1819, and adjustments were made to the boundary between the Louisiana Purchase and Spanish Texas. By the latter date, the demarcation of the southern boundary of the United States from the Atlantic to Texas was in place. Table 8.2 shows each state's growth.

Space was beginning to define national affairs. The economy was still driven in large part by Hamiltonian tax and banking formulas, and, as important as industry and commerce were to economic development, neither defined the nation as a society. America was about land, farms, mobility, and growing assumptions of egalitarianism. Land produced wealth as much as it afforded self-sufficiency, dignity, and political voice to the masses of westbound migrants. But economic classes existed on the frontier as they had always existed in the east. Slavery boomed, and the structure of the institution hardened into a fully developed racial caste system in the south and its western extensions. Also, wealthier planters held sway over the political and economic

Table 8.2: Population Growth by State, 1790-1820 (in 1,000s, rounded to nearest thousand)

Original New England States	1790	1800	1810	1820
New Hampshire	142 (1)	184 (1)	214 (1)	244 (1)
Massachusetts	379 (5)	423 (6)	472 (7)	523 (7)
Connecticut	238 (6)	251 (6)	262 (7)	275 (8)
Rhode Island	69 (4)	69 (4)	77 (4)	83 (4)

Original Mid-Atlantic States	1790	1800	1810	1820
New York	340 (26)	589 (31)	959 (40)	1,373 (39)
Pennsylvania	434 (10)	602 (16)	810 (23)	1,049 (30)
New Jersey	184 (14)	211 (17)	246 (19)	278 (20)

Original Southern States	1790	1800	1810	1820
Delaware	59 (13)	64 (14)	73 (17)	73 (17)
Maryland	320 (111)	342 (125)	381 (145)	407 (147)
Virginia	748 (306)	887 (367)	983 (426)	1,075 (465)
North Carolina	394 (106)	478 (140)	556 (179)	639 (220)
South Carolina	249 (109)	346 (149)	415 (201)	503 (265)
Georgia	83 (30)	163 (60)	252 (107)	341 (151)

New States (dates of admission)	1790	1800	1810	1820
Vermont (1792)	85 (0)	154 (0)	218 (0)	236 (0)
Kentucky (1792)	74 (13)	221 (41)	407 (82)	564 (129)
Tennessee (1796)	36 (4)	106 (14)	262 (46)	423 (83)
Ohio (1803)		45 (0)	231 (2)	581 (5)
Louisiana (1812)			77 (42)	153 (80)
Indiana (1816)		6 (0)	25 (1)	147 (1)
Mississippi (1817)		8 (4)	31 (17)	75 (33)
Illinois (1818)			12 (1)	55 (1)
Alabama (1819)		1 (0)	9 (0)	128 (42)
Maine (1820)	97 (1)	152 (1)	229 (1)	399 (1)
Missouri (1821)			20 (4)	67 (11)

Note: Figures are for the total population, and the figures in brackets are for the African American population, which is included in the whole.

Source: US Bureau of the Census, *Historical Statistics of the United States, Colonial Times to 1970* (Washington: Bureau of the Census, 1975), Part I, Section A, pp. 119ff.

lives of a large small-holding farm population in the south and southwest. In the northwest, merchants, speculators, and bankers rose to social, economic, and political prominence in the sprawling new agricultural communities. It must be remembered that the western boom was a real estate boom, and eastern investors, financiers, surveyors, and lawyers in many cases controlled the open land before the majority of settlers arrived. Yet there were real opportunities for economic security for most westbound Americans. What killed the Federalist Party was not the poverty of its ideas or the weakness of its leadership but the increasing irrelevance of its political economy to a majority of white male Americans. Federalists were being isolated in New England, as Ohio settlers and Alabama slaveholders saw the Democratic Republican Party as America's party, a party that would develop northern and southern wings.

In 1811, the 20-year charter of the Bank of the United States was set to expire. Congress's immersion in foreign affairs had deflected appeals for renewal or extension. The Bank had regulated the flow of capital and the value of American currency. It had attracted domestic and foreign, mostly British, subscriptions and in no small way had served to stabilize the economy. Jefferson's and Madison's treasury secretary, Albert Gallatin, endorsed plans for the charter's renewal. In financial circles, there was general approval, but, to some veteran Democratic Republicans, the Bank was an appalling reminder of Federalist power and an engine of class privilege. For many in Congress and in the population, the mere fact that the British, now a virtual enemy of the United States, held about two-thirds of the Bank's stock was reason enough to deny the Bank's charter renewal. There was also a new class of financial entrepreneurs at the state level. By 1811, the growth and distribution of population had resulted in a plethora of state banks whose assets would be greatly enhanced if they could parcel out the Bank's profits and exploit their own potential for investment. Renewal was denied with little trouble in the House, but the Senate vote was a tie, broken by Vice President Clinton's negative vote. As the Bank's charter lapsed in 1811, the United States and Great Britain were lurching towards a serious showdown.

In May 1811, a British frigate stopped an American frigate off Sandy Hook, New York and seized an American-born sailor. Mistaking a smaller British armed vessel *Little Bell* for the ship that had impressed the seaman, another American frigate disabled the *Little Belt* and killed nine British sailors. The United States government offered to compensate the British if the latter would suspend the practice of cruising off the American coast and seizing American seamen. The event coincided with a rising tide of Anglophobia in Congress. The term "war hawks" was being used to describe a minority group of southern and western Democratic Republicans in Congress that represented a growing voice in national affairs.

Tecumseh and the West

The Federalist rump was now buried in the northeast. Henry Clay (1777-1852), a Virginia-born Kentucky lawyer and a leading war hawk, became Speaker of the House. He was a staunch nationalist but also the first truly western American statesman, championing the west and becoming its principal spokesman for decades. He sought to reconcile the interests of the non-slave northwest with the southwestern slave states to form a distinct western bloc. What Clay and others saw as a new region with new ideas and distinctly western conditions was only partly accurate; the southern and northern tiers of the west would eventually declare their politics for south and north and not for the less than cohesive idea of the "west." In 1811, the main problem in the west was the ongoing pressure of white settlement on native territory.

By the summer of 1811, large numbers of settlers had moved as far west as Indiana Territory. More than 20 years earlier, in 1790, native attacks on settlements in eastern Ohio had led to revolutionary war veteran General "Mad Anthony" Wayne's victory over a native coalition at the Battle of Fallen Timbers. The Treaty of Greenville of 1795 resulted in the native concession of millions of acres in Ohio, which, in turn, encouraged rapid and large-scale white settlement. After statehood in 1803, Ohio's population soared and reached a quarter of a million by 1811 and nearly 600,000 by 1820. As Ohio boomed, it also became a throughway to the farther northwest, to Indiana and Illinois country. The trekking settlers were displacing the native populations along the way. The Shawnee chief Tecumseh (c1758-1813) was himself driven west from Ohio, as were thousands of others from the states of Kentucky and Tennessee and throughout the frontier zone.

At the junction of the Wabash and Tippecanoe Rivers sometime after 1808, Tecumseh established a native community and began to resist white encroachment by a strategy of intertribal cooperation. Tecumseh's logic was simple: all or any land ceded to white Americans by natives had to receive general native approval. According to Tecumseh's thesis, the principle of collective or communal native ownership of the land had been established at Greenville. More and more of the tribes in the northwest and even farther south were courted by the impressive Shawnee diplomat and leader. Alas, there was popular and political white resistance to any formal native federation. Tecumseh was well-known because of his military success in routing an American force in Ohio in 1791 and had joined his Shawnees with Cherokees, Creeks, and Chickasaws in the Tennessee area in raids on white settlers during the early 1790s. By 1810, Tecumseh was hoping, with the help of the British, to establish a buffer between the United States and British territory to the northwest. His vision of a vast native confederation was sustained by British aid and by his own energies. While he certainly entertained the possibility of full-scale war with the Americans, and although his model confederacy was not yet realized, Tecumseh was emboldened enough by the assumption of British support that he openly scorned the authority of Indiana Governor William Henry Harrison (1773-1841) at Vincennes. A year later, while Tecumseh was traveling in the southwest spreading his political message, his brother Tenskwatawa, the so-called "Prophet," was tricked into committing his warriors to a bloody battle with Harrison's militia. Tecumseh's dreams were shattered at the resulting Battle of Tippecanoe. While the battle was indecisive, the remnants of the

Prophet's army broke up and scattered. A period of dislocation, hunger, and deprivation followed for the natives of the region. Tecumseh, like another pro-British native leader before him, Joseph Brant, ended up in Upper Canada (Ontario) where he led a native contingent against the Americans in the War of 1812. He acquitted himself well before being killed at the Battle of the Thames in 1813. His dream of a huge native confederacy stretching from the Great Lakes to the southwest died with him. He was an imposing character, persuasive, brave, and visionary, but his failed scheme adds to the history of failure to resist the flood of whites to the old northwest. Sadly, the importance of Tecumseh's vision, albeit a desperate one, was largely ignored or at best slighted in the nineteenth century. Tecumseh's Tippecanoe was exploited by William Harrison when he ran for the presidency as a western Whig in 1840. He not only campaigned as a hero of the 1812 War but endorsed the slogan "Tippecanoe and Tyler too" (Tyler was the vice presidential candidate). A few weeks after his inauguration, Harrison died of pneumonia, but the slogan stuck, and "Tippecanoe" remained a quick reference to the memory of the "empire of freedom."

Conclusion

Between Jefferson's election in 1800 and Madison's re-election in 1812, the United States struggled to find a respectable place in the international community. It was buffeted by the great wars of Europe, and the abuses of American trading rights by Britain and France that had marked the 1790s continued into the new century. The problems with Britain increased in intensity until the tensions were released in the War of 1812. Domestically, the election of Jefferson in 1800 moderated the political turbulence of the 1790s and ushered in an era of national consolidation and growth. Under the leadership of John Marshall, the Supreme Court began to serve as a brake on arbitrary government and also emphasized national over state interests in disputes over legislative authority. But perhaps the most striking development of this period was the gradual filling in of the trans-Appalachian west and the spilling of American society over the Mississippi into the new American west, the trans-Mississippi west. Lewis and Clark, as emissaries of the republic, anticipated a continental United States with their great exploratory trek. While the agrarian tradition was being sustained, capitalism became a fixture in the national economy. The cotton economy was now tied to a textile industry and to the growth of the real estate, banking, and transportation sectors, and the trends that had been evident in the 1790s continued apace. As farms and plantations replaced native communities in the west, native populations declined. Native cultures were under constant stress. The end of the African slave trade had been anticipated, but the growth and refinement of the institution was guaranteed by cotton demand and the space for its expansion. Slavery became as fundamental to the American economy as any other economic and social characteristic. By the end of the first decade of the nineteenth century, problems in international relations continued to be the most compelling political issue.

Suggested Reading

For a picturesque overview of the early days of the nineteenth century, see Henry Adams, *America in 1800* (Ithaca, NY: Cornell University Press, 1955). (This short book is an extract from Adams's celebrated multi-volume *History of the United States of America during the Administrations of Jefferson and Madison,* first published in 1889.) While the Europhilic Henry Adams was at times appalled with what he saw as the crudity of American politics and society, he saw its color, freshness, and dynamism too. He was the great grandson of John Adams. While it is nearly sixty years old, Richard Hofstadter, "Thomas Jefferson: The Aristocrat as Democrat," in *The American Political Tradition and the Men Who Made It* (1948; New York: Vintage, 1973) is a brief, useful introduction to the complexities of Jefferson. See also Joseph Ellis, *American Sphinx: The Character of Thomas Jefferson* (New York: Knopf, 1997). On the relationship between Madison and Jefferson, see Lance Banning, *Jefferson and Madison* (Madison, WI: Madison House, 1995) and James Morton Smith, ed., *The Republic of Letters: The Correspondence between Thomas Jefferson and James Madison, 1776-1826,* vol. 3 (New York: W.W. Norton, 1995). On Madison, see Lance Banning, *The Sacred Fire of Liberty: James Madison and the Founding of the American Republic* (Ithaca, NY: Cornell University Press, 1995).

For the impact of growth on native peoples, see Frederick E. Hoxie, Ronald Hoffman, and Peter J. Albert, eds., *Native Americans in the Early Republic* (Charlottesville: University Press of Virginia, 1999); Douglas R. Hurt, *The Indian Frontier, 1763-1846* (Albuquerque: University of New Mexico Press, 2002); Colin G. Calloway, *Native Americans and the Early Republic* (Charlottesville: University Press of Virginia, 1999). On slavery, slaves, and racism, see Winthrop D. Jordan, *White Over Black: American Attitudes Towards the Negro, 1550-1812* (Chapel Hill: The University of North Carolina Press, 1968) and Berlin, *Many Thousands Gone,* cited previously. On the politics of the "three-fifths clause," see Garry Wills, *"Negro President": Jefferson and the Slave Power* (Boston: Houghton Mifflin Company, 2003). The most accessible study of America's economic neo-colonialism in this period is Drew McCoy, *The Elusive Republic: Political Economy in Jeffersonian America* (Chapel Hill: The University of North Carolina, 1980). See also John E. Crowley, *The Privileges of Independence: Neomercantilism and the American Revolution* (Baltimore: Johns Hopkins University Press, 1993). On class, see and compare Michael Merrill and Sean Wilentz, eds., *The Key of Liberty: The Life and Democratic Writings of William Manning, "A Laborer," 1747-1814* (Cambridge, MA: Harvard University Press, 1993) and Conrad Edick Wright, *The Transformation of Charity in Postrevolutionary New England* (Boston: Northeastern University Press, 1993).

CHAPTER NINE

THE WAR OF 1812 AND THE SECTIONAL REPUBLIC

The language of the declaration of independence is ... conclusive ... that the enslaved African race were not intended to be included, and formed no part of the people who framed and adopted this declaration.... The state of public opinion had undergone no change when the constitution was adopted.... The only two provisions [in the Constitution] which point to them ... treat them as property, and make it the duty of the government to protect it.

> — Chief Justice Roger Taney, offering his opinion in the Dred Scott case (1857) and renouncing the federal government's presumed authority to ban slavery by legislation in its territories, as in the Missouri Act of 1821

Time Line

1812-15	War of 1812.
1814	Treaty of Ghent.
1814-15	Hartford Convention.
1815	Battle of New Orleans.
1816	Election of James Monroe as president.
1817	Rush-Bagot Agreement.
1820	Election of James Monroe to second term.
1820-21	The Missouri Compromise.

The Origins of the War of 1812

The War of 1812 resulted from two decades of British interference with American trade, a continued British presence on American territory in the far west, and open disregard for American diplomacy. The neo-colonial status suggested by the Anglo-American relationship had long been an embarrassment. For example, during the 1807 *Chesapeake* incident, the citizens of far-off Washington County in the Mobile district of Mississippi Territory had sent a letter to the United States Senate to support both non-importation and war if it came to it. The letter included a very stirring announcement of American national pride.

> Our national ships are our territory in whatever quarter of the world they are found; much more so, then, when within our own ... limits and jurisdiction. We care not who the men were that were demanded from the *Chesapeake* ... no foreign force has a right to invade our

territory; no foreign officer … had a right to exercise his functions within our limits.…
England may count upon our divisions. She is mistaken. The violence of her conduct has
united all of America.… Our planters too, will hereafter find their market at home [and
Britain] will at length find that her tyranny on the ocean has given *commercial independence* to
those confederated States which British tyranny on the land first led to *political independence*.
[Italics in the original.]

Five years after that defiant endorsement, nothing had changed, and, if anything, the
situation had been aggravated by increased British insouciance. Moreover, despite
British assurances that they were not arming the northwest native tribes, clashes
between settlers and natives throughout late 1811 and 1812 indicated otherwise. By
the spring of 1812, the frontier issue was joined to the mounting diplomatic problems
to create grounds for "war hawk" action. In and out of Congress, there were cries to
push the British out of Canada, assert American neutrality, and confirm maritime
rights everywhere. James Madison, who had not seriously considered war, was obliged
to acknowledge the "hostile inflexibility" of the European powers. In November 1811,
in the same week as the Battle of Tippecanoe, he told Congress that the United States
must be prepared to defend its national integrity and territorial security with force if
necessary.

In April 1812, within days of Madison's recommendation, Congress passed an
embargo law. It was to last for 60 days with the prospects of military action if the
British did not rescind their punitive orders in council. In a deft move, moderate
Democratic Republicans managed to extend the embargo to 90 days to allow for further negotiations. Congress went ahead with a call for 100,000 militiamen for six-
month terms. Then, American trade problems resumed. Napoleon's trade decrees
continued to deny American neutrality. The British still refused to remove the orders
in council, but there were signs that they would not retain them indefinitely. War had
depleted British resources, and Napoleon's continued grip on Europe and his control
of the "Continental system" excluded British trade with most of allied or occupied
Europe. Moreover, there were clear signs that the removal of the American markets
from British manufactures and the non-intercourse acts were compounding Britain's
woes. The British cabinet was in a mood to abandon its orders, end naval interdictions,
and respect American neutrality. Ironically, in May 1812, when it appeared that a resolution to the dispute was imminent, British Prime Minister Spencer Perceval was
assassinated by a failed businessman, and, in the confusion, the decision was delayed.
Eventually, between June 16 and 23, the British worked to end the orders in council
formally, but before that news reached Congress, war was declared by clear majorities
in the Senate and House. Madison offered a set of reasons for the necessity of war.
These had to do with violations of American trading rights, citizenship (the impressments issues), British attacks on American maritime property, the blockading of
American ports, and the overall refusal to respect American neutrality. There was no
direct mention of frontier and western territorial tensions, and, while the war was seen

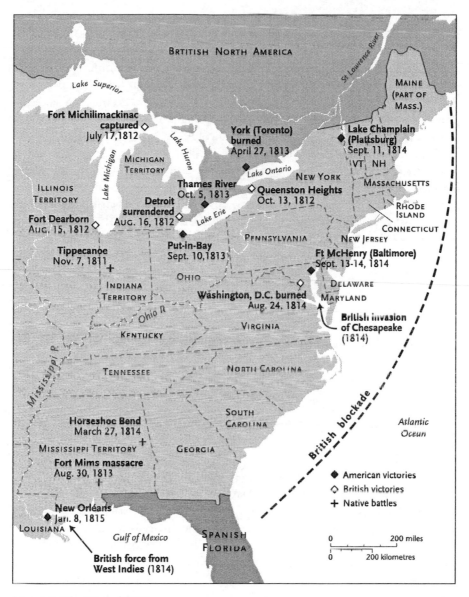

Map 9.1 The War of 1812

by many in the northeast as a Democratic Republican ploy to annex Canada (that is, Upper and Lower Canada, today's southern Ontario and southern Quebec) and expand American territory, the main theme of the war message was the assertion of the nation's international rights. These had been abused, it was felt, from the republic's creation. Madison announced that the United States was at war with Great Britain on June 19, 1812, four days before the British revoked the orders in council. The role of Napoleon and his double-dealing in trade relations with the United States added another level of complexity to the deterioration of Anglo-American relations.

Diplomatic fumbling drove Britain and the United States to war in 1812, and confused strategies and objectives dogged the belligerents thereafter. Had Britain expected a war to result from its trade restrictions, security measures, and diplomatic arrogance? Likely not. While the defense and development of British North America was a serious matter, Britain's major preoccupation between 1789 and 1815 was French revolutionary militarism and Napoleonic imperialism. From the American perspective, Britain had helped bring on the war with its intransigence. Yet Britain had begun to relax its restrictive policies when Madison announced a "state of war." The prosaic simplicity of "the War of 1812" indicates an absence of alternatives. For many, the war was "Mr. Madison's War," which is perhaps an exaggeration considering the president's cautious policies up to the fateful hour. It is more accurately the "Democratic Republican Party's war." Later, the term "Second War of Independence" refers to the postwar settlement with Britain and the generally amicable relations between the two nations thereafter. The mood of the Congress was split along sectional and party lines and, to some extent, by a generation gap; older republican idealists were opposed to the war, as were many Democratic Republicans in New England and New York. The decision for war was in large part encouraged by southerners and westerners. Federalists generally opposed it.

The War of 1812: The First Phase
The war comprised four main theaters: 1) American invasions of Canada from Lake St. Clair (at Detroit) in the west to Montreal in the east; 2) The British invasion of the Chesapeake; 3) Naval warfare on the Great Lakes; and 4) The British blockade of much of the American coastline. There was action in a variety of places from New Orleans in the south to the Strait of Mackinaw in the far northwest. To some extent, the tactical behavior of the belligerents was reminiscent of the Revolutionary War, but, in the end, there was no clear victor. Despite some initial opposition to the war, the American cause was sustained officially by the necessary assertion of its sovereignty. The United States had a territorial and demographic advantage, but its army was small, and most of it was untrained and commanded by inexperienced officers. The major British disadvantage was a logistical one, compounded by the great drain on resources caused by the war with Napoleon. Britain had to maintain an enlarged military establishment and also provide large financial subsidies to its European allies. After declaring war, the American strategy was limited to attacking British interests where possible. That

meant invading Canada, a strategy that obliged the British to defend its colony in the north from its former colonies to the south. Otherwise, the British benefited early from spotty American military participation and performance. The first American attempt to conquer Canada was immediately blunted. The impressive plan of 1812 called for crossings at Detroit, Niagara, and through the Lake Champlain corridor to Montreal. Before the invasion of Canada began, Tecumseh and his native supporters in the northwest went over to the British, and the United States lost the fort at Michilimackinac Island at the junction of Lake Huron and Lake Michigan.

At Detroit, General William Hull and 2,200 men crossed into Canada, hesitated in fear of losing a line of communication, were contained by British General Isaac Brock, and surrendered the fort at Detroit without offering resistance. Meanwhile, much farther west, near the present day site of Chicago, Fort Dearborn was overrun, and its garrison massacred by native allies of the British. The British took control of Lake Erie and the Michigan country to the northwest. A second front at Niagara proved to be just as disastrous for the Americans as Detroit had been. While General Brock was killed defending Queenston Heights on the Niagara Peninsula, his small mixed army of natives, provincial Canadian militia, and British regulars recovered the Heights and defeated American General Van Rensselaer's meager American force. The British were aided by the refusal of New York militia units to leave the state to enter Canada. The third of the Americans' invasion plans, the attack on Montreal, failed to materialize when General Dearborn's militia army refused to enter Lower Canada. As a result of even those limited American incursions, Anglo-Canadian anti-Americanism was reinforced and a greater spirit of imperial patriotism was encouraged in the approximately 75,000 people of Upper Canada. The French-speaking and smaller but substantial Anglophone population of Lower Canada had been indifferent or hostile to the republic since before the 1783 Treaty of Paris. It beggars logic to guess what the United States hoped to achieve with military success in Canada in 1812. There were over 200,000 people in Lower Canada. An American military victory might have brought Britain to the peace table, but more likely would have inspired an even greater commitment of British resources to the St. Lawrence Valley. It was doubtful that the United States could have subdued Canada in the first place, and, in any case, it was surely incapable of occupying any but small portions of it. The disasters revealed deep inefficiencies in the United States military command, operations planning, and combat training. The militia units of 1812 were ill prepared and suffered as a result. After one year of combat, it was clear that the United States lacked a sufficiently professional national military institution. The problem was not helped by the fact that the charter of the Bank of the United States had been annulled in 1811, making funding the war difficult.

In a clear reversal of military expectations, where American arms might have been expected to succeed, on land, they failed, and where the British had an ostensible advantage, at sea, the Americans achieved some success. A series of one-on-one encounters between American and British warships ranging from Nova Scotia waters to the coast of Brazil resulted in victories for American seamanship, courage, and gunnery. In at least five significant encounters, American warships defeated British opposition. The American frigate *Constitution* acquired the nickname "Old Ironsides" by the end of 1812, achieving victories in the north and south Atlantic against a backdrop of peace proposals. American Secretary of State James Monroe repeated American demands for an end to impressments, keeping in mind that the British had ended its orders in council at the start of the war. This was simply a call for a truce in order to negotiate the issues. The British rejected the proposal. In New England, antiwar sentiment was reinforced by the aborted invasions of Canada. In Massachusetts and Connecticut, there were proposals to deny militia support for the war, and New Hampshire's government speculated on the possibility of disunion. The hostility in the region carried over into the national election in the fall of 1812. While Madison's candidacy had been endorsed by the congressional caucus, New Englanders generally opposed him. New York Democratic Republicans nominated De Witt Clinton as presidential candidate, a move that was supported by Federalists. Together, the parties supported the Federalist Charles Jared Ingersoll for the vice presidency. Madison's first vice president, George Clinton, De Witt's uncle, had died in early 1812, and, to demonstrate a sectional balance on the ticket, Massachusetts's Elbridge Gerry, a revolutionary veteran, was chosen to run with Madison. The presidential race was closer than it should have been, but Madison beat Clinton by 128 to 89 electoral votes. The results, as in 1808, showed a sharp sectional divide; in 1812, Madison won only eight of his votes north of Pennsylvania, and, in a sign of post-independence change, the New England population now opposed a war with Britain. By 1812, the political culture of the northeast had seen its national role reduced by the rise of the Democratic Republicans. On the other hand, the political leadership in New England was not, as it turned out, wholly in tune with the popular mood in the region. While there were secessionist hints in the formal pronouncements of the New England assemblies, that extreme sentiment was not held by a majority of the population.

British naval hegemony inevitably asserted itself, and from 1813 on, the Royal Navy began an impressive blockade of the United States' coastline, including the vital Chesapeake. From Long Island south to Georgia and then to the mouth of the Mississippi, the blockade not only affected American trade but also presented the fearful prospect of British invasion; the Royal Navy did raid some communities along the shoreline of the upper Chesapeake. At the start of the war, the British did not tamper with neutral shipping into and out of New England ports, but, in 1814, after the expected antiwar dissent had not produced secession, Boston and the northeast ports were blockaded. By that time, in a policy reminiscent of the War for Independence, Congress sanctioned a large fleet of privateers. Their wide-ranging prowling caused Britain to resort to armed convoys for its merchant fleets. Several hundred British merchant ships were captured by American privateers. The naval war spread to the Pacific where United States Navy cruisers harassed British whalers and traders, but these were more irritants than serious threats to British maritime power. In a clear display of British naval superiority, the famous *Chesapeake* was defeated in a one-on-one engagement off the coast of Massachusetts in June 1813. The encounter with the British frigate *Shannon* had the semblance of a duel between two comparably armed vessels. The better-trained British crew triumphed. The dying American captain, James Lawrence, is reputed to have said "tell the men to fire faster and not give up the ship; fight her till she sinks" shortly before the *Chesapeake* was boarded and captured. There was a desolate mood in the United States when it was reported that the shattered *Chesapeake* was being taken to Halifax as a "prize," but the later response to the *Chesapeake* loss was to take Lawrence's alleged instructions and turn them into a patriotic slogan. "Don't give up the ship" was stitched onto the battle flag of the eponymous *Lawrence*, the flagship of Oliver Perry's Lake Erie squadron.

In the shadow of the loss of the *Chesapeake*, Perry's well-timed Lake Erie victory was the most decisive naval action of the war, a courageous and ingenious feat that boosted American hopes. Perry had made it to Lake Erie from Newport, Rhode Island with ships he had picked up along the way at Buffalo. He had added them to some newly constructed vessels at Presque Isle. The latter had been built from local timber but also from materials and appliances hauled overland from Philadelphia through the Allegheny Mountains to the south shore of Lake Erie. Perry's ten ships and 55 guns were too much for the British fleet of six ships and 65 guns. The sturdier American vessels wore down the British in a fierce encounter that lasted several hours. The victory gave Americans control of Lake Erie, and, though the British remained champions of the high seas, the United States controlled important inland waters adjacent to Canada. The year ended with another memorable dispatch when "don't give up the ship" was augmented by Perry's pithy message to General Harrison after his victory: "We have met the enemy and they are ours."

Perry's success at what was called the Battle of Put in Bay was tied to William Henry Harrison's attempt in 1813 to retake Detroit after the Hull debacle of 1812. The Kentucky government feared that the British might take control of areas to the west. They appointed the former Indiana Territory governor a major general of militia. James Madison later raised Harrison's rank to United States brigadier general (he was eventually commissioned as a major general) and put him in command of an American Army of about 10,000 men. However, at Frenchtown, southwest of Detroit, a force of Kentuckians was decimated by a British and native army. Five hundred Americans were taken prisoner and another 400 were killed, many of them massacred by native troops. But nearby at Fort Meigs and Fort Stephenson, the British were held off. With news of Perry's victory, Harrison moved on Detroit. Upper Canada was now threatened by Perry's control of Lake Erie and Harrison's control of the area around Detroit. The British all but abandoned the southwestern portion of Upper Canada between Niagara to the east and Detroit. Harrison's army caught the British and defeated them at the Battle of the Thames, near present day London, Ontario, in September 1813. The British defeat was compounded by the death of Tecumseh and the subsequent loss of the native alliance.

Earlier, in the spring of 1813, an amphibious American force left Sackett's Harbor at the eastern end of Lake Ontario on the American side and attacked York (later renamed Toronto) with the aim of seizing the British ships there, stifling British activity, and controlling the lake. The exercise at York must be counted a failure. A munitions accident caused over 300 American casualties, including the death of general Zebulon Pike, and, in an action that would come back to haunt the American cause, General Dearborn's troops burned the town's public buildings before departing across the lake to Niagara. The British would make a conspicuous display of reciprocity by destroying public buildings in Washington in the summer of 1814.

Meanwhile, the American campaign of 1813 ignored Kingston, on the Canadian side at the eastern end of Lake Ontario, and the opportunity to control a vital part of Upper Canada was lost. Military action continued around Niagara, but British authority was maintained in most of Upper Canada. In the summer and fall of 1813, American military reorganization and a substantial infusion of men and materiel led to a second attempt to take Montreal. Even then, the Americans were hobbled by confusion, poor communications, and indecision. Thus, the planned attack from Lake Ontario heading east linked to a northern campaign from Plattsburg, New York, collapsed in disarray. On the Niagara Peninsula at the end of the year, American troops burned a village and part of the town of Queenston, Upper Canada. The British retaliated by burning Buffalo and allowing native troops to go marauding through the countryside. Those actions underlined the fact that the war was often a dirty and callous affair, and the many small encounters, officially called battles, were often no more than bloody skirmishes. American efforts in Canada in 1813 were certainly more successful than in 1812, but Canada remained securely in British hands, and Fort Niagara was held by the British for the duration of the war.

One of the curiosities, or absurdities, of the War of 1812 was the fact that New England merchants continued to trade with the British. They sold foodstuffs to the British military in Canada and to the British Navy in the Atlantic. Congress's efforts to restrict this trade failed for want of compliance. The fact that New England beef was feeding British soldiers and sailors who were engaged in killing Americans should have been a national scandal. In many ways, however, this clumsily fought war itself seemed a sporadic, far-off affair for most Americans. For example, the British coolly set up a port of entry at Castine, Maine and collected duties from American merchants. While British goods continued to come into the United States through New England, the war did create a scarcity of some manufactured goods and boosted New England and other northern manufacturing enterprises. For most Americans, the war's most immediate effect was economic disruption and uncertainty. There were occasional bursts of patriotism, mostly at news of military successes, but the British blockade and the threat of invasion remained. The war was not as intrusive as it would have been had the British made a serious, sustained, and purposeful invasion of the United States. They did not, of course, because they could not hope to bring down the republic, even if they desired. Before 1814, the war's major offensives had been the American invasions of Canada, but with Napoleon's collapse, the British now deployed 14,000 veterans of the

European wars and tightened up their blockade of the American coast. At the same time, the United States Army was bolstered by a tighter and more efficient command structure, better communications, and an increase in the number of regular troops, from 11,000 in January to about 34,000 in October 1814. Yet even at that, the army did not reach the requested enlistments, and conscription was rejected by Congress.

Before the British could reinforce it, the Americans crossed the Niagara River for yet another invasion of Upper Canada. In two important encounters, they acquitted themselves well in formal, close combat with British Army regulars, winning at Chippewa and holding their own at Lundy's Lane in early 1814. They fell back to Fort Erie and, after resisting a siege of several weeks, burned the fort and abandoned it. That was the last meaningful foray into British territory. While these desultory maneuvers were going on, armistice talks began at Ghent in Belgium. Earlier, in the middle of 1813, Lord Castlereagh, the British prime minister, had become embroiled in a complex problem of supporting Russia's war against France while at the same time dealing with Russian attempts to end the Anglo-American war in order to strengthen allied capacities against Napoleon. Castlereagh had seen the futility of continuing the war with the United States, and the meeting at Ghent in Belgium was the result. The American delegation included John Adams's son John Quincy Adams (1767-1848), Henry Clay, and Albert Gallatin. The peace negotiations began in August 1814, just as the British were beginning major offensives. The timing underscores the war's tragicomic nature. There was now a fatalistic understanding on both sides that the war had been a mistake, but the British were bound to do something to force concessions at the negotiations table, and to exact a bit of revenge for the American vandalism in Upper Canada, especially for the burning of York. The British had set fire to Buffalo, but an assault on the capital at Washington seemed a more appropriate *quid pro quo*. After the failure of the Americans to control Upper Canadian territory in the summer of 1814, the British planned a major thrust into the upper Chesapeake to attack Washington and Baltimore. A second invasion force was scheduled to move south through the Lake Champlain corridor, following the approximate route of Burgoyne's ill-fated 1777 campaign. A third front was aimed at New Orleans and the lower Mississippi. These operations took place during the first months of peace talks at Ghent and drew on earlier plans. For the northern campaign, the British mustered an army of 11,000 regulars and launched a coordinated land and naval attack. In the two-hour naval encounter on Lake Champlain, a small American fleet defeated an equally small British fleet; the British land forces were mostly useless in the campaign, and the United States thus gained control of the Lake Champlain corridor. The British Army was withdrawn after leaving behind large numbers of deserters and tons of supplies. The well-worn invasion route, traversed by various armies in various wars, was now permanently in American hands. The invasion of the Chesapeake, on the other hand, challenged American sovereignty in the area, and was one of the most embarrassing experiences in the war for Americans.

The Chesapeake campaign involved an army of British veterans whose job was to alarm the population, destroy military supplies and facilities, and avenge the attack on York. Another feature of the strategy was to divert American attention away from Upper Canada and the Great Lakes, which was a concern in the summer of 1814 before the American failures at Lundy's Lane and Fort Erie. When they reached the mouth of the Patuxent River, before moving on to Baltimore and Washington, the British decided to seize the gunboats ostensibly guarding the capital. The Americans destroyed them, simply to keep them from the British, who then marched on Washington with little or no resistance. Indeed, the United States Army and many of the government officers, politicians, and other personnel had begun to scatter in panic or prudence into northern Virginia. At Bladensburg, the British defeated a large American force and then paused at the edge of Washington. Smaller units moved into the town and destroyed the Capitol and set fire to the president's residence (the "White House") and most of the public and many of the town's private buildings and homes. One of the few important buildings spared was the United States Patent Office. The naval yards were destroyed by the Americans themselves to prevent British use. The British had strolled into the heart of the republic's capital at will and dispersed its government. That humiliation was ameliorated somewhat by a remarkable defense of Baltimore. While the British were roaming through the capital, mocking American incompetence, the defenses of Baltimore had been strengthened. The defenders outnumbered the British and the harbor was blocked by the sinking of a line of ships. At Fort McHenry, the British bombardment failed, and Baltimore survived.

In mid-October the British withdrew to their transports and headed off to the West Indies, but not before another American patriotic symbol was minted. While witnessing the fierce bombardment of Fort McHenry, Francis Scott Key, a Maryland lawyer and volunteer in an artillery company, composed the poem "The Star Spangled Banner" with its stirring phrases and its coining of the celebratory "And the star-spangled banner in triumph doth wave/ O'er the land of the free and the home of the brave!" It remains a small irony but the tune that is used to accompany the poem, now the national anthem, is British.

Andrew Jackson, the Creek War, and the Battle of New Orleans

After the Washington mess, Madison had appointed fellow Virginian James Monroe as temporary secretary of war. New Englanders were wont to remind Madison and his cabinet of the westerners and southerners who had taken the lead in what was an ideologically driven and wasteful war. Daniel Boone, Henry Clay, and William Harrison were already westerners of national importance, and, in the wake of the War of 1812, another westerner by adoption, the southern-born Andrew Jackson (1767-1845), became an even more vivid stereotype. He was the vanguard politician for the "common man" in American national politics. Jackson led an expansive life from the time he fought as a youth and was captured by the British during the Revolutionary War, to his two-term presidency from 1828 to 1836. He was a shrewd original in so many ways, capable of making a quick study of any issue, and a highly focused activist.

He is remembered as a lawyer, local judge, politician, member of Congress, military commander and hero, land speculator, excellent duelist, and calculating individualist. Everything about him seemed larger than life, including his abrasive and confrontational political style. His militant approach to natives was extreme even in an era of popular belligerence. He was born and raised in South Carolina and, by the late 1780s, lived in the western section of North Carolina. When Tennessee was carved out of that territory and made a state in 1796, Jackson lived the rest of his life as a Tennessean. He surpassed Clay as the first major western political icon when he won the largest number of popular and electoral votes in the controversial 1824 presidential race. He lost that election, for, while he had the largest plurality, he did not win a majority. John Quincy Adams was selected by the House as president under the terms of Article II of the Constitution. In 1828, Jackson won the presidency in a clear endorsement of his 1824 performance, and he became the first president from outside the Virginia-Massachusetts axis. His entrée into national affairs began with his service in the War of 1812.

In 1812, Creek warriors began to disrupt settlement in the Alabama region. They had allegedly been aroused by Tecumseh a year earlier on one of his diplomatic missions. In the summer of 1813, these so-called "Red Sticks" (Upper Creeks) attacked a large Lower Creek, white and mixed blood settlement at Fort Mims near Mobile and massacred several hundred people. Andrew Jackson was then a major general of the Tennessee militia, and, by the fall of 1813, his forces had destroyed native settlements and killed hundreds of Creeks in retaliation. Early in 1814, despite some setbacks, Jackson's militia army eventually ended the Creek uprising with a decisive victory at Horseshoe Bend. Nearly 1,000 Creeks were killed and about 500 women and children taken captive. At the Treaty of Fort Jackson in August, a Creek minority signed away two-thirds of Creek lands to the United States and abandoned the southern and western areas of Alabama. At the same time, a second Treaty of Greenville was signed with several tribes in the northwest requiring the Shawnee, the Delaware, and others to go to war against the British. With the apparent pacification of the west, both north and south of the Ohio River, Jackson established his reputation as a military leader.

He was promoted to the rank of major general in the United States Army and to commander-in-chief of the United States Army in the southwest. Those were major stepping-stones in Jackson's career, but the *pièce de résistance* was yet to come. Two weeks after the Treaty of Ghent was signed on December 8, 1814, the United States won its greatest victory of the war at New Orleans, in January 1815. Andrew Jackson was the hero of a redundant victory that borders on the absurd. If the Creek War had brought him to public notice, the Battle of New Orleans made him famous. Jackson began his 1814 campaign by disobeying Secretary of War James Monroe's orders and invading Spanish Florida at Pensacola. He then moved from Mobile to New Orleans before learning that a large British invasion force was crossing the Gulf of Mexico from Jamaica to try to control the Mississippi. Jackson removed to Baton Rouge, but, when he learned that the British were east of New Orleans, he entered that city, declared martial law, and waited as the British force of some 7,500 men disembarked. Jackson then moved his defenses to a spot some five miles from New Orleans. After an artillery exchange on January 1, 1815, he awaited the British assault with an army of some 4,500 men. The British General Pakenham ordered close rank frontal attacks by his infantry. They were mowed down in alarming numbers by the Americans. That action and an ancillary engagement resulted in over 2,000 British soldiers being killed or wounded in about half an hour; also killed were three of the four British generals present.

Jackson's victory and the western warrior legend were enhanced by the reputation of the veteran frontiersmen from Kentucky and Tennessee among his troops who contributed to the slaughter with the deadly efficiency of their long rifles. The affair at New Orleans might be considered farce were it not for the shocking loss of British life in the most futile engagement of the war. The combatants did not know that the war was over, such was the slow movement of information, but rather than treat the battle as a tragedy of timing, chroniclers of the new republic have used it to create the durable impression of a great demonstration of unique American military prowess and British stupidity. An American popular song, "The Battle of New Orleans," written by a high school principal and history teacher, published in 1957, and recorded in 1959 could sell millions of copies with lines such as "They [the British] ran though the briars and they ran through the brambles/ And they ran through the bushes where a rabbit couldn't go/ And they ran so fast that the hounds couldn't catch 'em/ Down the Mississippi to the Gulf of Mexico." The legend of the Battle of New Orleans was accompanied by the legend of Andrew Jackson. American national integrity was fused to American military prowess, and the Treaty of Ghent was taken as an affirmation of America's independence.

The Treaty of Ghent and the Hartford Convention
The war had been the result, in part, of a delay in the transmission of trans-Atlantic information and then was settled weeks before the fighting ended, again because of slow communications. Despite improvised objectives and tepid support from significant sectors of the American and British publics, the Treaty of Ghent led to an arrangement between Great Britain and the United States that immediately pointed the way to American recognition of British territory in North America and a British acknowledgment of American territorial rights. American neutral rights were assured, but the agreements at Ghent were mostly concerned with territory and laid the groundwork for settlements of the northeastern boundary of Maine. The shape of the future Dominion of Canada had begun incidentally with the establishment of colonies in Nova Scotia and Prince Edward Island (formerly the French "Isle St. Jean") before the War for Independence. It had been advanced by the creation of New Brunswick in 1784 and with the (Canadian) Constitutional Act of 1791, which had created formal colonial structures in Upper and Lower Canada. In 1819, a settlement on the forty-ninth parallel as America's northern boundary resulted from negotiations to settle the issue of the military use of the Great Lakes. While there would be disputes over the

Oregon Territory lasting into the late 1840s and a much later quarrel over the Alaska-Canada boundary, there was at Ghent a general and mutual recognition of the permanence of British and American continental claims.

Was the war a delayed settling of the Revolution itself? Was it seriously expansionist? Was it the product of insulted national honor? It was, in some sense, all of those, but it was chiefly a product of the lingering problems of American trading rights, British power politics and economic ambition, and finally, the Napoleonic Wars. The issues that drove Madison and Congress to war were inextricably linked to the issue of neutrality and European wartime sanctions. The United States got caught up in someone else's conflict, in a global affair that set the United States in its place, as a marginal state in the Atlantic world. At the end of the war, Great Britain turned its attention to big power European diplomacy at the Congress of Vienna in 1815. The aftermath of the defeat of the greatest international player of the age, Napoleon, who had been toppled in 1814 and had returned and failed at Waterloo in 1815, left behind a world stage that he had helped create. American sovereignty was intact, but the war allowed future Canadian nationalism to use 1812 as the basis for its own sovereignty. Had not the Americans invaded Canada? Had not the republic's aggression and political ideology been repulsed? Modern Canada does find the roots of its alternate North American character, indeed the origins of its own independence, in the war and traces the historical development of its territorial integrity to the Treaty of Ghent. The repeated American incursions into Upper Canada had the unintended effect of permanently binding that community. Yet each belligerent could claim victory in the war's outcome. For the United States, an address to President Madison by the citizens of Baltimore in 1815 illustrates the general American view of the war: "[The war] has tried and vindicated our republican institutions: it has given us that moral strength, which consists in the well earned respect of the world, and in the just respect for ourselves. It has raised up and consolidated a national character, dear to the hearts of the people, as an object of honest pride and a pledge of future union, tranquility, and greatness."

The appearance of victory, even a symbolic one, crushed the political opponents of the war. The contemptuous Federalist term, "Mr. Madison's War" rebounded to further demoralize and hasten the demise of Hamilton's great political enterprise. The party had sagged and then declined after the 1800 election, and, even though it had done reasonably well in the elections of 1808 and 1812, it had become regionally isolated. By the end of the war, the Federalist Party was a New England party, retained by a weakened hierarchy of disaffected merchants, conservative lawyers, and cultural isolationists. While extremists called for secession, members of the party, encouraged by the state legislature of Massachusetts, met in Hartford, Connecticut from December 1814 to January 1815. They belatedly protested the war by condemning the national government's "infractions of the Constitution." They called for a restoration or redefinition of the sovereignty of the states and their roles in national affairs. Only the five New England states sent delegates to Hartford, underlining the wider irrelevance of the Federalist position. The 26 delegates issued a statement that resembled the Kentucky and Virginia Resolutions, stating that "In cases of deliberate, dangerous and palpable infractions of the Constitution, affecting the sovereignty of a State and liberties of the people; it is not only the right but the duty of such a State to interpose its authority for their protection, in the manner best calculated to secure that end."

The ironies were surely not lost on Madison. He had written something similar for Virginia to protest the Alien and Sedition Acts, and now his own government was being charged with similar abuses to "states rights" by representatives of a region that had been staunchly centralist in the late 1790s. While the extremists called for secession, moderates took a softer approach, attempting to "arraign" President Madison for his government's behavior. The convention issued a list of proposals, mostly requiring amendments to the Constitution, including these:

1. A method of protecting citizens of a state from unconstitutional military conscription.
2. Any money collected by the federal government in any state was to be used exclusively for the defense of that state.
3. An interstate system of national defense independent of federal control.
4. An amendment that would effectively remove the three-fifths clause as a basis for representation.
5. The raising to two-thirds the majority needed to declare war, sign treaties, restrict foreign trade, or admit new states to the union. It called for a 60-day limit on embargoes.
6. A ban on any naturalized citizen holding federal office.
7. The limiting of the president to one term in office.

The ideological temper of those proposals is obvious, but the entire exercise became patently useless when news of Jackson's victory at New Orleans and the signing of the Treaty of Ghent arrived. The moderate anti-secessionist, Harrison Gray Otis (1765-1848) of Massachusetts, the nephew of James Otis and of Mercy Otis Warren, had been authorized to present the convention's proposals to the federal government, but the end of the war precluded that. The Hartford Convention then became a target of popular derision, and the Federalist Party suffered further decline in the 1816 election.

The Hartford Convention was a sideshow of the nation's business in 1814-15. It represented the spiteful thrashings of a partisan and sectional minority. It was irrelevant and introspective, and its doctrines and proposals contradicted the nation's mood. It should be a footnote in the history of early nineteenth-century America, but it is important for what it tells us about the course and direction of the early republic. While the Hartford dissenters were declaiming on states' rights and the shift to a populist national government, they were reflecting on the declining influence of the first generation of revolutionary leaders in New England. The War of 1812 not only confirmed the power of the south (four of the first five presidents were Virginians) but revealed the rising influence of the west and a more "grassroots" agenda in national affairs. Andrew Jackson would very soon come to represent that shift. The major part of the Democratic Republican Party became, quite simply, the Democratic Party. The programs and policies of the Hamiltonian and New England Federalists had been and would continue to be absorbed or modified or rejected by the rising power of the Democrat Republican majority. A great example of that evolution resides in the person of James Madison, as the "last of the fathers," who with the War of 1812 demolished the founding "government" party of the United States, the Federalists. Before he left office, Madison demonstrated the ultimate fate of Jefferson's 1801 claim that "we are all republicans — we are all federalists" by overseeing the redundancy of the second clause, so that, for at least a generation, Americans would be "all Democratic Republicans."

Hamilton, had he lived, would have approved the retention of some of his economic mechanisms, but it is unlikely that even he could have saved the Federalist Party from extinction. The Democratic Republicans were the national party, and in 1815, Madison acted to correct the problems that had beset the nation in the early days of the war. He asked for a permanent *standing* army of 20,000, which was reduced to 10,000 by Congress; he oversaw a new commercial treaty with Great Britain, and waged a successful brief war against the Dey of Algiers for compensation for earlier Algerian collaboration with the British. Stephen Decatur's successes there and in neighboring Tunis and Tripoli ended a long-standing problem with the Barbary States. The most important reform enacted by the second Madison administration and the wartime Congress was the chartering of the second bank of the United States. Democratic Republicans reversed themselves in their approach to the Bank and, by 1814, had begun to consider a new 20-year charter for a bank on the principles of the 1791 model. By the end of 1816, the second Bank had been chartered, ultimately with 25 branches. It was capitalized at $35 million, a fifth of which was a federal deposit. It stabilized the nation's money supply and currency values. The president, a Democratic Republican, was authorized by a Democratic Republican Congress to name a fifth of the Bank's directors. The ghost of Hamilton might have been amused by the ironies of his old rival's role.

James Monroe and the "Era of Good Feelings"

The War of 1812 gave James Madison an exit from the national stage that befit his role in securing American nationhood. His immediate successor reaped the benefits of the war's ending. The war prepared the way for an "era of good feelings" as a Boston journal put it, when the national mood was buoyant, America's international status was improved, partisan politics were minimized, and economic opportunities were on the rise. The presidential election of 1816 was thus marked as much by the Democratic Republican nomination process as by the election itself. The newer generation of Democratic Republican Party members pushed for the nomination of Georgia's William H. Crawford, who was reluctant to accept. Monroe won the nomination narrowly but then won the election with a 183 to 34 electoral victory over the Federalist Rufus King. Only Massachusetts, Connecticut, and Delaware supported King.

The postwar reconciliations were evident within months of Monroe's inauguration. When the new president appeared in Hartford in the summer of 1817, at the site
of the recent Hartford Convention, the citizens were now eager to express their appreciation of the Democratic Republicans, the Constitution, and Monroe. They noted
smugly that, as New Englanders, they would "always be among the [Constitution's]
most firm and zealous supporters." The war that New England politicians had opposed
as late as 1814 and over which some had threatened secession was now seen as a great
national triumph. The citizens of Hartford told Monroe that "It is no less our happiness, sir, than yours, that your administration has commenced at a period gilded by the
recent exploits of our Army and Navy, and at the same time enjoying the tranquility
and security of peace." The "era of good feelings" began with a convenient revision of
recent New England politics and an apparent amnesia regarding the refusal of New
England legislatures to release militia for national service in the recent war. During the
same tour, the New England governors and other civic leaders also gushed with praise
for Monroe and the nation's health. It was clear that the Federalist Party was finished
as a national force. Stephen Decatur, the hero of the Algiers war, coined an appropriate
patriotic hurrah when he said in an after dinner speech in 1816, "Our Country! In her
intercourse with foreign governments may she always be in the right; *but our country,
right or wrong.*" (Emphasis added.) In 1820, Monroe won all but one of the 232 electoral votes cast (there were three abstentions) in a spectacular demonstration of the
power of Jefferson's party. Since 1800, Democratic Republican control of Congress had
fluctuated between two-to-one and four-to-one majorities. By 1820, the ratio in the
House was six to one (158-25), and only four of 48 Senators claimed Federalist affiliation. As the first party system in the United States receded, it coincided with a rap-
prochement in relations between the United States and Great Britain.

The demilitarization of the Great Lakes and border posts was agreed to in the
Rush-Bagot accord of 1817, which was unanimously accepted by the Senate in 1818.
This was an important moment in Anglo-American relations. Charles Bagot was the
British government's representative in the United States, and Richard Rush was the
United States' acting secretary of state. While mutual suspicions remained and while
wrangling over terms and borders would continue for decades, a first step had been
taken toward a reasonable coexistence in North America. The territorial consequences
of the War of 1812 went beyond the Rush-Bagot agreement, and, in the fall of 1818,
Rush, now serving as United States minister to Britain along with Albert Gallatin,
signed another agreement with the British. It established the forty-ninth parallel
as the northern boundary farther west, running from the Great Lakes to the Rocky
Mountains in a line that matched the northern extent of the Louisiana Purchase. By
agreement, the so-called "Oregon Country," roughly the present-day states of Oregon,
Washington, and the southern part of the Canadian province of British Columbia, was
left open to British and American interests alike for an initial period of ten years. The
forty-ninth parallel boundary was finally extended to the Pacific in 1846. The
Convention of 1818 reaffirmed Madison's 1815 commercial treaty with Britain and

allowed Americans access to fisheries off the British North American Atlantic coast.

In 1819, the United States acquired Florida and established a southern boundary with Spain that confirmed the southern and western limits of the Louisiana Purchase. The United States had taken over West Florida in 1810, but the whole of East Florida had remained under nominal Spanish control. During the War of 1812, the British had built a fort on the Apalachicola River near the southwestern Georgia state boundary. After the war, the fort became a gathering place for Seminoles, other natives, and runaway slaves. In 1816, an American military expedition burned the fort. The natives and former slaves then organized a resistance, and the first Seminole War was underway. Andrew Jackson took command of the United States forces in Florida in late 1817 and embarked on a vigorous campaign against the natives. His supreme self-confidence can be seen in the letter he sent to President Monroe wherein he asked that, if the United States wanted to possess all "the Floridas," he would act "and in sixty days it will be accomplished." When he did not get a reply, Jackson marched his army into Florida, capturing Pensacola and scattering the native resistance. He was not only decisive but bloody-minded too. He executed two British traders whom he accused of aiding the "enemy," thus applying his own standard of justice in territory that was outside United States legal jurisdiction.

While Jackson was rampaging through Florida, bringing the territory under military control and embellishing his popular image, the Cabinet was in an uproar and sought to censure him. He was criticized in the Senate, but, if his political reputation was damaged at that level, it was enhanced among the general population. Although the British condemned his killing of two British subjects and the British press had a field day attacking him, Jackson's actions actually influenced the boundary negotiations between the United States and Spain over the old Louisiana Territory line. The chief American negotiator, John Quincy Adams, defended Jackson's aggressions in Florida as a pre-emptive move against Spanish hostility, a specious claim, perhaps, but effective in the long term. In the Adams-Onis Treaty of February 1819, Spain ceded all of Florida. The United States dropped an earlier claim to part of Texas and agreed to a clarified version of the Louisiana Purchase boundaries. John Quincy Adams had shared Jackson's views in 1818 on Florida, but their contrasting backgrounds, dissimilar personalities, and opposing political manners were revealed in the 1824 presidential election, when the political establishment rejected Jackson's bluster and aggressiveness for the more conventional Adams.

New Englanders overwhelmingly re-elected Monroe in 1820, but the term "era of good feelings" should not be taken too seriously. The war had been concluded successfully, but beyond the platitudes, there were factions forming at all levels of politics in the wake of the moribund Federalist Party. The improving economy favored some but not all. Sectionalism was already a divisive cultural and political issue becoming lodged in the national character. Indeed, the future "bad feelings" in American sectional politics were beginning to show up, and, while the Democratic Republicans dominated after 1820, competition at the national level blunted the possibility of a one-party government. During his political career, Henry Clay ran for the presidency as a Democratic Republican, as a National Democratic Republican, and as a Whig. While the Jacksonians took a large section of the old Democratic Republican constituency into the Democratic Party, the rest of America found other political affiliations. As the franchise expanded at the state level, the emergence of class interests took the national political agenda in unforeseen directions all the way to the Civil War. States' rights and sectional interests remained politically charged. The Marshall court had confirmed the supremacy of national authority in areas of national concern in the 1819 *McCulloch v. Maryland* decision, where a state banking law that conflicted with a federal banking charter was overturned. But regional and ideological factions and personality conflicts contradicted the outward appearance of unity and harmony. Economically, the re-chartering of the Bank of the United States in 1816 led to a panic in 1819. The Bank's demand for specie payments created hardships for many smaller banks and individual debtors at the state level. Rural America was hostile to the Bank, and some western states enacted legislation to protect debtors. By 1820, the American economy was, in fact, overextended, and investments in land, agricultural commodities, and manufacturing were strained by inflated values and reduced credit. Foreign trade had not kept up with domestic growth and speculation.

Yet for all that, the nation was poised for a period of extraordinary growth. As native societies were breaking up under relentless white population growth, their lands were being converted into farms and plantations. The vexatious problems of competing interests seemed to be manageable with the exception of the deeper discords of sectionalism, at the root of which was slavery, or to be more precise slave society, planter culture, and southern political insecurity. For example, the populations of *neighboring* Ohio and Kentucky were each about 97 per cent rural in 1820, but different cultures and agricultural economies made for two kinds of rural communities. Not all rural Americans were engaged directly in agriculture, but the vast majority was. In 1800, about 75 per cent of Americans worked on farms; in 1820, the proportion had slipped to 72 per cent. In contrast to the western and southern societies, New England's farm population was at 68 per cent in 1800 and 63 percent in 1820. The mid-Atlantic states were moving in the same demographic direction, while the numbers for the south and southwest remained in the 79 per cent range in 1820. So, while most Americans were rural, and the vast majority of those agricultural, there was some economic diversity in all parts of the nation, with perhaps less diversity in the south and southwest. Variations within the social and cultural complexities of pre-revolutionary America accompanied the republic into the nineteenth century, and not least among them was cultural and economic sectionalism.

Massachusetts's changing economy affected the social character of the state, and as much as 20 per cent of the population was urban in 1820, while Georgia, for example remained at about 3 per cent. Even in the upper south, Virginia's urban population seemed stuck at a mere 4 per cent in 1820. Across the state line in Pennsylvania, some 15 per cent lived in urban settings, and the state's traditional agricultural economy was being modified by manufacturing. In the first two decades of the nineteenth century, population densities in the coastal counties of southern New England, New York, and Pennsylvania were in the 60 to 80 persons per square mile range, compared to 30 in eastern and central Virginia and about 12 per square mile in the Tidewater south. To the west, the densities fell rapidly, to about 5 per square mile in the populated parts of Tennessee, for example. The lure of the west was land and space. In 1820, the Federalists at Hartford had attacked the three-fifths clause as a Constitutional abomination, but the issue of slavery became more troublesome as a territorial matter. The major political issue for Americans in 1820 was space. There was apparently lots of it in the west, but what gripped the American political imagination in 1820 was the question of its utilization, not in terms of land use but in politics.

Missouri

A territorial government had been established for the Louisiana Purchase in 1805, and the State of Louisiana was created out of the extreme southern part of the Louisiana Territory in 1812. Its constitution allowing slavery was accepted by Congress. The admission of Louisiana restored the equal numbers of slave and non-slave states. As for the area acquired by the United States in the Treaty of Paris of 1783, Indiana in the north and Mississippi in the south were admitted as states in 1816 and 1817 respectively, and then Illinois in 1818 and Alabama in 1819 brought the number of states to 22. Michigan Territory did not receive statehood until 1837. By 1820, then, the 11 slave and 11 non-slave states maintained the senatorial balance in Congress, but the northern non-slave states had 105 seats in the House of Representatives, and the southern slave states had 81. Even with the three-fifths clause, the faster population growth in the north and northwest indicated an even wider representational gap in the future. West of the Mississippi, the Missouri Territory had been organized after Louisiana's admission as a state in 1812, and Arkansas Territory, lying between the State of Louisiana and Missouri, was established in 1819 while the debate over Missouri was going on. The American settlement of those areas included slaveholders and their slaves.

The question of slavery north of the State of Louisiana and west of the Mississippi River was raised in 1819. With slavery on the agenda, the Missouri territorial assembly had begun to petition for statehood in 1817. Missouri was a strong candidate for statehood and was strategically located where the Missouri River from the west and the Ohio River from the east ran into the Mississippi. The trading post at Saint Louis, established by the French in 1763, had become a jumping off point for the west after the Lewis and Clark expedition. Large numbers of settlers had moved into the eastern parts of the territory following the War of 1812, and the population was nearing the 60,000 number required for statehood. A glance at a map shows that the greatest part of the eastern boundary of the state of Missouri, as it was proposed in 1819 and as it is today, lies along the Mississippi River north of the mouth of the Ohio River across from the state of Illinois. Only a fraction of the eastern border lay next to the slave states of Kentucky and Tennessee. As a contiguous part of the United States in 1819, the proposed state was geographically more a northern than a southern extension. A New York Representative James Tallmadge attempted to amend the Missouri Act with a clause prohibiting slavery in the new state and adding a gradual emancipation clause for slaves who were already in the territory. The amendment was passed in the House and defeated in the Senate. A northern protest against the extension of slavery had been registered. At the same time, the bill for the establishment of Arkansas Territory with its northern boundary with Missouri at 36 degrees, 30 minutes north latitude came before Congress. Another New York Congressman, John Taylor, moved to ban slavery in the territory and that, too, was defeated. The debate over Missouri raised the question of whether Congress could in fact prohibit slavery in a new state in the Louisiana Territory. In the admissions process for new states, the only precedent for the pre-emptive banning of slavery had been the Northwest Ordinance of 1787, which had been passed under the Articles of Confederation. The question that came up as the Missouri Act was presented was whether Congress could actually rule in advance over a new state's position on slavery. The provisions of Article IV of the Constitution suggested that it could because of federal jurisdiction in territories.

The Missouri Compromise

In December 1819, while the question of jurisdiction was being debated in the Senate, the people of Maine petitioned Congress for admission as a separate state. Maine comprised the far northeastern counties of Massachusetts and, ever since the colonial period, had developed its own social and political identity. For decades, as a northern frontier extension of New England, it had attracted a steady flow of settlement, and the population was nearing 300,000 in 1819. The Senate proposed combining the admission of Maine and Missouri together without any restriction on slavery. Senator Jesse Thomas of Illinois proposed an amendment that would admit Missouri without a restriction on slavery but retain the earlier Taylor amendment regarding latitude 36° 30' north as the northern limit to slavery in the remainder of the Louisiana Purchase. The wrangling over the matter of slavery in Missouri in both houses of Congress was a harbinger of the more dangerous confrontations that widened the north-south gulf as the century wore on. In March 1820, Maine was admitted as the 23rd state. Missouri, which is actually north of 36° 30' was excluded from the slave prohibition, and its convention proposed a state constitution that not only allowed for slavery but prohibited *free* African Americans and "mulattoes" from settling in the state. Congress balked at the proposal, and the clause banning free African Americans was deleted. The debates over the state constitution dragged into 1821 before Missouri was admitted to the union in August 1821 as a slave state. Of its nearly 70,000 population, about 11,000 were African Americans, the majority of them slaves. The Missouri Compromise was eventually repealed in the Kansas-Nebraska Act of 1854 and then retroactively declared unconstitutional in the Dred Scott decision of 1857. The Supreme Court decided then that Congress could not deprive a person of property (in this case, slaves) under the terms of the due process clause of the Fifth Amendment. That clause superseded Congress's authority to regulate slavery by legislation as it had done by prohibiting slavery in the Louisiana Purchase territory above the 36° 30' line.

It is fitting that Thomas Jefferson's comments on the Compromise are often cited as the most prophetic. He was, by 1820, the nation's most venerated elder statesman, and his reaction to the Missouri Compromise contained a chilling prediction for the nation's sectional future. In a widely quoted letter, Jefferson lamented the deal:

> I had for a long time ceased to read newspapers, or pay any attention to public affairs, confident they were in good hands, and content to be a passenger in our bark to the shore from which I am not distant. But this momentous question, like a firebell in the night, awakened and filled me with terror. I considered it at once as the knell of the Union. It is hushed, indeed, for the moment. But this is a reprieve only, not a final sentence. A geographical line, coinciding with a marked principle, moral and political, once conceived and held up to the angry passions of men, will never be obliterated; and every new irritation will mark it deeper and deeper. I can say, with conscious truth, that there is not a man on earth who would sacrifice more than I would to relieve us from this heavy reproach, in any *practicable* way.

That eloquent and fearful comment was not a lament for the extension of slavery into Missouri but a condemnation of the banning of slavery north of 36° 30,' west of the Mississippi. Jefferson had endorsed the banning of slavery in the 1787 Northwest Ordinance, but had apparently reversed his position on the issue of the central government's intervention in the slavery issue. He now went on to say that, if left to the states, and to time and population dispersal, slavery would disappear. His point was that Congress had *constitutionally* marked the United States as a racially defined polity. Whether or not Jefferson was right in seeing the Compromise as threatening the unity of his beloved nation, he did identify the great flaw in the nation's design as the revolutionary generation disappeared from the scene. And while a divisive American drama was being rehearsed, one of the Revolution's few remaining leading actors, George III, died in January 1820. The "tyrant" had become blind, deranged, and immobilized. He had ascended the throne during the Seven Years' War, in an age that seemed distant to the generation of 1820, but, over six decades, he and his ministers had done much to shape the Revolution.

Conclusion

The War of 1812 was caused in large part by confused diplomacy and prosecuted in a mostly muddled and inconclusive way. Yet, if James Madison had been a reluctant belligerent in 1812, his later presidency was marked by rising American international status in international relations in the aftermath of the war. Such is the war's peculiar status that, while it seemed like a blunder in 1812, and was likely preventable by the use of common sense, it managed nevertheless to settle long-standing North American issues in the treaty that ended it. It produced no loser, unless we consider the fate of the native peoples who were caught up in the conflict. Each belligerent could find a satisfactory

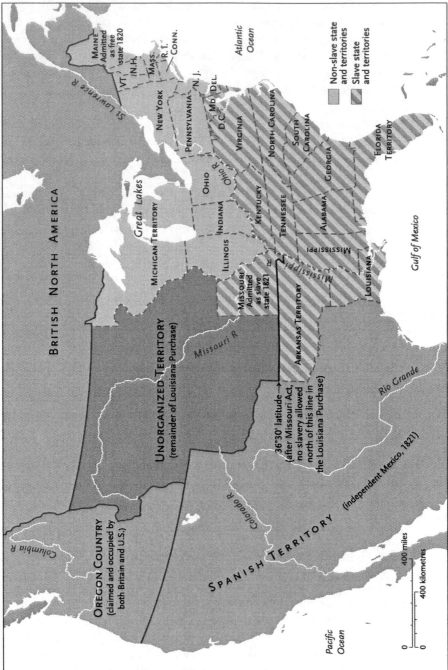

Map 9.2 The United States in 1821

explanation for the war, end their mutual hostilities, and fight no more. They became permanent trading allies and agreed to share North America. Thus, a major consequence of the War of 1812 was the confirmation of Canada's existence as a separate North American entity. That meant that the American Revolution, in the end, resulted in the creation of two new nations.

For the United States, the economics and politics of the age were also marked by the debates over space and the meaning and appropriate use of the vastness of the United States' continental identity and scope. The War of 1812 continued the erosion of native population on a shrinking native land base and further deprecated native cultures. Slavery became more deeply etched into the nation's business, politics, and culture and signaled a widening gulf between northern and southern cultures. James Monroe's "era of good feelings" can be seen now as a chimera, for a new set of potentially divisive political issues, most significantly the Missouri Compromise, began to emerge by 1820. By that time, two of the remaining founding fathers, John Adams and Thomas Jefferson, had eased into old age, and each would die, symbolically, on July 4, 1826, fifty years to the day from the official Declaration of Independence date. The third remaining leading founder, James Madison, was retired and would spend much time in the years to come compiling his notes of the Constitutional Convention of 1787. For all of their voluminous writings, the shy Madison and the often evasive, even indecisive Jefferson were really private persons whose formal behavior, along with that of John Adams, would seem almost dignified in contrast to the boisterous popular politics of the Jacksonians and their successors. Jefferson's "firebell in the night" spelled the end of a phase of the American Revolution, and suggested that it was not only incomplete but precarious in a way that would bring on the calamity of the Civil War. The Constitution had worked so far to resolve the crises of the booming new nation, but, after 1820, the Missouri Compromise and the sectional fault line would prove to be greater challenges to the republic's grand promise.

Suggested Reading

Recent scholarship on the period can be found in Jeffrey L. Pasley, Andrew W. Robertson, and David Waldstreicher, eds., *Beyond the Founders: New Approaches to the Political History of the Early American Republic* (Chapel Hill: University of North Carolina Press, 2004); Paul A. Gilge, ed., *Wages of Independence: Capitalism in the Early American Republic* (Madison, WI: Madison House, 1997); and Drew McCoy, *The Last of the Fathers: James Madison and the Republican Legacy* (Cambridge, England: Cambridge University Press, 1989). Monroe's presidency is examined in a recent brief biography by Gary Hart, *James Monroe* (New York: Times Books, 2005). Several older overviews are worth noting, including the clear and engaging treatment of the period by George Dangerfield, *The Era of Good Feelings* (New York: Harcourt Brace, 1952). The same author's *The Awakening of American Nationalism, 1815-1828* (New York: Harper and Row, 1965) is a well-written introduction to the mood and pace of American life. Another older essay of note is Marcus Cunliffe, *The Nation Takes Shape, 1789-1837*

(Chicago: University of Chicago Press, 1959). Useful economic studies are John R. Nelson, *Liberty and Property: Political Economy and Policymaking in the New Nation* (Baltimore: Johns Hopkins University Press, 1987) and Douglass North, *The Economic Growth of the United States, 1790-1860* (1961; New York: W.W. Norton, 1966). The literature on the War of 1812 is vast and a good introduction is Donald Hickey, *The War of 1812: The Forgotten Conflict* (Urbana, IL: University of Illinois Press, 1989). Canadian versions of the war are plentiful: see Wesley B. Turner, *The War of 1812: The War That Both Sides Won*, 2nd ed. (Toronto: Dundurn, 2000) and Victor Suthren, *The War of 1812* (Toronto: McClelland and Stewart, 1999). A study that combines issues of class, nationalism, and social structure is John Phillips Resch, *Suffering Soldiers: Revolutionary War Veterans, Moral Sentiment and Political Culture in the Early Republic* (Amherst, MA: University of Massachusetts Press, 1999). For the west, see Rohrbough, *The Trans-Appalachian Frontier*, cited previously.

EPILOGUE
THE GENERATION OF 1820

> Advance, then, ye future generations!...We welcome you to the blessings of good
> government and religious liberty... to the treasures of science and the delights of
> learning.... to the...sweets of domestic life...to the happiness of kindred, and
> parents, and children. We welcome you to the immeasurable blessings of rational
> existence, the immortal hope of Christianity, and the light of everlasting truth!
> — Daniel Webster (1782-1852), December 1820, on the 200th
> anniversary of the arrival of the Pilgrims

Change and Persistence: The Generation of 1820

To the generation of white male Americans who came of age after 1810, the world of
their grandparents, the colonial world of 1750, was a quaint, misty bygone place.
Regardless of their location in the expanding republic, the generation of 1820 lived in a
transformed world. They might be located in a state that had been a crown colony in
1750, or in a state that had never been a colony, or in a territory that was not yet a state.
Depending on where they were, they might be enjoying a more open, less deferential
existence than their predecessors with more active political roles and more economic
opportunity. They would have imbibed the ideology of republicanism and the right to
consent and also dissent in political matters, assuming a citizenship that promoted
those values. They would certainly have identified themselves with the language and
spirit of the Declaration of Independence and the clean, demonstrated symmetry of
constitutional government and law. They lived in a place that was a national, federated
system of recent creation but of proven ability, and with a future, as Daniel Webster
said, full of the promise and the treasures of "liberty...learning...happiness [and]
rational existence." These were the fruits of the great colonial experiment, the cultivation of new and potent political values, and the heroic rejection of (British) oppression. The generation of 1820 inhabited a nation state the shape of which would be
inconceivable to their grandparents. In 1750, the Appalachians were the west; in 1820,
America extended to the Rockies and the Pacific. Americans controlled the great
Mississippi for its entire length and had settled along the Gulf of Mexico. In the
extraordinary decades from 1750 to 1820, Americans had designed a unique and
vibrant new political system, had fought one war to bring it about and another to
affirm it, and, in doing so, had created a pantheon of national heroes. They celebrated
events such as the Boston Tea Party, and gathered in great throngs for Fourth of July
speeches and parades. A distinct and self-conscious American culture had begun. The
perception that prevailed in 1820s America was of an original historical experience,

the Revolution, and the uniqueness of its peoples and values. Social linkages were being forged as Ohio families traced their New England roots or Mississippi planters extended older plantation dynasties.

Americans had not only designed a political system for themselves but were forging a national economy and supervising a vast territorial hegemony. While the Americans of 1820 had not entirely turned their backs on the Atlantic and European worlds, they were now, for the most part, a westward-looking people. They would continue to need the "old world" for trade and would for some time continue to borrow scientific ideas, literary models, and the art and music of Europe. There was now little or no attachment to the trans-Atlantic cultures behind them and only the necessity of trade to notice them at all. In that sense, they were a less worldly generation than their grandparents had been, and would become even more self-consciously self-defining as the century wore on. The remainder of the British Empire in North America was Canada, and it began to turn the other way. The Canadian world was a more global one, tied to Britain, Europe, and the expanding British Empire of the nineteenth century. Americans, meanwhile, had created a *new* meaning for the New World with the first two generations of republican citizens. The 1.2 million British Americans of 1750 had become the 9.7 million Americans of 1820, and the land mass they controlled had been quadrupled.

There was great energy in the early republic, a release of ambition and expectation that suggested a buoyant present and a future of security, prosperity, and happiness. It is easy to imagine a society of vaguely defined statuses: free, proud, and mobile. Such was the perception of Daniel Webster, and we can be sure, most of his peers. In a 1988 essay "The Significance of the Early Republic," historian Gordon Wood sees the early republic as the culmination of "a basic social revolution, a fundamental shift in the way people related to one another.... In many respects the America of the 1820s was the exact opposite of the society the Founding Fathers had wanted to create. Never before or since has American society been so unsettled and the lines of authority so confused. Everything seemed up for grabs, and no ties that did not come from volitional allegiance seemed tolerable." Then, in a fulsome stretch, he claims that the society of the early republic "was...dominated by ordinary people — to a degree never duplicated by any nation in modern history." These are not entirely extravagant claims, but they are as *conceptual* as they are demonstrable. It is difficult to see President John Quincy Adams, Boston Mayor Josiah Quincy Jr., or Senator Henry Clay as "ordinary" or as being dominated by ordinary people in ever larger numbers of even more ordinariness. Also the comparison with all societies in the modern world might not be accurate. Nor might it apply to other periods in American history.

Webster's words reveal an epiphany, a sense that history had transformed America and created a new force in human affairs. Historians have tended to share that view, taking the Revolution as the genesis of American particularism. Wood, a learned and astute historian, is careful to exclude natives and African Americans from his assessment and limits his views to the condition of white, and one must note, male Americans. Yet by looking at 1820 America from the perspective of slavery or native culture, one might detect more persistence of elitism and deference than either Wood's analysis or Webster's 1820 grandiloquence indicate. Certain major features of the world of 1750 were continued into the new republic. For a start, the codification of slavery as national law and thus part of the national ethic set the racial agenda for the future. As the condition of the bondsman was legally and functionally tightened, it is difficult to see how there was "a basic social revolution" among the slaveholders of the south and the southwest. The white slaveholding cultures of 1820 resembled those of 1750 in quite concrete ways. Although the mass of white marginal farmers in the south, the Appalachian foothills, and the fields of Kentucky, Tennessee, and Alabama may have felt "republican" in 1820, how far had they moved from the deferential politics of their forebears? The south had charted its future social course by the end of the colonial period.

Native peoples in the new republic were being as relentlessly dislocated and marginalized as they had been in 1750, but now the process had reached the Mississippi River. The average Indiana farmer of 1820 was no more or less removed from the rigors of climate, market forces, and hard labor than his predecessor in New England or New Jersey of two generations earlier. The idea that the "America of the 1820s was the exact opposite" of what the founders intended is not obvious. Clearly, the founders of the national government had to accept state demands on rights, articulated, by the way, by a mostly colonial generation. Surely Jefferson and Madison allowed that the mass of the population had to be considered in any revolutionary settlement. Even John Hancock understood that the involvement of the "ordinary" colonial person in the resistance to British policy would have to be acknowledged. Did the high-toned rhetoric of the classical republicans, harnessed by the founders for their own ends, result in an unwanted and perhaps unpredictable trend to "democracy" by 1820? That seems unlikely, given that the war rather than independence opened up the social and political expectations of ordinary Americans. The 200,000 or so common soldiers who served in the Revolutionary War were *colonials*. Much is made of the impact of the First Amendment and its guarantee of free speech, but the Zenger trial of 1735 had set the stage for a colonial habit of dissent that was eloquently restated in James Otis's 1761 attack on British taxing authority. Much has been made also of the freedom of religion clause in the First Amendment and Jefferson's highly principled role in establishing religious freedom in Virginia. The separation of church and state in America had been in the making before the eighteenth-century Great Awakening. As for the Awakening, one could take some of Wood's description of 1820s America and use it for the religious upheavals of the 1740s and 1750s when observers probably could see a "society ... unsettled and the lines of authority ... confused."

The image of restless liberated masses making their way west certainly indicates a great release of human energy and produces the image of a revolution in social and economic mobility. But the opportunity for and the practice of mobility was not new to Americans. It was as old as the "swarming" immigrants of the early seventeenth century. Internal migration was as important a feature of 1750 America as it was later. The tens of thousands of opportunity seeking migrants into North Carolina in the late colonial period were as freewheeling and enthusiastic as were the throngs who headed to Kentucky and to Ohio in the wake of the Revolutionary War and to the trans-Mississippi frontier thereafter. It was, after all, real estate enterprise that had sent Virginians across the Appalachians in the 1740s and 1750s to confront the French and natives in the west. The "west" simply moved with the times. Andrew Jackson, a paradigm of the new frontier ethos, was weaned on migratory rights in the revolutionary period, encouraged by older colonial activists. When, in 1782, the French immigrant Crevecoeur eloquently described Americans in his oft-quoted phrase as "individuals of all nations melted into a new race of men," he was describing the generation that made the Revolution and not the one that inherited it. The first census of the United States in 1790 revealed that only 60 per cent of the white population was English in descent, ranging from about 82 per cent in Massachusetts to about 35 per cent in Pennsylvania. The early colonial national culture, the English, had been joined during the eighteenth century by a medley of other cultures and "nationalities." Only in New England was there ethnic homogeneity. If we include African Americans in the overall calculations, the proportion of Americans of English descent falls to about 50 per cent by the end of the Revolutionary War. Crevecoeur's "new man" could be found before the Revolution.

If American society in 1820 was unique in the world in its social makeup ("dominated by ordinary people to a degree never duplicated by any nation in modern history"), it was just as distinctive in 1750 if we compare colonial society — its political institutions and participation, land ownership rates, social mobility, and personal outlook — with any other society in the middle of the eighteenth century. But *expectations* had been radicalized so that by removing a king and replacing him with a civil constitution, the Revolution left "ordinary" Americans with a more appropriate means of dealing with their social futures. In the meantime, wealth would continue to influence the exercise of power, but wealth was now assumed to be accessible to most white males. Yet significant changes in the status of free blacks or white upper-class and lower-class women, for the most part, were not yet apparent. The Revolution did not eliminate classes in America but changed their functions. One of the early signs of social change in the new republic had very little to do with republicanism or egalitarianism, but was the embryonic stirring of industrial activity in the northeast and the appearance of wage labor and factory culture. A modern working class was in the making. The 200,000 ordinary veterans of the Revolutionary War clamored, mostly without success, for pensions and bonuses, perquisites that had already been extended to officers. The westbound migrants were settling into fluid but limited economies. The socio-economic ramp that Jackson Turner Main had described for the late eighteenth century persisted into the nineteenth. The rules were different, and the component parts of the society were extended over a greater range of territory and economies, but America was not a classless world for the "ordinary" citizen. For the great majority of small farmers (that is, the great majority of settlers), life was very hard. For every Lincoln who emerged from the marginal farms of Indiana and Illinois, hundreds of thousands of families left only the promise of more hard farming for their progeny. In

1820, the full promise of happiness for the majority of ordinary Americans was not yet a reality.

Still, for all the remnants and linkages to 1750, the world of 1820 was a new world. Gordon Wood is right to emphasize the energy that was in the air, and historian Alfred Young has astutely emphasized the radicalization of expectations. Before we make too much of the social revolution, we should remember that one of the ways we make sense of the past is to measure the degree and nature of change, or the absence of it, over time. The generation of 1820 was a product of a profound redefinition of politics, the creation of a unique national federation. What lay ahead for Americans in the *next* 70 years would also constitute a revolution in politics and in social and cultural conditions: the railroad, the mechanical reaper, the Mexican War, California and Colorado, abolitionism, the breakup of the union, the Civil War and the recovery of the union, the end of slavery and the subsequent horrors of Jim Crow segregation, the industrialization of the northeast, full-blown urbanism, monopoly capitalism, electric light and telephones, the new immigration that would truly transform America's ethnic makeup, women's rights movements, and the stirrings of an overseas American empire. What did Americans of 1890 see when they looked back to 1820? They saw a raw, mostly agrarian and unformed society, a boisterous and patriotic generation that was, unwittingly perhaps, sowing the seeds of disunion. But they might have chosen to see Abraham Lincoln preserving Thomas Jefferson's and the founders' political vision rather than to see the flaws in the real world of 1820.

Suggested Reading

A useful collection of essays on the early role of the Constitution in American society is Edward Countryman, ed., *What Did the Constitution Mean to Early Americans?* (Boston: Bedford/St. Martin's, 1999). The celebration of a national "American" character began long before the triumphant speeches of the early Republic and the end of the War of 1812. See Michel Guillaume Jean de Crevecoeur, *Letters from an American Farmer* (1782; Gloucester, MA: P. Smith, 1968). (He wrote under the name of J. Hector St. John Crevecoeur.) Gordon S. Wood, "The Significance of the Early Republic," *The Journal of the Early Republic* 8 (1988): 1-20 is a strongly stated thesis arguing that the Revolution's early legacy, its "significance," was an amalgam of self-conscious individualism, republican idealism, mobility, freedom, and exceptionalism. Wood's exuberant citizen of 1820s America is a white male one. The Wood article should be compared with Alfred F. Young, *The Shoemaker and the Tea Party: Memory and the American Revolution* (Boston: Beacon Press, 1999), which argues that the masses who helped forge the nation in war were largely co-opted by middle-and upper-class "patriots" in the first few decades after independence. David Brion Davis, *The Problem of Slavery in the Age of Revolution, 1770-1823* (Ithaca, NY: Cornell University Press, 1975) remains as the best single commentary on the conundrum of slavery in the wake of the Revolution. On the status of women in the new republic, see the relevant chapters in Carol Berkin, *Revolutionary Mothers: Women in the Struggle for America's Independence* (New York:

Hill and Wang, 2005) and for natives, see Colin G. Calloway, *Native Americans and the Early Republic* (Charlottesville: University Press of Virginia, 1999). A stimulating commentary on the changing west can be found in Stephen Aron, *How the West Was Lost: The Transformation of Kentucky from Daniel Boone to Henry Clay* (Baltimore: The Johns Hopkins University Press, 1996).

THE DECLARATION OF INDEPENDENCE
A TRANSCRIPTION

IN CONGRESS, July 4, 1776.

The unanimous Declaration of the thirteen united States of America,

When in the Course of human events, it becomes necessary for one people to dissolve the political bands which have connected them with another, and to assume among the powers of the earth, the separate and equal station to which the Laws of Nature and of Nature's God entitle them, a decent respect to the opinions of mankind requires that they should declare the causes which impel them to the separation.

We hold these truths to be self-evident, that all men are created equal, that they are endowed by their Creator with certain unalienable Rights, that among these are Life, Liberty and the pursuit of Happiness. — That to secure these rights, Governments are instituted among Men, deriving their just powers from the consent of the governed, — That whenever any Form of Government becomes destructive of these ends, it is the Right of the People to alter or to abolish it, and to institute new Government, laying its foundation on such principles and organizing its powers in such form, as to them shall seem most likely to effect their Safety and Happiness. Prudence, indeed, will dictate that Governments long established should not be changed for light and transient causes; and accordingly all experience hath shewn, that mankind are more disposed to suffer, while evils are sufferable, than to right themselves by abolishing the forms to which they are accustomed. But when a long train of abuses and usurpations, pursuing invariably the same Object evinces a design to reduce them under absolute Despotism, it is their right, it is their duty, to throw off such Government, and to provide new Guards for their future security. — Such has been the patient sufferance of these Colonies; and such is now the necessity which constrains them to alter their former Systems of Government. The history of the present King of Great Britain is a history of repeated injuries and usurpations, all having in direct object the establishment of an absolute Tyranny over these States. To prove this, let Facts be submitted to a candid world.

He has refused his Assent to Laws, the most wholesome and necessary for the public good.

He has forbidden his Governors to pass Laws of immediate and pressing importance, unless suspended in their operation till his Assent should be obtained; and when so suspended, he has utterly neglected to attend to them.

He has refused to pass other Laws for the accommodation of large districts of people, unless those people would relinquish the right of Representation in the Legislature, a right inestimable to them and formidable to tyrants only.

He has called together legislative bodies at places unusual, uncomfortable, and distant from the depository of their public Records, for the sole purpose of fatiguing them into compliance with his measures.

He has dissolved Representative Houses repeatedly, for opposing with manly firmness his invasions on the rights of the people.

He has refused for a long time, after such dissolutions, to cause others to be elected; whereby the Legislative powers, incapable of Annihilation, have returned to the People at large for their exercise; the State remaining in the mean time exposed to all the dangers of invasion from without, and convulsions within.

He has endeavoured to prevent the population of these States; for that purpose obstructing the Laws for Naturalization of Foreigners; refusing to pass others to encourage their migrations hither, and raising the conditions of new Appropriations of Lands.

He has obstructed the Administration of Justice, by refusing his Assent to Laws for establishing Judiciary powers.

He has made Judges dependent on his Will alone, for the tenure of their offices, and the amount and payment of their salaries.

He has erected a multitude of New Offices, and sent hither swarms of Officers to harrass our people, and eat out their substance.

He has kept among us, in times of peace, Standing Armies without the Consent of our legislatures.

He has affected to render the Military independent of and superior to the Civil power.

He has combined with others to subject us to a jurisdiction foreign to our constitution, and unacknowledged by our laws; giving his Assent to their Acts of pretended Legislation:

For Quartering large bodies of armed troops among us:

For protecting them, by a mock Trial, from punishment for any Murders which they should commit on the Inhabitants of these States:

For cutting off our Trade with all parts of the world:

For imposing Taxes on us without our Consent:

For depriving us in many cases, of the benefits of Trial by Jury:

For transporting us beyond Seas to be tried for pretended offences:

For abolishing the free System of English Laws in a neighbouring Province, establishing therein an Arbitrary government, and enlarging its Boundaries so as to render it at once an example and fit instrument for introducing the same absolute rule into these Colonies:

For taking away our Charters, abolishing our most valuable Laws, and altering fundamentally the Forms of our Governments:

For suspending our own Legislatures, and declaring themselves invested with power to legislate for us in all cases whatsoever.

He has abdicated Government here, by declaring us out of his Protection and waging War against us.

He has plundered our seas, ravaged our Coasts, burnt our towns, and destroyed the lives of our people.

He is at this time transporting large Armies of foreign Mercenaries to compleat the works of death, desolation and tyranny, already begun with circumstances of Cruelty & perfidy scarcely parallcled in the most barbarous ages, and totally unworthy the Head of a civilized nation.

He has constrained our fellow Citizens taken Captive on the high Seas to bear Arms against their Country, to become the executioners of their friends and Brethren, or to fall themselves by their Hands.

He has excited domestic insurrections amongst us, and has endeavoured to bring on the inhabitants of our frontiers, the merciless Indian Savages, whose known rule of warfare, is an undistinguished destruction of all ages, sexes and conditions.

In every stage of these Oppressions We have Petitioned for Redress in the most humble terms: Our repeated Petitions have been answered only by repeated injury. A Prince whose character is thus marked by every act which may define a Tyrant, is unfit to be the ruler of a free people.

Nor have We been wanting in attentions to our Brittish brethren. We have warned them from time to time of attempts by their legislature to extend an unwarrantable jurisdiction over us. We have reminded them of the circumstances of our emigration and settlement here. We have appealed to their native justice and magnanimity, and we have conjured them by the ties of our common kindred to disavow these usurpations, which, would inevitably interrupt our connections and correspondence. They too have been deaf to the voice of justice and of consanguinity. We must, therefore, acquiesce in the necessity, which denounces our Separation, and hold them, as we hold the rest of mankind, Enemies in War, in Peace Friends.

We, therefore, the Representatives of the united States of America, in General Congress, Assembled, appealing to the Supreme Judge of the world for the rectitude of our intentions, do, in the Name, and by Authority of the good People of these Colonies, solemnly publish and declare, That these United Colonies are, and of Right ought to be Free and Independent States; that they are Absolved from all Allegiance to the British Crown, and that all political connection between them and the State of Great Britain, is and ought to be totally dissolved; and that as Free and Independent States, they have full Power to levy War, conclude Peace, contract Alliances, establish Commerce, and to do all other Acts and Things which Independent States may of right do. And for the support of this Declaration, with a firm reliance on the protection of divine Providence, we mutually pledge to each other our Lives, our Fortunes and our sacred Honor.

The Signatories and their States:

Georgia: Button Gwinnett; Lyman Hall; George Walton
North Carolina: William Hooper; Joseph Hewes; John Penn
South Carolina: Edward Rutledge; Thomas Heyward, Jr.; Thomas Lynch, Jr.; Arthur Middleton
Massachusetts: John Hancock; Samuel Adams; John Adams; Robert Treat Paine Elbridge Gerry
Maryland: Samuel Chase; William Paca; Thomas Stone; Charles Carroll of Carrollton
Virginia: George Wythe; Richard Henry Lee; Thomas Jefferson; Benjamin Harrison; Thomas Nelson, Jr.; Francis Lightfoot Lee; Carter Braxton
Pennsylvania: Robert Morris; Benjamin Rush; Benjamin Franklin; John Morton; George Clymer; James Smith; George Taylor; James Wilson; George Ross
Delaware: Caesar Rodney; George Read; Thomas McKean
New York: William Floyd; Philip Livingston; Francis Lewis; Lewis Morris
New Jersey: Richard Stockton; John Witherspoon; Francis Hopkinson; John Hart Abraham Clark
New Hampshire: Josiah Bartlett; William Whipple; Matthew Thornton
Rhode Island: Stephen Hopkins; William Ellery
Connecticut; Roger Sherman; Samuel Huntington; William Williams Oliver Wolcott

THE CONSTITUTION OF THE UNITED STATES A TRANSCRIPTION

We the People of the United States, in Order to form a more perfect Union, establish Justice, insure domestic Tranquility, provide for the common defence, promote the general Welfare, and secure the Blessings of Liberty to ourselves and our Posterity, do ordain and establish this Constitution for the United States of America.

Article. I.

Section. 1.
All legislative Powers herein granted shall be vested in a Congress of the United States, which shall consist of a Senate and House of Representatives.

Section. 2.
The House of Representatives shall be composed of Members chosen every second Year by the People of the several States, and the Electors in each State shall have the Qualifications requisite for Electors of the most numerous Branch of the State Legislature.
No Person shall be a Representative who shall not have attained to the Age of twenty five Years, and been seven Years a Citizen of the United States, and who shall not, when elected, be an Inhabitant of that State in which he shall be chosen.
Representatives and direct Taxes shall be apportioned among the several States which may be included within this Union, according to their respective Numbers, which shall be determined by adding to the whole Number of free Persons, including those bound to Service for a Term of Years, and excluding Indians not taxed, three fifths of all other Persons. The actual Enumeration shall be made within three Years after the first Meeting of the Congress of the United States, and within every subsequent Term of ten Years, in such Manner as they shall by Law direct. The Number of Representatives shall not exceed one for every thirty Thousand, but each State shall have at Least one Representative; and until such enumeration shall be made, the State of New Hampshire shall be entitled to

chuse three, Massachusetts eight, Rhode-Island and Providence Plantations one, Connecticut five, New-York six, New Jersey four, Pennsylvania eight, Delaware one, Maryland six, Virginia ten, North Carolina five, South Carolina five, and Georgia three.

When vacancies happen in the Representation from any State, the Executive Authority thereof shall issue Writs of Election to fill such Vacancies.

The House of Representatives shall chuse their Speaker and other Officers; and shall have the sole Power of Impeachment.

Section. 3.

The Senate of the United States shall be composed of two Senators from each State, chosen by the Legislature thereof for six Years; and each Senator shall have one Vote.

Immediately after they shall be assembled in Consequence of the first Election, they shall be divided as equally as may be into three Classes. The Seats of the Senators of the first Class shall be vacated at the Expiration of the second Year, of the second Class at the Expiration of the fourth Year, and of the third Class at the Expiration of the sixth Year, so that one third may be chosen every second Year; and if Vacancies happen by Resignation, or otherwise, during the Recess of the Legislature of any State, the Executive thereof may make temporary Appointments until the next Meeting of the Legislature, which shall then fill such Vacancies.

No Person shall be a Senator who shall not have attained to the Age of thirty Years, and been nine Years a Citizen of the United States, and who shall not, when elected, be an Inhabitant of that State for which he shall be chosen.

The Vice President of the United States shall be President of the Senate, but shall have no Vote, unless they be equally divided.

The Senate shall chuse their other Officers, and also a President pro tempore, in the Absence of the Vice President, or when he shall exercise the Office of President of the United States.

The Senate shall have the sole Power to try all Impeachments. When sitting for that Purpose, they shall be on Oath or Affirmation. When the President of the United States is tried, the Chief Justice shall preside: And no Person shall be convicted without the Concurrence of two thirds of the Members present.

Judgment in Cases of Impeachment shall not extend further than to removal from Office, and disqualification to hold and enjoy any Office of honor, Trust or Profit under the United States: but the Party convicted shall nevertheless be liable and subject to Indictment, Trial, Judgment and Punishment, according to Law.

Section. 4.

The Times, Places and Manner of holding Elections for Senators and
Representatives, shall be prescribed in each State by the Legislature
thereof; but the Congress may at any time by Law make or alter such
Regulations, except as to the Places of chusing Senators.
The Congress shall assemble at least once in every Year, and such Meeting
shall be on the first Monday in December, unless they shall by Law appoint
a different Day.

Section. 5.

Each House shall be the Judge of the Elections, Returns and Qualifications
of its own Members, and a Majority of each shall constitute a Quorum to do
Business; but a smaller Number may adjourn from day to day, and may be
authorized to compel the Attendance of absent Members, in such Manner, and
under such Penalties as each House may provide.
Each House may determine the Rules of its Proceedings, punish its Members
for disorderly Behaviour, and, with the Concurrence of two thirds, expel a
Member.
Each House shall keep a Journal of its Proceedings, and from time to time
publish the same, excepting such Parts as may in their Judgment require
Secrecy; and the Yeas and Nays of the Members of either House on any
question shall, at the Desire of one fifth of those Present, be entered on
the Journal.
Neither House, during the Session of Congress, shall, without the Consent
of the other, adjourn for more than three days, nor to any other Place
than that in which the two Houses shall be sitting.

Section. 6.

The Senators and Representatives shall receive a Compensation for their
Services, to be ascertained by Law, and paid out of the Treasury of the
United States. They shall in all Cases, except Treason, Felony and Breach
of the Peace, be privileged from Arrest during their Attendance at the
Session of their respective Houses, and in going to and returning from the
same; and for any Speech or Debate in either House, they shall not be
questioned in any other Place.
No Senator or Representative shall, during the Time for which he was
elected, be appointed to any civil Office under the Authority of the
United States, which shall have been created, or the Emoluments whereof
shall have been encreased during such time; and no Person holding any
Office under the United States, shall be a Member of either House during
his Continuance in Office.

Section. 7.

All Bills for raising Revenue shall originate in the House of Representatives; but the Senate may propose or concur with Amendments as on other Bills.

Every Bill which shall have passed the House of Representatives and the Senate, shall, before it become a Law, be presented to the President of the United States: If he approve he shall sign it, but if not he shall return it, with his Objections to that House in which it shall have originated, who shall enter the Objections at large on their Journal, and proceed to reconsider it. If after such Reconsideration two thirds of that House shall agree to pass the Bill, it shall be sent, together with the Objections, to the other House, by which it shall likewise be reconsidered, and if approved by two thirds of that House, it shall become a Law. But in all such Cases the Votes of both Houses shall be determined by yeas and Nays, and the Names of the Persons voting for and against the Bill shall be entered on the Journal of each House respectively. If any Bill shall not be returned by the President within ten Days (Sundays excepted) after it shall have been presented to him, the Same shall be a Law, in like Manner as if he had signed it, unless the Congress by their Adjournment prevent its Return, in which Case it shall not be a Law.

Every Order, Resolution, or Vote to which the Concurrence of the Senate and House of Representatives may be necessary (except on a question of Adjournment) shall be presented to the President of the United States; and before the Same shall take Effect, shall be approved by him, or being disapproved by him, shall be repassed by two thirds of the Senate and House of Representatives, according to the Rules and Limitations prescribed in the Case of a Bill.

Section. 8.

The Congress shall have Power To lay and collect Taxes, Duties, Imposts and Excises, to pay the Debts and provide for the common Defence and general Welfare of the United States; but all Duties, Imposts and Excises shall be uniform throughout the United States;

To borrow Money on the credit of the United States;

To regulate Commerce with foreign Nations, and among the several States, and with the Indian Tribes;

To establish an uniform Rule of Naturalization, and uniform Laws on the subject of Bankruptcies throughout the United States;

To coin Money, regulate the Value thereof, and of foreign Coin, and fix the Standard of Weights and Measures;

To provide for the Punishment of counterfeiting the Securities and current

Coin of the United States;

To establish Post Offices and post Roads;

To promote the Progress of Science and useful Arts, by securing for limited Times to Authors and Inventors the exclusive Right to their respective Writings and Discoveries;

To constitute Tribunals inferior to the supreme Court;

To define and punish Piracies and Felonies committed on the high Seas, and Offences against the Law of Nations;

To declare War, grant Letters of Marque and Reprisal, and make Rules concerning Captures on Land and Water;

To raise and support Armies, but no Appropriation of Money to that Use shall be for a longer Term than two Years;

To provide and maintain a Navy;

To make Rules for the Government and Regulation of the land and naval Forces;

To provide for calling forth the Militia to execute the Laws of the Union, suppress Insurrections and repel Invasions;

To provide for organizing, arming, and disciplining, the Militia, and for governing such Part of them as may be employed in the Service of the United States, reserving to the States respectively, the Appointment of the Officers, and the Authority of training the Militia according to the discipline prescribed by Congress;

To exercise exclusive Legislation in all Cases whatsoever, over such District (not exceeding ten Miles square) as may, by Cession of particular States, and the Acceptance of Congress, become the Seat of the Government of the United States, and to exercise like Authority over all Places purchased by the Consent of the Legislature of the State in which the Same shall be, for the Erection of Forts, Magazines, Arsenals, dock-Yards, and other needful Buildings; — And

To make all Laws which shall be necessary and proper for carrying into Execution the foregoing Powers, and all other Powers vested by this Constitution in the Government of the United States, or in any Department or Officer thereof.

Section. 9.

The Migration or Importation of such Persons as any of the States now existing shall think proper to admit, shall not be prohibited by the Congress prior to the Year one thousand eight hundred and eight, but a Tax or duty may be imposed on such Importation, not exceeding ten dollars for each Person.

The Privilege of the Writ of Habeas Corpus shall not be suspended, unless

when in Cases of Rebellion or Invasion the public Safety may require it.
No Bill of Attainder or ex post facto Law shall be passed.
No Capitation, or other direct, Tax shall be laid, unless in Proportion to
the Census or enumeration herein before directed to be taken.
No Tax or Duty shall be laid on Articles exported from any State.
No Preference shall be given by any Regulation of Commerce or Revenue to
the Ports of one State over those of another; nor shall Vessels bound to,
or from, one State, be obliged to enter, clear, or pay Duties in another.
No Money shall be drawn from the Treasury, but in Consequence of
Appropriations made by Law; and a regular Statement and Account of the
Receipts and Expenditures of all public Money shall be published from time
to time.
No Title of Nobility shall be granted by the United States: And no Person
holding any Office of Profit or Trust under them, shall, without the
Consent of the Congress, accept of any present, Emolument, Office, or
Title, of any kind whatever, from any King, Prince, or foreign State.

Section. 10.
No State shall enter into any Treaty, Alliance, or Confederation; grant
Letters of Marque and Reprisal; coin Money; emit Bills of Credit; make any
Thing but gold and silver Coin a Tender in Payment of Debts; pass any Bill
of Attainder, ex post facto Law, or Law impairing the Obligation of
Contracts, or grant any Title of Nobility.
No State shall, without the Consent of the Congress, lay any Imposts or
Duties on Imports or Exports, except what may be absolutely necessary for
executing it's inspection Laws: and the net Produce of all Duties and
Imposts, laid by any State on Imports or Exports, shall be for the Use of
the Treasury of the United States; and all such Laws shall be subject to
the Revision and Controul of the Congress.
No State shall, without the Consent of Congress, lay any Duty of Tonnage,
keep Troops, or Ships of War in time of Peace, enter into any Agreement or
Compact with another State, or with a foreign Power, or engage in War,
unless actually invaded, or in such imminent Danger as will not admit of
delay.

Article. II.

Section. 1.
The executive Power shall be vested in a President of the United States of
America. He shall hold his Office during the Term of four Years, and,
together with the Vice President, chosen for the same Term, be elected, as
follows:

Each State shall appoint, in such Manner as the Legislature thereof may direct, a Number of Electors, equal to the whole Number of Senators and Representatives to which the State may be entitled in the Congress: but no Senator or Representative, or Person holding an Office of Trust or Profit under the United States, shall be appointed an Elector.

The Electors shall meet in their respective States, and vote by Ballot for two Persons, of whom one at least shall not be an Inhabitant of the same State with themselves. And they shall make a List of all the Persons voted for, and of the Number of Votes for each; which List they shall sign and certify, and transmit sealed to the Seat of the Government of the United States, directed to the President of the Senate. The President of the Senate shall, in the Presence of the Senate and House of Representatives, open all the Certificates, and the Votes shall then be counted. The Person having the greatest Number of Votes shall be the President, if such Number be a Majority of the whole Number of Electors appointed; and if there be more than one who have such Majority, and have an equal Number of Votes, then the House of Representatives shall immediately chuse by Ballot one of them for President; and if no Person have a Majority, then from the five highest on the List the said House shall in like Manner chuse the President. But in chusing the President, the Votes shall be taken by States, the Representation from each State having one Vote; A quorum for this purpose shall consist of a Member or Members from two thirds of the States, and a Majority of all the States shall be necessary to a Choice. In every Case, after the Choice of the President, the Person having the greatest Number of Votes of the Electors shall be the Vice President. But if there should remain two or more who have equal Votes, the Senate shall chuse from them by Ballot the Vice President.

The Congress may determine the Time of chusing the Electors, and the Day on which they shall give their Votes; which Day shall be the same throughout the United States.

No Person except a natural born Citizen, or a Citizen of the United States, at the time of the Adoption of this Constitution, shall be eligible to the Office of President; neither shall any Person be eligible to that Office who shall not have attained to the Age of thirty five Years, and been fourteen Years a Resident within the United States.

In Case of the Removal of the President from Office, or of his Death, Resignation, or Inability to discharge the Powers and Duties of the said Office, the Same shall devolve on the Vice President, and the Congress may by Law provide for the Case of Removal, Death, Resignation or Inability, both of the President and Vice President, declaring what Officer shall then act as President, and such Officer shall act accordingly, until the Disability be removed, or a President shall be elected.

The President shall, at stated Times, receive for his Services, a Compensation, which shall neither be increased nor diminished during the Period for which he shall have been elected, and he shall not receive within that Period any other Emolument from the United States, or any of them.

Before he enter on the Execution of his Office, he shall take the following Oath or Affirmation: — "I do solemnly swear (or affirm) that I will faithfully execute the Office of President of the United States, and will to the best of my Ability, preserve, protect and defend the Constitution of the United States."

Section. 2.

The President shall be Commander in Chief of the Army and Navy of the United States, and of the Militia of the several States, when called into the actual Service of the United States; he may require the Opinion, in writing, of the principal Officer in each of the executive Departments, upon any Subject relating to the Duties of their respective Offices, and he shall have Power to grant Reprieves and Pardons for Offences against the United States, except in Cases of Impeachment.

He shall have Power, by and with the Advice and Consent of the Senate, to make Treaties, provided two thirds of the Senators present concur; and he shall nominate, and by and with the Advice and Consent of the Senate, shall appoint Ambassadors, other public Ministers and Consuls, Judges of the supreme Court, and all other Officers of the United States, whose Appointments are not herein otherwise provided for, and which shall be established by Law: but the Congress may by Law vest the Appointment of such inferior Officers, as they think proper, in the President alone, in the Courts of Law, or in the Heads of Departments.

The President shall have Power to fill up all Vacancies that may happen during the Recess of the Senate, by granting Commissions which shall expire at the End of their next Session.

Section. 3.

He shall from time to time give to the Congress Information of the State of the Union, and recommend to their Consideration such Measures as he shall judge necessary and expedient; he may, on extraordinary Occasions, convene both Houses, or either of them, and in Case of Disagreement between them, with Respect to the Time of Adjournment, he may adjourn them to such Time as he shall think proper; he shall receive Ambassadors and other public Ministers; he shall take Care that the Laws be faithfully executed, and shall Commission all the Officers of the United States.

Section. 4.

The President, Vice President and all civil Officers of the United States, shall be removed from Office on Impeachment for, and Conviction of, Treason, Bribery, or other high Crimes and Misdemeanors.

Article III.

Section. 1.

The judicial Power of the United States shall be vested in one supreme Court, and in such inferior Courts as the Congress may from time to time ordain and establish. The Judges, both of the supreme and inferior Courts, shall hold their Offices during good Behaviour, and shall, at stated Times, receive for their Services a Compensation, which shall not be diminished during their Continuance in Office.

Section. 2.

The judicial Power shall extend to all Cases, in Law and Equity, arising under this Constitution, the Laws of the United States, and Treaties made, or which shall be made, under their Authority; — to all Cases affecting Ambassadors, other public Ministers and Consuls; — to all Cases of admiralty and maritime Jurisdiction; — to Controversies to which the United States shall be a Party; — to Controversies between two or more States; — between a State and Citizens of another State; — between Citizens of different States; — between Citizens of the same State claiming Lands under Grants of different States, and between a State, or the Citizens thereof, and foreign States, Citizens or Subjects.

In all Cases affecting Ambassadors, other public Ministers and Consuls, and those in which a State shall be Party, the supreme Court shall have original Jurisdiction. In all the other Cases before mentioned, the supreme Court shall have appellate Jurisdiction, both as to Law and Fact, with such Exceptions, and under such Regulations as the Congress shall make.

The Trial of all Crimes, except in Cases of Impeachment, shall be by Jury; and such Trial shall be held in the State where the said Crimes shall have been committed; but when not committed within any State, the Trial shall be at such Place or Places as the Congress may by Law have directed.

Section. 3.

Treason against the United States, shall consist only in levying War against them, or in adhering to their Enemies, giving them Aid and Comfort. No Person shall be convicted of Treason unless on the Testimony of two Witnesses to the same overt Act, or on Confession in open Court. The Congress shall have Power to declare the Punishment of Treason, but no Attainder of Treason shall work Corruption of Blood, or Forfeiture except during the Life of the Person attainted.

Article. IV.

Section. 1.

Full Faith and Credit shall be given in each State to the public Acts, Records, and judicial Proceedings of every other State. And the Congress may by general Laws prescribe the Manner in which such Acts, Records and Proceedings shall be proved, and the Effect thereof.

Section. 2.

The Citizens of each State shall be entitled to all Privileges and Immunities of Citizens in the several States.

A Person charged in any State with Treason, Felony, or other Crime, who shall flee from Justice, and be found in another State, shall on Demand of the executive Authority of the State from which he fled, be delivered up, to be removed to the State having Jurisdiction of the Crime.

No Person held to Service or Labour in one State, under the Laws thereof, escaping into another, shall, in Consequence of any Law or Regulation therein, be discharged from such Service or Labour, but shall be delivered up on Claim of the Party to whom such Service or Labour may be due.

Section. 3.

New States may be admitted by the Congress into this Union; but no new State shall be formed or erected within the Jurisdiction of any other State; nor any State be formed by the Junction of two or more States, or Parts of States, without the Consent of the Legislatures of the States concerned as well as of the Congress.

The Congress shall have Power to dispose of and make all needful Rules and Regulations respecting the Territory or other Property belonging to the United States; and nothing in this Constitution shall be so construed as to Prejudice any Claims of the United States, or of any particular State.

Section. 4.

The United States shall guarantee to every State in this Union a Republican Form of Government, and shall protect each of them against Invasion; and on Application of the Legislature, or of the Executive (when the Legislature cannot be convened), against domestic Violence.

Article. V.

The Congress, whenever two thirds of both Houses shall deem it necessary, shall propose Amendments to this Constitution, or, on the Application of the Legislatures of two thirds of the several States, shall call a Convention for proposing Amendments, which, in either Case, shall be valid to all Intents and Purposes, as Part of this Constitution, when ratified by the Legislatures of three fourths of the several States, or by Conventions in three fourths thereof, as the one or the other Mode of Ratification may be proposed by the Congress; Provided that no Amendment which may be made prior to the Year One thousand eight hundred and eight shall in any Manner affect the first and fourth Clauses in the Ninth Section of the first Article; and that no State, without its Consent, shall be deprived of its equal Suffrage in the Senate.

Article. VI.

All Debts contracted and Engagements entered into, before the Adoption of this Constitution, shall be as valid against the United States under this Constitution, as under the Confederation.
This Constitution, and the Laws of the United States which shall be made in Pursuance thereof; and all Treaties made, or which shall be made, under the Authority of the United States, shall be the supreme Law of the Land; and the Judges in every State shall be bound thereby, any Thing in the Constitution or Laws of any State to the Contrary notwithstanding.
The Senators and Representatives before mentioned, and the Members of the several State Legislatures, and all executive and judicial Officers, both of the United States and of the several States, shall be bound by Oath or Affirmation, to support this Constitution; but no religious Test shall ever be required as a Qualification to any Office or public Trust under the United States.

Article. VII.

The Ratification of the Conventions of nine States, shall be sufficient for the Establishment of this Constitution between the States so ratifying the Same.

The Word, "the," being interlined between the seventh and eighth Lines of the first Page, the Word "Thirty" being partly written on an Erazure in the fifteenth Line of the first Page, The Words "is tried" being interlined between the thirty second and thirty third Lines of the first Page and the Word "the" being interlined between the forty third and forty fourth Lines of the second Page.
Attest William Jackson Secretary

Done in Convention by the Unanimous Consent of the States present the Seventeenth Day of September in the Year of our Lord one thousand seven hundred and Eighty seven and of the Independence of the United States of America the Twelfth In witness whereof We have hereunto subscribed our Names,

G°. Washington
Presidt and deputy from Virginia
[Delaware]
Geo: Read
Gunning Bedford jun
John Dickinson
Richard Bassett
Jaco: Broom
[Maryland]
James McHenry
Dan of St Thos. Jenifer
Danl. Carroll
[Virginia]
John Blair
James Madison Jr.
[North Carolina]
Wm. Blount
Richd. Dobbs Spaight
Hu Williamson
[South Carolina]
J. Rutledge
Charles Cotesworth Pinckney
Charles Pinckney
Pierce Butler
[Georgia]
William Few
Abr Baldwin
[New Hampshire]
John Langdon
Nicholas Gilman
[Massachusetts]
Nathaniel Gorham
Rufus King
[Connecticut]
Wm. Saml. Johnson
Roger Sherman
[New York]

Alexander Hamilton
[New Jersey]
Wil: Livingston
David Brearley
Wm. Paterson
Jona: Dayton
[Pennsylvania]
B Franklin
Thomas Mifflin
Robt. Morris
Geo. Clymer
Thos. FitzSimons
Jared Ingersoll
James Wilson
Gouv Morris

Source: The proceeding text is a transcription of the Constitution in its original form taken from "The Charters of Freedom," The National Archives Experience available on the website of the United States National Archives at <http://www.archives.gov/national-archives-experience/charters/constitution_transcript.html>.

THE BILL OF RIGHTS, 1791

The first ten amendments to the Constitution are known collectively as the "Bill of Rights" and can be seen as an integral part of the founders' legacy and the values of the revolutionary generation. They are formally identified as Article I, Article II, Article III, et sequitur but are distinguished from the Constitution's Article I, II, and so on, by the use of the terms "First Amendment," "Second Amendment," etc. as follows.

Article I [First Amendment]
Congress shall make no law respecting an establishment of religion, or prohibiting the free exercise thereof; or abridging the freedom of speech, or of the press; or the right of the people peaceably to assemble, and to petition the Government for a redress of grievances.

Article II [Second Amendment]
A well regulated Militia, being necessary to the security of a free State, the right of the people to keep and bear Arms, shall not be infringed.

Article III [Third Amendment]
No Soldier shall, in time of peace be quartered in any house, without the consent of the Owner, nor in time of war, but in a manner to be prescribed by law.

Article IV [Fourth Amendment]
The right of the people to be secure in their persons, houses, papers, and effects, against unreasonable searches and seizures, shall not be violated, and no Warrants shall issue, but upon probable cause, supported by Oath or affirmation, and particularly describing the place to be searched, and the persons or things to be seized.

Article V [Fifth Amendment]
No person shall be held to answer for a capital, or otherwise infamous crime, unless on a presentment or indictment of a Grand Jury, except in cases arising in the land or naval forces, or in the Militia, when in actual service in time of War or public danger; nor shall any person be subject for the same offence to be twice put in jeopardy of life or limb; nor shall be compelled in any criminal case to be a witness against himself, nor be deprived of life, liberty, or property, without due process of law; nor shall private property be taken for public use, without just compensation.

Article VI [Sixth Amendment]

In all criminal prosecutions, the accused shall enjoy the right to a speedy and public trial, by an impartial jury of the State and district wherein the crime shall have been committed, which district shall have been previously ascertained by law, and to be informed of the nature and cause of the accusation; to be confronted with the witnesses against him; to have compulsory process for obtaining witnesses in his favor, and to have the Assistance of Counsel for his defence.

Article VII [Seventh Amendment]

In Suits at common law, where the value in controversy shall exceed twenty dollars, the right of trial by jury shall be preserved, and no fact tried by a jury shall be otherwise re-examined in any Court of the United States, than according to the rules of the common law.

Article VIII [Eighth Amendment]

Excessive bail shall not be required, nor excessive fines imposed, nor cruel and unusual punishments inflicted.

Article IX [Ninth Amendment]

The enumeration in the Constitution, of certain rights, shall not be construed to deny or disparage others retained by the people.

Article X [Tenth Amendment]

The powers not delegated to the United States by the Constitution, nor prohibited by it to the States, are reserved to the States respectively, or to the people.

REFERENCE BIBLIOGRAPHY

In addition to the suggested readings that accompany each chapter, the following are recommended as references.

Published, Edited Primary Sources

Bernard Bailyn, ed., *Pamphlets of the American Revolution, 1750-1776* (Cambridge, MA: Harvard University Press, 1965) is an important collection of sources on the intellectual, ideological, and political literature of the period. Two equally useful volumes of edited documents are Jack P. Greene, ed., *Colonies to Nation, 1763-1789* (New York: W.W. Norton & Company, 1975) and Jack P. Greene, ed., *Settlements to Society, 1607-1763: A Documentary History of Colonial America* (New York: W.W. Norton & Company, 1975). See also James Madison, *The Debates on the Federal Convention of 1787, which framed the Constitution of the United States of America*, ed. Gaillard Hunt and James B. Scott (New York: Oxford University Press, 1920); John Patrick Diggins, ed., *The Portable John Adams* (New York: Penguin, 2004); Merrill Peterson, ed., *The Portable Thomas Jefferson* (New York, Penguin, 1975); and Michael J. Dubin, *United States Presidential Elections: The Official Results by County and State* (Jefferson, NC: McFarland and Company, 2002).

The manuscripts left by many prominent figures of the revolutionary period continue to be published in multi-volume series that have been running for several decades. The founders were prolific writers and left behind thousands of pages of letters, commentary, official memoranda, and miscellany. See, for example, *The Adams Papers* (Massachusetts Historical Society/Belknap Press); *The Papers of Benjamin Franklin* (Yale University Press); *The Papers of Alexander Hamilton* (Columbia University Press); *The Papers of Thomas Jefferson* (Princeton University Press); *The Papers of James Madison* (University Press of Virginia); and *The Papers of George Washington* (University Press of Virginia). See also the *Presidents' Index Series* (Washington: Library of Congress, Manuscript Division). Some of the collections are so vast that the edited volumes have to be subdivided by subject. Many other revolutionaries left copious manuscripts, and some of those have been edited and published—Nathanael Greene, Albert Gallatin, and John Dickinson, for example. Official records, published and unpublished, exist in national repositories such as the United States Library of Congress and the Public Records Office in London. Some state records are available in published form. Most repositories are making their holdings available via the internet. See the examples available at http://archivegrid.org. There are many common web sites that afford access to published documents. An indispensable guide to the web for history materials is Alan Gevinson, Kelly Schrum, and Roy Rosezweig, *History Matters: A Student Guide to U.S. History Online* (Boston: Bedford/St. Martin's, 2005). The Avalon Project at Yale University Law School has a useful collection of commonly used revolutionary-era documents online at http://yale.edu/lawweb/avalon/avalon.htm. For images, cartoons, contemporary etchings, and other pictorial representation, see ttp://classroomclipart.com and follow the links to History, United States, American Revolution.

Statistics and Chronologies

Useful statistical material can be found in *Historical Statistics of the United States*, Parts 1 and 2 (Washington: Bureau of the Census, 1976). An enormous amount of miscellaneous economic, geographic, demographic, and sociological data can be found in Thomas L. Purvis, *Almanacs of American Life: Revolutionary America, 1763 to 1800* (New York: Facts on File, Inc., 1995). Purvis compiles common and obscure data in a way that is both valuable as information and fascinating by subject. Michael J. Dubin, *United States Presidential Elections: The Official Results by County and State* (Jefferson, NC: McFarland and Company, 2002) is an excellent political reference, as is Arthur M. Schlesinger, Jr. and Fred Israel, eds., *History of American Presidential Elections, 1789-1968*, vol. 1 (New York: Chelsea House, 1971), which is well organized and contains excellent analytical essays for each election. Percy Wells Bidwell and John Falconer, *History of Agriculture in the Northern United States, 1620-1860* (Washington: Carnegie Institute, 1925) and Lewis Cecil Grey, *History of Agriculture in the Southern United States to 1860* (Washington: Carnegie Institute, 1933) are superbly documented with a variety of agricultural data and are both thematically and statistically useful. The following are also recommended: Mark Mayo Boatner III, *Encyclopedia of the American Revolution* (New York: David McKay Company, Inc., 1974); Lester Cappon, ed., *Atlas of Early American History: The Revolutionary Era, 1760-1790* (Princeton, NJ: Princeton University Press, 1976); Wilbur Garrett, ed., *Historical Atlas of the United States*, with principal consultants D.W. Meinig, Sam Hilliard, and Michael Kammen (Washington: National Geographic Society, 1988); Ralph Louis Ketcham, *Presidents above Party: The First American Presidency, 1789-1829* (Chapel Hill: The University of North Carolina Press, 1984); Herbert S. Klein, *A Population History of the United States* (Cambridge, England: Cambridge University Press, 2004); Herbert S. Klein, *The Atlantic Slave Trade* (New York: Cambridge University Press, 1999); and Colin McEvedy, *The Penguin Atlas of North American History to 1870* (London: Penguin Books, 1988). A very well-organized and well-researched reference is Richard B. Morris and Jeffrey B. Morris, eds., *Encyclopedia of American History*, 7th ed. (New York: HarperCollins, 1996). The vexing issue of native populations is addressed in Russell Thornton, *American Indian Holocaust and Survival: A Population History Since 1492* (Norman: University of Oklahoma Press, 1987).

Anthologies

Recent scholarship is available in the following volumes: Richard Beeman, Stephen Botein, and Edward C. Carter, eds., *Beyond Confederation: Origins of the Constitution and American National Identity* (Chapel Hill: University of North Carolina Press, 1987); Jack P. Greene and J.R. Pole, eds., *Colonial British America: Essays in the New History of the Early Modern Era* (Baltimore, Johns Hopkins Press, 1984); Jack P. Greene and J.R. Pole, eds., *A Companion to the American Revolution* (Malden, MA: Blackwell, 2000); Jack Greene and J.R. Pole, *The Blackwell Encyclopedia of the American Revolution* (Oxford: Blackwell, 1991); Eliga H. Gould, and Peter S. Onuf, eds., *Empire and Nation: The American Revolution in the Atlantic World* (Baltimore: Johns Hopkins University Press, 2005); P.J. Marshall, ed., *The Oxford History of the British Empire*, vol. 2, *The Eighteenth Century* (New York: Oxford University Press, 1999); Lawrence Stone, ed., *An Imperial State at War: Britain from 1689-1815* (London: Routledge, 1994); and Alfred F. Young, ed., *Beyond the Revolution: Explorations in the History of American Radicalism* (DeKalb, IL: University of Northern Illinois Press, 1993). A collection of essays that includes much of the recent scholarship on the post-1789 period is Jeffrey L. Pasley, Andrew W. Robertson, and David Waldstreicher, eds., *Beyond the Founders: New Approaches to the Political History of the Early American Republic* (Chapel Hill: University of North Carolina Press, 2004).

Surveys (Recent General Overviews)

The first four titles listed here set the Revolution in a narrow time frame, usually 1763-89: Edward Countryman, *The American Revolution* (New York: Hill and Wang, 2003); Robert Middlekauff, *The Glorious Cause: The American Revolution, 1763-1789* (New York: Oxford University Press, 1982); Edmund S. Morgan, *The Birth of the Republic, 1763-89*, 3rd ed. (Chicago: The University of Chicago Press, 1992); and Gordon S. Wood, *The American Revolution: A History* (New York: Modern Library, 2002). The following titles take the Revolutionary period into the nineteenth century: Francis D. Cogliano, *Revolutionary America: A Political History* (London: Routledge, 2000); Paul A. Gilje, *The Making of the American Republic, 1763-1815* (Upper Saddle River, NJ: Prentice Hall, 2006) is especially strong on social issues; Reginald Horsman, *The New Republic: The United States of America, 1789-1815* (New York: Longman, 2000) is a good survey of development after the adoption of the Constitution; Cynthia A. Kierner, *Revolutionary America, 1750-1815: Sources and Interpretations* (Upper Saddle River, NJ: Prentice Hall, 2003) is the only survey that alternates documents with text; J. R. Pole, *Foundations of American Independence: 1763-1815* (Indianapolis: Bobbs-Merrill, 1972) is very useful, but out of print.

Biographies

While the older versions lack sufficient entries on women, African Americans, and natives, the most convenient source of biographical material is the *Concise Dictionary of American Biography* (*DAB*), 1st-3rd editions, (New York: Scribner's 1964; 1977; 1980). Over 15,000 persons are included in entries ranging from a few lines to a few thousand words. The paucity of entries on women and minorities that marked the earlier full and concise versions of the *DAB* is being corrected. Otherwise, see Edward T. James, *Notable American Women, 1607-1950: A Biographical Dictionary*, 3 vols. (Cambridge, MA: Belknap Press, 1971). The full *DAB* has been supplanted by the *American National Biography* (*ANB*), 25 vols. (New York: Oxford University Press, 1999-2002).

In addition to the generous space devoted to the revolutionary period in the *ANB*, a great many separate biographies exist for leading participants of the Revolution and an enduring feature of Revolution studies is the sheer volume of work on the founders, and especially on the half dozen most important of those. Full or partial biographies of Washington, for instance, run to the hundreds of titles. The practice of gracing founders with an individual "life" began in the early nineteenth century with biographies of George Washington and has continued unbroken, finally resulting in multi-volume studies such as Dumas Malone's *Jefferson and His Time*, 6 vols. (Boston, Little, Brown, 1948-81); Irving Brandt's *James Madison*, 6 vols. (Indianapolis: Bobbs-Merrill, 1941-61); and Douglas Freeman's *George Washington*, 7 vols. (New York: Scribners, 1948-52).

While the trend today is to focus on particular phases or aspects of the subject's life, conventional biographies on a much smaller scale continue to be published, and the founders still attract the attention of the leading scholars of the period. Some recent examples are Lance Banning, *The Sacred Fire of Liberty: James Madison and the Founding of the Federal Republic* (Ithaca, NY: Cornell University Press, 1995); Richard Brookheiser, *Alexander Hamilton's America* (New York, Touchstone, 2000); John Patrick Diggins, *John Adams* (New York: Henry Holt, 2003); Joseph Ellis, *His Excellency, George Washington* (New York: Knopf, 2004); Joseph Ellis, *American Sphinx: The Character of Thomas Jefferson* (New York: Knopf, 1997); and Edmund Morgan, *Benjamin Franklin* (New Haven: Yale University Press, 2002). (At least three scholarly biographies of Franklin appeared between 2002 and 2004.)

Useful collective biographies of less well known persons are Joyce Appleby, *Inheriting the Revolution: The First Generation of Americans* (Cambridge, MA: Belknap Press, 2000) and Bernard Bailyn, *Faces of Revolution: Personalities and Themes in the Struggle for Independence* (New York: Knopf, 1990). Biographical material for the mass of the American population is scant, although diaries provide some evidence of the lives and thoughts of ordinary Americans, male and female. The introduction to the following provides useful examples: Linda Kerber, *Women of the Republic: Intellect and Ideology in Revolutionary America* (Chapel Hill: The University of North Carolina Press, 1980). (Kerber cites 200 manuscript collections containing biographical material on women and identifies many of these.) The lives of ordinary Americans are represented in Michael Merrill, and Sean Wilentz, eds., *The Key of Liberty: The Life and Democratic Writings of William Manning, "A Laborer," 1747-1814* (Cambridge, MA: Harvard

University Press, 1993); Alfred F. Young, *The Shoemaker and the Tea Party: Memory and the American Revolution* (Boston: Beacon Press, 1999); and James Kirby Martin, *Ordinary Courage: The Revolutionary War Adventures of Joseph Plumb Martin*, 2nd ed. (Naugatuck, CT: Brandywine Press, 1999).

An essential bibliographic reference for the American Revolution is *The William and Mary Quarterly*; it presents the most recent research and reviews the vast literature on the period that runs from the late sixteenth to the early nineteenth centuries. The scholarship is first rate, and its geographical and cultural range is wide. *The Journal of the Early Republic* is recommended for its specific time frame, and the reviews in *Reviews in American History* and *The Journal of American History* are of the highest quality.

INDEX

14, 18-19, 34, 39-41, 45;
Spanish Armada, 38; in
American War for
Independence, 54-55, 77,
119-20, 134, 136, 142-43,
168-69, 179, 230, 235-36,
239, 242, 247; currencies,
178; in War of 1812, 263,
269. *See also* Spain
Spain: in colonial period, 37,
39, 41, 44; in Seven Years'
War, 44-45; in American
War for Independence,
120, 136, 143, 150; diplomacy, trade, economic
affairs, 178-79, 219, 235,
239, 247, 269. *See also*
Spanish
specie (hard currency), 117,
142, 178, 270
Spirit of the Laws (Baron
Montesquieu), 195
Springfield Armory, 180
St. Augustine, Florida, 40
St. John's (St Jean), Quebec,
87, 90, 131
St. Kitts, 8
St. Lawrence River, 8, 40, 44
St. Lawrence Valley, 39, 72,
257
St. Lucia, 45
Stamp Act Congress, 57, 63,
66, 73-74, 94, 99, 188,
194, 220
Stamp Act crisis, 42, 56-59,
65, 67, 70, 73, 76-77, 102,
106, 113, 142-43, 216,
227
standing army, 72, 82, 177, 267
"Star Spangled Banner"
(poem/song), 262
state constitutions, 153-57.
See also individual states
state land concessions, 149-
50, 181, 188
states' rights, 223, 231, 244-
45, 266, 270
Steuben, Baron von, 130,
132-33, 139

Stono Rebellion, 159
Strait of Mackinaw, 256
Stuarts, 38
subsistence agriculture, 23-
24, 106, 147, 172
Succession Act (1701), 34
Suffolk Resolves (1774), 81,
84
Sugar Act (Revenue Act), 49,
54
Sullivan, John, 125, 133
*Summary View of the Rights
of British-America*
(Thomas Jefferson), 74-
75, 93, 100
swarming (settlers), 14, 220,
279

Talleyrand, Charles Maurice
de, 221, 235
Tallmadge, James, 272
Taney, Roger, 253
Tarleton, Colonel Banastre,
138-39
Tecumseh, 233, 249-51, 257,
259, 263
Tennent, Gilbert, 33
Tennent, William, 32
Tennessee Company, 166
Tennessee, 166-67, 171, 208;
as a state, 216, 235; and
three-fifths clause, 224,
231; and natives, 250; and
Andrew Jackson, 263-64;
electors, 240; and the
west, 271, 279; popula-
tion, 248
Tenskwatawa, 250
Thompson, David, 236
Tidewater region, 20-21, 23,
64, 79, 159, 245, 271
Tippecanoe River, 250
tobacco, 4, 20, 23, 34, 50,
66, 101, 134
Tory, 60-61, 121, 130, 162-63
Townshend Duties, 49, 59-
60, 62-63, 67, 70
trade: in colonial era, 8, 11-
12, 18-20, 23, 34-35, 37;

French fur trade, 39-40;
Board of Trade, 51, 53,
124; imperial trade
reform, 54, 59, 62, 67, 75,
77; colonial resistance, 83,
85, 94-95, 103; in War for
Independence, 136, 152;
post-war trade, 168, 171,
175-79; United States
Constitution and inter-
state and international
trade, 189, 193-94, 205-
06; federalist theory and
policies, 202, 206, 218-19;
XYZ affair, 221; and the
west, 230, 236; during
Napoleonic Wars and
embargoes, 242-46; and
War of 1812, 253-54, 256,
258, 260; post-war, 270,
278. *See also* slave trade
Treaty of Aix-la-Chapelle
(1748), 41
Treaty of Ghent (1814), 253,
261, 266
Treaty of Greenville (1795),
250
Treaty of Greenville (1814),
263
Treaty of Paris (1763), 7, 44-
45, 49, 76
Treaty of Paris (1783), 112,
147, 149, 168, 257, 271
Treaty of Ryswick (1697), 39
Treaty of Utrecht (1713), 40
Trenchard, John, 31
Trinitarian, 229
Tryon, William, 64
Tucker, Josiah, 124
Tudors, 38
Tunis, 237, 267
Turner thesis (Frederick
Jackson Turner), 166
turnpikes, 208
Tuscarora (natives), 170

Unitarianism, 229
United States Congress, 5,
58, 194-97, 207, 210; and